The ABCs of Political Economy

The ABCs of Political Economy

A Modern Approach

Revised and Expanded Edition

Robin Hahnel

PlutoPress
www.plutobooks.com

First published 2002; revised and expanded edition 2014
by Pluto Press
345 Archway Road, London N6 5AA

www.plutobooks.com

British Library Cataloguing in Publication Data
A catalogue record for this book is available from the British Library

ISBN 978 0 7453 3498 1 Hardback
ISBN 978 0 7453 3497 4 Paperback
ISBN 978 1 7837 1206 9 PDF eBook
ISBN 978 1 7837 1208 3 Kindle eBook
ISBN 978 1 7837 1207 6 EPUB eBook

Library of Congress Cataloging in Publication Data applied for

This book is printed on paper suitable for recycling and made from fully
managed and sustained forest sources. Logging, pulping and manufacturing
processes are expected to conform to the environmental standards of the
country of origin.

10 9 8 7 6 5 4 3 2 1

Typeset in Minion
by Swales & Willis, Exeter, Devon

Text design by Melanie Patrick
Simultaneously printed digitally by CPI Antony Rowe, Chippenham, UK
and
Edwards Bros in the United States of America

Contents

x CONTENTS

List of Illustrations

Preface to the Revised and Expanded Edition

This revised and expanded edition of *The ABCs of Political Economy: A Modern Approach* is dedicated to the memory of Pete Seeger who died at the age of 94 on January 27, 2014 when I was finalizing the new edition. Through song and good cheer Pete Seeger helped five generations of Americans use the goodness within us to fight against injustice in all its forms – from the labor movement of the 1930s and 1940s, to the civil rights, anti-war, and women's movements of the 1960s and 1970s, to the environmental and global justice movements of the 1980s, and beyond. Pete Seeger, Presente! You are already missed by me and my children.

The ABCs of Political Economy was first published in 2002. Since then we have experienced the most tumultuous economic events in four generations. Whereas the spread of neoliberal globalization that took off after 1980 created severe crises in many less developed economies, the more advanced economies were relatively immune from crisis until 2008. However, the financial crisis of 2008, which triggered the Great Recession and continuing stagnation, has shaken the developed economies more than any events since the Great Depression of the 1930s. So there is much new for this new edition of a political economy primer to address.

Fortunately, *The ABCs of Political Economy* was intended to provide readers with analytical tools they can use to evaluate important economic issues for themselves, rather than provide my own critical analysis of current events. And fortunately, many of the tools developed turn out to be precisely what readers need to understand the cause of recent economic turmoil and pros and cons of different policy responses. So, fortunately for the author, no major rewrite is in order: the tools are ready and still sharp. What is needed mostly is to help readers see how to apply the tools to analyze recent events in the advanced economies.

No author can resist saying "I told you so." No, I did not predict the exact nature or timing of the recent events. And if I am to be honest, I must admit that I was surprised by the severity of the financial crisis, as well as the intransigence of ruling elites in response to a crisis of their making. However, I am gratified that while many economists in the advanced economies were celebrating neoliberal globalization in the early 2000s, the first edition of *The ABCs* drew attention to escalating inequality, financialization run amok, and unsustainable macroeconomic imbalances, and warned of dangers associated with these trends. And as it turns out, the financial and macroeconomic models in Chapter 9 are remarkably useful for analyzing financial crises and making sense of disagreements over whether fiscal stimulus or deficit reduction was the appropriate response to the Great Recession.

Chapter 1: The social theory outlined in this chapter contains an important role for economic dynamics and class relations. However, unlike traditional Marxist historical materialism, "liberating theory" or "complementary holism" also emphasizes the importance of the political, cultural, and kinship spheres of social life, racial, gender, religious, and political non-class "agents of history," and human agency. As core capitalist economies were shaken by economic trauma not seen in many generations it is interesting to consider what recent social uprisings have to teach us in this regard.

Chapter 2: The new version of this chapter about economic "goals" updates data on rising inequality over the past dozen years, elaborates considerably on what environmental sustainability means, and comments briefly on the goal of a "steady state economy" and the rise of the "de-growth movement."

Chapter 3: Occupy Wall Street erupted like a primal scream over escalating economic inequality. The corn model developed in this chapter provides an easy way to grasp the essential dynamics that permitted the top 1% to appropriate the lion's share of productivity gains in our economies over the past thirty years.

Chapter 4: In 2002 the "free market jubilee" was still in full swing. Six years later, after free market finance had created the greatest financial crisis in eighty years, and with carbon emissions on course to unleash cataclysmic climate change, many started to question whether free markets are as wonderful as we are usually told. In short, the "debate" over whether markets are guided by a beneficent invisible hand, or instead by a malevolent invisible foot described in the original version of this chapter, could no longer be swept under the rug by market enthusiasts. Now, in 2014, what should have been treated as perhaps the most crucial issue in all of economics has at long last become a full-fledged public debate.

Chapter 5: The biggest change in this chapter is the addition of a model illustrating the dilemmas faced when designing international climate treaties. As we race like lemmings toward climate disaster perhaps no subject is more important for the engaged public to understand clearly. The Sraffa model is now compared and contrasted to the neoclassical theory of income and price determination as well as the Marxian labor theory of value, closing with a "modern" argument for how we can distinguish between producers and parasites.

Chapter 6: The biggest policy debate since the economic crisis broke in 2008 is over fiscal stimulus vs. austerity. Government after government – conservative and liberal alike – has chosen austerity over stimulus despite the fact that competent macroeconomic theory and historical experience both teach that exactly the opposite is what is needed. The expanded version of this chapter shows how basic political macroeconomic theory, based on Keynes' insights, helps explain why government policy aggravated the Great Recession and continues to hamper recovery.

Chapter 7: In 2002 when this chapter was first written free market finance was in vogue. Despite numerous financial crises in lesser developed countries during the 1980s and 1990s, only the upside potential of financial deregulation and new financial "products" was discussed. When published, the explanations in the chapter about perverse incentives that plague banks and financial markets and the case for prudent regulation fell largely on deaf ears. In the aftermath of the greatest financial crisis since 1929 interest in the downside potentials of financialization has skyrocketed. The expanded version of this chapter includes a point-by-point explanation of what led to the financial crisis in 2008, as well as explanations of new monetary policy wrinkles like "quantitative easing" and "tapering."

Chapter 8: Globalization has continued to proceed unabated since 2002. However, crises have shifted from the "periphery" of the global economy to its "center" since 2008. In order to expand treatment of crisis in the advanced economies this chapter has been streamlined, with discussion focused more on the Trans-Pacific Partnership Agreement, the European Monetary Union, and austerity policies imposed on Portugal, Ireland, Greece, and Spain, the so-called PIGS in the Eurozone.

Chapter 9: The useful macroeconomic models in this chapter remain the same, but now the closed economy macro model is used to evaluate the weak fiscal stimulus applied by the newly elected Obama administration in early 2009. Tedious derivations of the reduced form solutions to the long-run political economy growth model and the comparative statics analysis have been replaced with a fuller explanation of the intuition behind the results and their political importance.

Chapter 10: The point-by-point critique of the economics of competition and greed in the original version of this chapter resonates quite differently now that the bloom is off the neoliberal rose, and hundreds of millions of dissident voices across the globe have risen to shout ENOUGH!

Chapter 11: An expanded version of this chapter includes material on what is known as the "new" or "future" economy," and why a "Green New Deal" is urgently needed to address both the economic and the ecological crises we face.

I would like to thank the Mesa Refuge Foundation for supporting me as a writer in residence during 2014. During my time there I was able to finish this revised and expanded edition as well as work on other writing projects.

1

Economics and
Liberating Theory

Unlike mainstream economists, political economists have always tried to situate the study of economics within the broader project of understanding how society functions. However, dissatisfaction with the traditional political economy theory of social change known as *historical materialism* has increased to the point where many modern political economists and social activists no longer espouse it, and most who still call themselves historical materialists have modified their theory considerably to accommodate insights about the importance of gender relations, race relations, and the "human factor" in understanding social stability and social change. The *liberating theory* presented in this chapter attempts to transcend historical materialism without throwing out the baby with the bath water. It incorporates insights from feminism, anti-colonial and anti-racist movements, and anarchism, as well as from mainstream psychology, sociology, and evolutionary biology where useful. Liberating theory attempts to understand the relationship between economic, political, kinship and cultural activities, and the forces behind social stability and social change, in a way that neither over nor underestimates the importance of economic dynamics, and neither over nor underestimates the importance of human agency compared to social forces. Whether the theory of people and society that follows accomplishes all this while avoiding unwarranted assumptions and unnecessary idiosyncrasies is for you, the reader, to judge.[1]

People and Society

People usually define and fulfill their needs and desires in cooperation with others – which makes us a *social species*. Because each of us assesses our options and

---

1 The original formulation can be found in *Liberating Theory* (South End Press, 1986) by Michael Albert, Leslie Cagan, Noam Chomsky, Robin Hahnel, Mel King, Lydia Sargent, and Holly Sklar.

chooses from among them on the basis of our evaluation of their consequences we are also a *self-conscious species*. Finally, in seeking to meet the needs we identify today, we choose to act in ways that sometimes change our human characteristics, and thereby change our needs and preferences tomorrow. In this sense people are *self-creative*.

Throughout history people have created *social institutions* to help meet their most urgent needs and desires. To satisfy our economic needs we have tried a variety of arrangements – feudalism, capitalism, and centrally planned "socialism" to name a few – that assign duties and rewards among economic participants in different ways. But we have also created different kinds of kinship relations through which people seek to satisfy sexual needs and accomplish child rearing and educational goals, as well as different religious, community, and political organizations and institutions for meeting cultural needs and achieving political goals. Of course the particular social arrangements in different *spheres of social life*, and the relations among them, vary from society to society. But what is common to all human societies is the elaboration of social relationships for the joint identification and pursuit of individual need fulfillment.

To develop a theory that expresses this view of humans – as a self-conscious, self-creative, social species – and this view of society – as a web of interconnected spheres of social life – we first concentrate on concepts helpful for thinking about people, or the *human center*, and next on concepts that help us understand social institutions, or the *institutional boundary* within which individuals function. After which we move on to explore the relationship between the human center and institutional boundary, and the possible relations between *four spheres of social life*.

The Human Center

Natural, Species, and Derived Needs and Potentials

All people, simply by virtue of being modern humans, have certain needs, capacities, and powers. Some of these, like the needs for food and sex, or the capacities to eat and copulate, we share with other living creatures. These are our *natural needs and potentials*. Others, however, such as the needs for knowledge, creative activity, and love, and the powers to conceptualize, plan ahead, evaluate alternatives, and experience complex emotions, are more distinctly human. These are our *species needs and potentials*. Finally, most of our needs and powers, like the desire for a particular singer's recordings, or the need to share feelings with a particular loved one, or the ability to play a guitar or repair a roof, we develop over the course of our lives. These are our *derived needs and potentials.*

In short, every person has natural attributes similar to those of other animals, and species characteristics shared only with other modern humans – both of which can be thought of as genetically "wired-in." Based on these genetic potentials people develop more specific derived needs and capacities as a result of their particular life experiences. While our natural and species needs and powers are the results of past human evolution and are not subject to modification by individual or social activity, our derived needs and powers are subject to modification by individual activity and are very dependent on social environment – as explained below. Since a few species needs and powers are especially critical to understanding how humans and human societies work, I discuss them before explaining how derived needs and powers develop.

Human Consciousness

Human beings have intellectual tools that permit them to understand and situate themselves in their surroundings. This is not to say that everyone accurately understands the world and her position in it. No doubt, most of us deceive ourselves greatly much of the time! But an incessant striving to develop some interpretation of our relationship with our surroundings is a characteristic of normally functioning human beings. We commonly call the need and ability to do this *consciousness,* a trait that makes human systems much more complicated than non-human systems. It is consciousness that allows humans to be self-creative – to select our activities in light of their preconceived effects on our surroundings and ourselves. One effect our activities have is to fulfill our present needs and desires, more or less fully, which we can call *fulfillment effects.* But another consequence of our activities is to reinforce or transform our derived characteristics, and thereby the needs and capacities that depend on them. Our ability to analyze, evaluate, and take what we can call the human *development effects* of our choices into account is why humans are the "subjects" as well as the "objects" of our histories.

The human capacity to act purposefully implies the need to exercise that capacity. Not only can we analyze and evaluate the effects of our actions, we need to exercise choice over alternatives, and we therefore need to be in positions to do so. While some call this the "need for freedom," it bears pointing out that the human "need for freedom" goes beyond that of many animal species. There are animals that cannot be domesticated or will not reproduce in captivity, thereby exhibiting an innate "need for freedom." But the human need to employ our powers of consciousness requires freedom beyond the "physical freedom" some animal species require as well. People require freedom to choose and direct their own activities in accord with their understanding and evaluation of the effects of that activity. In Chapter 2 I will define the concept "self-management" to express this peculiarly human species need in a way that subsumes the better known concept "individual freedom" as a special case.

Human Sociability

Human beings are a social species in a number of important ways. First, the vast majority of our needs and potentials can only be satisfied and developed in conjunction with others. Needs for sexual and emotional gratification can only be pursued in relations with others. Intellectual and communicative potentials can only be developed in relations with others. Needs for camaraderie, community, and social esteem can only be satisfied in relation with others.

Second, needs and potentials that might, conceivably, be pursued independently, seldom are. For example, people could try to satisfy their economic needs self-sufficiently, but we seldom have done so since establishing social relationships that define and mediate divisions of duties and rewards has always proved so much more efficient. And the same holds true for spiritual, cultural, and most other needs. Even when desires might be pursued individually, people have generally found it more fruitful to pursue them jointly.

Third, human consciousness contributes a special character to our sociability. There are other animal species which are social in the sense that many of their needs can only be satisfied with others. But humans have the ability to understand and plan their activity, and since we recognize this ability in others we logically hold them accountable for their choices, and expect them to do likewise. Peter Marin expressed this aspect of the human condition eloquently in an essay titled "The Human Harvest" published in *Mother Jones* (December, 1976: 38).

> Kant called the realm of connection the kingdom of ends. Erich Gutkind's name for it was the absolute collective. My own term for the same thing is the human harvest – by which I mean the webs of connection in which all human goods are clearly the results of a collective labor that morally binds us irrevocably to distant others. Even the words we use, the gestures we make, and the ideas we have, come to us already worn smooth by the labor of others, and they confer upon us an immense debt we do not fully acknowledge.

Bertell Ollman explains it is the individualistic, not the social interpretation of human beings that is unrealistic when examined closely (*Alienation,* Cambridge University Press, 1973: 108):

> The individual cannot escape his dependence on society even when he acts on his own. A scientist who spends his lifetime in a laboratory may delude himself that he is a modern version of Robinson Crusoe, but the material of his activity and the apparatus and skills with which he operates are social products. They are inerasable signs of the cooperation which binds men together. The very language in which a scientist thinks has been learned in a particular society. Social context also determines the career and other life goals that an individual adopts. No one becomes a scientist or even wants to become one in a society which does not have any. In short, man's consciousness of himself and of his relations with others and with nature is that of a social being, since the manner in which he conceives of anything is a function of his society.

In sum, there never was a Hobbesian "state of nature" where individuals roamed the wilds in a "natural" state of war with one another. Human beings have always lived in social units such as clans and tribes. The roots of our sociality – our "realm of connection" or "human harvest" – are both physical-emotional and mental-conceptual. The unique aspect of human sociality is that the "webs of connection" that inevitably connect all human beings are woven not just by a "resonance of the flesh" but by a shared consciousness and mutual accountability as well. Individual humans do not exist in isolation from their species community. It is not possible to fulfill our needs and employ our powers independently of others. And we have never lived except in active interrelation with one another. But the fact that human beings are inherently social does not mean that all institutions meet our social needs and develop our social capacities equally well. For example, in later chapters I will criticize markets for failing to adequately account for, express, and facilitate human sociality.

Human Character Structures

People are more than their constantly developing needs and powers. At any moment we have particular personality traits, skills, ideas, and attitudes. These *human characteristics* play a crucial mediating role. On the one hand they largely determine the activities we will select by defining the goals of these activities – our present needs, desires, or preferences. On the other hand, the characteristics themselves are merely the cumulative imprint of our past activities on our innate potentials. What is important regarding human characteristics is to neither underestimate nor overestimate their permanence. Although I have emphasized that people derive needs, powers, and characteristics over their life time as the result of their activities, we are never completely free to do so at any point in time. Not only are people limited by the particular menu of role offerings of the social institutions that surround them, they are constrained at any moment by the personalities, skills, knowledge, and values they have accumulated as of that moment themselves. But even though character structures may persist over long periods of time, they are not totally invariant. Any change in the nature of our activities that persists long enough can lead to changes in our personalities, skills, ideas, and values, as well as changes in our derived needs and desires that depend on them.

A full theory of human development would have to explain how personalities, skills, ideas, and values form, why they usually persist but occasionally change, and what relationship exists between these semi-permanent structures and people's needs and capacities. No such psychological theory now exists, nor is visible on the horizon. But fortunately, a few "low level" insights are sufficient for our purposes.

The Relation of Consciousness to Activity

The fact that our knowledge and values influence our choice of activities is easy to understand. The manner in which our activities influence our consciousness and the importance of this relation is less apparent. A need that frequently arises from the fact that we see ourselves as choosing among alternatives is the need to interpret our choices in a positive light. If we saw our behavior as completely beyond our own control, there would be no need to justify it, even to ourselves. But to the extent that we see ourselves as choosing among options, it can be very uncomfortable if we are not able to "rationalize" our decisions. This is not to say that people always succeed in justifying their actions, even to themselves. Nor is all behavior equally easy to rationalize! Rather, the point is that striving to minimize what some psychologists call "cognitive dissonance" is a corollary of our power of consciousness. The tendency to minimize cognitive dissonance creates a subtle duality to the relationship between thought and action in which each influences the other, rather than a unidirectional causality. When we fulfill needs through particular activities we are induced to mold our thoughts to justify or rationalize both the logic and merit of those activities, thereby generating consciousness-personality structures that can have a permanence beyond that of the activities that formed them.

The Possibility of Detrimental Character Structures

An individual's ability to mold her needs and powers at any moment is constrained by her previously developed personality, skills, and consciousness. But these characteristics were not always "givens" that must be worked with; they are the products of previously chosen activities in combination with "given" genetic potentials. So why would anyone choose to engage in activities that result in characteristics detrimental to future need fulfillment? One possibility is that someone else, who does not hold our interests foremost, made the decision for us. Another obvious possibility is that we failed to recognize important developmental effects of current activities chosen primarily to fulfill pressing immediate needs. But imposed choices and personal mistakes are not the most interesting possibilities. At any moment we have a host of active needs and powers. Depending on our physical and social environment it may not always be possible to fulfill and develop them all simultaneously. In many situations it is only possible to meet current needs at the expense of generating habits of thinking and behaving that prove detrimental to achieving greater fulfillment later. This can explain why someone might make choices that develop detrimental character traits even if they are aware of the long run consequences.

In sum, people are self-creative within the limits defined by human nature, but this must be interpreted carefully. At any moment each individual is constrained by her previously developed human characteristics. Moreover, as individuals we are powerless to change the social roles defined by society's major institutions within which most of our activity must take place. So as individuals we are to some extent powerless to affect the kind of behavior that will mold our future character traits. Hence, these traits, and any desires that may depend on them, may remain beyond our reach, and our power of self-generation is effectively constrained by the social situations in which we find ourselves. But in the sense that these social situations are ultimately human creations, and to the extent that individuals have maneuverability within given social situations, the potential for self-creation is preserved. In other words, we humans are *both* the subjects *and* the objects of our history.

We therefore define the concept of the *Human Center* to incorporate these conclusions:

- The **Human Center** is the collection of people who live within a society including all their needs, powers, personalities, skills, and consciousness. This includes our natural and species needs and powers – the results of an evolutionary process that occurred for the most part long before known history began. It includes all the structural human characteristics that are givens as far as the individual is concerned at any moment, but are, in fact, the accumulated imprint of her previous activity choices on innate potentials. And it includes our derived needs and powers, or preferences and capacities, which are determined by the interaction of our natural and species needs and powers with the human characteristics we have accumulated.

The Institutional Boundary

People "create" themselves, but only in closely defined settings which place important limitations on their options. Besides the limitations of our genetic potential and the natural environment, the most important settings that structure people's self-creative efforts are social institutions which establish the patterns of expectation within which human activity must occur.

Social institutions are simply conglomerations of interrelated roles. If we consider a factory, the land it sits on is part of the natural environment. The buildings, assembly lines, raw materials, and products are part of the "built" environment. Ruth, Joe, and Sam, the people who work in or own the factory, are part of society's human center. However, the factory *as an institution* consists of the roles and the relationships between those roles: assembly line worker, maintenance worker, foreman, supervisor, plant manager, union steward, minority stockholder, majority stockholder, etc. Similarly, the market as an institution consists of the roles of buyers and sellers. It is neither the place where buying and selling occurs, nor the actual people who buy and sell. It is not even the actual behavior of buying and selling. Actual behavior belongs in the sphere of human activity, or history itself, and is not the same as the social institution that produces that history in interaction with the human center. Rather, the market *as an institution* is the commonly held *expectation* that the social activity of exchanging goods and services will take place through the activity of consensual buying and selling.

We must be careful to define roles and institutions apart from whether or not the expectations that establish them will continue to be fulfilled, because to think of roles and institutions as *fulfilled* expectations lends them a permanence they may not deserve. Obviously a social institution only lasts if the commonly held expectation about behavior patterns is confirmed by repeated actual behavior patterns. But if institutions are defined as fulfilled expectations about behavior patterns it becomes difficult to understand how institutions might change. We want to be very careful not to prejudge the stability of particular institutions, so we define institutions as commonly held expectations and leave the question of whether or not these expectations will continue to be fulfilled – that is, whether or not any particular institution will persist or be transformed – an open question.

Why Must There Be Social Institutions?

If we were all mind readers, or if we had infinite time to consult with one another, human societies might not require mediating institutions. But if there is to be a "division of labor," and if we are neither omniscient nor immortal, people must act on the basis of expectations about other people's behavior. If I make a pair of shoes in order to sell them to pay a dentist to fill my daughter's cavities, I am expecting others to play the role of shoe buyer, and dentists to render their services for a fee. I neither read the minds of the shoe buyers and dentist, nor take the time to arrange and confirm all these coordinated activities before proceeding to make the shoes. Instead I act on the basis of expectations about others' behavior.

So institutions are the necessary consequence of human sociability combined with our lack of omniscience and our mortality – which has important implications for the tendency among some anarchists to conceive of the goal of liberation as the abolition of all institutions. Anarchists correctly note that individuals are not completely "free" as long as institutional constraints exist. *Any* institutional boundary makes some individual choices easier and others harder, and therefore infringes on individual freedom to some extent. But abolishing social institutions is impossible for the human species. The relevant question about institutions, therefore, should not be whether we want them to exist, but whether any particular institution poses unnecessarily oppressive limitations, or instead promotes human development and fulfillment to the maximum extent possible.

In conclusion, if one insists on asking where, exactly, the *Institutional Boundary* is to be found, the answer is that, as commonly held expectations about individual behavior patterns, social institutions are a very practical and limited kind of mental phenomenon. As a matter of fact they are a kind of mental phenomenon that other social animals share – baboons, elephants, wolves, and a number of bird species have received much study. But just because our definition of roles and institutions locates them in people's minds, where we have also located consciousness, does not mean there is not an important distinction between the two. It is human consciousness that provides the potential for purposefully changing our institutions. As best we know, animals cannot change their institutions since they did not create them in the first place. Other animals receive their institutions as part of their genetic inheritance that comes already "wired in." We humans inherit only the necessity of creating some social institutions due to our sociality and lack of omniscience. But the specific creations are, within the limits of our potentials, ours to design.[2]

- The **Institutional Boundary** is society's particular set of social institutions that are each a conglomeration of interconnected roles, or commonly held expectations about appropriate behavior patterns. We define these roles independently of whether or not the expectations they represent will continue to be fulfilled, and apart from whatever incentives do or do not exist for individuals to choose to behave in their accord. The Institutional Boundary is necessary in any human society since we are neither immortal nor omniscient, and is distinct from both human consciousness and activity. It is human consciousness that makes possible purposeful transformations of the Institutional Boundary through human activity.

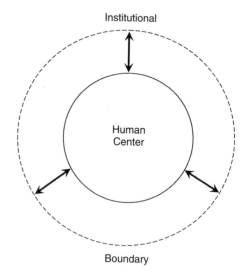

Institutional

Human
Center

Boundary

Figure 1.1 Human Center and Institutional Boundary

2 Thorstein Veblen, father of institutionalist economics, and Talcott Parsons, a giant of modern sociology, both underestimated the potential for applying the human tool of consciousness to the task of analyzing and evaluating the effects of institutions with a mind to changing them for the better. This led Veblen to overstate his case against what he termed "teleological" theories of history, i.e., ones that held onto the possibility of social progress. The same failure rendered Parsonian sociology powerless to explain the process of social change.

Complementary Holism

A social theory useful for pursuing human liberation must highlight the relationship between social institutions and human characteristics. But it is also important to distinguish between different areas, or spheres of social life, and consider the possible relationships between them. In *Liberating Theory* seven progressive authors called our treatment of these issues "complementary holism."

Four Spheres of Social Life

The economy is not the only "sphere" of social activity. In addition to creating economic institutions to organize our efforts to meet material needs and desires, people have organized community institutions for addressing our cultural and spiritual needs, intricate "sex-gender," or "kinship" systems for satisfying our sexual needs and discharging our parental functions, and elaborate political systems for mediating social conflicts and enforcing social decisions. So in addition to the *economic sphere* of social life we have what we call a *community sphere*, a *kinship sphere*,[3] and a *political sphere* as well. In this book we will be primarily concerned with evaluating the performance of the economic sphere, but the possible relationships between the economy and other spheres of social life are worthy of some consideration.

A *monist* paradigm presumes that one of the spheres of social life is always dominant in every society. For example, historical materialism considers the economic sphere to be dominant – even if only in the "last instance" – whereas feminist theories often treat the kinship or reproductive sphere as the most important, while anarchists trace all authority back to the political sphere. In contrast, *complementary holism* does not believe that any pattern of dominance among the four spheres of social life can be deduced from theoretical principles alone, and therefore known *a priori* to be true for all societies. Instead, complementary holism insists that any pattern of dominance (or non-dominance) is possible in theory, and therefore which sphere(s) are more or less dominant in any particular society can only be determined by an empirical study of that society.

All four spheres are socially necessary. Any society that failed to produce and distribute the material means of life would cease to exist. Many Marxists argue that this implies that the economic sphere, or what they call the economic "base"

---

3 Anthropologists often study what they refer to as "kinship systems." However, feminists more often use the phrase "reproductive sphere." In either case, this is the "sphere of social life" primarily concerned with the procreation and education of the next generation to become adult members of society.

or "mode of production," is necessarily dominant in any and all human societies. However, any society that failed to procreate and rear the next generation would also cease to exist. So the kinship or reproductive sphere of social life is just as socially necessary as the economic sphere. And any society that failed to mediate conflicts among its members would disintegrate. Which means the political sphere of social life is necessary as well. Finally, since all societies have existed in the context of other, historically distinct societies, and many contain more than one historically distinct community, all societies have had to establish some kind of relations with other social communities, and most have had to define relations among internal communities as well. This means that the community sphere of social life is as necessary as the political, kinship, and economic spheres.

Besides being necessary, each of the four spheres is usually governed by major social institutions which have significant impacts on people's characteristics and behavior. This, more than their "social necessity," is why complementary holism recognizes that all four spheres are important. But this does not imply any particular pattern of dominance. According to complementary holism there are a number of possible kinds of relations among spheres, and which possibility pertains in a particular society, at a particular time, must be determined by empirical investigation.

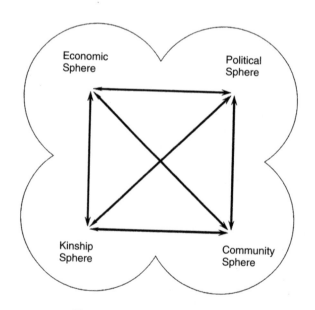

Figure 1.2 Four Spheres of Social Life

Relations between Center, Boundary, and Spheres

The human center and institutional boundary, together with the four spheres of social life, are useful conceptual building blocks for an emancipatory social theory. The concepts human center and institutional boundary include all four kinds of social activity, but distinguish between people and institutions. The spheres of social activity encompass both the human and institutional aspects of a kind of social activity, but distinguish between different primary functions of different activities. . The possible relations between center and boundary, and between different spheres, is obviously critical.

It is evident that if a society is to be stable people must generally fit the roles they are going to fill. Actual behavior must generally conform to the expected patterns of behavior defined by society's major social institutions. People must choose activities in accord with the roles available, and this requires that people's personalities, skills, and consciousness be such that they do so. We must be capable and willing to do what is required of us. In other words, there must be conformity between society's human center and institutional boundary for social stability.

Suppose this were not the case. For example, suppose South African whites had shed their racist consciousness overnight, but all the institutions of apartheid had remained intact. Unless the institutions of apartheid were also changed, rationalization of continued participation in institutions guided by racist norms would eventually regenerate racist consciousness among South African whites. Or, on a smaller scale, suppose one professor eliminates grades, makes papers optional, and no longer dictates course curriculum nor delivers monologues for lectures, but instead simply awaits student initiatives. If students arrive conditioned to respond to grading incentives alone, and wanting to be led or entertained by the instructor, then the elimination of authoritarianism in the institutional structures of a single classroom in the context of continued authoritarian expectations in the student body would result in very little learning indeed.

Social Stability and Social Change

Whether the result of any "discrepancy" between the human center and institutional boundary will lead to a re-molding of the center to conform with an unchanged boundary, or to changes in the boundary that make it more compatible with the human center cannot be known in advance. But in either case *stabilizing forces* within societies act to bring the center and boundary into conformity, and lack of conformity is a sign of social instability.

This is not to say that the human centers and institutional boundaries of all human societies are equally easy to stabilize. While we are always being socialized by the institutions we confront, this process can run into more or fewer obstacles depending on the extent to which particular institutional structures are compatible or incompatible with innate human potentials. In other words, just as there are always stabilizing forces at work in societies, there are often *destabilizing forces* as well resulting from institutional incompatibilities with fundamental human needs. For example, no matter how well oiled the socialization processes of a slave society, there remains a fundamental incompatibility between the social role of slave and the innate human potential and need for self-management. That incompatibility is a constant source of potential instability in societies that seek to confine people to slave status.

Similarly, it is possible for dynamics in one sphere to reinforce or destabilize dynamics in another sphere of social life. For example, it might be that the functioning of the nuclear family produces authoritarian personality structures that reinforce authoritarian dynamics in economic relations. Dynamics in economic hierarchies might also reinforce patriarchal hierarchies in families. In this case authoritarian dynamics in the economic and kinship spheres would be mutually reinforcing. Or, hierarchies in one sphere sometimes accommodate hierarchies in other spheres. For example, the assignment of people to economic roles might accommodate prevailing hierarchies in community and kinship spheres by placing minorities and women into inferior economic positions.

On the other hand, it is also possible for the activity in one sphere to disrupt the manner in which activity is organized in another sphere. For example, the educational system as one component of the kinship sphere might graduate more people seeking a particular kind of economic role than the economic sphere can provide under its current organization. This would produce destabilizing expectations and demands in the economic sphere, and/or the educational system in the kinship sphere. Some argued this was the case during the 1960s and 1970s in the US when college education was expanded greatly and produced "too many" with higher level thinking skills for the number of positions permitting the exercise of such potentials in the monopoly capitalist US economy – giving rise to a "student movement." In any case, at the broadest level, there can be either stabilizing or destabilizing relations among spheres.

Agents of History

The stabilizing and destabilizing forces that exist between center and boundary and among different spheres of social life operate constantly whether people in the society are aware of them or not. But these ever present forces for stability and change are usually complemented by self-conscious efforts of particular social groups seeking to maintain or transform the status quo. Particular ways of organizing the economy may generate privileged and disadvantaged *classes*. Similarly, the organization of kinship or reproductive activity may distribute the burdens and benefits unequally between *gender groups* – for example granting men more of the benefits while assigning them fewer of the burdens of kinship activity than women. And particular community institutions may not serve the needs of all community groups equally well, for example denying *racial or religious minorities* rights or opportunities enjoyed by majority communities. Therefore, apart from underlying forces that stabilize or destabilize societies, groups who enjoy more of the benefits and shoulder fewer of the burdens of social cooperation *in any sphere* have an interest in acting to preserve the status quo. While groups who suffer more of the burdens and enjoy fewer of the benefits under existing arrangements *in any sphere* can become agents for social change. In this way groups that are either privileged or disadvantaged by the rules of engagement *in any of the four spheres of social life* can become *agents of history*. The key to understanding the importance of classes without neglecting or underestimating the importance of privileged and disadvantaged groups defined by community, kinship or political relations is to recognize that *only some* agents of history are economic groups, or classes. Racial, ethnic, religious, and national "community" groups; women, men, heterosexual, and homosexual "gender" groups; and enfranchised, disenfranchised, bureaucrats, and military "political" groups can also be self-conscious agents working to preserve or change the status quo, which consists not only of the reigning economic relations, but the dominant gender, community, and political relations as well.[4]

Applications

Digesting this dense presentation of something as complicated as a theory of society is a challenge for any reader. Unfortunately we can only afford limited space here to briefly discuss a few examples of how it can be applied.

South Africa between 1948 and 1994 is a useful case to consider. Of course during those years the economy generated privileged and exploited classes – capitalists and

4 Broadly speaking the term "economism" means attributing greater importance to the economy than is warranted. It can take the form of assuming dynamics in the economic sphere are more important than dynamics in other spheres when this, in fact, is not the case in some particular society. It can also take the form of assuming that classes are more important agents of social change, and racial, gender, or political groups are less important "agents of history" than they actually are in a particular situation.

workers, landowners and tenants, etc. Patriarchal gender relations also disadvantaged women compared to men in South Africa, and undemocratic political institutions empowered a minority and disenfranchised the majority. But the most important social relations, from which the system derived its name, *apartheid*, were *rules for classifying citizens into different communities – whites, colored, blacks – and laws defining different rights and obligations for people according to their community status.* The relations of apartheid created oppressor and oppressed *racial community groups* who played the principal roles in the epic struggle to preserve or overthrow the status quo in South Africa. In other words, an open minded, reality-based analysis of what made this particular society "tick" would have rather easily come to the conclusion that the community sphere of social life was dominant, the struggle to preserve or overthrow apartheid relations between the white, colored, and majority black communities was central, racial dynamics affected class and gender dynamics more than the reverse, and during these years racial struggle was the "driving force" behind historical change. Because it holds that (1) any pattern of dominance is theoretically possible, and (2) empirical analysis is the only way to discover the pattern of dominance in a particular society, the complementary holist framework outlined in this chapter facilitates coming to this accurate evaluation.

This perspective need not deny that classes, or gender groups for that matter, also played significant roles in South Africa under apartheid. But a social theory that recognizes multiple spheres of social life, and understands that privileged and disadvantaged groups can emerge from any area where the burdens and benefits of social cooperation are not distributed equally, can help us avoid neglecting important agents of history. Unlike a monist theory like historical materialism which insists on prioritizing class, it can help us avoid misunderstanding what is actually going on in a situation like South Africa under apartheid. Complementary holism can also help us understand why not all forms of oppression will be redressed by a social revolution in only one sphere of social life – as important as that change may be. For example, while the overthrow of apartheid largely eliminated one form of oppression in South Africa, it has become apparent over the past two decades that it did little to change class oppression or exploitation.

But how might complementary holism be applied to help understand recent events? At the risk of underappreciating the severity of previous crises in the periphery of the global economy – such as the debt crisis and lost decade of the 1980s in Latin America and Africa, and the East Asian financial crisis in the late 1990s which Nobel Laureate Paul Krugman called "the greatest economic falling from grace since the Great Depression" – 2008 marked the beginning of economic turmoil unseen in the advanced economies since the 1930s. So if there was ever a time when economic dynamics and class struggle should have surged to the fore – or exhibited their "dominance" – this should be it.

Far from denying that economic dynamics and class struggle *can* be dominant, complementary holism holds that this is quite possible. Moreover, since according to complementary holism patterns of dominance can change, it is important for analysts using this social theory to be sensitive to any shifts. The response of the ruling class to an economic crisis of its making – bail out banks and creditors while subjecting the working majority to punishing austerity, no matter how counterproductive to economic recovery – demonstrates that far from being sated, ruling class appetite for class war has increased since 2008. We have also now seen popular uprisings in response such as Los Indignados in Spain, Un-Cut in the UK, and Occupy Wall Street in the US, screaming "no" to more economic deprivation. These are all signs that economic dynamics and class struggle are now more "front and center." However, even during these years of extreme economic crisis and heightened class struggle it would be a mistake to underappreciate the importance of dynamics in other spheres of social life and non-class agents of history prominent in recent struggles around the world.

It would be a mistake to interpret movements like Occupy as merely challenges to class exploitation. While the 1% versus the 99% slogan nicely captures the economic component, unlike the mainstream US labor movement, Occupy also challenged the pretense that the US political system is any longer remotely democratic. Occupy has been just as critical of money taking over politics symbolized by the *Citizens v. United* Supreme Court decision, and of the corporate dominated, two-party duopoly as it has been of escalating economic inequality. After several weeks reporters from the Public Broadcasting System covering the occupation at Zuccotti Park asked demonstrators there: "OK, we know what you're against – all the wealth going to the top 1% – but what are you for?" The demonstrators answered: "See our General Assembly? See us making decisions democratically? That is what we want. We want *real* democracy!" In other words, Occupy was a popular protest against a political system devoid of meaningful democracy as well as a protest against economic inequality.

Moreover, if we look around the world unencumbered by a monist theory which presumes economic dominance, it is apparent that more has changed in some non-economic spheres than in the economy since the onset of the economic crisis. And who is to say these changes are somehow of less significance? The truth is that at least as of the time of the writing of this second edition, there has been practically no change in the economic system, as neoliberalism remains on the throne everywhere it was prior to the crisis, despite its disastrous consequences. In the international economy the same kind of treaties are being negotiated. As a matter of fact, environmental provisions in the international economic treaties negotiated by the Bush administration between 2000 and 2008 had more teeth than environmental provisions do in the Trans-Pacific Partnership Agreement now being negotiated under even greater secrecy by the Obama administration. Domestically, center-left as well as right-wing governments in Europe and North America continue to preside over financial bailouts and fiscal austerity in one country after another, with only a difference in rhetoric. In short, despite all the economic turmoil, and change from "cold" to "hot" class war, there has been virtually no change in economic power or policy, and even less movement toward economic system change. At the same time, at least in the US we have seen a dramatic change in the kinship sphere of social life: The gay, lesbian, bisexual, and transgender (GLBT) movement, the only progressive movement which has been on the offensive instead of defensive recently, has achieved a major shift in popular consciousness regarding homosexuality and has made significant progress toward converting increasing popular tolerance toward sexual preference into greater political and institutional equality.

We have also witnessed dramatic changes in power and relations among major international "communities." The Latin America "community" of nations has continued to make historic strides in freeing itself from domination by the "northern colossus." Despite differences between the more "radical" bloc of Venezuela, Bolivia, Cuba, Ecuador, and Nicaragua, and the more moderate bloc of Uruguay, Argentina, Brazil, Chile, and Costa Rica, Latin America as a whole has greatly reduced US military power in the region, forged new international organizations of their own like ALBA and the Bank of the South while reducing US influence within the OAS, and reduced regional economic dependence on the US as well. By far the largest popular uprising in the past six years, the remarkable Arab Spring, was not primarily about economic issues in which protagonists were opposing classes.[5] The Arab Spring was primarily a revolt against corrupt, authoritarian political regimes and their quisling peace

---

5 Of course a majority who participated in the Arab Spring were from the working class, of course they were economically oppressed, and of course improvements in their economic conditions were called for. But this does not mean the Arab Spring was primarily a class movement, focused primarily on economic issues. Since ruling classes are small compared to working classes everywhere, the working class must necessarily comprise a large part of any movement that is popular, which does not mean that the movement is primarily about economic exploitation. A majority of African-Americans who participated in the civil rights movement of the 1960s were working class, and their deplorable economic conditions were among their grievances. But it would be inaccurate to conclude that the US civil rights movement of the 1960s was therefore primarily a class movement, focused primarily on economic exploitation. It was a movement in which an historically oppressed racial group, African-Americans, emerged as an agent of history and fought with some success against institutions and racist ideology that oppressed them specifically as a minority community.

with US–Israeli dominance over the region, i.e. it was primarily a revolt challenging the political status quo within several Arab countries, and disempowerment of the majority Arab "community" in the region as a whole. While, like Occupy, the Arab Spring has been quieted for the moment, combined with a partial US military retreat from the region, the Arab Spring has already shaken up relations among country, religious, and ethnic "communities" in the Mideast to an extent unseen since the end of World War II. Finally, the changes from a bipolar world between 1945 and 1989 where the US and Soviet Union "competed" as reigning superpowers, to a unipolar world between 1989 and 2010 with the US as lone superpower, to a world now adjusting to the rise of a new superpower, China, have all been transformations of historic importance in the community sphere of global society.

In any case, hopefully the conceptions of human beings, social institutions, and multiple spheres of social life comprising the skeleton of a "liberating" social theory summarized briefly in this chapter provide a proper setting for our study of "political economy" – one that neither overstates nor understates the role of economics in the social sciences. In Chapter 2 we proceed to think about how to evaluate the performance of any economy.

2

What Should We Demand from Our Economy?

It is easy enough to say we want an economy that distributes the burdens and benefits of social labor fairly, that allows people to make the decisions that affect their economic lives, that develops human potentials for creativity, cooperation and empathy, and that utilizes human and natural resources efficiently and sustainably. But what does all this mean more precisely?

Economic Justice

Is it necessarily unfair when some work less or consume more than others? Do those with more productive property deserve to work less or consume more? Do those who are more talented or more educated deserve more? Do those who contribute more, or those who make greater sacrifices, or those who have greater needs deserve more? By what logic are some unequal outcomes fair and others not?

Equity takes a back seat to efficiency for most mainstream economists, while the issue of economic justice has long been a passion of political economists. From Proudhon's provocative quip that "property is theft," to Marx's three volume indictment of capitalism as a system based on the "exploitation of labor," economic justice has been a major theme in political economy. After reviewing evidence of rising economic inequality within the United States and globally, we compare conservative, liberal and radical views of economic justice, and explain why political economists condemn most of today's growing inequalities as escalating economic injustice.

Increasing Inequality of Wealth and Income

I introduced this section in the 2002 edition saying: "As we begin the twenty-first century, escalating economic inequality makes all other economic changes pale in comparison. The evidence of increasing wealth and income inequality is overwhelming." While progressives lamented this trend, the major media, politicians in both the Democratic and Republican parties alike, and the mainstream of the economics profession ignored or belittled the issue. A dozen years, and a major economic crisis later, rising inequality continues unabated. However, it is no longer the case that few take notice. If Occupy Wall Street accomplished nothing else, it put this historic increase in economic inequality at front and center of public discourse. As a matter of fact, the Occupy slogan referring to the fact that the top 1% had captured almost all productivity gains for decades, leaving the bottom 99% no better off than they had been a generation earlier, turned out to be an understatement! Once attention was drawn to the issue, it turned out that it was the top one tenth of the top 1% who had managed to appropriate the lion's share of all productivity gains in the US economy for decades. I have left intact my summary of the evidence on increasing inequality published in the 2002 edition to show that what political economists had clearly documented by 2000 should have been more than enough to set off alarm bells a full decade before they finally went off in 2011. After that I have added a brief factual update on the first decade of the twenty-first century showing that despite the greatest economic crisis in eighty years rising inequality has continued unabated.

In a study published in 1995 by the Twentieth Century Fund, Edward Wolff concluded:

> Income inequality has increased over the past twenty years. Upper-income groups have continued to do well while others, particularly those without a college degree and the young have seen their real income decline. The 1994 *Economic Report of the President* refers to the 1979–1990 fall in real income of men with only four years of high school – a 21% decline – as stunning. But the growing divergence evident in income distribution is even starker in wealth distribution. Equalizing trends of the 1930s–1970s reversed sharply in the 1980s. The gap between haves and have-nots is greater now than at any time since 1929.[1]

In 2000 Chuck Collins and Felice Yeskel reported: "In 1976, the wealthiest one percent of the population owned just under 20% of all the private wealth. By 1999, the richest 1 percent's share had increased to over 40% of all wealth." And they

---

1 Edward N. Wolff, *Top Heavy: A Study of the Increasing Inequality of Wealth in America* (The Twentieth Century Fund, 1995): 1–2.

calculated that in the twenty-one years between 1976 and 1997 while the top 1% of wealth holders doubled their share of the wealth pie the bottom 90% saw their share cut almost in half.[2] In 1995 the Center for Popular Economics reported that between 1983 and 1989 the average wealth of households in the United States grew at an annual rate of 3.4% and the average financial wealth of households grew at 4.3% after being adjusted for inflation. But the top 1% of wealth holders captured an astounding 66.2% of the growth in financial wealth, the next 19% of wealth holders captured 36.8%, and the bottom 80% of wealth holders in the US lost 3.0% of their financial wealth. As a result the top 1% increased their share of total wealth in the US from 31% to 37% in those six years alone, and by 1989 the richest 1% of families held 45% of all nonresidential real estate, 62% of all business assets, 49% of all publicly held stock, and 78% of all bonds.[3]

In 1994 Lawrence Mishel and Jared Bernstein estimated that:

> most wealth growth arose from the appreciation (or capital gains) of pre-existing wealth and not savings out of income. Over the 1962 to 1989 period, roughly three-fourths of new wealth was generated by increasing the value of initial wealth – much of it inherited.[4]

The bi-annual economic report of the Economic Policy Institute concluded that the same pattern emerges when we look to see who benefited from the stock market boom between 1989 and 1997. The top 1% of wealth holders captured an astonishing 42.5% of the stock market gains over those years, the next 9% of wealth holders captured an additional 43.3% of the gains, the next 10% captured 3.1%, while the bottom 80% of wealth holders captured only 11% of the stock market gains.[5]

The Economic Policy Institute reported in its 1994–95 edition that while growing wealth inequality had been more dramatic, income inequality had been growing as well. Real wages fell starting in the mid-1970s to where the average hourly wage adjusted for inflation was lower in 1994 than it had been in 1968. And this decline in real hourly wages occurred despite continual increases in productivity per hour. Between 1973 and 1979 productivity rose at an annual rate of 0.6% while hourly

2 Chuck Collins and Felice Yeskel with United for a Fair Economy, *Economic Apartheid in America* (The New Press, 2000): 54–57.
3 *The New Field Guide to the US Economy*, by Nancy Folbre and the Center for Popular Economics (The New Press, 1995).
4 Lawrence Mishel and Jared Bernstein, *The State of Working America 1994–1995* (M.E. Sharpe, 1994): 246.
5 *The State of Working America 1998–1999*: 271.

wages fell by 0.1%; between 1979 and 1983 productivity rose by 1% per year and hourly wages rose by 1.1%; between 1983 and 1989 productivity rose by 0.8% and wages rose by 0.2%; and between 1989 and 1992 productivity rose by 1.5% per year while hourly wages fell by 0.9% per year.[6] Overall, between 1973 and 1998 labor productivity grew 33%. Collins and Yeskel calculated that if hourly wages had grown at the same rate as labor productivity the average hourly wage in 1998 would have been $18.10 rather than $12.77 – a difference of $5.33 an hour, or more than $11,000 per year for a full-time worker.[7] Moreover, the failure of real wages to keep up with labor productivity growth has been worse for those in lower wage brackets. Between 1973 and 1993 workers earning in the 80th percentile gained 2.7% in real wages while workers in the 60th percentile lost 4.9%, workers in the 40th percentile lost 9.0%, and workers in the 20th percentile lost 11.7%, creating much greater inequality of wage income.[8]

In contrast, I reported in the 2002 edition that corporate profit rates in the US in 1996 reached their highest level since these data were first collected in 1959. According to the Bureau of Economic Analysis the before-tax profit rate rose to 11.4% in 1996 yielding an eight-year period of dramatic, sustained increases in corporate profits unparalleled in US history. Moreover, whereas previous periods of high profits accompanied high rates of investment and economic growth, the average rate of economic growth over these eight years was just 1.9%. In short, whatever was good for corporate profits was clearly *not* so good for the rest of us.

While there are a number of different ways to measure inequality, the most widely used is a statistic called the gini coefficient. A value of 0 corresponds to perfect equality and a value of 1 corresponds to perfect inequality. In the 2002 edition I reported that the gini coefficient for the US had increased by 18.3% between 1966 and 1993, and noted that this 0.68% average annual rate of increase was "remarkable" and "historically unprecedented."

I also wrote in 2002 that trends in global inequality were just as disturbing, if not more so. Walter Park and David Brat reported in a study of gross domestic product per capita in 91 countries that the value of the gini rose steadily from 0.442 in 1960 to 0.499 in 1988.[9] In other words, between 1960 and 1988 there was an increase in the economic inequality *between* countries of 13%, which is an average annual increase of 0.72%.

6 *The State of Working America 1994–1995*, 112.
7 *Economic Apartheid in America*, 56.
8 *The State of Working America 1994–1995*, 121.
9 Walter Park and David Brat, "A Global Kuznets Curve?" *Kylos* 48, 1995: 110.

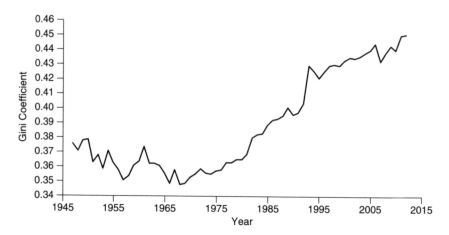

Figure 2.1 Gini Coefficients for US Household Income 1947–2012[10]

What does more recent data show? A quick check of the most recent data on the gini coefficient for the US shows that the "unprecedented" average annual rate of increase of 0.68% a year from the mid-1960s to the early 1990s has continued unabated. According to recent UN data the US gini coefficient increased from 0.428 in 1990 to 0.470 in 2006, which is an average annual increase of 0.60% a year. According to the latest World Bank estimates of gini coefficients for income for the entire world the most rapid rise in world history dating back to 1820 took place between 1980 and 2002, after which relatively strong economic performances in a few large developing countries like China, Brazil, and India seem to have slowed the trend.[11]

Nor is it hard to identify why inequality has continued to rise in the US since 2000. Despite increases in productivity wages have continued to stagnate so that profits have continued to grow. We can break the period from 2000 to 2012 into the pre-crisis boom period from 2000 to 2007, and the period after the crisis hit, from 2007 to 2012. In the pre-crisis "boom" productivity rose by 16% but average compensation rose by only 9.4%. Since the crisis productivity has risen by only 7.7% but average compensation has risen by only 0.9%. Over the entire twelve-year period

10 The data for Figure 2.1 is from the United States Census Bureau, www.census.gov/hhes/income/data/historical/fam Table F-4.
11 Branko Milanovic, "Global Inequality and the Global Inequality Extraction Ratio," *World Bank.* 2009.

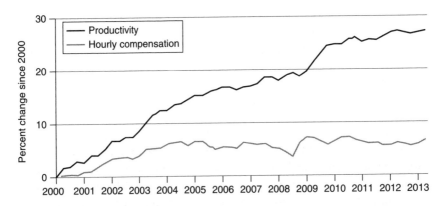

Figure 2.2 Real Average Hourly Compensation and Productivity Growth 2000–2013[12]

productivity rose by 24.9% but average hourly compensation rose by only 10.4%.[13] In contrast, according to data from the Bureau of Economic Analysis pre-tax US corporate profits as a percentage of GDP rose from 7% in 2000 to just over 12% – a record high – in 2007. When the crisis hit they fell back to 7% in 2009, but then rose just as quickly back to a new record high of 12.6% in the final quarter of 2011 and remained high ever since.[14] In short, since 2000 wages have lagged far behind productivity while profits have soared, and while profits recovered quickly and spectacularly from the crisis, wages have hardly recovered at all.

So the facts are clear: We have experienced an increase in economic inequality that is not only "reminiscent of the Robber Baron era," as I wrote in 2002, but now surpasses it. Nor did the greatest economic crisis in over eighty years reverse the trend. We are now ready to face the more difficult question of when unequal outcomes are also inequitable, and when they are not – which has long been a subject of much controversy.

Different Conceptions of Economic Justice

The subject of economic justice can be formulated as follows: What is an equitable distribution of the burdens and benefits of economic activity? Philosophers,

12 Lawrence Mishel and Heidi Shierholz, "A Decade of Flat Wages," EPI Briefing Paper #365, August 21, 2013: 6.
13 Ibid.: 4.
14 Ed Dolan, "US Corporate Profits at All Time High," *EconoMonitor*, September 26, 2013.

economists, and political scientists have offered three different distributive maxims attempting to define equity, which we can think of as the conservative, liberal, and radical definitions of economic justice.

Conservative Maxim 1: *Payment according to the value of one's personal contribution and the contribution of the productive property one owns.*

The rationale behind the conservative maxim is that people should get out of an economy what they and their productive possessions contribute to the economy. If we think of the goods and services, or benefits of an economy, as a giant pot of stew, the idea is that individuals contribute to how big and rich the stew will be by their labor and by the productive assets they bring to the kitchen. If my labor and productive assets make the stew bigger or richer than your labor and assets, then according to maxim 1 it is only fair that I eat more stew, or richer morsels, than you do.

While this rationale has obvious appeal, it has a major problem I call the *Rockefeller grandson problem.* According to maxim 1 the grandson of a Rockefeller with a large inheritance of productive property *should* eat 1000 times as much stew as a highly trained, highly productive, hard working son of a pauper – even if Rockefeller's grandson doesn't work a day in his life and the pauper's son works for fifty years producing goods or providing services of great benefit to others. This will inevitably occur if we count the contribution of productive property people own, and if people own different amounts of machinery and land, or what is the same thing, different amounts of stocks in corporations that own the machinery and land, since bringing a cooking pot or stove to the economy "kitchen" increases the size and quality of the stew we can make just as surely as peeling more potatoes and stirring the pot more does. So anyone who considers it *unfair* when the idle grandson of a Rockefeller consumes more than a hard working, productive son of a pauper cannot accept maxim 1 as the definition of equity.

A second line of defense for the conservative maxim is based on a vision of "free and independent" people, each with his or her own property, who, it is argued, would refuse to voluntarily enter a social contract on any other terms. This view is commonly associated with the writings of John Locke. But while it is clear why those with a great deal of productive property in Locke's imaginary "state of nature" would have reason to hold out for a social contract along the lines of maxim 1, why would not those who wander the state of nature with little or no productive property in their backpacks hold out for a very different arrangement? If those with considerable wherewithal can do quite well for themselves in the state of nature, whereas those without cannot, it is not difficult to see how requiring unanimity would drive the bargain in the direction of maxim 1. But then maxim 1 is the result of an unfair bargaining situation in which the rich are better able to tolerate failure to reach an agreement over a fair way to assign the burdens and benefits of economic cooperation than the poor, giving the rich the upper hand in negotiations over the terms of the social contract. In this case the social contract rationale for maxim 1 loses moral force because it results from an unfair bargain. This suggests that *unless those with more productive property acquired it through some greater merit on their part, the income which accrues to them from this property is unjustifiable, at least on equity grounds.* That is, while the unequal outcome might be desirable for some *other* reason such as improving efficiency or economic freedom, it would *not* be just or fair. In which case maxim 1 must be rejected as a definition of equity if we find that those who own more productive property did not come by it through greater merit.

One common way people acquire productive property is through inheritance. But it is difficult to see how those who inherit wealth are more deserving than those who don't. It is possible the person *making* a bequest worked harder or consumed less than others in her generation, and in one of these ways sacrificed more than others. Or it is possible the person *making* the bequest was more productive than others. And we might decide that greater sacrifice or greater contribution merited greater reward. But in these scenarios it is not the heir who made the greater sacrifice or contribution, it is the person who made the bequest, so the heir would not deserve greater wealth on those grounds. As a matter of fact, if we decide rewards are earned by sacrifice or personal contribution, inherited wealth violates either norm since inheriting wealth is neither a sacrifice nor a personal contribution. A more compelling argument for inheritance is that banning inheritance is unfair to those wishing to make bequests rather than that it is unfair to those who would receive them. One could argue that if wealth is justly acquired it is wrong to prevent anyone from disposing of it as they wish – including bequeathing it to their descendants. However, it should be noted that any "right" of wealthy members of older generations to bequeath their gains to their offspring would have to be weighed against the "right" of people in younger generations to start with "equal economic opportunities."[15] Indeed, these two "rights" are obviously in conflict, and some means of adjudicating between them is required. But no matter how this

---

15 We are not talking about willing personal belongings to decedents, which is unobjectionable, but passing on productive property in quantities that significantly skew the economic opportunities of members of the new generation.

matter is settled, it appears that those who receive income from inherited wealth do so unfairly.

A second way people acquire more productive property than others is through good luck. Working or investing in a rising or declining company or industry constitutes good luck or bad luck. But unequal distributions of productive property that result from differences in luck are not the result of unequal sacrifices, unequal contributions, or any difference in merit between people. Luck, by its very definition is not deserved, and therefore the unequal incomes that result from unequal distributions of productive property due to differences in luck appear to be inequitable as well.

A third way people come to have more productive property is through unfair advantage. Those who are stronger, better connected, have inside information, or are more willing to prey on the misery of others can acquire more productive property through legal and illegal means. Obviously if unequal wealth is the result of someone taking unfair advantage of another it is inequitable.

The last way people might come to have more productive property than others is by using some income they earned fairly to purchase more productive property than others can. What constitutes fairly earned income is the subject of maxims 2 and 3 which we discuss below. But there is a difficult moral issue regarding income from productive property even if the productive property was purchased with income we stipulate was fairly earned in the first place. In Chapter 3 we will discover that labor and credit markets allow people with productive wealth to capture part of the increase in productivity of *other people* that results when other people work with the productive wealth. Whether or not, and to what extent the profit or rent owners of productive wealth initially receive is merited we will examine very carefully. But even if we stipulate that some compensation is justified by a meritorious action that occurred *once* in the past, it turns out that labor and credit markets allow those who own productive wealth to parlay it into *permanently* higher incomes which *increase* over time with no further meritorious behavior on their parts. This creates the dilemma that ownership of productive property *even if justly acquired* may well give rise to additional income that, while fair initially, becomes unfair after some point, and increasingly so. The simple corn model we explore in Chapter 3 illustrates this moral dilemma nicely.

In sum, if unequal accumulations of productive property were the result only of meritorious actions, and if compensation ceased when the social debt was fully repaid, using words like "exploitation" to describe payments to owners of productive property would seem harsh and misleading. On the other hand, if those who own more productive property acquired it through inheritance, luck, unfair advantage –

or because once they have more productive property than others they can accumulate even more with no further above-average meritorious behavior by using labor or credit markets – then calling the unequal outcomes that result from differences in wealth unfair and exploitative seems perfectly appropriate.

Most political economists believe a compelling case can be made that differences in ownership of productive property which accumulate within a single generation due to unequal sacrifices and/or unequal contributions people make themselves are small compared to the differences in wealth that develop due to inheritance, luck, unfair advantage, and accumulation. Edward Bellamy put it this way in *Looking Backward*, written at the close of the nineteenth century:

> You may set it down as a rule that the rich, the possessors of great wealth, had no moral right to it as based upon desert, for either their fortunes belonged to the class of inherited wealth, or else, when accumulated in a lifetime, necessarily represented chiefly the product of others, more or less forcibly or fraudulently obtained.

One hundred years later Lester Thurow estimated that between 50 and 70% of all wealth in the US is inherited. Daphne Greenwood and Edward Wolff estimated that 50–70% of the wealth of households under age 50 was inherited. Laurence Kotlikoff and Lawrence Summers estimated that as much as 80% of personal wealth came either from direct inheritance or the income on inherited wealth.[16] A study published by United for a Fair Economy in 1997 titled "Born on Third Base" found that of the 400 on the 1997 Forbes list of wealthiest individuals and families in the US, 42% inherited their way onto the list; another 6% inherited wealth in excess of $50 million; and another 7% started life with at least $1 million. In any case, presumably what Proudhon was thinking when he coined the phrase "property is theft" was that most large wealth holders acquire their wealth through inheritance, luck, unfair advantage, or unfair accumulation. A less flamboyant radical might have stipulated that he was referring to productive, not personal property, and added the qualification "property is theft – more often than not."

---

16 Lester Thurow, *The Future of Capitalism: How Today's Economic Forces Will Shape the Future* (William Morrow, 1996), Daphne Greenwood and Edward Wolff, "Changes in Wealth in the United States 1962–1983," *Journal of Population Economics* 5, 1992, and Laurence Kotlikoff and Lawrence Summers, "The Role of Intergenerational Transfers in Aggregate Capital Accumulation," *Journal of Political Economy* 89, 1981.

Liberal Maxim 2: Payment according to the value of one's personal contribution only.

While those who support the liberal maxim find most property income unjustifiable, advocates of maxim 2 hold that all have a right to the "fruits of their own labor." The rationale for this has a powerful appeal: If my labor contributes more to the social endeavor it is only right that I receive more. Not only am I not exploiting others, they would be exploiting me by paying me less than the value of my personal contribution. But ironically, the same reason for rejecting the conservative maxim applies to the liberal maxim as well. Economists define the value of the contribution of any input as the "marginal revenue product" of that input. In other words, if we add one more unit of the input in question to all of the inputs currently used in a production process, how much would the value of output increase? The answer is defined as the marginal revenue product of the input in question. But mainstream economics teaches us that the marginal productivity, or contribution of an input, depends as much on the number of units of that input available, and on the quantity and quality of other, complementary inputs, as on any intrinsic quality of the input itself – which undermines the moral imperative behind any "contribution-based" maxim – that is, maxim 2 as well as maxim 1. Besides the fact that the marginal productivity of different kinds of labor depends mostly on the number of people in each labor category in the first place, and on the quantity and quality of non-labor inputs available for use, most differences in people's personal productivities are due to intrinsic qualities of people themselves which *cannot* be traced to differential sacrifices. No amount of eating and weight lifting will give an average individual a 6 foot 9 inch frame with 350 plus pounds of muscle. Yet professional football players in the United States receive hundreds of times more than an average salary because those attributes make their contribution outrageously high in the context of US sports culture. The famous British political economist Joan Robinson pointed out long ago, that however "productive" a machine or piece of land may be, that hardly constitutes a moral argument for paying anything to its owner. In a similar vein one could argue that however "productive" a high IQ or a 350 pound physique may be, that doesn't mean the owner of this trait deserves more income than someone less gifted who works as hard and sacrifices as much. The bottom line is that the "genetic lottery" greatly influences how valuable one's personal contribution will be. Yet the genetic lottery is no more fair than the inheritance lottery – which implies that as a conception of economic justice maxim 2 suffers from a similar flaw as maxim 1.[17]

17 Milton Friedman argued this point eloquently in *Capitalism and Freedom* (University of Chicago Press, 1964), Chapter 10. However, his conclusion was that since maxim 2 cannot be defended on moral grounds, critics of capitalism, which distributes the burdens and benefits of economic cooperation

In defense of maxim 2 it is frequently argued that while talent may not deserve reward, talent requires training, and herein lies the sacrifice that merits reward – doctor's salaries are compensation for all the extra years of education. But longer training does not necessarily mean greater personal sacrifice. It is important not to confuse the cost of someone's training to society – which consists mostly of the *trainer's* time and energy, and scarce social resources like books, computers, microscopes, libraries, and classrooms – with the personal sacrifice of the *trainee*. If teachers and educational facilities are paid for at public expense – that is, if we have a universal public education system – and if students are paid a living stipend – so they forego no income while in school – then the personal sacrifice of the student consists only of their discomfort from time spent in school. But even the personal suffering we endure as students must be properly compared. While many educational programs are less personally enjoyable than time spent in leisure, comparing discomfort during school with comfort during leisure is not the relevant comparison. The relevant comparison is with the discomfort others experience who are working instead of going to school. If our criterion is greater personal sacrifice than others, then logic requires comparing the student's discomfort to whatever level of discomfort others are experiencing who work while the student is in school. Only if schooling is more disagreeable than working does it constitute a greater sacrifice than others make, and thereby deserve reward. So to the extent that education is paid for publicly rather than privately, and the personal discomfort of schooling is no greater than the discomfort others incur while working, extra schooling merits no compensation on moral grounds.

In sum, I call the problem with maxim 2 the "*doctor–garbage collector problem.*" How can it be fair to pay a brain surgeon who is on the first tee at his country club golf course by 2 p.m. even on the four days a week he works, ten times more than a garbage collector who works under miserable conditions forty plus hours a week, if education is free all the way through medical school?

Radical Maxim 3: *Payment according to effort, or the personal sacrifices one makes.*

Which brings us to the radical maxim 3. Whereas differences in contribution will be due to differences in talent, training, job assignment, luck, and effort, the only factor that deserves extra compensation according to maxim 3 is extra effort. By "effort" is meant personal sacrifice for the sake of the social good. Of course effort can take many forms. It may be longer work hours, less pleasant work, or more

according to maxim 1, should mute their criticisms. Essentially Friedman reminded critics of capitalism who favor maxim 2 over maxim 1 that those who live in glass houses shouldn't throw stones!

intense, dangerous, unhealthy work. Or, it may consist of undergoing training that is less gratifying than the training experiences of others, or less pleasant than time others spend working who train less. The underlying rationale for maxim 3 is that people should eat from the stew pot according to the sacrifices they made to cook it. According to maxim 3 no other consideration, besides differential sacrifice, can justify one person eating more stew than another.

One argument for why sacrifice deserves reward is because people have control over how much they sacrifice. I can decide to work longer hours, or work harder, whereas I cannot decide to be 6 foot 9 or have a high IQ. It is commonly considered unjust to punish someone for something she could do nothing about. On those grounds paying someone less just because she is not large or smart violates a fundamental precept of fair play. On the other hand, if someone doesn't work as long or hard as the rest of us, we don't feel it is inappropriate to punish her by paying her less because she *could* have worked longer or harder if she had chosen to. In the case of reward according to effort, avoiding punishment is possible, whereas in the case of reward according to contribution it is largely not.

Moreover, the "punishment" meted out by maxim 3 to those who make fewer sacrifices than others is not even social disapproval. There is no reason for society to frown on those who prefer to make fewer sacrifices as long as they are willing to accept fewer economic benefits to go along with their lesser sacrifice. There is no reason that just because people enter into a system of equitable cooperation with others this precludes leaving the sacrifice/benefit trade-off to personal choice. Maxim 3 simply balances any differences in the burdens people choose to bear with commensurate differences in the benefits they receive. I think this is the strongest argument for reward according to sacrifice. Even if all were not equally able to make sacrifices, receiving extra benefits to compensate for extra burdens seems only fair. When people enter into economic cooperation with one another, for the arrangement to be just should not all participants benefit equally? Since each participant bears burdens as well as enjoys benefits, it is equalization of *net* benefits, i.e. benefits enjoyed minus burdens borne, that makes the economic cooperation fair. So if some bear more of the burdens justice requires that they be compensated with benefits commensurate with their greater sacrifice. Only then will all enjoy equal *net* benefits. Only then will the system of economic cooperation be treating all participants equally, i.e. giving equal weight or priority to the interests of all participants. Notice that even if some are more able to sacrifice than others, the outcome for both the more and less able to sacrifice is the same when extra sacrifices are rewarded. In this way all receive the same net benefits from economic cooperation irrespective of any differences in their abilities to contribute *or* to sacrifice.

Many who object to maxim 3 as a distributive principle raise questions about measuring sacrifice, or about conflicts between reward according to sacrifice and economic efficiency. But measurement problems, or conflicts between equity and efficiency, are *not* objections to maxim 3 as a definition of what is fair, i.e. they are *not* objections to maxim 3 *on equity grounds*. To reject maxim 3 because effort or sacrifice may be difficult to measure, or because rewarding sacrifice may reduce efficiency is not to reject maxim 3 because it is unfair. No matter how weighty these arguments may prove to be, they are not arguments against maxim 3 on grounds that it somehow fails to accurately express what it means for the distribution of burdens and benefits in a system of economic cooperation to be just, or fair. Moreover, even should it prove that economic justice is difficult to achieve because it is difficult to measure something accurately, or costly to achieve because to do so generates inefficiency, one presumably would still wish to know exactly what this elusive or costly economic justice *is*.

Even for those who reject contribution-based theories of economic justice like maxims 1 and 2 as inherently flawed because people's abilities to contribute are different through no fault of their own, there is still a problem with maxim 3 from a moral point of view that I call the "*AIDS victim problem*." Suppose someone has made average sacrifices for 15 years, and consumed an average amount. Suddenly they contract AIDS through no fault of their own. In the early 1990s a medical treatment program for an AIDS victim often cost close to a million dollars. That is, the cost to society of providing humane care for an AIDS victim was roughly a million dollars. If we limit people's consumption to the level warranted by their efforts, we would have to deny AIDS victims humane treatment, which many would find hard to defend on moral grounds.

Of course this is where another maxim comes to mind: *payment according to need.* Whether taking differences in need into consideration is required by economic justice or is required, instead, for an economy to be *humane* is debatable. But as long as we conclude that ignoring either effort or need is morally indefensible it reduces to a question of semantics.

Efficiency

As long as resources are scarce relative to human needs and socially useful labor is burdensome, in part, efficiency is preferable to wastefulness. Political economists do not have to imitate our mainstream colleagues and concentrate on efficiency to the detriment of other important criteria such as economic justice and democracy in order to recognize that people have every reason to be resentful if their sacrifices are wasted or if limited resources are squandered.

The Pareto Principle

Economists usually define economic efficiency as Pareto optimality – named after the late nineteenth-century Italian economist Wilfredo Pareto. A **Pareto optimal outcome** *is one where it is impossible to make anyone better off without making someone else worse off.* The idea is simply that it would be inefficient or wasteful not to implement *a change that made someone better off and nobody worse off.* Such a change is called a **Pareto improvement**, and another way to define a Pareto optimal, or efficient outcome, is an outcome where there are no further Pareto improvements possible.

This does not mean a Pareto optimal outcome is necessarily wonderful. If I have 10 units of happiness and you have 1, and there is no way for me to have more than 10 unless you have less than 1, and no way for you to have more than 1 unless I have less than 10; then my having 10 units of happiness and your having 1 is a Pareto optimal outcome. But you would be right not to regard it very highly, and being a reasonable person, I would even agree with you. Moreover, there are usually *many* Pareto optimal outcomes. For instance, if I have 7 units of happiness and you have 6, and if there is no way for me to have more than 7 unless you have less than 6, and no way for you to have more than 6 unless I have less than 7; then my having 7 and your having 6 is also a Pareto optimal outcome. And we might both regard this second Pareto optimal outcome as better than the first, even though I am personally better off under the first. So the point is not that achieving a Pareto optimal outcome is necessarily wonderful – that depends on which Pareto optimal outcome we have achieved. Instead the point is that *non*-Pareto optimal outcomes are clearly undesirable because we could make someone better off without making anyone worse off – and it is "inefficient" or wasteful not to do that. In other words, it is hard to deny that there is something wrong with an economy that systematically yields non-Pareto optimal outcomes, i.e. fails to make some of its participants better off when doing so would make nobody worse off.

It is important to recognize that the Pareto criterion, or definition of efficiency, is not going to settle most of the important economic issues we face. Most policy choices will make some people better off but others worse off, and in these situations the Pareto criterion has nothing to tell us. Consequently, if economists confine themselves to the narrow concept of efficiency as Pareto optimality, and only recommend policies that are, in fact, Pareto improvements, we would be rendered silent on most issues! For example, reducing greenhouse gas emissions makes a lot of sense because the future benefits of stopping global warming and avoiding dramatic climate change far outweigh the present costs of reducing emissions. But since a relatively few people in the present generation will be made somewhat worse off no matter how we go about it, the fact that many more people in future generations will be much, much better off does not allow us to recommend the policy as a Pareto improvement – that is, on efficiency grounds in the narrow sense.

The Efficiency Criterion

The usual way around this problem is to broaden the notion of efficiency from Pareto improvements to changes where the benefits to some outweigh the costs to others. This broader notion of efficiency is called the **efficiency criterion** and serves as the basis for *cost–benefit analysis*. Simply put, the efficiency criterion says *if the overall benefits to any and all people of doing something outweigh the overall costs to any and all people of doing it, it is "efficient" to do it. Whereas, if the overall costs to any and all people outweigh the overall benefits to any and all people of doing something it is "inefficient" to do it.*

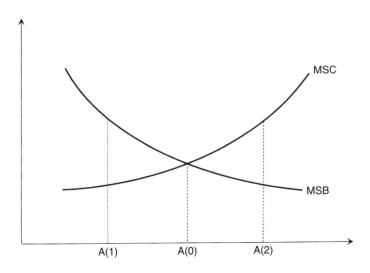

Figure 2.3 The Efficiency Criterion

We can illustrate the efficiency criterion using a very useful graph. Suppose we knew the cost to society of growing each and every apple. That is, suppose we knew how much of society's scarce land, labor, fertilizer, etc. it took to grow each and every apple, and we also knew how much pesticide it took, and how much it "cost" society when more pesticide seeped into our ground water, etc. We call this the *social cost* of producing apples, and we call the social cost of the last (or next) apple produced the *marginal social cost* of apples, or MSC for short. Suppose we also knew the benefit to society of having another apple available to consume. The *social benefit* of the last (or next) apple consumed is called the *marginal social benefit* of apples, or MSB for short. Now let us assume that the more apples we have consumed already the less beneficial an additional apple will be, and the more apples we have produced already the more it costs society to produce another one. In this case if we plot the number of apples on the horizontal axis and measure the marginal social benefit and marginal social cost of apples on the vertical axis, the MSB curve will be downward sloping and the MSC curve will be upward sloping as it is in Figure 2.3. What is incredibly useful about this diagram is it allows us to determine how many apples we *should* produce and consume, i.e. the socially efficient or "optimal" quantity of apples to produce, A(0). It is the amount where the marginal social cost, of producing the last apple, MSC is equal to the marginal social benefit from consuming the last apple, MSB. We can demonstrate that the socially efficient, or optimal level of apple production and consumption is the level below which the MSC and MSB curves cross by showing that any lower or higher level of production and consumption allows for an increase in net social costs and therefore violates the efficiency criterion.

Suppose someone thought we should produce fewer apples than the level where MSC equals MSB, such as A(1) < A(0). For any level of production less than A(0), such as A(1), what would be the effect of producing one more apple than we are already producing? To see what the additional cost to society would be, we go up from A(1) to the MSC curve. To see what the additional benefit to society would be we go up from A(1) to the MSB curve. But when we produce and consume at A(1) the MSB curve is higher than the MSC curve, indicating that producing and consuming another apple increases social benefits more than it increases social costs. In other words, there are positive net social benefits from expanding production and consumption of apples.

Suppose someone thought we should produce more apples than the level where MSC equals MSB, such as A(2) > A(0). For any level of production greater than A(0), such as A(2), what would be the effect of producing one less apple than we are already producing? To see what the savings in social cost would be we go up from A(2) to the MSC curve. To see what the lost social benefit would be we go up from

A(2) to the MSB curve. But when we produce and consume at A(2) the MSC curve is higher than the MSB curve indicating that producing and consuming one less apple reduces social benefits by less than it reduces social costs. In other words, there are potential positive net social benefits from reducing production and consumption of apples.

The conclusion is for all A < A(0) we should expand apple production and consumption, and for all A > A(0) we should reduce apple production and consumption. Therefore the only level of apple production that is efficient from society's point of view is the level where the marginal social benefit of the last apple consumed is equal to the marginal social cost of the last apple produced, A(0). In any other case we could increase net social benefits by expanding or reducing apple production and consumption.

Mainstream economists do not like to admit that policies recommended on the basis of the efficiency criterion are usually *not* Pareto improvements since they *do* make some people worse off. The efficiency criterion and all cost–benefit analysis necessarily (1) "compares" different people's levels of satisfaction, and (2) attaches "weights" to how important different people's levels of satisfaction are when we calculate overall, or *social benefits* and *social costs*. Notice that when I stipulated that a few would be worse off in the present generation if we reduce greenhouse gas emissions while many will be benefited in the future I was attributing greater weight to the gains of the many in the future than the losses of a few in the present. I think it is perfectly reasonable to do this, and do not hesitate to do so. But I am attaching weights to the wellbeing of different people – in this case roughly equal weights, which I also believe is reasonable. If one refuses to attach weights to the wellbeing of different people the efficiency criterion cannot be used. I also stipulated that the benefits of preventing global warming to people in the future were large compared to the cost of reducing emissions to people in the present. I was willing to compare how large a gain was for one person compared to how small a loss was for a different person. If one refuses to compare the size of benefits and costs to different people the efficiency criterion cannot be used. In other words, unlike the narrow Pareto principle, the efficiency criterion requires comparing the magnitudes of costs and benefits to *different* people and deciding how much importance to attach to the wellbeing of *different* people.

Put differently, it requires *value judgments* beyond what are required for the Pareto criterion. So when mainstream economists pretend they have imposed no value judgments, and have separated efficiency from equity issues when they apply cost–benefit analysis and recommend policy based on the *efficiency criterion* they misrepresent themselves. While a Pareto improvement makes some better off at the expense of none – and therefore does not require comparing the sizes of gains and losses to different people or weighing the importance of wellbeing to different people – policies that satisfy the efficiency criterion generally make some better off precisely at the expense of others, which necessarily requires comparing the magnitudes of costs and benefits to different people and making a value judgment regarding how important the interests of the "winners" are compared to the interests of the "losers."

Mainstream economists like to point out that if a policy passes the efficiency criterion that means the magnitude of benefits enjoyed by the winners is necessarily larger than the magnitude of costs suffered by the losers, which means it would be *theoretically possible* for the winners to fully compensate the losers and still be better off themselves. But first, this requires a comparison of the magnitude of gains to some compared to the magnitude of losses to others – already a large step beyond the narrow conceptualization of efficiency enshrined in the Pareto principle that does not permit comparing different people's satisfactions. Secondly, either compensation is paid, or it is not paid. If a policy requires winners to fully compensate losers then it *is* a Pareto improvement and we do not need the weaker efficiency criterion to recommend it. If, on the other hand, a policy does not require that losers be fully compensated from the gains to winners, then it requires a value judgment that those who win deserve to do so, and those who lose deserve to do so, before it can be recommended – however much economists who claim to forswear "value judgments" may wish otherwise. In the end, the only reason we need the efficiency criterion in the first place is precisely because so many important choices fall outside the purview of the Pareto principle, i.e. cannot be reduced to efficiency defined narrowly.

Seven Deadly Sins of Inefficiency

How might an economy be wasteful in the sense that it fails to achieve a Pareto optimal outcome? It turns out there are seven different ways that any economy might be inefficient. I facetiously call them the seven "deadly sins" of inefficiency.

The production sector of an economy will be inefficient if:

1. It leaves productive resources idle. (Example: unemployed workers, or idle crop land.)
2. It uses inefficient technologies, that is, uses more of some input than necessary to get a given amount of output. (Example: The same number of shoes can be made with less leather and the same amount of labor by more careful cutting.)

3. It misallocates productive resources so that swapping inputs between two different production units would lead to increases in output in both. (Example: Employing carpenters on a farm and agronomists in the construction industry.)

The consumption sector will be inefficient if:

1. There are undistributed or idle consumption goods. (Example: Wheat rotting in silos while people go hungry.)
2. Final goods are misdistributed so that two consumers could exchange goods and both be better off than under the original distribution. (Example: Apples are distributed to orange lovers while oranges are distributed to apple lovers.)

And the production and consumption sectors will be inefficiently integrated with one another if:

1. Goods are misallocated between consumers and producers so it is possible for a producer and consumer to swap goods and have the output of the producer rise and the satisfaction of the consumer increase as well. (Example: Personal computers are distributed to households that suffer for lack of heat while employees at accounting firms are unproductive in overheated offices without personal computers to work with.)
2. Resources are misallocated to different industries so it is possible to shift productive resources from one industry to another to produce a different mixture of outputs more to consumers' tastes. (Example: Most land suitable for orchards is planted in pear trees even though most consumers prefer apples to pears.)

The seven deadly sins of inefficiency provide an orderly, and not overly intimidating, procedure for checking to see if an economy will be inefficient in the narrow sense of the Pareto criterion. All we need to do is check if the economy is prone to "sinning" in any of these seven ways. If not, we can conclude the economy is efficient, or will achieve Pareto optimality, whatever other desirable or undesirable qualities it may possess. Moreover, if the economy is prone to inefficiency we will know what *kind* of inefficiency it suffers from.

Endogenous Preferences

But there is an important issue traditional treatments ignore which complicates how we should think about efficiency. When people make choices in light of their present preferences, the actions they take not only fulfill their present preferences (to a greater or lesser degree), they also change people's characteristics to some extent, and thereby change their future needs and desires. In Chapter 1 we saw this is what it means to say people have "consciousness" and are "self-creative." While traditional treatments of efficiency take account of the first effect of people's choices – the "preference fulfillment effect" – the second effect – the "preference development effect" – is usually ignored. But evaluating the effect of economic choices and institutions on people's human development patterns may be as important as evaluating how well those choices and institutions succeed in fulfilling present preferences. However, when economic choices have human development effects that means they also change people's preferences, creating the following dilemma: How are we to judge the efficiency of economic institutions using people's preferences as our yard stick if those preferences are in part a product of those same economic institutions in the first place? While this may appear to be a vicious circle giving rise to a philosophical conundrum that cannot be resolved, it turns out that there are some conclusions we can draw about economic efficiency even when we recognize that people's preferences are influenced by the economic institutions that purport to satisfy those preferences.

The view that people are self-conscious agents whose characteristics and preferences develop can be summarized in a model of "endogenous preferences." Using such a model it is possible to demonstrate that if an economy is *biased* against a certain kind of activity – that is, if people must pay more than the true cost to society to engage in the activity:

1. The degree of inefficiency in the economy will be greater than recognized by traditional theory that fails to treat preferences as endogenous, and the inefficiency will increase or "snowball" over time.
2. Individual human development patterns will be "warped" in the sense that they will not develop in ways that could generate the most fulfillment they could enjoy, and the warping will increase or "snowball" over time.
3. These detrimental, non-traditional effects of the bias in the economy will be disguised to the participants who adjust unconsciously, or forget they have adjusted after the fact.

The intuition behind these political economy welfare theorems[18] is that to the extent people recognize the "preference development" as well as the "preference fulfillment"

---

18 For a rigorous derivation of these results see Chapter 6 in Robin Hahnel and Michael Albert, *Quiet Revolution in Welfare Economics* (Princeton University Press, 1990).

effects of their economic choices, it is sensible for them to take both effects into account when making decisions. If an economic institution is biased against some activity – charging people more than the true social cost of making the activity available – then rational people will choose activities in part to develop a lower preference for that activity than if they were only charged the lower, true social cost for engaging in it. It follows that the demand for the activity will be less than had people not adjusted their preferences. But this reduced demand implies that even fewer resources will be allocated to supplying the activity than had people not adjusted their preferences, thereby aggravating the inefficiency. The more time people have to make these individually rational adjustments the lower the demand for, and therefore the supply of, the activity will be, leading to ever greater misallocation of resources as time goes on, and ever greater deviations of people's human development trajectories from those that would have maximized their wellbeing under a system of unbiased prices. If after the fact people forget that they adjusted their preferences to conform to the biased prices, they will only see themselves as getting what they want.

In other words, if an economic institution introduces a systematic bias in the terms of availability of an activity, the consequence will be a "snowballing" divergence from efficient allocations. This implies *that a major criterion for judging the efficiency of economic institutions should be determining whether they exert any systematic biases on individual choice*, because to the extent that people's preferences are "endogenous" any biases are more detrimental than traditionally recognized.

While traditional economists limit their evaluations of economies to efficiency (without considering the complication of endogenous preferences) and equity (about which they have little to say), political economists have good reason to take other criteria into account as well. Specifically, *how* and *by whom* decisions are made, as well as the *social and environmental effects* of economic activities.

Self-management

I define **self-management** as *decision-making input in proportion to the degree one is affected*, and believe more self-management is desirable, all other things being equal, or as economists like to say, *ceteris paribus*.

The first thing to notice is that, defined in this way, self-management is seldom equivalent either to individual freedom or majority rule. Only if a single individual were the only person affected by a decision would self-management be the same as individual freedom, i.e. the right of an individual to decide whatever she pleases. And only if all were equally affected by a decision would self-management be the same as majority rule, i.e. one person one vote. Since most economic decisions affect more than one person, but affect people to different degrees, self-management as I have defined it usually requires that some people have more decision-making power while others have less regarding any particular economic decision.

But why is more self-management a good thing? For the last ten thousand years most humans have lived in circumstances with few opportunities for self-management. So admittedly, people don't die without it. However, political economists contend that just as denial of material means of subsistence conflicts with human "natural" needs for food, shelter, and clothing, denial of self-management opportunities is in conflict with our "species nature." The capacity to analyze and evaluate the consequences of our actions, and choose among alternatives based on our assessments, in conjunction with the need to employ this capacity is what we called "consciousness." Development of the capacity and desire for self-management is nothing more than development of the capacity to garner satisfaction from this innate human potential. For that reason, economic institutions that satisfy this need and nurture this capacity are preferable to economic institutions that stifle self-management. In brief, we human beings have the ability to analyze and evaluate the consequences of our actions and choose accordingly, and we garner considerable satisfaction from doing so.

Solidarity

By **solidarity** I simply mean *concern for the wellbeing of others, and granting others the same consideration in their endeavors as we ask for ourselves.* Empathy and respect for others has been formulated as a "golden rule" and "categorical imperative," and outside the economics profession solidarity is widely held to be a powerful creator of wellbeing. Solidarity among family members, between members of the same tribe, or within an ethnic group frequently generates wellbeing far in excess of what would be possible based on material resources alone. But in mainstream economics concern for others is defined as an "interpersonal externality" – a nasty sounding habit – and justification is demanded for why it is necessarily a good thing.

In addition to consciousness, sociability is an important part of human nature. Our desires develop in interaction with others. One of the strongest human drives is the never ending search for respect and esteem from others. All this is a consequence of our innate sociability. Because our lives are to a great extent joint endeavors, it makes sense we would seek the approval of others for our part in group efforts. Since many of our needs are best filled by what others do for/with us, it makes sense to want to be well regarded by others.

Now compare two different ways in which an individual can gain the esteem and respect of others. One way grants an individual status by elevating her above others, by positioning the person in a status hierarchy that is nothing more than a pyramid of relative rankings according to established criteria – whatever they may be. For one individual to gain esteem in this way it is necessary that at least one other – and usually many others – lose esteem. We have at best a zero-sum game, and most often a negative-sum game since underlings in hierarchies far outnumber superiors. The second way grants individuals respect and guarantees that others are concerned for their wellbeing out of group solidarity. Solidarity establishes a predisposition to consider others' needs as if they were one's own, and to recognize the value of others' diverse contributions to the group's social endeavors. Solidarity is a positive-sum game. Any group characteristic that enhances the overall wellbeing members can obtain from a given set of scarce material resources is obviously advantageous. Solidarity is one such group characteristic. So political economists consider economic institutions that enhance feelings of solidarity are preferable to economic institutions that undermine solidarity among participants.

Variety

I define **economic variety** as *achieving a diversity of economic life styles and outcomes*, and believe it is desirable *ceteris paribus*. The argument for variety as an economic goal is based on the breadth of human potentials, the multiplicity of human natural and species needs and powers, and the fact that people are neither omniscient nor immortal.

First of all, people are very different. The fact that we are all human means we have genetic traits in common, but this does not mean there are not differences between people's genetic endowments. So the best life for one is not necessarily the best life for another. Second, we are each individually too complex to achieve our greatest fulfillment through relatively few activities. Even if every individual were a genetic carbon copy of every other, the complexity of this single human entity, her multiplicity of potential needs and capacities, would require a great variety of different human activities to achieve maximum fulfillment. To generate this variety of activities would in turn require a rich variety of social roles even in a society of genetic clones. And with a variety of social roles we would discover that even genetic clones would develop quite different derived human characteristics and needs.

While the above two arguments for the desirability of a variety of outcomes are "positive," there are "negative" reasons that make variety preferable to conformity as well. Since we are not omniscient nobody can know for sure which development path will be most suitable for her, nor can any group be certain what path is best. John Stuart Mill astutely pointed out long ago in *On Liberty* that this implies the majority should be *thankful* to have minorities testing out different life styles, because every once in a while every majority is wrong. Therefore, it is in the majority's interest to have minorities testing their dissident notions of "the good life" in case one of them turns out to be a better idea. Finally, since we are not immortal, each of us can only live one life trajectory. Only if others are living differently can each of us vicariously enjoy more than one kind of life.

Sustainability

In the 2002 edition I introduced this section with the observation: "It took a massive movement to raise the issue of whether or not economies were 'environmentally sustainable,' or instead, on course to destroy the natural environment upon which they depend." Let me begin this section in the 2014 edition by apologizing for providing as little guidance on this crucial subject as I did a dozen years ago.[19] Like most of my fellow political economists, I have been far too slow to recognize the severity of the ecological crisis our economies have created. I tried to make amends in *Green Economics: Confronting the Ecological Crisis* published by M.E. Sharpe in 2011 which interested readers should consult for a fuller treatment of environmental economic issues. However, more needs to be said here than briefly distinguishing between "weak" and "strong" conceptions of sustainability, as I did in the 2002 edition.

First we need to amend Figure 1.1 which was our representation of society as comprised of a human center and an institutional boundary. We need to add another circle, or boundary, called the natural environment around the outside of both the

---

19 In particular I am ashamed to have written in the 2002 edition: "It is not clear that if we leave aside the political question of how to popularize important ideas, there is anything in the notion of 'sustainability' that is not already implicit in the values of efficiency, equity and variety. If an economy uses up natural resources too quickly, leaving too little or none for later, it has violated the efficiency criterion. If an economy sacrifices the basic needs of future generations to fulfill desires for luxuries of some in the present generation, it has failed to achieve intergenerational equity. If we chop down tropical forests with all their biodiversity and replace them with single species tree plantations, we have destroyed, rather than promoted variety." While these observations may be logically sound, they are unworthy of anyone well versed in the severity of the ecological crisis we have created. Failure to include *sustainability* as an explicit economic goal on grounds that other goals already subsume it would be a colossal mistake.

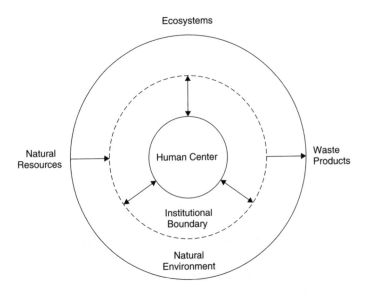

Figure 2.4 Human Society as Part of a Natural Ecosystem

human center and institutional boundary because human societies always interact with their natural environment, and we ignore the nature of that interaction at our peril.

However, this does not settle how best to conceptualize the interaction. Economists initially thought of the natural environment simply as the source of raw materials, or *natural capital* – minerals, fossil fuels, fertile soil, forests, fresh water, etc. – and saw resource depletion as what threatens sustainability. Belatedly economists came to appreciate that the natural environment also serves as a useful *sink* – and recognized limits to its capacity to absorb economic waste products as a threat to sustainability. Ecologists, who study the natural environment as their primary job rather than as a side-line, think of the environment as interconnected *ecosystems* – and see destabilization of vital ecosystems as what threatens sustainability. If we consider climate change, for example, the economic perspective sees the problem as humans exhausting the capacity of the upper atmosphere as a sink to absorb more greenhouse gases. The ecological perspective sees the problem as humans destabilizing a vital ecosystem, the carbon cycle. In general the economic perspective sees society taking raw material "inputs" from, and releasing waste "outputs" back into the natural environment, while the ecological perspective sees earth as a single network of ecosystems that includes one rather recent arrival, a species that has become a major destabilizing force – a veritable bull in the china closet.

In *Green Economics* I wrote a whole chapter to answer the question: "What on earth is sustainable development?" I began by noting that it is tempting to follow the lead of former Supreme Court Justice Potter Stewart who, when asked to define pornography, famously quipped, "I shall not today attempt to define it, but I know it when I see it," and answer with regard to sustainable development, "I am not sure what it is, but I am quite sure what it is *not!*" The problem is that delving into the meaning of sustainable development opens several Pandora's boxes: How does one reconcile the notion of sustaining a status quo with progress? When is adding more of something an adequate substitute for less of something else? How can we measure the value of a capital stock whose composition is heterogeneous?

The most famous definition of sustainable development is from the report of the United Nations World Commission on Environment and Development, better known as the Brundtland Commission, after its chair: "Sustainable development is development that meets the needs of the present without compromising the ability of future generations to meet their own needs." However, this delightfully concise definition has been criticized from every angle. It has been ridiculed as so vague that it says nothing. As the philosopher Luc Ferry remarked: "Who would like to be a proponent of an untenable development!" When the definition is reworded as sustainable growth and interpreted broadly to anticipate new technologies and permit full substitution of produced capital for natural capital, many environmentalists regard it as a license to continue to kill the planet. When interpreted strictly as requiring that stocks of different categories of natural capital not be permitted to decline, it is criticized by business leaders and many economists as imposing unreasonable and unnecessary restrictions.

Weak versus Strong versus Environmental Sustainability

The core idea of sustainability as intergenerational equity is that we must leave future generations in conditions at least as favorable as those we enjoy.[20] If we interpret "conditions" as "assets," and "assets" as "capital," this reduces to leaving future generations with an overall capital stock at least as "valuable" as what we have today.

---

20 This is clearly what critics would call an anthropocentric view of sustainability which says nothing *per se* about preserving the present natural environment. For instance, if it were possible to transform planet earth beyond recognition, but the new planet was still as accommodating to humans as it is today, this would be consistent with sustainability interpreted as intergenerational equity.

It is now common to talk of produced capital, natural capital, human capital, and sometimes social capital. If we ignore problems of how to incorporate technical knowhow, and how to aggregate heterogeneous components to calculate a value for the overall capital stock – problems which are, in fact intractable, even if they are often dismissed as merely technical – *weak sustainability* simply *requires maintaining the value of the overall capital stock per capita*, and is the definition mainstream economists are most comfortable with. *Strong sustainability requires, in addition, maintaining the overall value of the natural capital stock as well,* which environmentalists prefer to weak sustainability which allows substituting produced for natural capital without limit. And what is sometimes called *environmental sustainability requires, in addition, maintaining the physical stocks of every important category of natural capital,* which many environmentalists are even more comfortable with.

The critical issue is obviously what we might call "fungibility." To what extent can one kind of capital be substituted for another? There is a large literature debating how realistic it is to assume that produced capital can adequately substitute for different components of natural capital, where differences of opinion between so-called technological "optimists" and "pessimists" play a central role. Economists are generally optimistic about technical progress and long accustomed to assuming that everything is infinitely substitutable for everything else at the margin, albeit with diminishing effects, of course. Ecologists generally begin with the opposite assumption, namely that key components of natural systems are irreplaceable without destabilizing the entire system. Since in many cases attempts to substitute produced capital for natural capital are irreversible, and since our understanding of ecosystem complexity is often imperfect, many environmentalists argue that the *precautionary principle* should be applied: *Do not assume some part of natural capital can be adequately replaced by produced capital until it has been proven beyond any reasonable doubt to be the case.*

A Workable Definition of Sustainable Development

Sustainable means repeatable. However, humans in the modern age have not been content with mere survival – repeating the same activities, with the same results, year after year. We have grown accustomed to aspire for more. We hope to progress, or develop, and we hope to progress along many dimensions. I think the word *sustainable* can best be used as *a warning about dangers we must avoid during our quest for progress, or development, if we do not wish to compromise the prospects of those who will follow us in ways that cannot be morally justified.* For our behavior to be sustainable we must operate under constraints as we struggle to develop.

If the prospects of the next generation depended only on how much seed corn they had to work with, the traditional economic concept of maintaining the seed stock would be a sufficient condition for intergenerational equity. When "seed stock" became hoes and plow horses as well as seeds, the idea became that as long as the capital stock *as a whole* equipped our descendants with the means to be as productive as we were, intergenerational equity was observed. But when we came to our senses and realized that the earth was filling fast – that is, that per capita stocks of different components of natural capital were already scarce and shrinking fast – necessary conditions for intergenerational equity became more complicated and more stringent. In truth, methodological problems associated with aggregation of different components of the capital stock, as well as practical questions of substitutability, became troublesome issues as soon as hoes were added to seed corn. But these problems became acute as soon as we realized that the prospects of the next generation depend on how much natural capital they will have to work with as well as how much produced capital we have left them. And since the environment also provides amenities, as well as a variety of vital sink services that do not neatly fit the metaphor of capital as enhancer of human productivity, the problem of defining how development – that is, human progress – could simultaneously be sustainable – that is, not compromise the ability of future generations to continue to develop – became even more problematic. So I suggest something more along the lines of an intergenerational social contract as a lawyer would draft it, rather than a traditional definition of sustainability:

WHEREAS the natural environment provides valuable services as amenities, as the source of resources, and as sinks to process wastes,

WHEREAS the regenerative capacity of different components of the natural environment and ecosystems contained therein are limited,

WHEREAS ecosystems are complex, contain self-reinforcing feedback dynamics that can accelerate their decline, and often have thresholds that are difficult for us to pinpoint,

And WHEREAS passing important environmental thresholds can be irreversible,

WE, the present generation, now understand that while striving to meet our economic needs democratically, fairly, and efficiently we must not impair the ability of future generations to meet their needs and continue to progress.

In particular, WE, the present generation, understand that intergenerational equity requires leaving future generations conditions at least as favorable as those we enjoy. These conditions include what are commonly called produced capital, natural capital, ecosystem sink services, environmental amenities, human capital, social capital, and technical knowhow.

Moreover, SINCE the degree to which different kinds of capital and sink services can or cannot be substituted for one another is uncertain, and since some changes are irreversible,

WE, the present generation, also understand that intergenerational equity requires us to apply the precautionary principle with regard to what is an adequate substitution for some favorable part of overall conditions we permit to deteriorate. The burden of proof must lie with those among us who argue that a natural amenity, resource, or sink service that we permit to deteriorate on our watch is fully and adequately substituted for by some other component of the inheritance we bequeath our heirs.

Growth

Most economists regard economic growth as something positive, and for many it continues to be their primary goal. On the other hand, many environmentalists view growth as the ultimate cause of our environmental problems. Growth is good? Growth is bad? What are we to think? A good place to start is by asking precisely what it is that is growing, because usually environmentalists and economists are not talking about the same thing at all.

When economists talk about economic growth they mean the growth of *gross domestic product*, or **GDP**, *defined as the value of all the goods and services produced during a year. Net domestic product*, NDP, *is then defined as GDP minus any deterioration in the value of the productive capital stock, which, as we have seen, should include natural, human, and perhaps social "capital" as well as produced capital like plant and machinery.* Putting aside a host of important issues about ways in which GDP and NDP are miscalculated, the rate of growth of NDP per capita should therefore, at least in theory, represent the sustainable increase in the *value* of what we produce per person in the economy from one year to the next, which we measure in dollars. However, when the ecological economist Kenneth Boulding said: "Anyone who believes in indefinite growth in anything physical, on a physically finite planet, is either mad or an economist,"[21] he was talking about growth of throughput, which is defined as *quantities of physical matter humans draw from the natural environment as "inputs" for our production processes – things like tons of coal, tons of iron ore, cubic meters of top soil, clean water drawn from aquifers, etc. – as well as quantities of physical matter we release as side-product or "outputs" back into the natural environment – things like cubic meters of carbon dioxide released into the upper atmosphere, tons of slag left in heaps, and deposition of dirt into water or air, measured in parts per million, etc.* Net domestic product and throughput are not the same thing at all. They are not even measured in the same units.

Throughput has been growing mightily over the past few hundred years not only because population has grown, but because throughput per capita has grown among all but the most impoverished, and as a result we are nearing crucial limits on the ability of important components of throughput to continue to grow much longer without serious adverse consequences. Contrary to what environmentalists believed in the early 1970s, it is the ability of the planet as a "sink" to absorb throughputs we release as wastes that we seem to be exhausting more rapidly, rather than the ability of the planet to continue to provide natural resources we use as inputs. Either way, there is strong evidence that we left the "frontier economy" where our impact on the natural environment was not yet significant long ago, and we are now well into a "bull in the china closet economy" where we are a serious threat to ecosystem resilience, and are fast approaching a "spaceman" economy where every aspect of our natural environment will have to be meticulously managed. In short, we are pressing up against limits on some components of throughput, and have surpassed limits for others, threatening sustainability.

This is where the goal of a "steady state economy" first proposed by a founder of the school of ecological economics, Herman Daly, comes in. Daly argued that if throughput continues to grow we will soon destroy the planet irreparably, and therefore our goal should be what he called a **steady state economy**, i.e. *an economy where throughput, in general, does not grow any further, but remains constant, or "steady."* However, it has now become clear that holding some parts of throughput "steady" is not good enough. For example, climate scientists tell us that unless we decrease emissions of greenhouse gases substantially over the next few decades we risk triggering cataclysmic climate change. In other words, with regard to greenhouse gas throughput at least, we must lower throughput every year, which is where the

---

21 This is the actual quote, which is almost universally misquoted as: "Anyone who believes in infinite economic growth on a finite planet is either a mad man or an economist."

de-growth movement comes in. *Sustainability now requires not only keeping some components of throughput "steady," but shrinking other components as well.*

However, throughput is *not* gross domestic product. What economists call "real GDP" is measured in "constant" dollars in order to prevent inflation from deceiving us into thinking that the quantity of goods and services produced is rising when really all that is happening is the price of goods and services is rising. However, the word *real* in front of GDP should not be taken to mean "physical" because it does not. Nor should valid arguments that we systematically mismeasure GDP and NDP, or that many exaggerate its importance compared to other economic and non-economic goals, be interpreted as demonstrating that the value of what we produce per hour of work cannot, at least in theory, rise without limit – because it does not.

Limiting throughput to sustainable levels need not prevent us from increasing economic wellbeing per capita. The question is how to increase the *value* of goods and particularly services people enjoy even while the throughput used to produce them, and the throughput released as by-products in their production and consumption, do not increase, and in some cases even decline. For example, in the computer industry, throughput per unit of computing capacity has dropped dramatically since the 1940s. Suppose it had dropped by a factor of 10. This would mean that we could consume five times more computing capacity now than in 1940 while cutting throughput for computing services in half. It is also possible that before we exhaust one kind of throughput, we can change production technologies to substitute a different input that is still plentiful or, if necessary, we can consume a different good or service instead. As noted, we must become carbon neutral well before the end of the century in order to avoid risking cataclysmic climate change. That means those planning to prevent climate change believe it is possible to substitute renewable sources for fossil fuels before we run out of atmospheric storage space for greenhouse gases. Meanwhile, GDP could still grow 5% a year while carbon emissions decrease 10% a year as long as energy efficiency grew at 15% a year.[22]

So instead of sterile debates where people fail to specify what is growing and talk past one another, what we should be asking ourselves is this: *Is there something about our economic system that keeps us on a trajectory to produce the kinds and quantities of goods and services that **will** continue to increase throughput?* In other words, is there a

---

22 Strictly speaking, this conclusion assumes that the ratio of fossil fuels to renewables in our energy system remains constant. If we also substitute more renewables for fossil fuels a 15% increase in energy efficiency combined with 5% growth of GDP would decrease carbon emissions by even more than 10%.

growth imperative in our economic system that is environmentally unsustainable? In the words of Herman Daly, is there something about our economic system that generates **uneconomic growth** – *growth that is environmentally destructive and fails to yield real economic development?* If so, what are the causes of uneconomic growth, and what can be done to stop it? Of course, this is the question concerned environmentalists thought they were asking all along, which we will take up in Chapter 10: What is to be undone?

Conclusion

So the criteria political economists should consider when evaluating the performance of an economy, or evaluating the consequences of different economic policies, or comparing the desirability of different economic systems are: (1) *Equity*, defined as reward according to sacrifice and need; (2) *efficiency*, defined narrowly as Pareto optimality, and more broadly as the efficiency criterion, but with the preference development effect accounted for rather than ignored; (3) *self-management*, defined as decision-making power in proportion to the degree one is affected; (4) *solidarity*, defined as concern for the wellbeing of others; (5) *variety*, defined as achieving a variety of economic life styles and outcomes; and (6) *sustainability*, which may be difficult to define in a few words, but at a minimum rules out behavior which is environmentally destructive to the point of jeopardizing the wellbeing of future generations.

3

Efficiency and Economic Justice: A Simple Corn Model

This is the first of three chapters presenting theoretical models and analyses that are useful for political economists. The two simple corn models presented here require no more sophisticated mathematical skill than simple arithmetic. Chapter 5 contains four useful microeconomic models, and Chapter 9 five useful macroeconomic models. All the models sharpen the logical basis of subjects treated verbally in the eight, non-technical chapters. More importantly, all three technical chapters are well within the grasp of anyone with a high school education, and they permit readers who master them to be "players" rather than "spectators" in the field of political economy. Since the primary purpose of this book is to equip readers to practice political economy on their own, rather than have to rely on someone else's analysis and conclusions, I highly recommend these chapters to readers willing to invest a little extra time to become more intellectually independent.

Model 3.1 of a domestic corn economy allows us to explore efficiency, inequality, and the relationship between them in a very simple setting. It allows us to see how economic institutions like labor markets and credit markets which establish relationships between employers and employees, and borrowers and lenders, can affect efficiency and inequality simultaneously. It also provides a convenient context to see how different conceptions of economic justice such as the conservative, liberal, and radical "maxims" discussed last chapter give rise to different conclusions about when unequal outcomes are unfair and when they are not. Model 3.2 of a global corn economy allows us to see how international financial investment and direct foreign investment affect global efficiency and global inequality.

Model 3.1: A Domestic Corn Economy

Imagine an economy consisting of 1000 members. There is one produced good, corn, which all must consume. Corn is produced from inputs of labor and seed corn. All members of this society are equally skilled and productive, and all know how to use the two technologies that exist for producing corn. We assume each person needs to consume exactly 1 unit of corn per week. After their "necessary consumption" we assume people care about leisure. That is, after consuming 1 unit of corn, people care about working as few days as possible in order to enjoy as many days of the week in leisure activities as possible. Finally, we assume that after consuming 1 unit of corn and minimizing the number of days they have to work, i.e. maximizing their leisure, if people have the chance to accumulate more corn rather than less they will want to do so.[1] There are two ways to make corn: a *labor intensive technique* (LIT) and a *capital intensive technique* (CIT):

Labor Intensive Technique:
6 days of labor + 0 units of seed corn yields 1 unit of corn

Capital Intensive Technique:
1 day of labor + 1 unit of seed corn yields 2 units of corn

In either case the corn produced appears only at the end of the week. That is, if I work Monday through Saturday using the labor intensive technology I will get a yield of one unit of corn on Sunday. If I work with a unit of seed corn on Tuesday using the capital intensive technology the unit of seed corn is tied up for the whole week and is gone by Sunday, and I will get a yield of 2 units of corn on Sunday. There is no need to replace seed corn used in the labor intensive process since none is used. On the other hand, if we are to get back to where we started after using the capital intensive process, we need to use 1 of the 2 units of corn produced to replace the unit of seed corn used up. Another way of saying this is that the capital intensive process produces 2 gross units of corn but only 1 net unit of corn. So each technique produces one net unit of corn available at the end of the week. The labor intensive process uses 6 days of labor and requires no seed corn to get 1 unit of corn, net. The capital intensive process uses 1 unit of labor and requires 1 unit of seed corn to get 1 unit of corn, net. Finally, we

---

1 This simple model deviates from real world conditions in many respects. The assumption that people only wish to consume 1 unit of corn, after which they wish to minimize work time, after which they wish to maximize accumulation, is convenient for now. We will consider the implications of people's preferences for how they work, and who decides how they work, and discuss the effects of more realistic assumptions about consumption and savings later.

assume either technique can be used in any "scale" desired. For example, if I work only 1 day in the LIT I will get 1/6 unit of corn on Sunday. If I work half a day in the CIT I will get 1 unit of corn gross, and half a unit of corn net on Sunday.[2]

But why would anyone ever produce corn the labor intensive way? If I work 1 day using the capital intensive technique I can produce 2 units of corn, and after replacing the 1 unit of seed corn I used up I have 1 unit left over. On the other hand, I would have to work 6 days to end up with 1 unit of corn if I used the labor intensive technique. So no one would ever use the labor intensive technique if she could use the capital intensive technique instead.[3] However, a key feature of the model is you cannot use the capital intensive technology unless you have seed corn to begin with. So if someone does not have access to seed corn at the beginning of the week, yet needs to produce corn, they have no choice but to use the labor intensive technology. This is how the model nicely captures one critical feature of modern economies – the role of *capital*, represented in our model by seed corn.

In our simple corn economy there is an easy way to measure economic efficiency. What people want is net corn production. In other words, the only benefit people get from the economy is net corn production. On the other hand, what people don't like is working since it detracts from their leisure. In other words, the only burden people bear in the economy is the amount of time they have to work. In this simple situation the economy is more efficient the lower the average number of days of work per unit of net corn produced.[4] So *we can measure the **efficiency** of the economy by the average number of days worked per unit of net corn produced*. There is also a simple way to measure the ***degree of inequality*** in the economy. Since everyone consumes the same amount of corn, 1 unit, the only difference in outcomes that people care about is the number of days they have to work. So we can define the degree of inequality in the economy as the difference between the maximum number of days anyone works and the minimum number of days anyone works.[5]

---

2 In other words, we are assuming what economists call "constant returns to scale."
3 Remember we are assuming for now that people don't care whether they work an hour in the labor intensive process or the capital intensive process.
4 Efficiency means minimizing the ratio of "pain" to "gain." "Pain" in our simple economy has been reduced to total number of days worked, and "gain" has been reduced to the total number of units of net corn produced. So average days worked per unit of net corn, or total days worked divided by total net corn production, is the obvious measure of efficiency in our simple corn economy.
5 Shortly we will discover that our measure of the degree of inequality is imperfect whenever people accumulate different amounts of corn. Our measure also fails to address changes in the degree of inequality between people who are not at the upper and lower extremes. But this imperfect measure is sufficient for our purposes, so we avoid unnecessary complications involved in devising a better measure.

To explore how the distribution of seed corn and economic institutions like a labor market and credit market affect efficiency and inequality in the economy we explore *two different* **situations** and *three different sets of* **rules** for how people can behave in the economy. In situation 1 we give some people more of the economy's scarce seed corn than others. This situation is obviously most relevant to real world circumstances where some people have more capital than others. In situation 2 we give everyone equal amounts of scarce seed corn. While there has never been a capitalist economy in which everyone started out with the same amount of capital, nonetheless, it is interesting to explore what would happen in this situation as compared to the real world of unequal endowments of scarce capital.[6] In each situation we explore what people would do under three different sets of rules. First *we do not permit people to enter into any kind of economic relationship with each other at all.* That is, we require people to be completely self-sufficient. This rule, or way of running the economy, we call **autarky.** Next we permit people to enter into an employment relationship where *anyone who wishes to hire someone, and anyone who wishes to work for someone else, for a wage the employer and employee both agree to, are free to do so.* In other words, we legalize, or open up a **labor market.** Finally, instead of opening a labor market, we open up a **credit market.** Under this third set of rules *people are free to borrow corn from others and lend corn to others at a rate of interest both borrower and lender agree to.*

Political economists define **classes** as *groups of people who play the same economic role as one another but enter into economic relationships with other groups of people playing a different role with whom they have conflicting interests of one sort or another.* So under the rules of autarky there can be no "classes" because nobody enters into any relationship with anyone else. In autarky it may, or may not be the case that everyone suffers or benefits to the same degree from their economic activity, but any differences that might occur cannot be the result of relationships people enter into with one another because under the rules of autarky everyone works for herself using her own seed corn. There are no employers (a class), nor employees (a class) with conflicting interest over how high or low the wage rate will be. Nor are there lenders (a class), nor borrowers (a class) with conflicting interests over how high or low the interest rate will be. Clearly if we open a labor market and some people become

6 What does it mean to say capital is "scarce" in our simple economy? As long as the total amount of seed corn in the economy is insufficient to allow us to produce all of the corn people need to consume using the more efficient, capital intensive technology, and thereby avoid having to use the less efficient labor intensive technology at all, seed corn is "scarce." So as long as we have less than 1000 units of seed corn initially, seed corn is scarce in the sense that we could reduce the amount of days people had to work if we had more.

employers and others become employees classes will emerge. And if we open a credit market and some become lenders and others borrowers classes will emerge as well.

Finally, political economists distinguish between *outcome* – in our simple model, does one person work more or less than another – and *decision-making process* – in our simple model, who decides how the work will be done.[7] In the simple corn model if I decide how I will go about my work we say my work is **self-managed**. *If someone else decides how I will go about my work, we say my labor is other-directed or **alienated**.* Political economists believe being human means being able to make one's own decisions regarding how to use one's productive capabilities. Therefore, irrespective of whether the outcome is deemed fair or unfair, many political economists believe people are being denied a "species right" to exercise their capacity of self-management when their work is other-directed or alienated. Most political economists consider self-managed decision-making processes more desirable than other-directed, or alienated decision-making processes – independent of whether or not the distribution of (consumption) benefits and (work) burdens, i.e. the outcome, is fair or unfair.

Situation 1: Inegalitarian Distribution of Scarce Seed Corn

We begin with a situation that reflects real world conditions, namely that some people begin with more of the economy's scarce capital than others. We give 100 people 5 units of seed corn each, leaving the other 900 people no seed corn at all,[8] and proceed to analyze what the 100 "seedy" people and 900 "seedless" people would do under three different rules for running the economy.

Autarky

Having no seed corn and needing 1 unit of corn to consume, each of the 900 seedless people have no choice but to work 6 days (Monday through Saturday) for themselves using the labor intensive technology. On the other hand, each of the 100 seedy people have plenty of seed corn and can avoid the less productive labor intensive process. Each seedy person needs only to work 1 day (Monday) using the capital intensive

7 Besides differences in work time, differences in outcome would include differences in consumption, accumulation, or desirability of working with different technologies, or under one's own or another's management, if we allow for such differences in our model.
8 This is obviously a dramatic degree of inequality in the distribution of capital. However, *qualitatively* none of our results depend on the degree of inequality in the initial distribution of scarce capital.

technology, using one of their units of seed corn. This yields 2 units of corn on Sunday. If she uses 1 to replace the unit of seed corn used up, there is one unit of corn left over for consumption. How efficient is this outcome? The total number of days worked is 900(6) + 100(1) or 5550 days (of work "pain"). The total amount of net corn produced is 1000 units (of consumption "gain"). So the average days worked (pain) per unit of net corn produced (gain) is 5550/1000 or 5.500 days per unit of net corn. The maximum number of days anyone works is 6 while the minimum number of days anyone works is 1, so the degree of inequality in the economy under autarky would be 6 – 1 or 5 days.

Labor Market

If we legalize a labor market the first thing to consider is if people would use it, and if so, what the wage rate would be. If I am one of the 100 seedy people I might consider becoming an employer. If I hire someone to work for me for a day with one of my units of seed corn in the capital intensive process, my employee would produce 2 units of corn on Sunday that would be mine. After using one of those units of corn to replace the one used up in the capital intensive production process, there would still be one unit of corn net of replacement. As long as the wage rate were less than 1 unit of corn per day I would have some corn *profit* without having worked myself at all.[9] Provided the daily wage rate were less than a unit of corn I would be eager to become an employer. Of course if profits are positive anyone would like to be an employer, including any of the 900 seedless. But having no seed corn, if a seedless person hired an employee they would have to put them to work in the labor intensive process. Since a day's work in the labor intensive process only produces 1/6 unit of net corn, the daily wage rate would have to be less than 1/6 unit of corn for it to be profitable for the seedless to become employers.

Who would be willing to be an employee? Since employees work (while employers do not) and receive no profits (which employers do) this appears the less attractive role to play in the labor exchange.[10] Why would anyone agree to be an employee when they have the option of becoming an employer or working for themselves? If the wage rate is sufficiently high it might not be profitable for you to be an employer, and/or you might be able to get more corn for a day's work as someone else's employee than

---

9 For simplicity we assume that supervisory time is zero for employers.
10 Employees also have to put up with being told how to do their work by their employers. But for now we are assuming that none of our 1000 people care whether they engage in self-managed or alienated labor.

you could working for yourself. How high would the wage rate have to be to make it worthwhile for a seedy person to become an employee? If the daily wage rate is less than 1 unit of corn the seedy will want to be employers, not employees, because they can earn positive profits as employers without working at all. Moreover, for any wage rate less than 1 unit of corn per day the seedy are better off working for themselves using the capital intensive process since they get 1 unit of net corn per day they work. So unless the daily wage rate were higher than 1 unit of corn the seedy will not willingly become employees. On the other hand, for any wage rate higher than 1/6 unit of corn per day the seedless are better off becoming employees than they would be becoming either employers or working for themselves. If the daily wage rate, w, is greater than 1/6 the seedy would receive negative profits as employers since lacking seed corn they can only put employees to work in the less productive labor intensive process. And if w is greater than 1/6 the seedy are better off working as someone else's employee than they would be working for themselves since they only get 1/6 unit of corn under self-employment in the labor intensive process. Another way of summing up the situation is: For any w < 1/6 neither seedy nor seedless will be willing to be employees. Instead everyone would want to be an employer. For any 1 ≤ w neither seedy nor seedless will be willing to be employers. Instead everyone would want to be an employee. Since we define a labor market to be one in which people agree to be employers and employees voluntarily, only for 1/6 ≤ w < 1 would the labor market be used.

Consider some daily wage between 1/6 and 1, say w = 1/3. Would there be willing employers and willing employees at this wage rate? The seedless would not be willing to be employers since when w = 1/3 profits are negative for seedless employers who could only put their employees to work in the labor intensive process. But the seedy would gladly be employers since every day of labor a seedy person hired would yield her a profit of 2/3 units of corn. [1 day of labor working with one unit of seed corn in the capital intensive process yields 2 units of corn, gross, and 1 unit of corn net, leaving 2/3 units profits after paying 1/3 units in wages.] None of the seedy would be willing to be employees for a daily wage of 1/3 units of corn since they can get 1 unit of corn per day of self-employment in the capital intensive process. But all the seedless would be willing to be employees since a daily wage of 1/3 is twice as much as the 1/6 per day they get by self-employment in the labor intensive process. As a matter of fact, for any 1/6 ≤ w < 1 all the seedy would be willing to be employers and all the seedless would be willing to be employees.

But this does not mean that any daily wage rate equal to or higher than 1/6 and lower than 1 could become the permanent, stable, or what economists call *equilibrium wage* in our economy. As a matter of fact, 1/3 is not an equilibrium wage. At w = 1/3 all 900 seedless people would want to work 3 days each as employees. That would be a total supply of labor of 900(3) = 2700 days. But the total demand for labor would only be 500 days. This is because while each seedy person would like to hire as many days of labor as possible since profits are positive at w = 1/3, profits are only positive if you put your employees to work in the capital intensive process, and each seedy person only has 5 units of capital, which is only sufficient to put 5 days of labor to work in the CIT. So the maximum possible demand for labor in our economy is 5 days of labor per seedy employer times 100 seedy employers, or 500 days of labor. So if w were equal to 1/3, the supply of labor (2700 days) would greatly exceed the demand for labor (500 days). In any market where excess supply prevails, all buyers will be able to buy all they want at the going price, but only some of the sellers will succeed in selling all they want to sell at the going price. There is an incentive for frustrated sellers, i.e. those who find they cannot sell all they would like to at the going price, to offer to sell at a lower price in order to move from the group of frustrated sellers who could not find buyers to the group of satisfied sellers who do find buyers. But this will drive the price down.[11] For any daily wage rate higher than 1/6 there will be excess supply in the labor market in our economy, and the self-interested behavior of seedless people who cannot get all the days of work they want, combined with the self-interested behavior of seedy people who see that they could find willing employees at an even lower wage rate, will push the wage rate down. Presumably this downward pressure on the wage rate would continue until the daily wage was 1/6, at which there would no longer be excess supply in the labor market. We have found the equilibrium wage for our economy. If we legalize a labor market there would be some people willing to become employees and some people willing to be their employers for any wage rate between 1/6 and 1. But for all wage rates higher than 1/6 there would be excess supply in the labor market which would push w down to 1/6 – the equilibrium daily wage rate.

At w = 1/6 what will each seedless person do? She will work 6 days and end up with 1 unit of corn to eat. Some may work all 6 days in the capital intensive process as employees. Some may work all 6 days for themselves in the labor intensive process. Some may be self-employed for some days and employees for other days, but all of the seedless will work a total of 6 days each in any case.

At w = 1/6 what will each seedy person do? She will hire as many days of labor as she can put to work in the capital intensive process, i.e. 5 days of labor; 5 days of labor

11 There is also an incentive for savvy buyers who notice there are more sellers than buyers at the going price to lower the price they are willing to pay. We study the logic of this micro law of supply and demand further in Chapter 4.

working with her 5 units of seed corn in the capital intensive process will produce 10 units of corn, gross, on Sunday. Five of the 10 units will be used to replace the 5 units used up.[12] Since our seedy employer hired 5 days of labor at a daily wage rate of 1/6 she must pay $(1/6)(5) = 0.833$ units of corn in wages, leaving $5 - 0.833 = 4.167$ units of corn in profits. Each seedy person consumes 1 unit out of her profits and therefore will be able to accumulate, or add to her stock of seed corn for the following week 3.167 units of corn, beginning the second week with $5 + 3.167 = 8.167$ units of seed corn.

How has opening up a labor market affected the degree of inequality and efficiency of our economy? The maximum number of days anyone works is still 6. But now the minimum number of days worked is 0, giving a degree of inequality of $6 - 0 = 6$ which is greater than 5 under autarky. In fact, opening the labor market has increased the degree of inequality in the economy by more than the difference between 6 and 5 would indicate. The seedless continue to work 6 days and consume 1 unit of corn. But the seedy not only reduce their work time from 1 day to 0 while continuing to consume 1 unit of corn, they each accumulate 3.167 units of corn as well while the seedless accumulate nothing. In other words, a more accurate measure of the degree of inequality in the economy which accounted for differences in accumulation would tell us that the degree of inequality had risen to something greater than the 6 indicated by our imperfect measure.

We calculate the efficiency of the economy as before, dividing the total number of days worked (pain) by total net corn production (gain). The seedless work 900(6) days while the seedy work 100(0) days, or 5400 total days worked —100 less than under autarky because the 100 seedy people no longer work 1 day each. But when counting total net corn production we have to remember that not all net corn produced got consumed this time. Some net corn produced gets consumed. As before, there are 1000 units of net corn consumed since each of the 1000 people consumes one each. But unlike under autarky, the seedy also accumulate corn when we legalize a labor market. Each seedy person accumulates 3.167 units of corn for a total of 100(3.167) = 316.7 units of corn accumulated. So the average number of days worked per unit of net corn produced is now $[900(6) + 100(0)]$, or 5400 total days worked divided by $[1000 + 316.7]$, or 1316.7 units of net corn = 4.101 days worked, on average, per unit of net corn produced, our measure of efficiency for the economy.

---

12 We require replacement of seed corn used because we want to explore what economists call "reproducible solutions," i.e. we want outcomes that could be repeated indefinitely, week after week.

Credit Market

What if wage slavery is made illegal – just as chattel slavery was abolished by law in the United States after the Civil War – but borrowing and lending seed corn is legal instead? That is, what if instead of opening a labor market we open a credit market? What does it mean to open, or legalize a credit market, and under what circumstances would people use it? In our simple economy a credit market means that someone lends seed corn to someone else on Monday morning and the borrower pays the lender back on Sunday not only the amount she borrowed on Monday, i.e. the principal, but some additional amount of corn in interest as well that the borrower and lender agree to. Are there weekly interest rates per unit of borrowed corn at which we would find some people willing to be lenders and other people willing to be borrowers? Is there an **equilibrium weekly rate of interest**, r, that we might expect to eventually prevail in our simple economy?

The first thing to consider is why anyone would ever want to be a borrower rather than a lender. After all, the lender gets back more than she lent and the borrower has to give back more than she borrowed! The reason to borrow in our economy is to avoid having to work in the less productive, labor intensive process for lack of seed corn. If I have a unit of seed corn I can get 1 unit of corn, net, for a day of self-employed labor in the capital intensive process. Whereas, if I have no seed corn, a day of self-employment only yields 1/6 unit of corn. As outrageous as a 5/6 or 83.3% weekly rate of interest may seem, for any r < 5/6 the seedless in our economy are better off borrowing seed corn at the beginning of the week and using it to work for themselves in the capital intensive process instead of working for themselves in the labor intensive process. If a seedless person borrows 1 unit of seed corn and works with it for a day she will get 2 units of corn on Sunday. She can use 1 of the 2 units to pay back the principal and still have 1 unit of corn, net, for 1 day of work. As long as the rate of interest is less than 5/6 she will still have more than 1/6 unit of corn left after paying interest as well as principal – which is better than had she not borrowed at all and worked the day in the labor intensive process instead. So there will be plenty of willing seedless borrowers if r < 5/6. And it is not hard to imagine that the seedy will be willing to lend. As long as r > 0 the seedy do better for themselves by lending and collecting interest for no work on their part.[13]

---

13 If the interest rate became low enough a seedy person would not want to lend out all 5 units of her seed corn. If the interest rate was so low she could not get 1 unit in interest for all 5 units lent, she should keep enough seed corn (something less than 1 unit out of her stock of 5) to do however much work she had to do herself in the capital intensive rather than the labor intensive process. However, we are about to discover that the equilibrium interest rate in our simple economy is high enough, by a considerable margin, to rid our seedy lenders of this technical worry.

So we will have willing (seedy) lenders and willing (seedless) borrowers for any $0 < r \leq 5/6$.

But is any of the above interest rates that would yield willing lenders and borrowers an equilibrium weekly rate of interest? Suppose $r = \frac{1}{2}$. Each seedless person would want to borrow 2 units of seed corn since they would end up with $\frac{1}{2}$ unit of corn after repaying principal and interest for each unit they borrowed and worked with in the capital intensive process for a day, and 2 units of borrowed corn along with 2 days of work would get them the 1 unit of corn they need to consume. That is a total demand for seed corn in our Monday morning credit market of $900(2) = 1800$ units of corn. But the maximum total supply of seed corn in our Monday morning credit market is only $100(5) = 500$ units of seed corn available to be lent. This large excess demand for seed corn at $r = \frac{1}{2}$ would put upward pressure on the interest rate as frustrated (seedless) borrowers unable to borrow all they want would offer to pay a slightly higher rate of interest, and savvy (seedy) lenders who recognized they could get more than half a unit would begin to demand more. At any $r < 5/6$ there would be excess demand in our credit market pushing the interest rate up until it reached $5/6$, our equilibrium weekly interest rate.

At $r = 5/6$ what will each seedless person do? She will work 6 days and consume 1 unit of corn whether she borrows or not. If she does not borrow and works for herself in the labor intensive technology she nets $1/6$ unit of corn per day's work. If she borrows a unit of seed corn and works with it herself in the capital intensive technology she also nets $1/6$ unit of corn per day's work after paying principal and interest. So whether she borrows 0, 1, 2, 3, 4, 5, or 6 units of corn in the Monday credit market she will end up working 6 days during the week. She will be working under her own management all 6 days, the only difference being how many of those days she will be working in the labor or the capital intensive technology. At $r = 5/6$ what will each seedy person do? She will lend all 5 units of corn, receive $(5/6)(5)$ $= 4.167$ units of corn in interest in addition to being repaid her 5 units of corn principal, consume 1 unit, and have 3.167 units of corn to add to her corn stock for the following week.

As in the case of the labor market, the degree of inequality in the economy will be 6 – the seedless work 6 days and the seedy 0 – but this imperfect measure underestimates how much opening the credit market increases the degree of inequality because it does not account for the fact that now the seedy accumulate 3.167 units per week while the seedless accumulate nothing.

Opening a credit market also increases the efficiency of the economy exactly to the same extent as opening a labor market. Total days worked is $900(6) +$ $100(0) = 5400$. Total net corn produced is 1000 for consumption and $100(3.167) =$

316.7 for accumulation, or 1316.7. So the average days worked per unit of net corn is 5400/1316.7 = 4.101 once again. Obviously opening a credit market has exactly the same effect as opening a labor market on outcomes, i.e. the efficiency and degree of inequality in our simple economy.[14]

While there is much to consider regarding the explanation and interpretation of these results, before turning to these substantive issues it is instructive to see what the effects of opening a labor or credit market in the same simple economy would be if the 500 units of scarce seed corn were distributed equally among people in the first place.

Situation 2: Egalitarian Distribution of Scarce Seed Corn

In situation 2 we distribute the same 500 units of seed corn in an egalitarian manner. We give each of the 1000 people ½ unit of seed corn and examine what people would do under autarky, with access to a labor market, and with access to a credit market.

Autarky

In autarky each person must work entirely for herself and can only have access to her own half unit of seed corn. What would each of our 1000 people do? As long as you have seed corn you will use the capital intensive process. So the first thing every person would do is work a half day (Monday morning), using their half unit of seed corn in the capital intensive process to produce 1 unit of corn, gross, available on Sunday. After replacing the half unit of seed corn they used up, they would have a half unit of corn left for consumption. But everyone needs 1 unit of corn per week for consumption. Under autarky, to get the other half unit of corn she needs to consume each person would then have to work 3 more days (3(1/6) = 3/6 = 1/2) using the labor intensive technology, for a total of 3.50 days of work per week. So with an egalitarian distribution of 500 units of scarce seed corn, under autarky the efficiency of the economy – or average number of days worked per unit of net corn produced

14 While credit and labor markets have the same effect on outcomes in our simple economy they do *not* have the same effect on the decision-making process. The labor market turns seedless people who were self-employed under autarky into employees who engage in other-directed, or alienated labor. The credit market allows lenders to benefit materially from the increased efficiency that comes from borrowers working in the capital instead of labor intensive process, but leaves borrowers working under their own management.

– will be 3.50(1000)/1000 or 3.500, and the degree of inequality in the economy will be 3.50 – 3.50 = 0.

Labor Market

The equilibrium wage will be exactly the same if we open a labor market in situation 2 as it was in situation 1. This might seem surprising, but the equilibrium wage does not depend on the distribution of the scarce seed corn but only on the comparative efficiencies of the capital and labor intensive technologies and whether or not seed corn is scarce. Since neither productive technology nor the scarcity of seed corn has changed between situations 1 and 2, the equilibrium wage will still be 1/6.[15]

Suppose a person decides she wants to be an employer. With only half a unit of seed corn she can only profitably employ somebody for half a day. Her employee working half a day with that half unit of seed corn produces 1 unit of corn on Sunday. Half of that unit must go to replace the half unit used up leaving ½ or 6/12 units net of replacement. Since she has only hired half a day of labor she only has to pay half the daily wage rate, or ½(1/6) = 1/12 unit of corn in wages. Subtracting 1/12 in wages from 6/12 leaves 5/12 units of corn profits. So far this looks very attractive – 5/12 units of corn profits without having to work at all – and we might suspect that all 1000 people will want to be employers. But our employer still needs 7/12 more units of corn for her consumption. And the bad news is that she has no alternative but to work in the labor intensive process herself to produce this 7/12 because her employee has tied up her half unit of seed corn for the week. How many days will it take working in the labor intensive technology to produce 7/12 units of corn? Each day she works she produces 1/6, or 2/12. So it will take her three and a half days to produce 7/12 units of corn.

If someone decides not to be an employer the first thing she will do is work half a day with her own half unit of corn in the capital intensive technology which we know yields half a unit of corn net of replacement on Sunday. At that point she will still need another half unit for consumption and has two ways to get it: She can work as somebody else's employee or she can work for herself in the labor intensive process. With w = 1/6 it will take her three more days of work no matter whether she is self-employed or someone else's employee, or some combination of the two. So under an egalitarian distribution of scarce seed corn, while employers would reap positive

---

15 Whether or not seed corn is scarce depends on the productivity of the capital intensive technology, the total amount of seed corn available, and the amount of corn each must consume, none of which has changed between situation 1 and situation 2.

profits, surprisingly it turns out that employers and employees would end up working the same number of days, 3.5, and consuming the same amount as one another, 1 unit of corn. This means that under an egalitarian distribution of scarce seed corn the degree of inequality in the economy would remain the same as it was under autarky if we opened a labor market, i.e. zero. And the efficiency of the economy would remain the same as well, 3.500 days of work per unit of net corn produced.

Credit Market

Just as the equilibrium wage depends only on the relative productivity of the capital and labor intensive technologies and on whether or not capital is scarce, the equilibrium weekly interest rate depends only on these factors, not on the distribution of the scarce seed corn. So if we opened a credit instead of a labor market in situation 2 the interest rate would be 5/6 just as it was in situation 1. And while it might seem like all would wish to be lenders at this attractive rate of interest it turns out that lenders and borrowers alike would end up having to work the same number of days to get their unit of corn to consume, 3.5.

Anyone who lends her half unit of corn will get $(\frac{1}{2})(5/6) = 5/12$ units of corn interest at the end of the week. But to get the other 7/12 units of corn she needs to consume she will have to work three and a half days using the labor intensive technology. Before anyone would borrow seed corn she will first work with her own half unit for half a day using the capital intensive process, netting half a unit for consumption. Only then would she borrow seed corn in order to work in the more productive capital intensive process rather than the less productive labor intensive process. But if the weekly interest rate is 5/6 she only ends up with 1/6 unit per day she works with borrowed corn, which is neither better nor worse than the 1/6 she gets working in the labor intensive process without borrowing corn. In either case, or in any combination, she would have to work three more days after working for half a day with her own seed corn, for a total of 3.5 days of work. Again, opening a credit market under an egalitarian distribution of scarce seed corn does not change the degree of inequality in the economy from what it was under autarky, zero. Nor does it change the efficiency of the economy which remains 3.500 days of work on average per unit of net corn.

Conclusions from the Domestic Corn Model

The main results from the simple corn model are:

1. As long as there is an unequal distribution of scarce seed corn there will be unequal outcomes under autarky, with a labor market, or with a credit market. Some will have to work more days than others to consume the same amount of corn. (In situation 1 under autarky the degree of inequality was 5 and with a labor market or credit market it was 6.)

2. With an inegalitarian distribution of scarce seed corn, opening a labor or a credit market increases the efficiency of the economy, but increases the degree of inequality in the economy as well. (In situation 1 opening either a labor or credit market reduced the average number of days of work needed to produce a unit of net corn from 5.500 to 4.101, while it increased the degree of inequality from 5 to 6.)

3. Whether scarce seed corn is initially distributed unequally or equally, opening a credit market and opening a labor market have identical effects on efficiency and the degree of inequality in the economy, i.e. on economic outcomes. (In both situation 1 and 2 outcomes were affected identically when we opened a labor market and when we opened a credit market.)

4. However, opening a labor market has a different effect on who manages labor than does opening a credit market. (Opening a labor market shifts some of the seedless from self-managed to alienated labor, whereas opening a credit market does not.)

The first result is easy to understand. If seed corn allows people to produce corn with less work, and if seed corn is scarce, having more seed corn than someone else is an advantage under any of our rules for running the economy.

The second result may seem less intuitive. Why would a change in rules that increases the efficiency of the economy also increase the degree of inequality in the economy? In situation 1 much of the scarce seed corn does not get used to put people to work in the more productive, capital intensive process under autarky. This is because there is no incentive for the seedy to work with more than 1 of their 5 units of seed corn themselves under autarky – leaving 100(4) = 400 of our 500 units of seed corn idle. Opening a labor market creates an incentive for the seedy to use all their seed corn to hire employees at a profit. A side effect of the seedy's search for individual profit is that all the scarce seed corn in the economy gets used to put people to work in the more productive, capital intensive process rather than the less productive, labor intensive process. Not surprisingly this yields an efficiency gain for the economy. Similarly, opening a credit market creates a different but equally effective incentive for the seedy to lend all their seed corn for a positive rate of interest, which also means that all of the scarce seed corn in the economy will be used to put people who otherwise would have worked in the less productive, labor intensive technology to work instead in the more productive, capital intensive technology. Opening either a labor or credit market yields the same efficiency gain for the economy.

The reason opening a labor or credit market also increases the degree of inequality in the economy is that as long as seed corn is scarce the seedy as the employers (or lenders) will be able to capture the efficiency gain of the increased productivity of their employees (or debtors). Since the seedy were already better off under autarky – working 1 day instead of 6 – if they capture the efficiency gain from opening a labor or credit market the difference between them and the seedless must increase. In situation 1 the efficiency gain from opening a labor or credit market takes the form of less days worked by the seedy – each works 1 less day than under autarky for a total reduction of 100 days of work – and more corn accumulated by the seedy – each accumulates 3.167 units more than under autarky for a total increase of 316.7 units of corn accumulated. Once we realize that the outcome for the seedless is the same with a labor or credit market as under autarky – under all three sets of rules the seedless work 6 days and consume 1 unit of corn – it is obvious that the entire efficiency gain from opening a labor or credit market must have gone to the seedy. And since the seedy were already better off under autarky, the degree of inequality must now be greater.

The reason the seedy capture the entire efficiency gain in our model is because seed corn is scarce, so when the seedless compete among themselves for access to seed corn through a credit market they bid the interest rate up to the point where the lenders capture the entire efficiency gain from opening the credit market. Similarly, when the seedless compete for access to work with scarce seed corn through a labor market they bid the wage rate down to the point where the entire efficiency gain from opening a labor market goes to their employers.[16] In either case it is the labor of the seedless that becomes more productive when we open a credit or labor market. But as long as seed corn is scarce it will be their employers or their creditors who capture the lion's share of their increased productivity. In our simple model the lenders and employers will capture the entire efficiency gain. But even in more complicated and realistic models it is generally the case that employers and lenders capture the lion's share of efficiency gains from the employment and credit relationships as long as

16 In our simple model only if seed corn were in excess supply and labor were therefore scarce would the seedless in the economy be able to capture the benefits of the employment and credit relationships. If labor were scarce seedy employers competing for employees would bid the wage rate up to 1, and seedy lenders competing for borrowers would bid the interest rate down to zero – and their seedless employees and debtors would capture the entire efficiency gain from opening labor and credit markets. But just as capital has always been distributed unequally, capital has always been scarce, and will remain so as long as more capital can improve the productivity of any working in the economy.

seed corn, or capital, is scarce. As long as the seedy capture more than 50% of the increase in their employees' or creditors' productivity, the degree of inequality in the economy necessarily rises.

The reason there are no efficiency gains from opening a labor or credit market under an egalitarian distribution of scarce seed corn is that there is no inefficiency in the first place! In situation 2 all 500 units of seed corn are used to put people to work in the more productive, capital intensive technology under autarky because each person has an incentive to use her half unit of seed corn to work in the capital intensive process before working in the less productive, labor intensive process. The reason the degree of inequality does not rise above zero when we open a labor or credit market in situation 2 is that everyone is free to walk away from the labor and credit markets if they can do better by themselves, which means none must accept a worse outcome than they get under autarky. With no efficiency gain, when none accepts a worse outcome none can achieve a better outcome.

While the third result may be surprising at first, when properly interpreted it makes intuitive sense. Opening a credit market has exactly the same effect on outcomes as opening a labor market in our simple economy because we have abstracted from all the factors that make labor and credit markets different in the real world! For example, our model has no economies of scale. One person working one day with one unit of seed corn in the capital intensive technology produces just as much corn per day worked (and per unit of corn used) as 5 people working one day each with 5 units of seed corn in the capital intensive technology. So in our model there is no advantage for an employer gathering 5 employees to work together, compared to 5 borrowers borrowing 1 unit of seed corn each and working in isolation from one another. This is often not the case in the real world where there *are* economies of scale. Our model also abstracts from any differences in the productivity of self-managed and other-directed or alienated labor, and from any supervisory costs of monitoring employees. Consequently the model fails to capture differences in outcomes due to these factors. Finally, there is no uncertainty and therefore no risk in our model. Since there are different kinds and degrees of uncertainty and risk in real world labor and credit relations, our model also fails to capture differences in outcome due to these differences between credit and labor markets. In short, whereas labor and credit markets do not affect outcomes differently in our simple model, this does not mean they do not affect outcomes differently in the real world. However, even our simple model highlights one important difference between the effects of real labor and credit markets – who manages labor. Only opening a labor market transforms self-managed labor into other-directed, or alienated labor for the seedless, whereas opening a credit market does not.

Generalizing Conclusions

The simple corn model is quite different from the real world. And as we have already observed, some results are more extreme in the corn model than would be the case in real world settings. What are the effects of relaxing simplifying assumptions in the model? What conclusions from the corn model *can* we generalize to real world situations?

The assumption that people only want to consume 1 unit of corn per week after which they want to work as few days as possible is not critical. We could change the model to allow for the fact that people are happier the more they consume as well as the less they work without changing any of the above conclusions.[17]

We could also allow for many different goods without affecting any conclusions. However, in a multi-good world there would be one interesting difference. The analog to the autarkic solution in the simple corn model in a world where people consume many goods, not all of which they produce themselves, is a solution where people trade goods but do not trade labor or credit. In this case there *are* relationships people enter into with one another even when they do not employ one another or borrow from one another. They enter into a division of labor where people produce different goods which they trade with one another. Just as unequal outcomes resulted in the one-good model when people start with different amounts of seed corn even under autarky where people enter into no "relations" with one another at all; it turns out that unequal outcomes result when people with different initial stocks of goods trade goods with one another *even when the markets for all goods are completely competitive.* In the simple corn model when scarce seed corn is initially distributed unequally unequal outcomes occur without any institutionalized relationship as a transmission vehicle. In a more realistic model of a multi-good world, unequal outcomes occur simply through the exchange of goods in competitive markets when people start with different initial stocks of goods.[18] In any case, all conclusions from the one-good corn model do generalize to a multi-good model.

---

17 We have already seen that, when people accumulate corn, how we measure inequality must be modified to take differences in corn accumulated into account as well as differences in days worked.

18 This result surprised many political economists as well as mainstream economists when it was first demonstrated by John Roemer in *A General Theory of Exploitation and Class* (Harvard University Press, 1982). In Appendix B of *Panic Rules! All You Need to Know About the Global Economy* (South End Press, 1999) I add a second good, machines, to the simple corn model in order to demonstrate that international trade, even if markets are competitive, is likely to increased global inequality. The effects of international trade on global efficiency and inequality are discussed in Chapter 8 of this book.

Finally, we could modify the model to eliminate the "knife edge" effect that all of the efficiency gain from opening a labor or credit market must rebound *entirely* to the seedy as long as seed corn is scarce (only to switch over and be captured *entirely* by the seedless in an instant should seed corn cease to be scarce). Qualitatively, none of our conclusions hinge on the fact that 100% of the efficiency gain is captured by the seedy as employers, or creditors. As long as those who were worse off in the first place receive less than half the efficiency gain, the degree of inequality will increase as use of labor and credit markets expands, which will be the case as long as having more capital would allow someone in the economy to work more productively. So results from the simple model do generalize to more realistic settings where efficiency gains from labor and credit markets are shared by both parties.

To summarize regarding the most crucial issue: How can voluntary, mutually beneficial exchanges aggravate inequalities? Nobody is forcing employees to work for employers when we open up a labor market, or debtors to borrow from lenders when there is a credit market. An opportunity exists for anyone to take advantage of – or not – as they choose. Moreover, we have assumed competitive interaction in all market exchanges. So any increase in inequality that results is not because a buyer can insist on an unduly large share of the benefit from the exchange because sellers have no other buyers to sell to; or because a seller can insist on an unduly large share of the benefit because buyers have no other sellers to buy from. Not only are all exchanges voluntary, and therefore should not leave either party worse off than they would have been not making the exchange, the exchanges take place under competitive conditions where both parties can choose a different exchange partner should they find the one they are dealing with unreasonable. The answer to how rising inequality can result from voluntary, competitive exchanges is ultimately simple, and hopefully now intuitive: If those who are initially better off capture a higher percentage of the increased economic efficiency that results from exchange than those who are initially worse off, although exchange will be voluntary and mutually beneficial, it will also increase the degree of inequality in the economy. Moreover, this can occur through competitive as well as noncompetitive markets, and goods markets as well as labor and credit markets. So despite its simplicity, the model helps explain:

1. How unequal ownership of productive assets, or wealth, leads to inequalities in work time, consumption, and accumulation.
2. How both the employment and credit relationships can be mutually beneficial and lead to increasing inequality at the same time.

3. How economic relationships can simultaneously promote more efficient uses of scarce productive resources *and* be transmission vehicles for increasing economic inequality.
4. Why making markets competitive – be they labor, credit, or goods markets – may improve outcomes, but will *not* prevent them from aggravating economic inequality nonetheless.
5. Why the employment relation is particularly problematic from the perspective of economic justice since it aggravates inequalities in economic outcomes *and* inequalities in decision-making power, i.e. causes alienation.

Political economists believe that understanding these issues is important to understanding what is going on in the real world when some people "choose" to work in other people's factories, when farmers "choose" to mortgage their land to borrow operating funds from banks, when third world nations "choose" to borrow from international banks, when workers in less developed countries flock to work for subsidiaries of multinational companies, and when less developed countries willingly trade raw materials for manufactured goods from more developed countries. Who will be employer and who will be employee; who will lend and who will borrow; and who will sell and who will buy which kinds of goods are not accidents in these situations. Nor is it ignorance or short-sightedness that leads the exploited in these situations to "choose" to participate in their own fleecing. Moreover, the model suggests there is good reason to believe that while even more unequal outcomes can be expected from non-competitive and coercive conditions, as long as parties to exchanges have different amounts of wealth, or scarce capital, to begin with, inequalities would be aggravated even if all the above economic relations were fully informed, strictly voluntary, and took place under perfectly competitive conditions.

Economic Justice in the Corn Model

To translate conclusions regarding unequal outcomes into conclusions about economic injustice requires applying an ethical framework to the corn model. It is tempting to label unequal outcomes in the corn model unfair, or exploitative. Indeed, in many circumstances we can do this, but it is important to be clear how and why we judge unequal outcomes to be inequitable, and when outcomes that are unfair are also exploitative. In the simple corn model making ethical judgments about unequal outcomes requires focusing first on *how* people came to have unequal stocks of seed corn in the first place, since it is the unequal initial distribution of seed corn that gives rise to the unequal outcomes.

If the inegalitarian distribution of scarce seed corn were due to unequal inheritances, then supporters of both liberal maxim 2 and radical maxim 3 would judge the unequal outcomes that result to be unfair. In the liberal and radical views nobody should have to work more simply because someone else inherited more seed corn than they did. Only a supporter of conservative maxim 1 would see things differently. In the conservative view calling outcomes where those who inherited seed corn work less than those without seed corn unfair is unwarranted because according to maxim 1 those who "contribute" seed corn should not have to "contribute" as much labor as those who "contribute" no seed corn.

What if some have more seed corn than others simply because of luck? In the simple corn model we can imagine that even if people began in situation 2 where everyone has a half unit of seed corn, after a few weeks some would enjoy good luck and produce more than 1 net unit of corn in 3 and a half days' work, allowing them to accumulate more than half a unit of seed corn, while others would suffer bad luck and produce less than 1 net unit of corn in 3 and a half days' of work. If the unlucky still consumed 1 unit of corn they would be unable to fully replace their half unit of seed corn and therefore have to work more than the lucky every week subsequently – even if all were equally lucky after the first week. Since good luck entails no greater sacrifice than bad luck, unequal outcomes due to unequal stocks of seed corn resulting from unequal luck in a previous week would be deemed unfair by supporters of radical maxim 3. If supporters of conservative maxim 1 consider acquisition through luck blameless, they would be inclined to view unequal outcomes from this cause perfectly fair and equitable. The attitude of supporters of liberal maxim 2 is not clear cut. During the week when the good or bad luck took place differences in outcome might well be considered as differences in the productivity of people's work which, according to maxim 2 justify different outcomes. But once any initial differences in luck were translated into differences in corn stocks, since liberal maxim 2 gives no moral credit for contributions from productive property, different outcomes in subsequent weeks would be seen as inequitable.

Inequalities due to unfair advantage are also easy to visualize in the simple corn model. Suppose those who are stronger take the land closer to the village where everyone lives by force, allowing them to consistently produce more than 1 unit of corn in three and a half days of work because they don't have to walk as far to get to and from the fields. The weaker people, however, are forced to walk farther to and from work each day so they consistently produce less than 1 unit of corn in three and a half days of work. The strong will end up with more seed corn than the weak because they used their greater physical strength to achieve an unfair advantage. And as we saw in situation 1, those who begin with more seed corn can easily acquire even more seed corn with no additional work of their own if they can hire others in a "free" labor market or lend to others in a "free" credit market. Not surprisingly in this case all three maxims condemn unequal outcomes that result from unfair advantage as unfair. Since there is no unequal sacrifice unequal outcomes are unfair according to radical maxim 3. Since the greater productivity of the strong is achieved unfairly, the unequal outcomes are unfair according to liberal maxim 2. And if productive property is unjustly acquired, presumably supporters of conservative maxim 1 would view any rewards to the unfairly acquired property as unjust as well.

But the most difficult scenario from an ethical perspective is the following: What if we start in situation 2, and while most people work 3 and a half days a week – half a day using the CIT and 3 days using the LIT – 100 enterprising souls work an extra 3 days using the LIT. That is, what if instead of taking 3 and a half days of leisure like their 900 counterparts, these 100 go-getters use 3 of their leisure days in week one to work longer in the LIT, and thereby add an extra half unit of corn to their seed stock to start week two? In this case they would not have acquired their greater stock of seed corn through inheritance, luck, or unfair advantage. Instead, they would have more seed corn than the other 900 people at the start of week two because they made the sacrifice of working longer than others had in week one. Or, the greater sacrifice might take the form of working the same number of days but working harder, with greater intensity in week one. Or, it might take the form of tightening their belt and consuming less than a whole unit of corn, and therefore saving more than others do in week one. In the case of extra seed corn acquired through some greater sacrifice, the fact that the seedy can work less than 3 and a half days in week two would not seem unfair, and even radicals should refrain from criticizing the unequal outcome in week two when our industrious (or thrifty) 100 end up working less than their 900 sisters. One could view their shorter work week in week two simply as compensation for their extra days of work in week one. However, before giving a moral "thumbs up" to unequal outcomes even in this situation it is important to consider three issues very carefully.

First of all, it is common for supporters of capitalism to rationalize inequalities as being entirely of this nature even though overwhelming evidence suggests this is the *least* important cause of unequal outcomes in capitalist economies. Edward Bellamy put it this way in 1897:

Why, dear me, there never would have been any possibility of making a great fortune in a lifetime if the maker had confined himself to the product of his own efforts. The whole acknowledged art of wealth-making on a large scale consisted in devices for getting possession of other people's product without too open breach of the law. It was a current and a true saying of the times that nobody could honestly acquire a million dollars. Everybody knew that it was only by extortion, speculation, stock gambling, or some other form of plunder under pretext of law that such a feat could be accomplished.

(Equality, republished by AMS Press, 1970)

Clearly, inherited wealth is not due to any sacrifices on the part of the heir. Readers should go back and check to see that every study cited in Chapter 2 about the origins of wealth inequality in the US in modern times concluded that 50% or more can be attributed to unequal inheritance.

Second, it is not necessarily the case that all 1000 people had an equal opportunity to work more than 3 and a half days the first week. For example, what if some of the 1000 people are single mothers who are hard pressed to arrange for day care for even 3 and a half days a week? Would not that change our attitude about whether or not the unequal outcomes in week two were fair?

But the most troubling problem is the following: Suppose all have equal opportunity to work extra days the first week but only 100 choose to do so. On Monday of the second week the industrious 100 who chose to work 3 extra days the first week would have 1 unit of seed corn, while everyone else would still have only a half. Even under the rules of autarky this would permit the industrious to work only 1 day a week, *forever*, while everyone else would continue to have to work 3 and a half days a week, *forever*. After only two weeks of this the industrious would have worked 5 days fewer than the rest, and therefore already have more than "made up" for their extra three days work the first week. *At what point does their compensation become excessive, and the continued inequality therefore become inequitable?*

More troubling still is the fact that if there is a labor or credit market the 100 who were more industrious the first week can soon accumulate enough seed corn to never have to work themselves again, *and* accumulate more and more of the corn produced by others every week thereafter. Under autarky an extra sacrifice in week one does not eliminate the necessity of continuing to work oneself, and can only be parlayed into a 2 and a half day leisure advantage that remains constant every week thereafter. On the other hand, a labor or credit market allows any who make an extra sacrifice in week one to "leverage" it into never having to work again, living instead entirely off the labor of others, and appropriating ever more of what others produce as each week passes. Why do labor and credit markets complicate the situation both quantitatively and qualitatively?

The personal advantages of working more in early weeks are greater if one can use the extra seed corn to get profits by becoming an employer (paying w = 1/6), or to get interest by becoming a lender (charging r = 5/6). With labor and credit markets extra sacrifices early give rise not only to permanent advantages, but to permanent advantages that steadily increase in size. Under autarky the most advantage one can attain is 2 and a half days more leisure per week for ever. On the other hand if the industrious 100 work an extra three days in the LIT the first week, and in the second week work 1 day in the CIT and 6/5 days in the LIT – for a total of 2 and 1/5 days the second week – they will be able to start the third week with 6/5 units of seed corn. By either lending 6/5, or using it to hire labor, they would never have to work again. If they work any amount more than 2 and 1/5 days the second week, they would not only never have to work again, they would be able to accumulate ever increasing amounts of seed corn each week thereafter, indefinitely.

This is not to say that we cannot devise rules for where and how to draw the line between just and unjust compensation for extra sacrifice in early weeks. But it should be clear that merely because the initial reason for unequal corn stocks – an unequal sacrifice in some earlier week – might merit a legitimate compensating inequality in later weeks, this does *not* mean that *whatever* compensation, or advantage, results from a greater sacrifice in an earlier week is just and fair.

Labor and credit markets also complicate the situation qualitatively. Unlike under autarky, with labor and credit markets there is an explicit social relationship through which increasingly unfair outcomes occur. Employers who make no further sacrifices can enjoy ever larger profits by capturing the increased productivity of more and more employees. Lenders who make no further sacrifices can enjoy ever larger interest payments by capturing the increased productivity of more and more borrowers. This qualitative difference suggests a useful way to distinguish between outcomes that are merely unfair, unjust, or inequitable, and outcomes that are not only unjust but also exploitative.

Economic Justice, Exploitation, and Alienation

If asked if the seedy can "exploit" the seedless if they never enter into any relationship with them whatsoever, I believe most would be inclined to say "no." Under the rules of autarky our 1000 people could literally live on 1000 separate islands. They might not even be aware of each other's existence. Nonetheless, if the 100 seedy acquired their extra seed corn through no greater sacrifice on their part, the radical maxim suggests that the longer work week of the seedless is still objectively unfair. Yet even if we think the advantages of the seedy are unfair, under autarky most would hesitate to say the seedy are exploiting the seedless. We can preserve this useful difference in common usage by reserving the word *exploitation* for *unfair economic outcomes that result from explicit social relationships*. In this case the unequal outcomes in autarky are unfair, but we do not say the seedy are exploiting the seedless. Whereas the unequal outcomes resulting from the employment relationship and the credit relationship are not only unfair, but we say employers are exploiting their employees, and creditors are exploiting borrowers.[19] While this is ultimately simply semantics, we can define clear rules of usage making it possible to draw distinctions many have found to be meaningful between different kinds of economic injustice.

To summarize: First we focus on outcomes – days worked, consumption, accumulation. We define economic justice solely in terms of outcomes. Then we draw a distinction between two kinds of unjust outcomes, ones that occur through an explicit social relationship that benefits one party more than the other, and unjust outcomes that are not the result of explicit social relationships. We say employers exploit employees and creditors exploit borrowers because the differences in outcome are not only unfair, but a social relationship plays a crucial role in producing the unfair outcome. Whereas we call unequal outcomes under autarky unfair, but not exploitative. Finally we recognize that besides outcomes, and whether or not an unjust outcome is the result of an explicit social relationship, who gets to decide how someone's labor is expended is also important. If a worker has the right to work as she sees fit, we say her labor is self-managed, whether or not she is working in the LIT or the CIT, whether or not she is working with her own corn or with borrowed corn, and whether or not she is exploited. On the other hand *if labor is performed as an employee then it is the employer who has the legal right to say how the employee will use her time and perform her labor*. In this case we could say the employee's labor is no longer self-managed, but "other-directed," but it is more common for political economists to say the employee's labor is *alienated*, whether or not she is also exploited.

This theory of economic justice, exploitation, and alienation allows us to identify some outcomes as unfair even when there is no relationship through which some are

---

19 These rules of usage imply that we should refer to unfair outcomes that result when parties trade goods with one another also as exploitative since there is an explicit social relationship through which the unjust outcome occurs. In which case if we come to the conclusion that the outcomes of international trade between capital-poor countries and capital-rich countries is unfair, we should also criticize international trade as "exploitative" rather than merely as "unequal exchange."

"exploiting" others. It allows us to identify unfair outcomes where there are people who are exploiting others through particular social relationships, and to raise the issue of culpability in these cases. And finally, this theory allows us to distinguish between unfair outcomes and undemocratic economic decision-making procedures whereby some have the power to decide how others will use their laboring capacities. In this framework, the capitalist employment relationship is revealed as particularly problematic since it leads to alienation as well as economic injustice and exploitation.

Occupy Wall Street

More than anything else Occupy Wall Street was a primal scream about inequality in America. Protesters in Zuccotti Park dared to point their finger straight at the elephant in the room and say: "We see you! We see that for over three decades the wealthiest top 1% have managed to appropriate almost all productivity increases, while the economic interests of the 99% have been increasingly neglected." Their scream hit a nerve that had long been numbed, and soon there were Occupy encampments in hundreds of cities and towns across the US, and economic discourse ever since has been forced to acknowledge the presence of the elephant. No simple model can provide a full explanation of what caused the historic increase in inequality.[20] But the corn model provides a good starting point because it teaches us what happens when capital and labor markets are left to function according to the laws of supply and demand. When capital makes our labor more productive, when capital is scarce, and when people are "free" to hire and be hired, lend and borrow, initial differences in wealth – however they may have arisen – will be parlayed into ever growing inequality.

But is our explanation too good? Why does inequality not *always* increase in economies with labor and credit markets? Inequality has increased in the US and almost every other country over the past thirty years, and continues to do so. But this was not always the case. In the middle third of the twentieth century wealth and income inequality was reduced in the US and most of the more advanced economies. Here as well the corn model provides a hint: If wage rates and interest rates are determined by the laws of supply and demand growing inequality will be the result. But what if wage and interest rates are determined by some other process? In our example, what if the 900 seedy formed a union and negotiated with an employers'

20 For a comprehensive treatment see *Capital in the Twenty-First Century* (Belknap Press, 2014) by Thomas Piketty.

organization representing the 100 seedy? Is there any reason the union could not win a contract where all employers would have to agree to pay a wage of 1/4, or 1/2, or 2/3 units of corn per day? Or, is there any reason the 900 seedy could not elect a government that passed a minimum wage law setting the minimum wage at 1/4, or 1/2, or 2/3 units of corn per day? Similarly, is there any reason governments cannot outlaw "usurious" interests rates as high as 5/6 units of corn per week, or cap interest rates at 3/4, or 1/2, or 1/3 units of corn per week?

Readers should check to see that for any of the above wage or interest rates: (1) The increase in the productivity of the economy from introducing a labor or credit market would be exactly the same as under the "free market" wage rate of 1/6 and interest rate of 5/6. And (2) employers would still be willing to hire employees even at these higher wage rates, and lenders would still be willing to lend at these lower rates of interest. The only difference is that at these higher wage rates and lower interest rates the seedless would capture part of the increase in their productivity.

In general, there are always wage rates that are "feasible" under collective bargaining or a minimum wage law that would divide the efficiency gain from a labor market equally between employer and employee, in which case inequality would not increase but remain constant. And there are even higher wage rates that are "feasible," i.e. still leave employers with positive profits, and therefore an incentive to hire employees, that would decrease inequality by awarding more than 50% of the efficiency gain from the employment relation to employees, and less than 50% to employers.[21] These, and other interventions in labor and credit markets to improve outcomes which were more prevalent in the advanced economies prior to the onset of neoliberalism, are discussed in Chapter 11 where we take up ideas about "What Is to Be Done?"

Model 3.2: A Global Corn Economy

A simple corn model of the global economy can also provide insights about some of the predictable effects of international financial investment – where multinational banks or mutual funds lend to foreign instead of domestic borrowers – and direct foreign investment – where a multinational company opens a subsidiary in a "host" country. In our global corn economy instead of 1000 people we have 100 countries,

---

21 The Sraffa model elaborated in Chapter 5 also makes clear that different combinations of wage and profit rates are equally possible from a purely technological perspective, and therefore that minimum wage laws, unions, and bargaining power can have a significant effect on wage rates in the real world.

each with the same number of inhabitants. Instead of a domestic credit market where people can borrow from one another we have an international credit market where countries can borrow from one another. Instead of a labor market where people can hire one another, we have direct foreign investment (DFI) where companies based in one country can establish subsidiaries in other countries and hire employees there. The only produced good is corn. Corn is produced from inputs of labor and seed corn. All countries are equally skilled and productive, and all have knowledge of the technologies that exist for producing corn. Each country needs to consume 1 unit of corn per year, after which they wish to maximize their leisure and only accumulate corn if they can do so without loss of leisure. There are two ways of producing corn, the "labor intensive technique" and the "capital intensive technique."

Labor intensive technique, LIT:
6 units of labor + 0 units of seed corn yield 1 unit of corn

Capital intensive technique, CIT:
1 unit of labor + 1 unit of seed corn yield 2 units of corn

In either case it takes a year for the corn to be produced and seed corn is tied up for the entire year disappearing by year's end. *Our measure of global inequality is the difference between the number of units of labor worked by the country that works the most, and the number of units of labor worked by the country that works the least. Our measure of global efficiency is the average units of labor worked per unit of net corn produced in the world.* There are 50 units of seed corn in the world. 10 "northern" countries each have 5 units of seed corn, and 90 "southern" countries have no seed corn at all.

We compare outcomes under three international economic regimes: (1) Under autarky there is no international investment of any kind permitted. In other words, there is neither international financial investment nor direct foreign investment. (2) An international credit market allows countries to lend and borrow seed corn as they please. We generously assume that when we open an international credit market all mutually beneficial deals between lending and borrowing countries are discovered and signed, i.e. that the credit market functions perfectly without crises and efficiency losses of any kind.[22] (3) Direct foreign investment (DFI) permits northern countries to hire labor from southern countries in subsidiaries owned

---

22 We drop this assumption in model 9.2 which substitutes a more realistic version of international finance for the ideal but naïve international credit market assumed here. The more realistic model 9.2 allows for efficiency losses as well as efficiency gains from extending the international credit system.

by the northern country. By assuming the labor market inside southern countries equilibrates we implicitly assume foreign and domestic employers pay the same wage rate. If northern multinational companies paid higher wages than domestic employers in southern countries our results would be slightly less unequal.

Under **autarky** each southern country will work 6 units of labor in the LIT while each northern country will work 1 unit of labor in the CIT. The degree of global inequality will be $6 - 1$ or 5. The average number of days worked per unit of net corn produced globally will be $[90(6) + 10(1)]/[100] = 5.500$.

If we legalize an **international credit market** the interest rate, r, on international loans will be 5/6 unit of seed corn per year. Each southern country will work 5 units of labor either in the LIT or with borrowed seed corn in the CIT. Each northern country will lend 5C, collect (5/6)5 or 4.167C in interest, consume 1C and accumulate 3.167C without having to work at all. The degree of global inequality would increase from 5 to 6, although the degree of inequality would really be greater than 6 if we took into account corn accumulated by the northern countries. The efficiency of the global economy would increase since the average number of days worked per unit of net corn produced in the world would fall from 5.500 to $[90(6) + 10(0)]/[100 + 10(3.167)]$ or 4.101. The intuition behind these results is that under autarky northern countries do not have any incentive to put all their seed corn to productive use. Each northern country uses only 1 of its 5 units of seed corn – the other 4 units are an idle productive resource. The international credit market gives northern countries an incentive to lend their seed corn to southern countries where the borrowed seed corn increases the productivity of southern labor. Because seed corn is scarce globally, the northern countries are able to capture the entire efficiency gain from the increased productivity in the southern countries.

If some technical change improved the efficiency of the LIT so it only required 4 units of labor to produce a unit of corn, the international rate of interest, r, would fall from 5/6 to 3/4 units of corn per year. Global efficiency would increase since the average number of days needed to produce a unit of net corn in the world would fall to $[90(4) + 10(0)]/[100 + 10(2.75)] = 2.824$ which is less than 4.101. The international rate of interest, r, decreases because the difference between the productivity of the CIT and LIT technologies is now less so southern countries are not willing to pay as much for the seed corn they need to use the CIT. Global efficiency increases because all production in LIT is more productive, or efficient. Inequality decreases because lenders get less of the efficiency gain and borrowers more when r is lower. *Notice that improving the productivity of more labor intensive technologies not only increases global efficiency, it ameliorates global inequality.*

On the other hand, if some technical change improved the efficiency of the CIT so that it only required half a unit of labor together with 1 unit of seed corn to produce 2 units of corn, gross, or one unit of net corn, the international interest rate would rise to from 5/6 to 11/12 units of corn per year. Global efficiency would increase since the average number of days needed to produce a unit of net corn in the world would fall to $[90(6) + 10(0)]/[100 + 10(3.583)] = 3.975$ which is less than 4.101. The international rate of interest, r, increases because the difference between the productivity of the CIT and LIT technologies is now greater so southern countries are willing to pay more to get access to the seed corn they need to use the CIT. Global efficiency increases because all production in the CIT is more productive, or efficient. Inequality increases because lenders get more of the efficiency gain and borrowers less when r is higher. *Notice that improving the productivity of more capital intensive technologies increases global efficiency but aggravates global inequality.*

If, instead of an international credit market, we legalize **direct foreign investment** the wage rate in southern economies will be w = 1/6. Each southern country will have to work 6 units of labor, whether in the LIT in domestic owned businesses or in the CIT in northern owned businesses located in the southern, or "host" country. Each northern country will hire 5 units of southern labor to work in the northern country's businesses located in southern countries, producing 10C gross, 5C net, paying $(1/6)(5) = 0.8333C$ in wages, and receiving 4.167C profits. So each northern country will consume 1C and accumulate 3.167C without working at all. The degree of global inequality would increase from 5 to 6, although inequality would now really be greater than 6 if we took into account corn accumulated by the northern countries. The efficiency of the global economy would increase since the average number of days worked per unit of net corn produced in the world would fall from 5.500 to $[90(6) + 10(0)]/[100 + 10(3.167)] = 4.101$. Again, the intuition behind these results is that direct foreign investment gives northern countries an incentive to use seed corn that was idle under autarky to employ southern labor that was previously working in the LIT under autarky, in northern businesses located in the south using the CIT – thereby raising the productivity of some southern labor. Because seed corn is scarce globally, the northern countries are able to capture the entire efficiency gain from the increased productivity in the southern countries.

4

Markets: Guided by an Invisible Hand or Foot?

Adam Smith and his modern disciples see markets working as if they were guided by a beneficent, invisible hand, providing consumers freedom of choice while allocating scarce productive resources and distributing goods and services efficiently. Critics, on the other hand, see markets often working as if they were guided by a malevolent, invisible foot, misrepresenting people's preferences and misallocating resources to the detriment of social needs. After explaining the basic laws of supply and demand on which economists of all stripes more or less agree, this chapter explains the logic behind these opposing views and points out what determines where the truth lies.

How Do Markets Work?

If we leave decisions to markets about what to produce, how to produce it, and how to distribute it, what will happen? Only after we know what markets *will* do can we decide if they are leading us to do what we would choose to do, or instead, misleading us to do things we would not choose to do.

What Is a Market?

A market is a social institution in which participants can exchange a good or service with one another on terms they find mutually agreeable. It is part of the institutional boundary of society located in the economic sphere of social life. If a good is exchanged in a "free" market, anyone can play the role of seller by agreeing to provide the good for a particular amount of money. And anyone can play the role of buyer by agreeing to purchase the good for a particular amount of money. The market for the good consists of all the potential buyers and sellers. Our analysis of the market consists of examining all the potential deals these buyers and sellers would be willing to make and predicting which deals will occur and which ones will not. We do this by using four "laws" concerning supply and demand.

The "Law" of Supply

The first "law" we use to analyze a market is called the "*law of supply*" which states that *we usually expect the number of units of the good suppliers will offer to sell to increase if the price they receive for the good is higher.* There are two reasons for this: (1) At higher prices there are likely to be more suppliers. That is, at a low price some potential suppliers may choose not to play the role of seller at all, but at a higher price they may decide it is worth their while to "enter the market." So, at higher prices we may have a greater number of individual suppliers. (2) Individual suppliers who were already selling a certain quantity at the lower price may wish to sell more units at the higher price. If the individual seller produces the good under conditions of rising cost a higher price means they can produce more units than before whose cost will be covered by their selling price. Or, if the seller has a fixed amount of the good in hand they may be induced to part with a larger portion of it once the price is higher. In any case, the "law of supply" tells us to expect the quantity of a good potential suppliers will be willing to supply to be a positive function of price.

The "Law" of Demand

The second "law" is the "*law of demand*" which states that *we usually expect the number of units of the good demanders will offer to buy to decrease if the price they have to pay is higher.* There are two reasons for this as well: (1) At the higher price some who had been buying before may become unable or unwilling to buy any of the good at all and may therefore "drop out of the market." So at higher prices we may have a smaller number of individual demanders. (2) Individual demanders who continue to buy may wish to buy fewer units at the higher price than they did at the lower price. If the usefulness of the good to an individual buyer decreases the more units they already have, the number of units whose usefulness outweighs the price the buyer must pay will decrease the higher the price the buyer must pay. So the "law of demand" tells us to expect the quantity of a good that potential buyers will be willing to buy to be a negative function of price.

It is important to understand that these so-called "laws" should not be interpreted like the laws of physics. No economist believes that the demand of every individual demander in every market decreases as market price rises, or that the amount every seller offers to supply in every market increases as market price rises. In other words, economists recognize that individuals may well "disobey" these "laws" of supply and demand. Moreover, there may be particular markets that disobey these laws at particular times so that the market supply fails to rise, or market demand fails to fall when market price rises. Markets for stocks and markets for currencies, for example, display annoying propensities to violate the "law of supply" and "law of demand." A rise in the price of Amazon.com stock can unleash a rush of new buyers who demand more of the stock anticipating further increases in price, and can shrink the supply of sellers who become even more reluctant to part with Amazon.com while its price is increasing. The "laws" of supply and demand do not help us understand market "bubbles" and "crashes." In 1997 a drop in the price of Thailand's currency, the baht, triggered the East Asian financial crisis when buyers disappeared from the market not wanting to buy baht while its price was falling, and sellers flooded the market hoping to unload their baht before it fell even farther in value. Clearly the "laws" of supply and demand are not going to help us understand the logic behind currency crises.

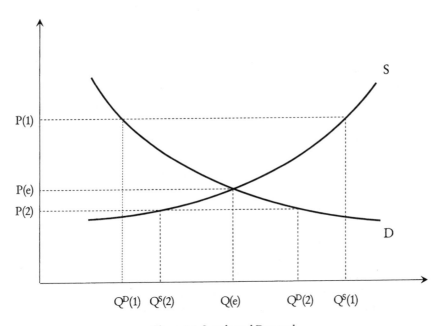

Figure 4.1 Supply and Demand

We will take up these annoying "anomalies" when participants interpret changes in market prices as *signals* about what direction a price is moving in when we examine disequilibrating forces than can operate in markets later in this chapter. But for now it is sufficient to note that the "laws" of supply and demand should be interpreted simply as plausible hypotheses about the behavior of buyers and sellers in many markets under many conditions.

At this point economists invariably use a simple graph to illustrate the laws of supply and demand. We plot market price on a vertical axis and the quantity, or number of units all potential suppliers, in sum total, would be willing to supply in a specified time period on the horizontal axis. According to the law of supply as we go up the vertical axis, at ever higher prices, the number of units all potential suppliers would be willing to supply in a given time period, or the "market supply," increases. This gives us an upward sloping market supply curve, or in different words a market supply curve with a positive slope. Similarly, we plot market price on a vertical axis and the quantity, or number of units all potential demanders, in sum total, would be willing to buy in a given time period on the horizontal axis. According to the law of demand as we go up the vertical axis, at ever higher prices, the number of units all potential demanders would be willing to buy, or the "market demand," decreases. This gives us a downward sloping market demand curve, or in different words, a market demand curve with a negative slope.

While these are logically two separate graphs, illustrating two different "laws" or functional relationships, since the vertical axis is the same in both cases, and the horizontal axis is measured in units of the same good supplied or demanded in the same time period, we can combine the two graphs into one with an upward sloping market supply curve and a downward sloping market demand curve. In this most familiar of all graphs in economics one must remember: (1) the independent variable is price, and this is measured (unconventionally) on the vertical axis, while the dependent variable, quantity supplied or demanded by market participants, is measured (unconventionally) on the horizontal axis. (2) When using the market supply curve the horizontal axis measures the number of units of the good all potential suppliers would be willing to sell at different prices. (3) When using the market demand curve the horizontal axis measures the number of units of the good all potential demanders would be willing to buy at different prices. (4) There is an implicit time period buried in the units of measurement on the horizontal axis. For example, the supply and demand curves and the graph will look different if the horizontal axis is measured in bushels of apples supplied and demanded per week than if it is measured in bushels of apples supplied and demanded per month.

The "Law" of Uniform Price

The "*law of uniform price*" says that *all units of a good in a market will tend to sell at the same price no matter who are the buyers and sellers.* This might seem surprising since some of the deals struck will be between high cost producers and buyers who are very desirous of the good, and some of the deals will be struck between low cost producers and buyers who are luke warm about buying at all. Nonetheless, the law of uniform price says a good will tend to sell at the same price no matter who the seller and buyer may be. The logic of this law can be illustrated by asking what would happen if some buyers and sellers were arranging deals at a lower price than others for the same good. In this case it would pay for anyone to enter the part of the market where the good was selling at the lower price as a buyer and buy up all they could, and then enter the part of the market where deals were being struck at the higher price as a seller to re-sell at a profit. This activity is called "arbitrage," and in a free market where any who wish can participate as buyers or sellers the activity of arbitrage should drive all deals to be struck at the same price. Where prices are lower arbitrage increases demand and raises price, and where prices are higher arbitrage increases supply and lowers price – driving divergent prices for the same good in a market closer together. Of course, this assumes that "a rose is a rose is a rose is a rose" in the words of one of the great French *literati*, Gertrude Stein – that is, that there are no qualitative differences between different units of the good. But subject to this assumption, and the energy levels of those who would profit from doing nothing other than buying "cheap" to sell "dear," economists expect all units of a good that is bought and sold in a "well ordered" market to sell more or less at the same price.

The Micro "Law" of Supply and Demand

I call the last "law" the "*micro law of supply and demand*" to distinguish it from a different law we study in Chapter 6 that I call the "macro law of supply and demand." The micro law of supply and demand states that *in a free market the uniform market price will adjust until the number of units buyers want to buy is equal to the number of units sellers want to sell, i.e. until quantity demanded is equal to supplied.* In terms of the supply and demand graph in Figure 4.1, the micro law of supply and demand says that the market will settle at the price across from where the market supply and demand curves cross, and at the quantity bought and sold beneath where the supply and demand curves cross. This price and this quantity bought and sold are called the *equilibrium price* and *equilibrium quantity,* so another way of stating the micro law of supply and demand is: *markets will settle at their equilibrium prices, and if left to the free market the quantity of any good that will be produced and consumed will be the equilibrium quantity.*

The rationale for the micro law of supply and demand is as follows: Suppose the going market price, $P(1)$, is higher than the equilibrium price, $P(e)$. In this case if we read across from this price to find out how much buyers are willing to buy, $Q^D(1)$, as compared to how much suppliers are willing to sell, $Q^S(1)$, we discover from the market demand and supply curves that buyers are not willing to buy all that sellers are willing to sell at this price, $Q^D(1) < Q^S(1)$. In other words, at this price there will be excess supply in the market for the good. What can we expect sellers to do? In conditions of excess supply sellers fall into two groups: those who are happily succeeding in selling their goods at $P(1)$ and those who cannot sell all they want and are therefore frustrated. Those who are not able to sell their goods have an incentive to lower their asking price below the going market price in order to move from the group of frustrated sellers to the group of successful sellers, thereby driving the market price down in the direction of the equilibrium price. Buyers also have an incentive to only agree to buy at a price below the going market price when they notice there is excess supply in the market since they know that there are some frustrated sellers out there who should be willing to accept less than the going market price, providing another reason market price should start to fall in the direction of the equilibrium price.

On the other hand, suppose the going market price, $P(2)$, is lower than the equilibrium price, $P(e)$. If we read across from this price to find out how much buyers are willing to buy, $Q^D(2)$, as compared to how much suppliers are willing to sell, $Q^S(2)$, we discover from the market demand and supply curves that sellers are not willing to sell all that buyers are willing to buy this price, $Q^S(2) < Q^D(2)$. In other words, at this price there will be excess demand in the market for the good. What can we expect buyers to do? In conditions of excess demand buyers fall into two groups: those who are happily able to buy all the good they want at $P(2)$, and those who are not able to buy all they want and are therefore frustrated. Those who are not able to buy all they want have an incentive to raise their offer price above the going market price in order to move from the group of frustrated buyers to the group of successful buyers, thereby driving the market price up in the direction of the equilibrium price. Sellers also have an incentive to only agree to sell at a price above the going market price when they notice there is excess demand in the market since they know that there are some frustrated buyers who should be willing to pay more than the going market price, providing another reason market price should rise in the direction of the equilibrium price.

So for actual market prices above the equilibrium price there are incentives for frustrated sellers to cut their asking price and buyers to offer a lower price, driving the market price down toward the equilibrium price. And as the market price drops the amount of excess supply will decrease, since the law of supply says that supply decreases as price falls and the law of demand says that demand increases as price falls. And for market prices below the equilibrium price there are incentives for frustrated buyers to raise their offer price and for sellers to raise their asking price driving the market price up toward the equilibrium price. And as the market price rises excess demand will decrease, since the law of demand says that demand decreases as price rises and the law of supply says that supply increases as price rises. So according to the micro law of supply and demand, the only stable price will be the equilibrium price because self-interested behavior of frustrated sellers or buyers will lead to changes in price under conditions of both excess supply and excess demand, and only at the equilibrium price is their neither excess supply nor excess demand. This particular kind of self-interested behavior of buyers and sellers – individually rational responses to finding oneself unable to sell or buy all one wants at the going market price – can be thought of as "equilibrating forces" that economists expect to operate in markets. So the micro law of supply and demand can be thought of as a "law" explaining why there should be equilibrating forces at work in markets. We will discover below that market enthusiasts and critics disagree about how strong these "equilibrating forces" are compared to "disequilibrating forces" the micro law of supply and demand does not alert us to that operate alongside equilibrating forces. There are a few things worth noting at this point:

(1) There are different senses in which buyers or sellers are "satisfied." All buyers would always like to pay a lower price, and all sellers would always like to receive a higher price. So in that sense, neither buyers nor sellers are ever "satisfied" no matter what the price. But when the price is above the equilibrium price, while successful sellers will be pleased, there will be unsuccessful sellers who will be displeased. Moreover, there is something the non-sellers can do about their frustration: they can offer to sell at a lower price. Similarly, when the price is below the equilibrium price, while successful buyers will be pleased, there will be unsuccessful buyers who will be displeased. And what the non-buyers can do about their frustration is offer to pay a higher price.

(2) It is always the case that the quantity bought will be equal to the quantity sold no matter what the price, and whether or not the market is in equilibrium. This follows because every unit that was bought was sold and every unit that was sold was bought! But that is not the same as saying that the quantity demanders *want* to buy at the going price is equal to the quantity suppliers *want* to sell at the going price. There is only one price at which the quantity demanded will equal the quantity supplied – the equilibrium price. At all other prices there will be either excess supply or excess demand.

(3) Since not all markets are always in equilibrium, how much will be bought and sold when a market is out of equilibrium? This is where the assumption of non-coercion in our definition of a market comes in: buyers cannot be forced to buy if they don't want to, and sellers can't be forced to sell if they don't want to. When there is excess supply the sellers would like to sell more than the buyers want to buy at the going price. So under conditions of excess supply it is the buyers who have the upper hand, in a sense, and they will determine how much is going to be bought, and therefore sold. In Figure 4.1 when market price is P(1) and there is excess supply buyers will only buy Q^D (1) and therefore, that is all sellers will be able to sell. When there is excess demand the buyers would like to buy more than the sellers want to sell. So under conditions of excess demand it is the sellers who have the upper hand and will determine how much is going to be sold, and therefore bought. In Figure 4.1 when market price is P(2) and there is excess demand sellers will only sell Q^S (2) and therefore, that is all buyers will be able to buy.

Elasticity of Supply and Demand

The law of demand just says that as price rises we expect the quantity demanded to fall. It doesn't say whether demand will fall a lot or a little. *If a 1% increase in price leads to more than a 1% fall in quantity demanded, we say that market demand is* **elastic**. *If a 1% increase in price leads to less than a 1% fall in quantity demanded, we say that market demand is* **inelastic**. Similarly, the law of supply just says that as price rises we expect the quantity supplied to rise, it doesn't say whether supply will rise a lot or a little. If a 1% increase in price leads to more than a 1% rise in quantity supplied, we say that market supply is *elastic*. If a 1% increase in price leads to less than a 1% rise in quantity supplied, we say that market supply is *inelastic*.

The elasticities of supply and demand allow us to predict how much prices of goods and quantities bought and sold will change when a demand or supply curve shifts. Elasticity also holds the key to how revenues of sellers will be affected by changes in supply. For example, the demand for corn is usually elastic. So when a drought hits the corn belt and the supply curve for corn shifts back to the left, the price will rise and the equilibrium quantity bought and sold will fall. But the percentage fall in sales will be greater than the percentage increase in price because demand for corn is elastic. Since the revenue of corn farmers is simply equal to the market price times the quantity sold, the fact that sales drop by a greater percent than price rises means revenues must fall. On the other hand, the demand for oil is usually inelastic. So if war breaks out in the Middle East and a country such as Iraq, Kuwait, Iran, Libya, or Saudi Arabia is temporarily eliminated as a potential supplier, the world supply curve for oil shifts back to the left, and the price will rise and the equilibrium quantity bought and sold will fall as before. But because demand for oil is inelastic the percentage fall in sales will be less than the percentage increase in price. In this case the revenue of oil suppliers will increase because the rise in price outweighs the drop in sales when supply decreases.

You can use your understanding of elasticity to predict whether more or less involuntary unemployment will result from a rise in the minimum wage, and whether more or fewer shortages in rental units will result from lowering the price ceiling under rent control. Readers should draw a labor market diagram with one "flat" (elastic) labor demand curve and one "steep" (inelastic) labor demand curve where both demand curves cross the labor supply curve at the same point. Where both demand curves cross the supply curve determines the equilibrium wage rate and the equilibrium level of employment. Now draw in a minimum wage *above* the equilibrium wage and see what happens to employment as buyers (employers) determine the quantity that will be bought and sold in a market with excess supply. Notice that the drop in employment is greater if the demand for labor is more elastic, and smaller if the demand for labor is more inelastic.[1] Readers should also draw a diagram for rental units with one "flat" or elastic supply curve and one "steep" or inelastic supply curve where both supply curves cross the demand curve for rental units at the same point. Where both supply curves cross the demand curve determines the equilibrium rental price and the equilibrium quantity of rental units. Now draw a price ceiling *below* the equilibrium price and see what happens to the supply of rental units when suppliers determine the amount that will be sold and bought in a market with excess demand. Notice that the shortage of rental units is greater if the supply curve for rental units is more elastic, and smaller if the supply is more inelastic.

1 This is the standard treatment of the effect of minimum wages in all mainstream textbooks, which thereby conclude that raising the minimum wage must necessarily reduce employment to some extent. However, this treatment and conclusion is quite misleading, as will be discussed in Chapter 11. Note that this conclusion is based on microeconomic considerations alone. Macroeconomic theory, on the other hand, suggests it is quite possible that raising the minimum wage can cause a significant increase in the aggregate demand for goods and services, which can, in turn, cause an increase in the demand for labor to produce more goods. This "macro" effect of a higher minimum wage would be represented as a shift in the labor demand curve to the right, which would increase employment, counteracting the employment reducing "micro" effect of moving to a point higher up on the labor demand curve. So while all agree that the size of the employment shrinking micro effect depends on how elastic the labor demand curve is, when the employment enhancing "macro" effect is also taken into account it is impossible to predict based on theory alone whether or not raising the minimum wage will reduce or increase employment.

The principal factors that determine the elasticity of market demand are the availability and closeness of substitutes for the good, and the organization and bargaining power of potential buyers. The principal factors that determine the elasticity of market supply are the time period under consideration, the mobility of productive factors into and out of the industry, and the organization and bargaining power of potential sellers.

The Dream of a Beneficent Invisible Hand

Adam Smith noticed something strange but wonderful about free markets. He saw competitive markets as a kind of beneficent, "invisible hand" that guided "the private interests and passions of men" in the direction "which is most agreeable to the interest of the whole society." Smith expressed this view in perhaps the most widely quoted passage in all of economics in *The Wealth of Nations* published in 1776:

> Every individual necessarily labours to render the annual revenue of the society as great as he can. He generally, indeed, neither intends to promote the public interest, nor knows how much he is promoting it. He intends only his own gain, and he is in this, as in many other cases, led by an *invisible hand* to promote an end which was no part of his intention. Nor is it always the worse for the society that it was no part of it. By pursuing his own interest he frequently promotes that of the society more effectually than when he really intends to promote it.... It is not from the benevolence of the butcher, the brewer, or the baker that we expect our dinner, but from their regard to their self-interest. We address ourselves, not to their humanity, but to their self-love, and never talk to them of our necessities, but of their advantages.

In the words of Robert Heilbroner:

> Adam Smith's laws of the market are basically simple. They show us how the drive of individual self-interest in an environment of similarly motivated individuals will result in competition; and they further demonstrate how competition will result in the provision of those goods that society wants, in the quantities that society desires.[2]

2 Robert Heilbroner, *The Worldly Philosophers* (Simon and Schuster, 1992).

But how does this miracle happen?

Suppose consumers' taste for apples increases and their taste for oranges decreases – for whatever reason. Assuming consumers know best what they like, how would we want the economy to respond to this new situation? If there were an omniscient, beneficent God in charge of the economy she would shift some of our scarce productive resources – land, labor, fertilizer, etc. – out of orange production and into apple production. What would a system of free markets do? These changes in consumer tastes would shift the market demand curve for apples out to the right indicating that consumers would now like to buy more apples than before at each and every price of apples. And they would shift the market demand curve for oranges back to the left, indicating that consumers are now only willing to buy fewer oranges than before at each and every price of oranges. This would lead to excess demand for apples and excess supply of oranges at their old equilibrium prices. The micro law of supply and demand would drive the price of apples up until the excess demand for apples was eliminated and the price of oranges down until the excess supply of oranges was eliminated. At the new higher price of apples the law of supply tells us former apple growers, and any new ones drawn into the industry by the higher price of apples, would increase production of apples by purchasing more land, labor, fertilizer, etc. At the new lower price of oranges the law of supply tells us orange growers would decrease their production of oranges by using less land, labor, and fertilizer, etc. to grow oranges. Bingo! As if guided by an invisible hand, without anyone thinking or planning at all, the free market does what a beneficent God would have done for us!

Or, suppose agronomists develop a new strain of apple that can be grown with less land between the trees than before. This is a technical change that reduces the amount of a scarce productive resource it takes to grow apples compared to the past. An omniscient, beneficent God would have consumers buy more apples and fewer oranges now that apples are less socially costly than previously. What will free markets do? The cost-reducing change in apple growing technology will shift the market supply curve for apples out to the right because apple growers can cover the cost of growing more apples than before at each and every price, producing excess supply of apples at the old equilibrium price. The micro law of supply and demand will lower apple prices until the excess supply is eliminated and we reach the new equilibrium in the apple market. And the law of demand tells us that consumers will buy more apples at the lower price. Meanwhile, over in the orange market, the fall in the price of apples leads some fruit buyers to substitute apples for oranges which shifts the demand curve for oranges back to the left indicating that fewer oranges will be demanded at each and every price of oranges now that the price of apples is lower, creating excess supply in the orange market. This will lead to a fall in the price of oranges and lower levels of orange production. Bingo! The free market will bring about an increase in apple production and consumption and a decrease in orange production and consumption when the social cost of producing apples decreases relative to the social cost of producing oranges – just what we would have wanted to happen.

We can combine Figure 2.3: The Efficiency Criterion (p. 35) and Figure 4.1: Supply and Demand (p. 85) to see what Smith's conclusion that markets harness individually rational behavior to yield socially rational outcomes amounts to. According to the micro law of supply and demand, the market outcome will be the equilibrium outcome, and the number of apples produced and consumed can be found directly below where the market supply curve crosses the market demand curve. According to the efficiency criterion, the optimal number of apples to produce and consume can be found directly below where the marginal social cost curve crosses the marginal social benefit curve. So the market outcome will yield the socially efficient outcome if and only if the market supply curve coincides with the MSC curve and the market demand curve coincides with the MSB curve. Another way to put it is that if and only if market supply closely approximates marginal social cost and market demand closely approximates marginal social benefits will free market outcomes be socially efficient outcomes.

But do market supply and demand reasonably express marginal social costs and benefits? That is one way to see the debate between those who see market allocations as being guided by an invisible hand versus those who see them as being misguided by an invisible foot. If market supply and demand closely approximate true marginal social costs and benefits then the individually rational behavior of buyers and sellers and the workings of the micro law of supply and demand would be working in the social interest because they would be driving production and consumption of goods and services toward socially efficient levels. Moreover, whenever conditions changed social costs or benefits these equilibrating forces would move us to the new socially efficient outcome. In other words, markets would yield efficient reallocations of scarce productive resources. On the other hand, if there are significant discrepancies between market supply and marginal social costs, and/or market demand and marginal social benefits, individually rational behavior of buyers and sellers and the micro law of supply and demand work against the social interest by driving us to produce too little of some goods and too much of others. In other words, by relying on market forces we would consistently get inefficient allocations of productive resources.

Mainstream and political economists agree on one part of the answer before parting company. *They agree that what market supply captures and represents are the costs borne by the actual sellers of goods and services; and what market demand represents are the benefits enjoyed by the actual buyers of goods and services.* We call these **private costs** and **private benefits**. A rational buyer will keep buying more of a good as long as the private benefit to her of an additional unit is at least as great as the price she must pay for it. In other words, her marginal private benefit curve is her individual demand curve. Since the market demand curve is simply the summation of all individual demand curves, the market demand curve is simply the sum of all marginal private benefit curves. A rational seller will keep selling more of a good as long as the cost to her of producing another unit of output is no greater than the price she will get from selling it. In other words, her marginal private cost curve is her individual supply curve. Since market supply is simply the summation of all individual supply curves, the market supply curve is simply the sum of all marginal private cost curves. So the question becomes when do private costs and benefits differ from social costs and benefits?

In fairness to Adam Smith, the distinction between private and social costs and benefits was not clear in his life time. Smith, and the "classical economists" who lived and wrote after him as well, conflated social and private costs and benefits and never asked if anyone other than the seller bore part of the cost of increased production, or anyone other than the buyer enjoyed part of the benefit of increased consumption of different kinds of goods and services. The modern terminology for *differences between social and private costs of production* is a **production externality**. And the name for *the difference between social and private benefits from consumption* is a **consumption externality**. These *external effects* can be negative if someone other than the seller suffers a cost associated with production, in which case social costs exceed private costs, or if someone other than the buyer is adversely affected by the buyer's consumption, in which case private benefits exceed social benefits. Or external effects can be positive if the private costs of production exceed the social costs or social benefits of consumption exceed private benefits. Adam Smith's vision of the market as a mechanism that successfully harnesses individual desires to the social purpose of using scarce productive resources efficiently hinges on the assumption that external effects are insignificant. And, indeed, this is precisely the un-emphasized assumption that lies behind the mainstream conclusion that markets are remarkable efficiency machines that require little social effort on our part. In fact, the mainstream view today is a strident echo of Adam Smith's conclusion that the only "effort" required on our part is the "effort" to resist the temptation to tamper with the free market and simply *laissez faire.*

The Nightmare of a Malevolent Invisible Foot

Mainstream economic theory teaches that the problem with externalities is that the buyer or seller has no incentive to take the external cost or benefit for others into account when deciding how much of something to supply or demand. And mainstream theory teaches that the problem with public goods is that nobody can be excluded from benefiting from a public good once anyone buys it, and therefore everyone has an incentive to "free ride" on the purchases of others rather than reveal their true willingness to pay for public goods by purchasing them in the marketplace. In other words, mainstream economics concedes that the market will lead to inefficient allocations of scarce productive resources when public goods and externalities come into play because important benefits or costs go unaccounted for in the market decision-making procedure. If anyone cares to listen, standard economic theory predicts that if decisions are left to be decided by market forces we will produce too much of goods whose production and/or consumption entail negative externalities, too little of goods whose production and/or consumption entail positive externalities, and much too little, if any, public goods. We can see the problem of negative externalities by looking at the automobile industry, and the problem of public goods by considering pollution reduction.

Externalities: The Auto Industry

The micro law of supply and demand tells us how many cars will be produced and consumed if we leave the decision to the free market. The price of cars will adjust until there is neither excess supply nor excess demand at which point the "equilibrium" number of cars will be produced and consumed. The question is whether this will be more, less, or the same number of cars that is socially efficient, or optimal to produce and consume. As we saw, the socially efficient level of auto production and consumption is where the MSB curve crosses the MSC curve. If the market supply curve for cars coincides with the MSC curve for cars, and if the market demand curve for cars coincides with the MSB curve for cars, the market outcome will be the efficient outcome. Otherwise, it will not be.

Let us assume that the market supply curve for cars does a reasonably good job of approximating the marginal private costs the makers and sellers of cars incur. If they can get a price for a car that is something above what it costs them to make it, presumably they will produce and sell the car. So the market supply curve, S, equals the marginal private cost curve for making cars, MPC: S = MPC. But if there are costs to external parties above and beyond the costs of inputs car makers must pay for, there is no reason to expect the sellers of cars to take them into account. So if the corporations making cars in Detroit also pollute the air in ways that cause acid rain, the costs that take the form of lost benefits to those who own, use, or enjoy forests and lakes in Eastern Canada and the United States will not be taken into account by those who make the decisions about how many cars to produce. Nevertheless, along with the cost of steel, rubber and labor – which are costs borne by car manufacturers – the costs of acid rain are part of the social costs of making cars even if they are not borne by car makers. To the cost of steel, rubber, and labor that comprise the private costs of making a car must be added the damage from acid rain that occurs when we make a car if we are to have the full cost to society of making a car. In other words, the marginal social cost of making a car, MSC, is equal to the marginal private cost of making the car, MPC, *plus* the marginal external costs associated with making the car, MEC: MSC = MPC + MEC. Since MEC is positive for automobile production marginal social costs always exceed marginal private costs, which means the marginal social cost curve for producing cars lies above the marginal private cost curve for cars, which is roughly equal to the market supply curve for cars: MSC = MPC + MEC = S + MEC with MEC > 0.

When car buyers consider whether or not to purchase a car they presumably compare the benefit they expect to get in the form of ease and speed of transportation with the price they will have to pay out of their limited income. If the private benefit exceeds the price, they will buy the car, and if it does not, they won't. This means

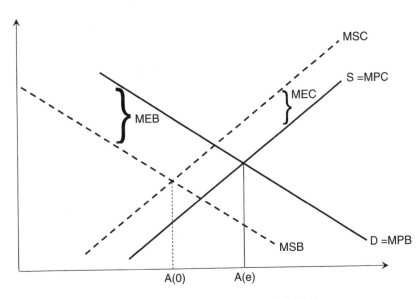

Figure 4.2 Inefficiencies in the Automobile Market

the market demand curve, D, represents the marginal private benefit curve from car consumption, MPB, reasonably well: D = MPB. But I am not the only person affected when I "consume" my car. When I drive my car the exhausts add to the greenhouse gases in the atmosphere and contribute to global warming. When I drive from the suburbs through inner city neighborhoods I contribute to urban smog, noise pollution, and congestion. In other words, when I consume a car there are others who suffer negative benefits which means that the social benefit of consuming another car is less than the private benefit of consuming another car. So even if the market demand curve for cars reasonably represents the marginal private benefits of car consumption, it overestimates the marginal social benefits of car consumption because it ignores the negative impact of car consumption on those not driving them. The marginal social benefit from consuming another car, MSB, is equal to the marginal private benefit to the car buyer, MPB, plus the external benefits to others, MEB: MSB = MPB + MEB. But in the case of car consumption the marginal external "benefits," MEB, are *negative*. This implies that the marginal social benefit curve lies somewhere *below* the market demand curve for automobiles: MSB = MPB + MEB = D + MEB with MEB < 0.

But as can be seen in Figure 4.2, if the MSC curve lies above the market supply curve, and the MSB curve lies below the market demand curve for cars, MSC and MSB will cross to the left of where the market supply and demand curves cross. Therefore the socially efficient, or optimal level of automobile production and consumption, A(0), will be less than the equilibrium level of production and consumption, A(e), which the micro law of supply and demand will drive us toward. In other words, the market will lead us to produce and consume more cars than is socially efficient, or optimal. The market will produce too many cars because sellers and buyers decide how many cars to produce and consume and they have no reason to take anything other than the costs and benefits to them into account. They have no incentive to consider the external effects of producing and consuming cars. In fact, they have good reason to ignore these external effects because taking them into account would make them individually worse off. Not surprisingly we discover that if decision makers ignore negative consequences of doing something – in this case the negative external effects of car production and consumption on people *other* than the car producer and buyer – they will decide to do too much of it – in this case they will decide to produce and consume too many cars.

External effects are notoriously hard to measure in market economies. This is of great significance since their magnitude tells us how inefficient a market will be, and how large a pollution tax must be to correct the inefficiency. In a 1998 report the Center for Technology Assessment estimated that when external effects are taken into account the true social cost of a gallon of gas consumed in the US might have been as high as $15. In that same year when I filled up my car in St. Mary's County Maryland I paid a little over one dollar a gallon. That price already included some hefty federal and state gasoline taxes, but obviously they were not nearly hefty enough!

Public Goods: Pollution Reduction

A public good is a good produced by human economic activity that is consumed, to all intents and purposes, by everyone rather than by an individual consumer. Unlike a private good such as underwear that affects only its wearer, public goods like pollution reduction affect most people. In different terms, nobody can be excluded from "consuming" – or benefiting from the existence of the public good. This is not to say that everyone has the same preferences regarding public goods any more than people have the same preferences for private goods. I happen to prefer apples to oranges, and I value pollution reduction more than I value so-called national defense. There are others who place greater value on national defense than they do on pollution reduction, just as there are others who prefer oranges to apples. But unlike the case of apples and oranges where those who prefer apples can buy more apples and those who like oranges more can buy more oranges, all US citizens have to "consume" the same amount of federal spending on the military and federal spending on pollution reduction. We cannot provide more military spending for the US citizens who value that public good more, and more pollution reduction for the US citizens who value the environment more. Whereas different Americans can consume different amounts of private goods, we all must live in the same "public good world."

What would happen if we left the decision about how much of our scarce productive resources to use to devote to producing public goods to the free market? Markets only provide goods for which there is what we call "effective demand," that is, buyers willing and able to put their money where their mouth is. But what incentive is there for a buyer to pay for a public good? First of all, no matter how much I value the public good, I only enjoy a tiny fraction of the overall, or social benefit that comes from having more of it since I cannot exclude others who do not pay for it from benefiting as well. In different terms: Social rationality demands that an individual purchase a public good up to the point where the cost of the last unit she purchased is as great as the benefits enjoyed by *all* who benefit, *in sum total*, from her purchase of the good. But it is only rational for an individual to buy a public good up to the point where the cost of the last unit she purchased is as great as the benefit she, herself enjoys from the good. When individuals buy public goods in a free market they have no incentive to take the benefits others enjoy when they purchase public goods into account when they decide how much to buy. Consequently they "demand" far less than is socially efficient, if they purchase any at all. In sum, market demand – the sum of all individual demands – will grossly under represent the marginal *social* benefit of public goods.

Another way to see the problem is to recognize that each potential buyer of a public good has an incentive to wait and hope that someone else will buy the public good. A patient buyer can "free ride" on others' purchases since non-payers cannot be excluded from benefiting from public goods. But if everyone is waiting for someone else to plunk down their hard earned income for a public good, nobody will demonstrate "effective demand" for public goods in the market place. Free riding is individually rational in the case of public goods – but leads to an effective demand for public goods that grossly underestimates their true social benefit. In Chapter 5 we explore this logic formally in "the public good game."

What prevents a group of people who will benefit from a public good from banding together to express their demand for the good collectively? The problem is there is an incentive for people to lie about how much they benefit. If the associations of public good consumers are voluntary, no matter how much I truly benefit from a public good, I am better off pretending I don't benefit at all. Then I can decline membership in the association and avoid paying anything, knowing full well that I will, in fact, benefit from its existence nonetheless. Even if membership is not voluntary there is a problem if contributions are based on how much members declare they benefit. In this case it would be in the interest of every member of the coalition to underreport how much they benefit, and difficult to know when to challenge a member's declaration since we know not all truly do benefit to the same extent. So even if the coalition of consumers does include all who benefit, if its effective demand is based on member's individually rational underrepresentations, it will still underrepresent the true social benefits people enjoy from the public good, and consequently demand less than the socially efficient, or optimal amount of the public good.

In sum, because of what economists call the "free rider" incentive problem and the "transaction costs" of organizing and managing a coalition of public good consumers, market demand predictably under represents the true social benefits that come from consumption of public goods. If the production of a public good entails no external effects so that the market supply curve accurately represents the marginal social costs of producing the public good, then since market demand will lie considerably under the true marginal social benefit curve for the public good, the market equilibrium level of production and consumption will be significantly less than the socially efficient level. In conclusion, if we left it to the free market and voluntary associations precious little, if any, of our scarce productive resources would be used to produce public goods no matter how valuable they really were. As Robert Heilbroner succinctly put it: "The market has a keen ear for private wants, but a deaf ear for public needs." Which is why, when the need for some particular public good is painfully obvious and failure to provide it would be seriously dysfunctional, even governments most devoted to free market principles have found it necessary to substitute a completely different decision-making procedure for the market mechanism – the "draft!" In effect the government "drafts" everyone into the public good consumer coalition and collects taxes from members to pay for the public goods according to some formula *not* based on what members report they would be willing to pay.

Green Consumerism

The fact that pollution reduction is a public good has important implications for *green consumerism* in market economies. There are a number of cheap detergents that get my wash very white but cause considerable water pollution. "Green" detergents, on the other hand, are more expensive and leave my whites more gray than white, but cause less water pollution. *Whether or not I end up making the socially responsible choice,* because pollution reduction is a public good the market provides *too little incentive* for me to make the socially efficient choice. My own best interests are served by weighing the disadvantage of the extra cost and grayer whites *to me* against the advantage *to me* of the diminution in water pollution that would result if I use the green detergent. But presumably there are many others besides me who also benefit from the cleaner water if I buy the green detergent – which is precisely why we think of "buying green" as socially responsible behavior. Unfortunately the market provides no incentive for me to take *their* benefit into account. Worse still, if I suspect others may consult only their own interest when they choose which detergent to buy, i.e. if I think they will ignore the benefits to me and others if they choose the green detergent, by choosing to take their interest into account and consuming green myself I risk not only making a choice that was detrimental to my own interest, I risk being played for a sucker as well.[3]

This is not to say that many people will not choose to "do the right thing" and "consume green" in any case. Moreover, there may be incentives *other than the socially counterproductive market incentives* that may overcome the market disincentive to consume green. The fact that I am a member of several environmental organizations and fear I would be ostracized if a fellow member saw me with a polluting detergent

3 Most detergents call for a full cup per load of wash. Church & Dwight canceled a 1/4 cup laundry detergent product when consumer demand for this "green" product proved insufficient. Christine Canning, "The Laundry Detergent Market," in *Household and Personal Products Industry,* April 1996.

in my shopping basket in the checkout line is apparently a powerful enough incentive in my own case to lead me to buy a green detergent despite the market disincentive to do so. (Admittedly I have only a slight preference for white over gray clothes, and who knows how long I will hold out if the price differential increases!) But the point is that because pollution reduction is a public good, market incentives are *perverse*, i.e. lead people to consume less "green" and more "dirty" (dirty environment, not clothes) than is socially efficient. The extent to which people ignore the perverse market incentives and act on the basis of concern for the environment, concern for others, including future generations, or in response to non-market, social incentives such as fear of ostracism is important for the environment and the social interest, but does not make the market incentives any less perverse.

The Prevalence of External Effects

In face of these concessions – markets misallocate resources when there are externalities and public goods – how do market enthusiasts continue to claim that markets allocate resources efficiently – as if guided by a beneficent invisible hand? The answer lies in an assumption that is explicit in the theorems of graduate level microeconomic theory texts but only implicit in undergraduate textbooks and in the advice of most economists. The fundamental theorem of welfare economics states that if all markets are in equilibrium the economy will be in a Pareto optimal state *only if there are no external effects or public goods*. The assumption that there are no public goods or external effects is explicit in the statement of the theorem that is the modern incarnation of Adam Smith's two hundred year-old vision of an invisible hand – because otherwise the theorem would be false! Since everyone knows there are externalities and public goods in the real world, the conclusion that markets allocate resources reasonably efficiently in the real world therefore rests on the assumption that external effects and public goods are few and far between. This assumption is usually unstated, and its validity has never been demonstrated through empirical research. It is a *pre*sumption implicit in an untested paradigm that lies behind mainstream economic theory – a paradigm that pretends that the choices people make have little effect on the opportunities and wellbeing of others.

If we replace the implicit paradigm at the basis of mainstream economics with one that sees the world as a web of human interaction where people's choices often have far reaching consequences for others, both now and in the future, the presumption that external effects and public goods are the exception rather than the rule is reversed. Since political economists have long seen the world in just this way, and everything we have learned about the relation between human choices and ecological systems over the past thirty years reinforces this vision of interconnectedness, there is every reason for political economists to expect external and public effects to be the rule rather than the exception. What is surprising is that so few political economists have recognized the far reaching implications of their own beliefs when it comes to assessing the efficiency of markets. One stellar exception is E. K. Hunt. In an article remarkable for its lack of impact on other political economists when published in June 1973 in the *Journal of Economic Issues*, Hunt stated the "reverse" assumption as follows:

> The Achilles heel of welfare economics [as practiced by mainstream pro-market economists] is its treatment of externalities. . . . When reference is made to externalities, one usually takes as a typical example an upwind factory that emits large quantities of sulfur oxides and particulate matter inducing rising probabilities of emphysema, lung cancer, and other respiratory diseases to residents downwind, or a strip-mining operation that leaves an irreparable aesthetic scar on the countryside. The fact is, however, that most of the millions of acts of production and consumption in which we daily engage involve externalities. In a market economy any action of one individual or enterprise which induces pleasure or pain to any other individual or enterprise . . . constitutes an externality. Since the vast majority of productive and consumptive acts are social, i.e., to some degree they involve more than one person, it follows that they will involve externalities. Our table manners in a restaurant, the general appearance of our house, our yard or our person, our personal hygiene, the route we pick for a joy ride, the time of day we mow our lawn, or nearly any one of the thousands of ordinary daily acts, all affect, to some degree, the pleasures or happiness of others. *The fact is . . . externalities are totally pervasive.* . . . Only the most extreme bourgeois individualism could have resulted in an economic theory that assumed otherwise.

If the social effects of production and consumption frequently extend beyond the sellers and buyers of those goods and services, as Hunt argues above, and if these external effects are not insignificant, markets will frequently *mis*allocate resources leading us to produce too much of some goods and too little of others. By ignoring negative external effects markets lead us to produce and consume more of goods like automobiles than is socially efficient. By ignoring positive external effects markets lead us to consume less of goods like tropical rain forests that recycle carbon dioxide and thereby reduce global warming than is socially efficient – instead we clear cut them or burn them off to pasture cattle. And while markets provide reasonable opportunities for people to express their preferences for goods and services that can be enjoyed individually with minimal "transaction costs," they do not provide efficient, or what economists call "incentive compatible" means for expressing desires for goods that are enjoyed, or consumed socially, or collectively – like public space and pollution reduction. Instead, markets create perverse free rider disincentives for those who would express their desires for public goods individually, and pose daunting transaction costs for those who attempt to form a coalition of beneficiaries. In other words, *markets have an anti-social bias.*

Worse still, markets provide powerful incentives for actors to take advantage of external effects in socially counterproductive ways, and even to magnify external effects or create new ones. Increasing the value of goods and services produced, and decreasing the unpleasantness of what we have to do to get them, are two ways producers can increase their profits in a market economy. And competitive pressures will drive producers to do both. But maneuvering to appropriate a greater share of the goods and services produced by externalizing costs and internalizing benefits without compensation are also ways to increase profits. Competitive pressures will drive producers to pursue this route to greater profitability just as assiduously. Of course the problem is, while the first kind of behavior serves the social interest as well as the private interests of producers, the second kind of behavior does not. Instead, when buyers or sellers promote their private interests by externalizing costs onto those not party to the market exchange, or internalizing benefits without compensation, their "rent seeking behavior" introduces inefficiencies that lead to a misallocation of productive resources and consequently decreases the value of goods and services produced.

Questions market admirers seldom ask are: Where are firms most likely to find the easiest opportunities to expand their profits? How easy is it to increase the quantity or quality of goods produced? How easy is it to reduce the time or discomfort it takes to produce them? Alternatively, how easy is it to enlarge one's slice of the economic pie by externalizing a cost, or by appropriating a benefit without compensation? In sum, why should we assume that it is infinitely easier to expand profits by productive behavior than by rent seeking behavior? Yet this implicit assumption is what lies behind the view of markets as efficiency machines.

Market enthusiasts fail to notice that the same feature of market exchanges primarily responsible for small transaction costs – excluding all affected parties but two from the transaction – is also a major source of potential gain for the buyer and seller. When the buyer and seller of an automobile strike their convenient deal, the size of the benefit they have to divide between them is greatly enlarged by externalizing the costs onto others of the acid rain produced by car production, and the costs of urban smog, noise pollution, traffic congestion, and greenhouse gas emissions caused by car consumption. Those who pay these costs, and thereby enlarge car maker profits and car consumer benefits, are "easy marks" for car sellers and buyers because they are geographically and chronologically dispersed, and because the magnitude of the effect on each of them is small and unequal. Individually they have little incentive to insist on being party to the transaction. Collectively they face transaction cost and free rider obstacles to forming a voluntary coalition to represent a large number of people – each with little, but different amounts at stake.

Moreover, the opportunity for socially counterproductive rent seeking behavior is not eliminated by making markets perfectly competitive or entry costless, as is commonly assumed. Rent seeking *at the expense of buyers or sellers* may be eliminated by making markets more competitive, i.e. increasing the number of sellers for buyers to choose from and the number of buyers for sellers to choose from. But even if there were countless perfectly informed sellers and buyers in every market, even if the appearance of the slightest differences in average profit rates in different industries induced instantaneous self-correcting entries and exits of firms, even if every economic participant were equally powerful and therefore equally powerless – in other words, even if we embrace the full fantasy of market enthusiasts – as long as there are numerous external parties with small but unequal interests in market transactions, those external parties will face greater transaction costs and free rider obstacles to an effective representation of their collective interest than faced by the buyer and seller in the exchange. And it is this unavoidable inequality that makes external parties easy prey to rent seeking behavior on the part of buyers and sellers.

Even if we could organize a market economy so that buyers and sellers never faced a more or less powerful opponent in a market exchange, this would not change the fact that each of us has smaller interests at stake in many transactions in which we are neither the buyer nor seller. Yet the sum total interest of all external parties can be considerable compared to the interests of the buyer and the seller. It is the transaction cost and free rider problems of those with lesser interests that create an unavoidable inequality in power, which, in turn, gives rise to the opportunity for individually profitable but socially counterproductive rent seeking on the part of buyers and sellers even in the most competitive markets. A sufficient condition for the opportunity to profit in socially counterproductive ways from maneuvering, rent seeking, or cost shifting behavior is that each one of us has diffuse interests that make us affected external parties to many exchanges in which we are neither buyer nor seller – no matter how competitive markets may be.

But socially counterproductive rent seeking behavior is not only engaged in at the expense of parties external to market exchanges. The real world bears little resemblance to a game where all buyers and sellers are equally powerful, in which case it would be pointless for sellers or buyers to try to take advantage of one another. In the real world it is often easier for powerful firms to increase profits by lowering the prices they pay less powerful suppliers and raise the prices they charge powerless consumers than it is to search for ways to increase the quality of their products. In the real world there are consumers with little information, time, or means to defend their interests. There are small, capital poor, innovative firms for giants like IBM, Microsoft, and Google to buy up instead of tackling the hard work of innovation themselves. There are common property resources whose productivity can be appropriated at little or no cost to be over exploited at the expense of future generations. And finally, there is a government run by politicians whose careers rely largely on their ability to raise campaign money, begging to be plied for tax dodges and corporate welfare programs financed at taxpayer expense. In other words, in the real world where buyers and sellers are usually not equally powerful, the most effective profit maximizing strategy is often to out maneuver less powerful market opponents and expand one's slice of the pie at their expense rather than work to expand the economic pie.

Snowballing Inefficiency

To the extent that consumer preferences are endogenous the degree of misallocation that results from uncorrected external effects in market economies will increase, or "snowball" over time. As people adjust their preferences to the biases created by external effects in the market price system, they will increase their preference and demand for goods whose production and/or consumption entails negative external effects, but whose market prices fail to reflect these costs and are therefore lower than they should be; and they will decrease their preference and demand for goods whose production and/or consumption entails positive external effects, but whose market prices fail to reflect these benefits and are therefore higher than they should be. While this reaction, or adjustment is individually rational it is socially irrational and inefficient since it leads to even greater demand for the goods that market systems tend to overproduce, and even less demand for the goods that market systems tend to underproduce. As people have greater opportunities to adjust over longer periods of time, the degree of inefficiency in the economy will grow, or "snowball."[4]

Market Disequilibria

Nobody knows where the equilibrium price in a market is. What the micro law of supply and demand says is that self-interested behavior on the part of frustrated

---

4 For a rigorous demonstration that endogenous preferences imply snowballing inefficiency when there are market externalities see theorems 7.1 and 7.2 in Hahnel and Albert, *Quiet Revolution in Welfare Economics* (Princeton University Press, 1990).

sellers when there is excess supply because the actual price is higher than the equilibrium price, and self-interested behavior on the part of frustrated buyers when there is excess demand because market price is below the equilibrium price, will tend to move markets toward their equilibria. But as long as a market is out of equilibrium the quantity bought and sold will be less than the quantity that would be bought and sold if the market were in equilibrium. Since the equilibrium quantity is the same as the socially efficient quantity to produce and consume in absence of external effects, this means markets do not yield efficient outcomes when they are out of equilibria even in absence of external effects. So the first problem is *the slower markets equilibrate the more inefficiency we will endure while they do.*[5]

The second problem is if market participants interpret changes in prices as *signals* about further changes in prices it is *unlikely* they will obey the "laws" of supply and demand. If I believe that even though the price of apples just rose, any further change in the price of apples is just as likely to be down as up, that is, if I do *not* interpret the rise in price as a signal that the price is rising, I will probably demand fewer apples at the new higher price as the law of demand predicts. But if I think that because the price just rose it is more likely to go up than down the next time it changes, I should buy more apples now that I think the chances are greater than I thought before that the price of apples will rise. If I want to consume apples I should buy more apples now before they become even more expensive later. And even if I don't want to consume apples myself, I should buy more now and sell them tomorrow when the price is even higher. Similarly, if sellers in a market interpret price changes as signals of what direction prices are headed in, they should offer to sell more when the price falls and sell less when it rises, the law of supply notwithstanding.[6] In this case, when actual buyers' behavior is represented by an upward sloping demand curve and actual sellers' behavior is represented by a downward sloping supply curve, self-interested

5 The technical name for this is "false trading" whenever deals are struck at a price other than the equilibrium price. Moreover, whenever we have false trading, and inefficiency in one market, we will have false trading and inefficiencies in related markets as well. In general when markets are out of equilibrium there will be disequilibrating "quantity" adjustments as well as equilibrating "price" adjustments. The degree of inefficiency in a market economy due to "false trading" depends on the relative speeds of price and quantity adjustments, and only if price adjustments are infinitely fast so that no quantity adjustment, i.e. false trade, ever takes place, would we avoid these inefficiencies.

6 Mainstream texts persist in treating such behavior as if it was not the obvious violation of the "laws" of supply and demand that it clearly is. Instead of admitting that demand is not always negatively related to market price, and supply is not always positively related to market price, mainstream texts resort to the subterfuge of saying that the change in expectations about the likely direction of future price changes *shifts* demand curves and supply curves that *still do* obey the laws of supply and demand, yielding actual results that contradict what those laws lead us to expect. This is sophistry at its worst.

behavior on the part of frustrated buyers when there is excess demand will raise a price that is higher than the equilibrium price, not lower it. And self-interested behavior on the part of frustrated sellers will lower a price that is lower than the equilibrium price, not raise it. In other words, there will be disequilibrating forces in the market pushing it farther away from equilibrium, not toward it.

A rising price that becomes, at least temporarily, a self-fulfilling prophesy is commonly called a market "bubble," and a falling price that becomes a self-fulfilling prophesy is often called a market "crash." This kind of disequilibrating dynamic occurs more often than market enthusiasts like to admit. Until recently enthusiasts liked to pretend that bubbles and crashes were few and far between and largely confined to financial markets – currency markets, stock markets, bond markets, etc. – with little effect on normal people. But the prominent role played by the bubble and crash in the US housing market in the latest economic crisis, and similar housing bubbles and crashes in Spain and Ireland, have made it increasingly difficult to pretend that market disequilibria are not a serious problem. Moreover, even when they occur in financial markets where most of us are not players they often have disastrous effects on what is called the "real economy," i.e. on employment, investment, and production and consumption of goods and services, as model 9.2 demonstrates. Finally, there can be a different kind of disequilibrating dynamic that operates between markets that are connected in a particular way. In Chapter 6 we will see how the market for labor and the market for goods in general can interact in a way that pushes both markets farther away from their equilibrium. Recognizing this particular disequilibrating dynamic was one of Keynes' greatest insights, and allowed him to explain why production and employment may keep dropping in a recession even though there are more and more workers willing to work, if only someone would hire them, and more and more employers anxious to produce goods, if only someone would buy them.

Conclusion: Market Failure Is Significant

In sum, convenient deals with mutual benefits for buyer and seller should not be confused with economic efficiency. When some kinds of preferences are consistently underrepresented because of transaction cost and free rider problems, when consumers adjust their preferences to biases in the market price system and thereby aggravate those biases, and when profits can be increased as often by externalizing costs onto parties external to market exchanges as from productive behavior, theory predicts free market exchange will often result in a *mis*allocation of scarce productive resources. Theory tells us free market economies will allocate too much of society's resources to goods whose production or consumption entail negative external effects, and too little to goods whose production or consumption entail positive external effects, and there is every reason to believe the misallocations are significant. When markets are less than perfectly competitive – which they almost always are – and fail to equilibrate instantaneously – which they always do – the results are that much worse.

Markets Undermine the Ties That Bind Us

While political economists criticize market inefficiencies and inequities, many others have complained, in one way or another, that markets are *socially destructive*. In effect markets say to us: You cannot consciously coordinate your economic activities efficiently, so don't even try. You cannot come to efficient and equitable agreements among yourselves, so don't even try. Just thank your lucky stars that even such a hopelessly socially challenged species such as yourselves can still benefit from a division of labor thanks to the miracle of the market system. Markets are a decision to punt in the game of human economic relations, a no-confidence vote on the social capacities of the human species. Samuel Bowles explained market's antisocial bias eloquently in an essay titled "What Markets Can and Cannot Do" published in *Challenge Magazine* in July 1991:

Even if market allocations *did* yield Pareto-optimal results, and even if the resulting income distribution *was* thought to be fair (two very big "ifs"), the market would still fail if it supported an undemocratic structure of power or if it rewarded greed, opportunism, political passivity, and indifference toward others. The central idea here is that our evaluation of markets – and with it the concept of market failure – must be expanded to include the effects of markets on both the structure of power and the process of human development. As anthropologists have long stressed, how we regulate our exchanges and coordinate our disparate economic activities influences what kind of people we become. Markets may be considered to be social settings that foster specific types of personal development and penalize others.... The beauty of the market, some would say, is precisely this: It works well even if people *are* indifferent toward one another. And it does not require complex communication or even trust among its participants. But that is also the problem. The economy – its markets, work places and other sites – is a gigantic school. Its rewards encourage the development of particular skills and attitudes while other potentials lay fallow or atrophy. We learn to function in these environments, and in so doing become someone we might not have become in a different setting. . . . By economizing on valuable traits – feelings of solidarity with others, the ability to empathize, the capacity for complex communication and collective decision making, for example – markets are said to cope with the scarcity of these worthy traits. But in the long run markets contribute to their erosion and even disappearance. What looks like a hardheaded adaptation to the infirmity of human nature may in fact be part of the problem.

Markets and hierarchical decision making economize on the use of valuable but scarce human traits like "feelings of solidarity with others, the ability to empathize, the capacity for complex communication and collective decision making." But more importantly, markets and hierarchical relations contribute to the erosion and disappearance of these worthy traits by rewarding those who ignore democratic and social considerations and penalizing those who try to take them into account. It is no accident that despite a monumental increase in education levels, the work force is less capable of exercising its self-management potential than it was a hundred years ago, or that people feel more alone, alienated, suspicious of one another, and rootless than ever before. Robert Bellah, Jean Bethke Elshtain, and Robert Putnam among others have documented the general decay of civic life and weakening of trust and participation across all income and educational levels in the United States. There is no longer any doubt that "the social fabric is becoming visibly thinner, we don't trust one another as much, and we don't know one another as much" in Putnam's words.[7] While it is easier to blame the spread of television than a major economic institution, the atomizing effect of markets as they spread into more and more areas of our lives bears a major responsibility for this trend.

Market prices are systematically biased against social activities in favor of individual activities. Markets make it easier to pursue wellbeing through individual rather than social activity by reducing the transaction costs associated with the former compared to the latter. Private consumption faces no obstacles in market economies where joint, or social consumption runs smack into the free rider problem. Markets harness our creative capacities and energy by arranging for other people to threaten our livelihoods. Markets bribe us with the lure of luxury beyond what others can have and beyond what we know we deserve. Markets reward those who are the most

---

7 Putnam made this remark when interviewed at the 1995 annual meeting of the American Association of Political Scientists in Chicago. *The Washington Post*, September 3, 1995: A5.

efficient at taking advantage of his or her fellow man or woman, and penalize those who insist, illogically, on pursuing the golden rule – do unto others as you would have them do unto you. A mathematics instructor at a small college in Liaoyang China who had doubled his income running a small fleet of taxis summarized his experience with marketization as follows: "It's really survival of the fittest here. If you have a cutthroat heart, you can make it. If you are a good person, I don't think you can."[8]

Of course, we are told we can personally benefit in a market system by being of service to others. But we know we can often benefit more easily by tricking others. Mutual concern, empathy, and solidarity are the appendixes of human capacities and emotions in market economies – and like the appendix, they continue to atrophy as people respond sensibly to the *rule of the market place – do others in before they do you in.*

8 Reported in "With Carrots and Sticks, China Quiets Protesters," *The Washington Post*, March 22, 2002: A24.

5

Microeconomic Models

This chapter contains four microeconomic models that illustrate important themes in political economy. Readers who want to be able to analyze economic problems themselves from a political economy perspective are encouraged to work through these models.

Model 5.1: The Public Good Game

The "public good game" illustrates why markets will allocate too few of our scarce productive resources to the production of public, as opposed to private goods. Assume 0, 1, or 2 units of a public good can be produced and the cost to society of producing each unit is $11. Either Ilana or Sara can purchase 1 unit, or none of the public good – each paying $11 if she purchases a unit, and nothing if she does not. Suppose Sara gets $10 of benefit for every unit of the public good that is available and Ilana gets $8 of benefit for every unit available. We fill in a game theory "payoff matrix" for each woman buying, or not buying, one unit of the public good as follows: We calculate the net benefit for each woman by subtracting what she must pay if she purchases a unit of the public good from the benefits she receives from the total number of the public good produced and therefore available for her to consume. Ilana's payoff is listed first, and Sara's second in each "cell." For example, in the case where both Ilana and Sara buy a unit of the public good, and therefore each gets to consume 2 units of the public good, Ilana's net benefit is 2($8) – $11, or $5, and Sara's net benefit is 2($10) – $11, or $9.

(1) Will Sara buy a unit? No. Sara is better off free riding no matter what Ilana does. If Ilana buys, Sara is better off not buying and free riding since $10 > $9. If Ilana does not buy Sara is also better off not buying than buying since $0 > – $1.

		SARA	
		Buy	Free Ride
ILANA	Buy	($5, $9)	(–$3, $10)
	Free Ride	($8, –$1)	($0, $0)

(2) Will Ilana buy a unit? No. Ilana is also better off free riding no matter what Sara does since $8 > $5 and $0 > – $3.

(3) Assuming that Sara and Ilana's benefits are of equal importance to society, what is the socially optimal number of units of the public good to produce? 2 units since $5 + $9 = $13 is greater than $10 – $3 = $8 – $1 = $7 which is greater than $0 + $0 = $0.

Suppose the social cost and price a buyer is charged is $5 instead of $11. The game theory payoff matrix for buying or not buying one unit of the public good now is:

		SARA	
		Buy	Free Ride
ILANA	Buy	($11, $15)	($3, $10)
	Free Ride	($8, $5)	($0, $0)

(4) Will Sara buy a unit? Yes. Buying is best for Sara no matter what Ilana does since $15 > $10 if Ilana buys, and $5 > $0 if Ilana does not buy.

(5) Will Ilana buy a unit? Yes. Buying is best for Ilana no matter what Sara does since $11 > $8 if Sara buys, and $3 > $0 if Sara does not buy.

(6) Assuming that Sara and Ilana's benefits are of equal importance to society, what is the socially optimal number of units of the public good to produce? 2 units yields the largest possible net social benefit of any of the four possible outcomes: $11 + $15 = $26.

Finally, suppose the social cost and price a buyer is charged is $9. Now the game theory payoff matrix for buying or not buying one unit of the public good is:

		SARA	
		Buy	*Free Ride*
ILANA	*Buy*	($7, $11)	(–$1, $10)
	Free Ride	($8, $1)	($0, $0)

(7) Will Sara buy a unit? Yes, since Sara is better off buying no matter what Ilana does: $11 > $10 when Ilana buys, and $1 > $0 when Ilana does not buy.

(8) Will Ilana buy a unit? No, since Ilana is better off free riding no matter what Sara does: $8 > $7 when Sara buys, and $0 > –$1 when Sara does not buy.

(9) Assuming that Sara and Ilana's benefits are of equal importance to society, what is the socially optimal number of units of the public good to produce? 2 units since $7 + $11 = $18 is greater than $8 + $1 = $10 – $1 = $9, which is greater than $0 + $0 = $0.

What the "public good game" demonstrates is the following conclusion: Unless the private benefit *to each* consumer of a unit of a public good exceeds the *entire social cost* of producing a unit, the free rider problem will lead to underproduction of the public good. When the cost is $11 the private benefit for both Sara and Ilana is less than the social cost, and neither buys, although buying and consuming two units is socially beneficial. When the cost is $9 the private benefit for Ilana is still less than the social cost so she does not buy, and only one unit is bought (by Sara) and consumed (by both women), although producing and consuming two would be more efficient. Only when the cost is $5 is the private benefit to both Sara and Ilana sufficient to induce each to buy, and *then and only then* do we get the socially efficient level of public good production. Obviously for most public goods the private benefit to most individual buyers will not outweigh the entire social cost of producing the public good, and we will therefore get significant "underproduction" of public goods if resource allocation is left to the free market.

Model 5.2: The Price of Power Game

When people in an economic relationship have unequal power the logic of preserving a power advantage can lead to a loss of economic efficiency. This dynamic is illustrated by the "Price of Power Game" which helps explain phenomena as diverse as why employers sometimes choose a less efficient technology over a more efficient one, and why patriarchal husbands sometimes bar their wives from working outside the home even when household wellbeing would be increased if the wife did work outside.

Assume P and W combine to produce an economic value and divide the benefit between them. They have been producing a value of 15, but because P has a power advantage in the relationship P has been getting twice as much as W. So initially P and W jointly produce 15, P gets 10 and W gets 5. A new possibility arises that would allow them to produce a greater value. Assume it increases the value of what they jointly produce by 20%, i.e. by $(0.20)(15) = 3$, raising the value of their combined production from 15 to $15 + 3 = 18$. But taking advantage of the new, more productive possibility also has the effect of increasing W's power relative to P. Assume the effect of producing the greater value renders W as powerful as P eliminating P's power advantage in their relationship. The obvious intuition is that if P stands to lose more from receiving a smaller slice than P stands to gain from having a larger pie to divide with W, it will be in P's interest to block the efficiency gain. We can call this efficiency loss "the price of power." But constructing a simple "game tree" helps us understand the obstacles that prevent untying this Gordian knot as well as the logic leading to the unfortunate result.

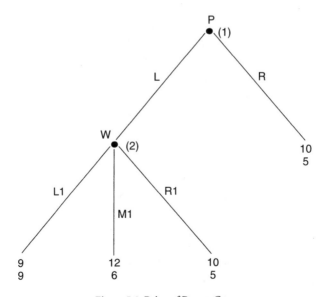

Figure 5.1 Price of Power Game

As the player with the power advantage P gets to make the first move at the first "node." P has two choices at node 1: P can reject the new, more productive possibility and end the game. We call this choice R (for "right" in the game tree diagram in Figure 5.1), and the payoff for P is 10 (listed on top) and the payoff for W is 5 (listed on the bottom) if P chooses R. Or, P can defer to W allowing W to choose whether or not they will adopt the new possibility. We call this choice L (for "left" in the game tree diagram in Figure 5.1), and the payoffs for P and W in this case depend on what W chooses at the second node. If the game gets to the second node because P deferred to W at the first node, W has three choices at node 2: Choice R1 is for W to reject the new possibility in which case the payoffs remain 10 for P and 5 for W as before. Choice L1 is for W to choose the new, more productive possibility and insist on dividing the larger value of 18 equally between them since the new process empowers W to the extent that P no longer has a power advantage, and therefore W can command an equal share with P. If W chooses L1 the payoff for P is therefore 9 and the payoff for W is also 9. Finally, choice M1 (for "middle" in the game tree in Figure 5.1) is for W to choose the new, more productive possibility but to offer to continue to split the pie as before, with P receiving twice as much as W. In other words, in M1 W promises P not to take advantage of her new power, which means that P still gets twice as much as W, but since the pie is larger now P's payoff is 12 and W's payoff is 6 if W chooses M1 at node 2.

We solve this simple dynamic game by backwards induction. If given the opportunity, W should choose L1 at node 2 since W receives 9 for choice L1 and only 5 for choice R1 and only 6 for choice M1. Knowing that W will choose L1 if the game goes to node 2, P compares a payoff of 10 by choosing R with an expected payoff of 9 if P chooses L and W subsequently chooses L1 as P has every reason to believe she will. Consequently P chooses R at node 1 ending the game and effectively "blocking" the new, more productive possibility.

The outcome of the game is not only unequal – P continues to receive twice as much as W – it is also inefficient. One way to see the inefficiency is that while P and W could have produced and shared a total value of 18 they end up only producing and sharing a total value of 15. Another way to see the inefficiency is to note that there is a Pareto superior outcome to (R). (L, M1) is technically possible and has a payoff of 12 for P and 6 for W, compared to the payoff of 10 for P and 5 for W that is the "equilibrium outcome" of the game.

It is the existence of L1 as an option for W at node 2 that forces P to choose R at node 1. Notice that if L1 were eliminated so that W had only two choices at node 2, R1 and M1, W would choose M1 in this new game, in which case P would choose L instead of R at node 1. While this outcome would remain unequal it would not be inefficient. So one could say the inefficiency of the outcome to the original game is because W cannot make a *credible* promise to P to reject option L1 if the game gets to node 2. Since there is no reason for P to believe W would actually choose M1 over L1 if the game gets to node 2, P chooses R at node 1. In effect P will block an efficiency gain whenever it diminishes P's power advantage sufficiently. If P stands to lose more from a loss of power than he gains from a bigger pie to divide, P will use his power advantage to block an efficiency gain.[1]

If we turn our attention to how the efficiency loss might be avoided, two possibilities arise. The most straightforward solution, which not only avoids the efficiency loss but generates equal instead of unequal outcomes for P and W, is to eliminate P's power advantage. If P and W have equal power and divide the value of their joint

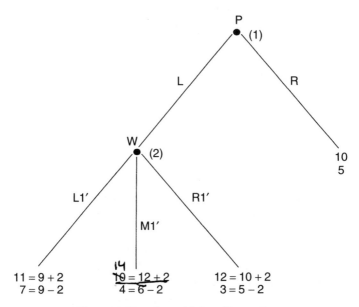

Figure 5.2 Transformed Price of Power Game

---

1 If the new opportunity completely eliminates P's power advantage but only increases efficiency by 20%, P will veto the change, as we have just seen. Readers can check to see that if the efficiency gain were 30% P would still block the change, but just barely. However, for a 40% efficiency gain P would no longer block because P's smaller share of the larger pie would finally be greater than the larger share of the smaller pie.

production equally they will always choose to produce the larger pie and there will never be any efficiency losses. The more convoluted solution is to accept P's power advantage as a given, and search for ways to make a promise from W not to take advantage of her enhanced power *credible.* Is there some way to transform the initial game so that a promise from P not to choose L1 is credible?

What if W offered P 2 units to choose L rather than R at node 1? If a contract could be devised in which W had to pay P 2 units, if and only if P chose L at node 1, then the new game would have the following payoffs at node 2: If W chose R1' P would get $10 + 2 = 12$ instead of 10, and W would get $5 - 2 = 3$ instead of 5. If W chose M1' P would get $12 + 2 = 14$ instead of 12 and W would get $6 - 2 = 4$ instead of 6. Finally, if W chose L1' P would get $9 + 2 = 11$ and W would get $9 - 2 = 7$ instead of 9. Under these circumstances, in the transformed price of power game illustrated in Figure 5.2 W would choose L1' since 7 is greater than both 4 and 3. But when W chooses L1' at node 2 that gives P 11 which is more than P gets by choosing R at node 1. Therefore a bribe of 2 paid by W to P if and only if P chooses R over L would give us an efficient but unequal outcome. It is efficient because P and W produce 18 instead of 15 and because (L, L1') is Pareto superior to (R). It is still unequal because P receives 11 while W receives only 7.

There are many economic situations where implementing an efficiency gain changes the bargaining power between collaborators and therefore the Price of Power Game can help illustrate aspects of what transpires. Below are two interesting applications.

The Price of Patriarchy

If P is a patriarchal head of household and W is his wife, the game illustrates one reason why the husband might refuse to permit his wife to work outside the home even though net benefits for the household would be greater if she did.[2] Patriarchal power within the household can be modeled as giving the husband the "first mover advantage" in our model. Patriarchal power in the economy can be modeled as a gender wage gap for women with no labor market experience. If we assume as long as the wife has not worked outside the home she cannot command as high a wage as her husband in the labor market, her exit option is worse than her husband's should the marriage dissolve. This unequal exit option makes it possible for a patriarchal

---

2 I do not mean to imply there are not many *other* reasons husbands behave in this way. Nor am I suggesting *any* of the reasons are morally justifiable, including the reason this model explains.

husband to insist on a greater share of the household benefits than the wife as long as she has no outside work experience.[3] But after she works outside the home for some time the unequal exit option can dissipate, and with it the husband's power advantage within the home.

The obstacles to eliminating efficiency losses in this situation by eliminating patriarchal advantages are not economic. Gender-based wage discrimination can be eliminated through effective enforcement of laws outlawing discrimination in employment such as those in the US Civil Rights Act. The psychological dynamics that give "first mover" advantages to husbands within marriages require changes in the attitudes and values of both men and women about gender relations. Of course eliminating the efficiency loss due to patriarchal power by eliminating patriarchal power has the supreme advantage of improving economic justice as well as efficiency.

Trying to eliminate the efficiency loss by making the wife's promise not to exercise the power advantage she gets by working outside the home credible has a number of disadvantages. Most importantly it is grossly unfair. The bribe the wife must pay her husband to be "allowed" to work outside the home is obviously the result of the disadvantages she suffers from having to negotiate under conditions of unequal and inequitable bargaining power in the first place. Second, it may not be as "practical" as it first appears. Those who believe this solution is more "achievable" than reducing patriarchal privilege should bear in mind how unlikely it is that wives with no labor market credentials could obtain what would amount to an unsecured loan against their future expected productivity gain! Nor could their husbands co-sign for the loan without effectively changing the payoff numbers in our revised game. Third, even if wives obtained loans from some outside agent – presumably an institution like the Grameen Bank in Bangladesh that gives loans to women without collateral but holds an entire group of women responsible for non-payment of any individual – there would have to be a binding legal contract that prevented husbands from taking the bribe and reneging on their promise to allow their wives to work outside the home. Notice that if P can take the bribe and still choose R he gets 10 + 2 = 12 which is greater than the 11 he gets if he keeps his promise to choose L.

---

3 I am not suggesting the wife's lack of work experience in the formal labor market makes her a less productive employee than her husband. If employers do not evaluate the productivity enhancing effects of household work fairly, or use previous employment in the formal sector as a screening device, the effect is the same as if lack of formal sector work experience did, in fact, mean lower productivity. The husband enjoys a power advantage no matter what the reason his wife is paid less than he is initially.

Finally, notice that any bribe between 1 and 4 would successfully transform the game from an inefficient power game to a conceivably efficient, but nonetheless inequitable power game. If W paid P a bribe of 4 the entire efficiency gain would go to her husband. But even if W paid P only a bribe of 1 and kept the entire efficiency gain for herself, she would still end up with less than her husband. In that case W would get $9 - 1 = 8$ compared to $9 + 1 = 10$ for P. So even if we conjure up a Grameen Bank to give never employed women unsecured loans, even if we ignore all problems and costs of enforcement, there is no way to transform our power game into a game that would deliver efficient and equitable outcomes. Since P gets 10 by choosing R and ending the game, he must receive at least 10 in order to choose L. But if the productivity gain is only 3 when both work outside, and therefore total household net benefits are only 18, W can receive no more than 8 if P must have at least 10, and no transformation of the game that preserves patriarchal power will produce equitable results. Whether or not this morally inferior solution is actually easier to achieve than reducing patriarchal privilege also seems to be an open question.

Conflict Theory of the Firm

If P represents an employer, or "Patron," and W represents his employees or "Workers," the Price of Power Game illustrates why an employer might fail to implement a new, more productive technology if that technology is also "worker empowering." A host of factors influence the bargaining power between employers and employees, and therefore the wages employees will receive and the efforts they will have to exert to receive them. But one factor that can affect bargaining power in the capitalist firm is the technology used. For example, if an assembly line technology is used and employees are physically separated from one another and unable to communicate during work, it may be more difficult for employees to develop solidarity that would empower them in negotiations with their employer as compared to a technology that requires workers to work in teams with constant communication between them. Or it may be that one technology requires employees themselves to have a great deal of know-how to carry out their tasks, while another technology concentrates crucial productive knowledge in the hands of a few engineers or supervisors, rendering most employees easily replaceable and therefore less powerful. If the technology that is more productive is also "worker empowering," employers face the dilemma illustrated by our Price of Power Game and may have reason to choose a less efficient technology over a more efficient one that is more worker empowering.

When we consider possible solutions in this application an interesting new wrinkle arises. In capitalism there is inevitably a conflict between employers and employees over wages and effort levels. If new technologies not only affect economic efficiency but the relative bargaining power of employers and employees as well, we cannot "trust" the choice of technology to *either* interested party without running the risk that a more productive technology might be blocked due to detrimental bargaining power effects for whoever has the power to choose. I pointed out above how P might block a more efficient technology if it were sufficiently employee empowering, so we cannot trust employers to choose between technologies. But if W had the power to do so, W might block a more efficient technology if it were sufficiently employer empowering, so it appears we cannot resolve the dilemma by giving unions the say over technology in capitalism either. Since we cannot change the fact that new more productive technologies sometimes affect bargaining power, the solution seems to lie in eliminating the conflict between employers and employees. This can only happen in economies where there are no employers and no division between profits and wages, that is, in economies where employees manage and pay themselves. We consider economies of this kind in Chapter 11.

Model 5.3: Climate Control Treaties

This exercise is designed to illustrate some of the key issues when designing an international climate treaty that is *effective* – reduces global emissions sufficiently – *equitable* – distributes responsibility for reductions according to differential responsibility and capability – and *efficient* – minimizes the global cost of averting climate change. Imagine three countries sitting down to negotiate a climate treaty: the United States, Russia, and India. Consider the United States and Russia as more developed countries (MDCs), termed Annex-1 countries in the Kyoto Protocol, and India as a less developed country (LDC), or a non-Annex-1 country. Below are equations for both the marginal costs (MCs) and total costs (TCs) of reducing greenhouse gas (GHG) emissions for all three countries. As a country reduces emissions more and more, the MC of reducing emissions rises. This is because presumably a country will use the least costly options for reducing emissions first, and move on to higher-cost methods as more emission reductions are required. It is also typically the case that the MC of emission reduction is lower in developing countries. This is because LDCs have engaged in relatively little *emission reduction*, or **abatement**, so many low-cost opportunities for reducing emissions are still available in LDCs. The MC and TC of emissions reduction (abatement) for the three countries are expressed in billions of dollars, where X is the number of tons of GHG emissions reduced:

United States $MC_{us} = 5X_{US}$ $TC_{us} = 2.5X_{US}^2$

Russia $MC_R = 2X_R$ $TC_R = X_R^2$

India $MC_I = X_I$ $TC_I = X_I^2/2$

No Treaty

Initially there is no treaty. And while each country has potentially unlimited "rights" to emit carbon into the upper atmosphere, the United States chooses only to "exercise" its "right" to emit 400 tons, Russia chooses only to exercise its right to emit 250 tons, and India chooses only to exercise its right to emit 200 tons. As a result, global emissions are 850 tons. Suppose the international community has identified a 10% reduction in global carbon emissions as necessary to reduce the risk of dangerous climate change to an acceptable level.

Treaty 1 requires each country to reduce its emissions by 10%

(1) How much emission reduction would each country have to do?

United States: $(0.10)400 = 40 = X_{US}$
Russia: $(0.10)250 = 25 = X_R$
India: $(0.10)200 = 20 = X_I$
Global: $(40 + 25 + 20) = 85 = X_G = (0.10)850$

(2) What would be the cost of the last ton of emission reduced in each country?

United States: $MC_{US} = 5X_{US} = 5(40) = \$200$
Russia: $MC_R = 2X_R = 2(25) = \$50$
India: $MC_I = X_I = 1(20) = \$20$

(3) What would be the total cost for each country?

United States: $TC_{US} = 2.5X_{US}^2 = 2.5(40)^2 = \$4,000$
Russia: $TC_R = X_R^2 = (25)^2 = \$625$
India: $TC_I = X_I^2/2 = (20)^2/2 = \$200$

(4) What would be the total cost of emission reduction for the world?

$TC_G = \$4,000 + \$625 + \$200 = \$4,825$

Efficiency After each country has reduced its emissions by 10%, the MC of reduction is different in the three countries. We therefore know we failed to minimize the global cost of reduction, which means the pattern of reductions this treaty yields is *inefficient*. To illustrate: The last ton reduced in the United States (the 40th ton reduced) cost $200, while the last ton reduced in Russia (the 25th ton reduced) cost only $25. Had we reduced 39 tons in the United States (instead of 40) and 26 tons in Russia (instead of 25), we would have achieved the same level of global reductions, 85, but global cost would have been $200 – $25 = $175 lower.

Equity For simplicity assume the benefits of achieving a global reduction of 85 tons are the same for all three countries. While the United States is paying more than Russia, which is paying more than India to achieve this global reduction, we might argue that it is still unfair for India to bear this much of the cost because (1) India did much less to create the problem in the first place since Indian per capita cumulative emissions are much lower than per capita cumulative emissions of the United States and Russia, and (2) India is less able to bear the cost of preventing climate change since per capita gross domestic product (GDP) is much lower there. We could also argue that the treaty now explicitly limits each country's "right" to release carbon into the upper atmosphere but distributes the remaining rights very unfairly. The treaty implicitly awards the United States rights to emit (400 – 40) = 360 tons, but awards Russia only rights to emit (250 – 25) = 225 tons, and India only rights to emit (200 – 20) = 180 tons. Other ways to see why this treaty is unfair are: (1) Since per capita cumulative emissions are highest in the United States and lowest in India, India should be awarded the most rights to emit more carbon dioxide in the future and the United States should be awarded the fewest rights to emit more – whereas this treaty does just the opposite. (2) Since emission rights are a new form of wealth and per capita wealth is lowest in India and highest in the United States, India should receive the most emission rights and the United States the fewest – whereas this treaty does just the opposite. (3) It is more difficult to achieve economic development when consumption of fossil fuel is limited. Since India is least developed and the United States is most developed, India should receive the most emission rights and the United States the fewest – whereas this treaty does just the opposite.

Treaty 2 calls for a 10% reduction in global emissions, but exempts India from making any reductions and permits no trading of emission rights

(1) How much emission reduction would each country have to do?
To make the two treaties equally *effective* global reductions must be the same: X_G must again be 85, but now $X_I = 0$. Assume we require the United States and Russia to make the same percentage reduction, p, in their emissions. In this case we have:

$X_{US} + X_R = 85; 400p + 250p = 85$

Solving the second equation for p: $650p = 85$; $p = 85/650 = 0.13077$; that is, the United States and Russia must each reduce their emissions by 13.077%.

United States: $(0.13077)400 = 52.308 = X_{US}$
Russia: $(0.13077)250 = 32.692 = X_R$
India: $0 = X_I$
Global: $52.308 + 32.692 + 0 = 85 = X_G$

(2) What would be the cost of the last ton of emission reduced in each country?

United States: $MC_{US} = 5X_{US} = 5(52.308) = \$261.54$
Russia: $MC_R = 2X_R = 2(32.692) = \$65.38$
India: [Note: $MC_I = X_I = 1(1) = \$1$ if India reduced emissions by 1 ton]

(3) What would be the total cost for each country?

United States: $TC_{US} = 2.5X_{US}^2 = 2.5(52.308)^2 = \$6,840.32$
Russia: $TC_R = X_R^2 = (32.692)^2 = \$1,068.77$
India: $TC_I = X_I^2/2 = (0)^2/2 = \$0.00$

(4) What would be the total cost of emission reduction for the world?

$TC_G = \$6,840.32 + \$1,068.77 + \$0 = \$7,909.09$

Efficiency Treaty 2 is even less efficient than Treaty 1 since $\$7,909.09 > \$4,825$. This is why people sometimes argue that achieving equity can come at the expense of efficiency. The cost of treating India fairly – not requiring it to reduce emissions at all – has raised the global cost of reducing emissions by 85 tons by $\$7,909.09 - \$4,825 = \$3,084.09$. The reason is that none of the reduction is taking place in India, where the costs of reduction are lowest. Note that the first unit reduced in India would have cost only $1! We are also distributing reductions inefficiently between the United States and Russia since the MCs are different in these two countries. We could lower TC_G by having more of the reductions in Russia, where the last unit of abatement cost only \$65.38, and fewer of the reductions in the United States, where the last unit of abatement cost \$261.54. But since Treaty 2 does not permit carbon trading between the United States and Russia, the inefficient pattern of abatement in those two countries will not be eliminated.

Equity Clearly Treaty 2 treats India more fairly than Treaty 1 does. The implicit distribution of emissions rights – that is, new wealth – is now, for the United States,

$400 - 52.308 = 347.692$ (which is less than 360), and for Russia, $250 - 32.692 = 217.308$ (which is less than 225). While India is given potentially limitless emission rights, under Treaty 2 India will only "exercise" its rights to emit 200 tons. That is all India chose to exercise before there was any treaty, and since this treaty does not allow India to sell any of its new wealth, India will continue to emit 200 tons, as before.

Treaty 3 calls for a 10% reduction in global emissions, exempts India from making any reductions, reduces US and Russian emission rights by the same percentage – 13.077 – but permits unlimited trading of emission rights between Annex-1 countries (that is, between the United States and Russia)

(1) How much would each country have to reduce its emissions?

Once again $X_{US} + X_R = 85$ and $X_I = 0$. But now instead of $400\,p + 250\,p = 85$, meaning that the United States and Russia will each reduce its emissions by the same percentage, p, the pattern of emissions reductions will be determined by the condition: $MC_{US} = MC_R$. This is because the United States and Russia will keep trading emission rights until there are no longer any mutually beneficial deals to be struck, which will be the case only when MC_{US} becomes equal to MC_R. So $5X_{US} = MC_{US} = MC_R = 2X_R$, or $X_{US} = (2/5)X_R$. Substituting for X_{US} in the first equation above, $(2/5)X_R + X_R = 85$, and $X_R = (5/7)85 = 60.714$, and therefore $X_{US} = 24.286$.

United States: $24.286 = X_{US}$
Russia: $60.714 = X_R$
India: $0 = X_I$
Global: $24.286 + 60.286 + 0 = 85 = X_G$

(2) What would be the cost of the last ton of emission reduced in each country?

United States: $MC_{US} = 5X_{US} = 5(24.286) = \$121.43$
Russia: $MC_R = 2X_R = 2(60.714) = \$121.43$
India: [Note: $MC_I = X_I = 1(1) = \$1$ if India reduced emissions by 1 ton]

(3) What would be the total cost of the reductions carried out in each country?

United States: $TC_{US} = 2.5X_{US}^2 = 2.5(24.286)^2 = \$1{,}474.52$
Russia: $TC_R = X_R^2 = (60.714)^2 = \$3{,}686.19$
India: $TC_I = X_I^2/2 = (0)^2/2 = \$0.00$

However, the total cost to the United States is not just the cost of reducing its own emissions by 24.286 tons. That reduction is not sufficient to achieve a 13.077% reduction from 400, i.e. to get down to 347.692 tons, which is all the United States has the "right" to emit. Consequently, the United States will have to buy emission rights from Russia to meet its treaty obligations: $400 - 24.286 = 375.714$ tons emitted $- 347.692$ tons allowed $= 28.022$ emission permits the US must buy from Russia. The price of each emission right will be $121.43 because Russia would accept no less (since that is what it will cost Russia to reduce its last ton), and the United States will pay no more (since the United States could reduce another ton itself for that amount). So $121.43(28.022) = $3,402.71$, and the total cost to the United States – that is, the cost of reducing emissions internally by 24.286 tons, *plus* the cost of buying 28.022 emission rights from Russia – is $1,474.52 + $3,402.71 = $4,877.23$.

The total cost to Russia of reducing emissions by 60.714 – which exceeds a 13.077% reduction from 250 by 28.022 tons – is reduced by the amount Russia gains from selling 28.022 emission rights to the United States. At a price of $121.43 each, Russia reduces its total costs by $121.43(28.022) = $3,402.71$. So the total cost to Russia – that is, the cost of reducing emissions internally by 60.714 tons, *minus* the revenue received from selling 28.022 emission rights to the United States – is $3,686.19 - $3,402.71 = 283.48.

(4)   What would be the total cost of emissions reduction for the world?

$TC_G = $4,877.23 + $283.48 + $0 = $5,160.71$
(Alternatively: $TC_G = $1,474.52 + $3,686.19 + $0 = $5,160.71$)

Efficiency Treaty 3 is more efficient than Treaty 2 because it allows reductions to be reallocated from the United States to Russia until the marginal reduction costs are equal in the two countries. TC_G are lowered by $7,909.09 - $5,160.71 = $2,748.38$. However, Treaty 3 is still not as efficient as it might be. The 85th ton reduced costs $121.43 (whether it is reduced in the United States or in Russia). If instead the 85th ton were reduced in India, it would cost only $1!

Equity The distribution of emission rights under Treaty 3 is the same as under Treaty 2, so the equity implications of the wealth distribution are the same. The efficiency gain ($7,909.09 - $5,160.71 = $2,748.38) from reallocating reductions from the United States to Russia until the marginal reduction costs are equal in the two countries achieved by Treaty 3 is divided between the United States ($6,840.32

– \$4,877.23 = \$1,963.09) and Russia (\$1,068.77 – \$283.48 = \$785.29). There is no change for India. Under both Treaty 2 and Treaty 3, India benefits from prevention of climate change at no cost.

Treaty 4 calls for a 10% reduction in global emissions, continues to exempt India from *responsibility* for any reductions, reduces US and Russian emission rights by the same percentage – 13.077 – but permits unlimited trading of emissions rights between all countries, including India; that is, full use of a Clean Development Mechanism (CDM). This treaty most closely resembles the treaty negotiated in Kyoto in 1997 which was in effect from 2005 through 2012

(1) How much emission reduction would each country have to do? Treaty 4 does not require India to reduce emissions; however, since India can now sell emission reduction credits to the United States and Russia, India will benefit by reducing emissions, as illustrated below.

We now have two conditions: $X_{US} + X_R + X_I = 85$, and $MC_{US} = MC_R = MC_I$. Since $MC_{US} = 5X_{US}$, $MC_R = 2X_R$, and $MC_I = X_I$, from the second condition we get $5X_{US} = 2X_R = X_I$, or $X_R = (5/2)X_{US}$ and $X_I = 5X_{US}$.

Substituting into the first equation,

$X_{US} + (5/2)X_{US} + 5X_{US} = 85$, giving $X_{US} = 10$. And $X_R = (5/2)X_{US} = (5/2)(10) = 25$, and $X_I = 5X_{US} = 5(10) = 50$.

United States:	$10 = X_{US}$
Russia:	$25 = X_R$
India:	$50 = X_I$
Global:	$10 + 25 + 50 = 85 = X_G$

(2) What would be the cost of the last ton of emission reduced in each country?

United States:	$MC_{US} = 5X_{US} = 5(10) = \$50$
Russia:	$MC_R = 2X_R = 2(25) = \$50$
India:	$MC_I = X_I = 1(50) = \$50$

(3) What would be the total cost for each country?
Total costs for each country associated with the reductions it carries out itself are as follows:

United States: $TC_{US} = 2.5X_{US}^2 = 2.5(10)^2 = \$250$
Russia: $TC_R = X_R^2 = (25)^2 = \$625$
India: $TC_I = X_I^2/2 = (50)^2/2 = \$1,250$

However, the United States and Russia will have to buy emission rights from India as follows:

The United States will buy: $400 - (1 - 0.13007)400 - 10 = 42.308$
Russia will buy: $250 - (1 - 0.13007)250 - 25 = 7.692$
India will sell: $42.308 + 7.692 = 50$

Emission rights will sell for $50 each because the MC of reductions is now $50 in all three countries, so no country will pay more than $50 for a credit or sell a credit for less than $50. Therefore, it will cost the United States an additional $50(42.308) = $2,115.40, it will cost Russia an additional $50(7.692) = $384.60, and India will gain $50(50) = $2,500 from selling emission rights through the CDM, and therefore the total costs for the three countries are:

United States: $TC_{US} = \$250 + \$2,115.40 = \$2,365.40$
Russia: $TC_R = \$625 + \$384.60 = \$1,009.60$
India: $TC_I = \$1,250 - \$2,500.00 = -\$1,250.00$

(4) What would be the total cost of emission reductions for the world?

$TC_G = \$2,365.40 + \$1,009.60 - \$1,250 = \$2,125$
(also $TC_G = \$250 + \$625 + \$1,250 = \$2,125$)

Efficiency: Treaty 4 has minimized the global cost of reducing global emissions by 85 tons: TC_G for Treaty 4 = $2,125 < TC_G for Treaty 1 = $4,825 < TC_G for Treaty 3 = $5,160.71 < TC_G for Treaty 2 = $7,909.09. We also know this because the marginal costs of reduction are the same in all three countries, so there is no way to reallocate emission reductions and lower global costs. Comparing the total cost of reducing emissions by 85 tons under Treaty 4 and Treaty 3, the efficiency gain produced by the CDM is $5,160.71 - $2,125 = $3,035.71. It is distributed as follows: US total costs have fallen by $4,877.23 - $2,365.40 = $2,511.83. Russian total costs have risen by $1,009.60 - $283.48 = $726.12. (This is because the CDM allowed India to replace Russia as the seller in the lucrative market for emission rights.) And India now enjoys a profit of $1,250.

Equity Treaty 4 awards the same emission rights – that is, new wealth – as Treaty 2 and 3: the United States (347.692), Russia (217.308), and India (potentially limitless). However, the CDM in Treaty 4 allows India to make more profitable use of its emission rights by selling some of them to the United States and Russia. Under Treaty 2 and 3, India could not sell any of its new wealth to the United States and Russia. The CDM allows India to sell emission rights, which it has every incentive to do as long as reducing emissions costs less than the price India receives. In the market for emission rights, supply (50 emission rights supplied by India) will equal demand for emission rights (42.308 from the United States plus 7.692 from Russia) when the price of an emission right is $50. So under Treaty 4 the reduction of 50 of the 85 tons reduced globally will take place in India, which will presumably (see below) cut back on its emissions from 200 to 150 tons. However, even though the reductions are taking place in India (where they are cheaper), the costs of achieving those reductions are being paid for by the United States and Russia.

The United States and Russia are paying more than it costs India to reduce 50 tons. The total cost of reducing the 50 tons in India is $50^2/2 = \$1,250$. The United States and Russia pay India $50(50) = \$2,500$. But this does not mean the United States and Russia are overpaying India by $1,250. We could just as easily argue the United States and Russia are underpaying India because it would have cost the United States and Russia much more than $2,500 to reduce those 50 tons themselves. By comparing the total costs under Treaty 3 and Treaty 4, we can calculate how much more it would have cost the United States and Russia: From Treaty 3 we know the total cost to the United States and Russia combined of reducing all 85 tons themselves is $5,160.71. From Treaty 4 the total cost to the United States and Russia combined (when they can purchase 50 of the 85 tons from India) is $2,365.40 + $1,009.60 = $3,375. Therefore the United States and Russia have saved $5,160.71 − $3,375 = $1,785.71 by purchasing 50 emission rights from India. Rather than speak of over or underpaying, it is more accurate to say that the United States and Russia are sharing with India the efficiency gain from relocating 50 tons of reduction from the United States and Russia to India. In this case, the United States and Russia are getting $1,785.71 of the efficiency gain, and India is getting $1,250 of the efficiency gain.

Warning There is an important implicit assumption in the above analysis and an explicit warning is in order. *We have assumed that India will actually reduce its emissions by 50 tons when it sells 50 emission rights to the United States and Russia, and therefore India will only emit 200 − 50 = 150 tons.* Of course this is what the executive board of the CDM in the Kyoto Protocol is supposed to ensure when it certifies emission rights for sale, namely that there was actually that number of tons reduced additional to what would have occurred in any case, which was 200. But Treaty 4 gives India unlimited emission rights. When India could not sell emission rights, it only found it in its interest to "exercise" its right to emit 200 tons. But since India can now sell emission rights at $50 apiece, why would India not want to "exercise" its right to emit more than 200 tons – in which case global emissions would no longer decline by 85 tons? As long as India has unlimited emission rights, there will be what economists call a perverse incentive for India to try to sell bogus emission rights. Selling a real reduction that cost only $15, say, for $50 is a good deal. But if you can sell a "pretend" reduction that cost nothing for $50, that is an even better deal!

The simple way to solve this problem is not to give India unlimited emission rights. Requiring India to reduce its emissions by 0.0% means requiring India to maintain its emissions at 200 tons. So all we have to do is give India the right to emit 200 tons – all it wanted to emit initially. Then if India decides it wants to sell 50 of those 200 emission rights to the US and Russia – which it clearly has an incentive to do – it must cut its own emissions back to 150 tons.

This is only an exercise for illustrative purposes. However, readers can find out for themselves what truly fair reductions are for every country in the world by going to the EcoEquity website www.ecoequity.org, and using their "equity calculator." Readers can chose among three global reduction scenarios, three different weights for responsibility and capability, three different development thresholds, and three different dates from which to calculate historic responsibility. For any combination of choices the calculator will tell you how much each country has a right to continue to emit, and how much each country is responsible for reducing. What the above exercise demonstrates is that when there are significant differences in marginal reduction costs in different countries, if the treaty you design using the EcoEquity calculator – that is the treaty you believe is both effective and fair – permits country governments to authorize the sale and purchase of emission rights by sources: (1) there will be a great deal of trading, (2) which will significantly reduce global reduction costs, and (3) generate a significant flow of payments from sources in MDCs to sources in LDCs.

Model 5.4: The Sraffa Model of Income Distribution and Prices

Mainstream economic theory explains the prices of goods and services in terms of consumer preferences, production technologies, and the relative scarcities of different productive resources. Political economists, on the other hand, have long insisted that wages, profits, and rents are determined by power relations among classes in addition to factors mainstream economic theory takes into account, and therefore that the relative prices of goods in capitalist economies depend also on power relations between classes as well as on consumer preferences, technologies, and resource scarcities.

The labor theory of value Karl Marx developed in *Das Kapital* was the first political economy explanation of "wage, price and profit"[4] determination. In *Production of Commodities by Means of Commodities* (Cambridge University Press, 1960) Piero Sraffa presented an alternative political economy framework that avoided logical inconsistencies and anomalies in the labor theory of value, and extends easily to include different wage rates for different kinds of labor and rents on different kinds of natural resources – which the labor theory of value cannot accommodate. The model below is based on Sraffa, and is often called "the modern surplus approach."

The "surplus approach" is only one part of a political economy explanation of the determination of wages, profits, rents, and prices. The surplus approach does *not* explain why consumers come to have the preferences they do, *nor* what determines the relative power of employers, workers, and resource owners. Instead the surplus approach takes consumer demand and the power relationships between workers, employers, and resource owners as givens, and seeks to explain what prices will result under those conditions. While it does not explain what causes changes in the power relations between workers, employers, and resource owners, the surplus approach does explain how any changes in power between them will affect prices as well as income distribution. And while it does not explain what causes technological innovations, it does explain which new technologies will be chosen, and how their implementation will affect wages, profits, rents, prices, and economic efficiency. Logically, the surplus approach is the *last* part of a micro political economy. Other political economy theories must explain the factors that influence preference formation and power relations between different classes. In Chapters 2, 4 and 10 the effects of institutional biases on preference formation are explained briefly. In Chapter 10 factors affecting the bargaining power of workers and capitalists are explored. But once consumer demand and the bargaining power between classes is given, the "surplus approach" provides a rigorous explanation of price formation and income distribution in capitalism.[5]

---

4 Marx wrote a pamphlet under this title in which he presented a popularized version of the labor theory of value from *Das Kapital.*
5 For a more rigorous political economy theory of preference formation see Chapter 6 in Hahnel and Albert, *Quiet Revolution in Welfare Economics.* For a more thorough presentation and defense of the political economy "conflict theory of the firm" and extensive examination of factors that influence the bargaining power of capitalists and workers see Chapters 2 and 8.

The Sraffa Model

Assume a two sector economy defined by the technology below where a(ij) is the number of units of good i needed to produce one unit of good j, and L(j) is the number of hours of labor needed to produce one unit of good j. Suppose:

a(11) = 0.3 a(12) = 0.2
a(21) = 0.2 a(22) = 0.4
L(1) = 0.1 L(2) = 0.2

The first column can be read as a "recipe" for making one unit of good 1: It takes 0.3 units of good 1 itself, 0.2 units of good 2, and 0.1 hour of labor to "stir" these inputs to get 1 unit of good 1 as output. Similarly, the second column is a recipe for making one unit of good 2: It takes 0.2 units of good 1, 0.4 units of good 2 itself, and 0.2 hours of labor to make one unit of good 2.

Let p(i) be the price of a unit of good i, w be the hourly wage rate in the economy, and r(i) be the rate of profit received by capitalists in sector i. The first step is to write down an equation for each industry that expresses the truism that revenue minus cost for the industry is, by definition, equal to industry profit. If we divide both sides of this equation by the number of units of output the industry produces we get the truism that revenue per unit of output minus cost per unit of output must equal profit per unit of output. Another way of saying this is: cost per unit of output plus profit per unit of output must equal revenue per unit of output. This is the equation we want to write for each industry.

The second step is to write down what cost per unit of output and revenue per unit of output will be for each industry. For industry 1 it takes a(11) units of good 1 itself to make a unit of output of good 1. That will cost p(1)a(11). It also takes a(21) units of good 2 to make a unit of output of good 1. That will cost p(2)a(21). So [p(1)a(11) + p(2)a(21)] are the non-labor costs of making one unit of good 1. Since it takes L(1) hours of labor to make a unit of good 1 and the wage per hour is w, the labor cost of making a unit of good 1 is wL(1). Revenue per unit of output of good 1 is simply p(1).

What is profit per unit of output in industry 1? By definition profits are revenues minus costs, so profits per unit of output must be equal to revenues per unit of output minus cost per unit of output. Also by definition the rate of profit is profits divided by whatever part of costs a capitalist must pay for in advance. Dividing both the numerator, profits, and denominator, costs advanced, by the number of units of output in industry 1 gives us the truism that the rate of profit in industry 1 is equal to the profit per unit of output in industry 1 divided by whatever part of costs per unit of output capitalists must advance in industry 1. Therefore, (multiplying both sides of this identity by costs advanced per unit of output) the profit per unit of output in industry 1 must be equal to the rate of profit for industry 1 times the cost per unit of output capitalists must advance in industry 1.

We will assume (with Sraffa) that capitalists must pay for non-labor costs in advance but can pay their employees after the production period is over out of revenues from the sale of the goods produced. So the cost per unit of output capitalists must advance in industry one is only the non-labor costs per unit, or [p(1)a(11) + p(2)a(21)]. We will also assume (with Sraffa) that the rate of profit capitalists receive is the same in both industries, r.[6] Therefore:

profit per unit of output in industry one = r[p(1)a(11) + p(2)a(21)]

And we are ready to write the accounting identity, or truism, that cost per unit of output plus profit per unit of output equals revenue per unit of output in industry 1:

$$[p(1)a(11) + p(2)a(21)] + wL(1) + r[p(1)a(11) + p(2)a(21)] = p(1)$$

Which can be rewritten for convenience as:

(1) $(1+r) [p(1)a(11) + p(2)a(21)] + wL(1) = p(1)$

Similarly for industry 2:

(2) $(1+r) [p(1)a(12) + p(2)a(22)] + wL(2) = p(2)$

We call equations (1) and (2) the *price equations* for the economy. They are 2 equations with 4 unknowns: w, r, p(1), and p(2). (The a(ij) and L(j) are technological "givens.") But we are only interested in relative prices, i.e. how many units of one good trade for how many units of another good. If we set the price of good 2 equal to 1,

---

6 These assumptions are both convenient because they simplify the analysis. However, they are not necessary, and one of the strengths of the surplus approach is that we could change them and still solve the model. In particular, if capitalists in different industries had different bargaining power, or if some industries were more competitive and others less so, or if there were barriers to entry for some industries, so capitalists were not always free to flee lower profit industries to enter higher profit industries until profit rates were equal everywhere, we could easily complicate our model and stipulate different rates of profit r(1) and r(2) for the two industries.

$p(2) = 1$, then $p(1)$ tells us how many units of good 2 one unit of good 1 exchanges for, and w tells us how many units of good 2 a worker can buy with her hourly wage. So we now have 2 equations in 3 unknowns: w, r, and $p(1)$, the price of good 1 *relative* to the price of good 2. We proceed to discover: (1) that the wage rate and profit rate must be negatively related, (2) that the relative prices of goods can change even when there are no changes in consumer preferences, productive technologies, or the relative scarcities of resources, (3) which new technologies will be adopted and which will not be, (4) when the adoption or rejection of a new technology will be socially productive or counterproductive, and (5) how the adoption of new technologies will affect the rate of profit in the economy.

(1) What would the wage rate be in this economy if the rate of profit were zero? We simply substitute $r = 0$, $p(2) = 1$, and the values representing our technologies (or recipes) for producing the two goods, the a(ij)'s and L(j)'s, into the two price equations and solve for $p(1)$ and w:

$(1+0)[0.3p(1) + 0.2(1)] + 0.1w = p(1); 0.3p(1) + 0.2 + 0.1w = p(1)$
$(1+0)[0.2p(1) + 0.4(1)] + 0.2w = 1; 0.2p(1) + 0.4 + 0.2w = 1$
$0.1w = 0.7p(1) - 0.2; w = 7p(1) - 2$
$0.2w = 0.6 - 0.2p(1); w = 3 - p(1)$
$7p(1) - 2 = w = 3 - p(1); 8p(1) = 5; p(1) = 5/8; p(1) = 0.625$
$w = 3 - p(1) = 3 - 0.625; w = 2.375$

(2) Suppose the actual conditions of class struggle are such that capitalists receive a 10% rate of profit. Again, with $p(2) = 1$, what will the wage rate be under these socio-economic conditions?

$(1 + 0.10)[0.3p(1) + 0.2(1)] + 0.1w = p(1)$
$(1 + 0.10)[0.2p(1) + 0.4(1)] + 0.2w = 1$

Solving these two equations as we did above yields: $p(1) = 0.649$ and $w = 2.086$.

(3) Suppose the actual conditions of class struggle are such that capitalists receive a 20% rate of profit. Again, with $p(2) = 1$, what will the wage rate be under these socio-economic conditions?

$(1 + 0.20)[0.3p(1) + 0.2(1)] + 0.1w = p(1)$
$(1 + 0.20)[0.2p(1) + 0.4(1)] + 0.2w = 1$

Solving these two equations as we did above yields: $p(1) = 0.658$ and $w = 1.811$.

The answers to the first three questions reveal an interesting relationship between the rate of profit and the wage rate in a capitalist economy. As the rate of profit rises from 0% to 10% to 20% the wage rate falls from 2.375 to 2.086 to 1.811 units of good 2 per hour.[7] Moreover, the change in r and w is not due to changes in the productivity of either "factor of production" since productive technology did not change in either industry. It is possible the fall in w (and consequent rise in r) was caused by an increase in the supply of labor making it less scarce relative to capital – which mainstream microeconomic models do recognize as a reason there would be a change in returns to the two "factors." But this is by no means the only reason wage rates fall and profit rates rise in capitalist economies. A decline in union membership, a decrease in worker solidarity, a change in workers' attitudes about how much they "deserve," or an increase in capitalist "monopoly power" leading to a higher "markup" over costs of production on goods workers buy are also reasons real wages fall and profit rates rise in capitalist economies. Political economy theories like the conflict theory of the firm explore how changes in the human characteristics of employees affect wage rates (and consequently profit rates), and how employer choices regarding technologies and reward structures affect their employees characteristics. Political economy theories like monopoly capital theory explore factors that influence the size of markups in different industries and the economy as a whole.

The answers to the first three questions also reveal something interesting about relative prices in a capitalist economy. As we changed from one possible combination of (r,w) to another – from (0, 2.375) to (0.10, 2.086) to (0.20, 1.811) – p(1), the price of good 1 relative to good 2, changed from 0.625 to 0.649 to 0.658 even though there were no changes in productive technologies (or consumer preferences for that matter). In other words, the relative prices of goods are *not* determined solely by preferences, technologies, and factor supplies. Relative prices are also the product of power relationships between capitalists and workers (and owners of natural resources in an extended version of the model).

Technical Change in the Sraffa Model

One of the conveniences of the Sraffa model is that it allows us to determine when capitalists will implement new technologies and when they will not, and what the long-run effects of their decisions on the economy will be.

---

7 This negative relationship between w and r holds in more sophisticated versions of the model and appears again in our long-run political economy macro model 9.5.

(4) Under the conditions of question 1, [r = 0%, w = 2.375, p(1) = 0.625, and p(2) = 1], suppose capitalists in sector 1 discover the following new capital-using but labor-saving technique:

a'(11) = 0.3
a'(21) = 0.3
L'(1) = 0.05

Will capitalists in sector 1 replace their old technique with this new one?

The new technique is capital using since a'(21) = 0.3 > 0.2 = a(21). But it is labor saving since L'(1) = 0.05 < 0.10 = L(1). The extra capital raises the private cost of making a unit of good 1 by: (0.3 − 0.2)p(2) or (0.3 − 0.2)(1) = 0.100. The labor savings lowers the private cost of making a unit of good 1 by: (0.1 − 0.05)w or (0.1 − 0.05)(2.375) = 0.119. Which means that when the rate of profit in the economy is zero and therefore w = 2.375, this new capital-using, labor-saving technology lowers the private cost of producing good 1 and would be adopted by profit maximizing capitalists in sector 1.

(5) Under the conditions in question 3, [r = 20%, w = 1.811, p(1) = 0.6579, and p(2) = 1], suppose capitalists in sector 1 discover the *same* new technique: Will they replace their old technique with this new one?

As before the extra capital raises the private cost of making a unit of good 1 by: (0.3 − 0.2)p(2), or (0.3 − 0.2)(1) = 0.100. But now the labor savings lowers the private cost of making a unit of good 1 by: (0.1 − 0.05)w, or (0.1 − 0.05)(1.8106) = 0.091. Which means the new technique now raises rather than lowers the private cost of making a unit of good 1, and would *not* be adopted by profit maximizing capitalists.

The model permits us to easily deduce what new technologies would be adopted by profit maximizing capitalists. And if a new technology is adopted we can use the model to calculate how the new technology will affect wages, profits, and prices in a very straightforward way – as we do below. But the answers to questions 4 and 5 above reveal a surprising conundrum worth considering before we proceed. The new technique either improves economic efficiency, and is therefore socially productive, or it does not. If it improves economic efficiency, capitalists in industry 1 serve the social interest by adopting it, as we discovered they would under the conditions stipulated in question 4. But then, capitalists will obstruct the social interest by *not* adopting the new, more efficient technique, as we discovered they will *not* under the conditions stipulated in question 5. On the other hand, if the new technique reduces economic efficiency, capitalists will serve the social interest by *not* adopting it, as we discovered they will *not* under the conditions stipulated in question 5, but will obstruct the social interest by adopting it, as we discovered they will under the conditions stipulated in question 4. In other words, no matter whether the new technique is or is not more efficient, capitalists will act contrary to the social interest in one of the two sets of socio-economic circumstances above!

Adam Smith actually envisioned *two* invisible hands, not one, at work in capitalist economies: One invisible hand promoted *static* efficiency, and the other one promoted *dynamic* efficiency. He not only hypothesized that the micro law of supply and demand would lead us to allocate scarce productive resources to the production of different goods and services efficiently at any point in time, he also believed that competition would drive capitalists to search for and implement new, socially productive technologies, thereby raising economic efficiency over time. Smith assumed that *all* new technology that reduced capitalists' costs of production – and *only* technologies that reduced capitalists' production costs – improved the economy's efficiency. We have just discovered that apparently Smith's second "invisible hand" is imperfect just like his first! In some circumstances capitalists will serve the social interest by adopting new technologies that lower their costs of production, but in some circumstances they will not. And in some circumstances capitalists will serve the social interest by rejecting new technologies that lower their costs of production, but in some circumstances they will not.

To sort out the logic of when the first invisible hand works, and when it does not, we needed to be able to identify the socially efficient level of output for any good. We used the efficiency criterion to do that: The socially efficient amount of anything to produce is the amount where the marginal social benefit of the last unit consumed is equal to the marginal social cost of the last unit produced. To sort out the logic of when the second invisible hand works, and when it does not, we need to be able to identify when a new production technology is efficient, or socially productive. The surplus approach proves remarkably adept at helping us identify when a new technology improves economic efficiency and is therefore socially productive, and when it reduces economic efficiency, and is therefore socially counterproductive. The only thing we care about in the simple economy in this model is how many hours of labor, in grand some total, it takes to get a unit of a good. There is only one primary input to "economize on" in the simple version of the model – labor. As long as labor is less pleasurable than leisure, being able to get a unit of a good with less work is socially productive. Whereas any new technology that meant we had to work more hours to get a unit of a good would be socially counterproductive.

It may seem like we have the answers ready made in $L(1)$ and $L(2)$. Since $L'(1)'$ < $L(1)$ and $L(2)$ does not change, it may appear that the new technique is obviously socially productive. But unfortunately $L(1)$ is *not* the amount of labor it takes to get a unit of good 1. L(1) is the number of hours of labor it takes to make a unit of good 1 *once you already have a(11) units of good 1 and a(21) units of good 2. But since it takes some labor to get a(11) units of good 1 and a(21) units of good 2, it takes more labor than L(1) to produce a unit of good 1.* We call L(1) the amount of labor it takes "directly" to get a unit of good 1 – once we have a(11) units of 1 and a(21) units of 2 for L(1) to work with. The amount of labor it took to get a(11) units of 1 and a(21) units of 2 is called the amount of labor needed "indirectly" to produce a unit of good 1. The total amount of labor it takes society to produce a unit of good 1 is the amount of labor necessary directly *and* indirectly. And while the new technique in question reduces direct labor needed to make a unit of good 1, i.e. is labor-saving, it unfortunately increases the amount of indirect labor it takes to make a unit of good 1, i.e. is capital-using.

Fortunately it is not terribly complicated to calculate the amount of labor, directly and indirectly necessary to produce a unit of good 1 and a unit of good 2. Let v(1) represent the total amount of labor needed directly and indirectly to make a unit of good 1, and v(2) represent the total amount of labor needed directly and indirectly to make a unit of good 2. Since v(i)a(ij) represents the amount of labor it takes to produce a(ij) units of good i we can write the following equations for the total amount of labor needed both directly and indirectly to make each good:

(3) $v(1) = v(1)a(11) + v(2)a(21) + L(1)$

Similarly for good 2:

(4) $v(2) = v(1)a(12) + v(2)a(22) + L(2)$

These are 2 equations in 2 unknowns, so v(1) and v(2) can be solved for as soon as we know the technology, or "recipe" for production in each industry. All we have to do is solve for the original v's, or "values," for the initial technologies – v(1) and v(2) – solve for the new values with the new technologies – v(1)' and v(2)' – and compare them. If v'(1) < v(1) and v'(2) < v (2) the new technology is socially productive. If v'(1) > v(1) and v'(2) > v(2) the new technology is socially counterproductive.[8]

8 It is obvious why the new technology for industry 1 will change v(1) since it changes L(1) and a(21). But why would v(2) also change? Even though there is no change in technology in industry 2, *since good 1 is an input used to produce good 2 and since v(1) will change, v(2) will also change.* This also resolves another potential concern. If the new technology lowers v(1) then it necessarily lowers v(2), whereas if it raises v(1) it necessarily raises v(2). So we will never face the dilemma that a new technology in one industry will lower v in one industry but raise v in others – and thereby make it impossible for us to conclude whether or not the technology was socially productive or counterproductive.

For the old technologies we write:

$$v(1) = 0.3v(1) + 0.2v(2) + 0.1$$
$$v(2) = 0.2v(1) + 0.4v(2) + 0.2$$

Which can be solved to give: $v(1) = 0.2632$ and $v(2) = 0.4211$.
For the new technologies we write:

$$v'(1) = 0.3v'(1) + 0.3v'(2) + 0.05$$
$$v'(2) = 0.2v'(1) + 0.4v'(2) + 0.2$$

Which can be solved to give: $v'(1) = 0.2500$ and $v'(2) = 0.4167$.

Since the new v's are smaller than the old v's the new technology is truly more efficient, or socially productive, because it lowers the amount we have to work to get a unit of either good to consume. Why is it capitalists will serve the social interest by adopting the new, more efficient technology when w = 2.375 and r = 0%, but obstruct the social interest by rejecting this technology that would make the economy more efficient when w = 1.811 and r = 20%?

To solve the puzzle we start with what we know: We now know the new technology made the economy more efficient. We know the new technology was capital-using and labor-saving. And we know capitalists in industry 1 embraced it when the wage rate was 2.375 (and the rate of profit was zero), but rejected it when the wage rate was 1.811 (and the rate of profit was 20%). The reason for the capitalists' seemingly contradictory behavior is clear: When the wage rate was higher the savings in labor costs because the new technology is labor-saving was greater – and great enough to outweigh the increase in non-labor costs because the new technology was capital-using. But when the wage rate was lower the savings in labor costs was less and no longer outweighed the increase in non-labor costs. Apparently the price signals [p(1), p(2), w, and r] in the economy in the first case led capitalists to make the socially productive choice to adopt the technology, whereas different price signals in the second case led capitalists to make the socially counterproductive choice to reject the technology.

No matter how efficient, or socially productive a new-capital using, labor-saving technology may be, it is clear that if the wage rate gets low enough (because the rate of profit gets high enough) the efficient technology will become cost-increasing, rather than cost-reducing, and capitalists will reject it. Similarly, no matter how inefficient, or socially counterproductive a new capital saving, labor-using technology may be, if the wage rate gets low enough (because the rate of profit gets high enough) the inefficient technology will become cost-reducing, rather than cost-increasing, and capitalist will embrace it.[9] In other words, Adam Smith's second invisible hand works perfectly when the rate of profit is zero but cannot be relied on when the rate of profit is greater than zero. Moreover, as the rate of profit rises from zero (and consequently the wage rate falls), the likelihood that socially efficient capital-using, labor-saving technologies will be rejected, and the likelihood that socially counterproductive capital-saving, labor-using technologies will be adopted by profit maximizing capitalists increases.

Technical Change and the Rate of Profit

In any case, clearly it is cost-reducing technological changes that capitalist will adopt – whether they be capital-using and labor-saving or capital-saving and labor-saving, and whether they be socially productive or counterproductive. Can we conclude anything definitive about the effect of any cost-reducing technical change on the rate of profit? Marx hypothesized that capitalist development would tend to introduce capital-using, labor-saving changes more often than capital-saving, labor-using changes. Since Marx's labor theory of value led him to believe that a capitalist's profits came only from exploiting the amount of "living labor" he hired, and not from exploiting his non-labor inputs, i.e. the "dead labor" he used, this led Marx to believe there would be a tendency for the rate of profit to fall in capitalist economies in the long run. In other words, Marx reasoned that if the ratio of living to dead labor tended to shrink, capitalists' rate of profit would eventually shrink as well. For over a hundred years some Marxist political economists searched for evidence of this phenomenon in real world capitalist economies, often thinking the tendency had finally manifested itself when a new crisis hit and profit rates sank. But in 1961 a Japanese political economist, Nobuo Okishio, published a theorem proving that if the wage rate did not fall, no cost-reducing technical change would lower the rate of profit. Instead, cost-reducing changes, *including capital-using, labor-saving changes*, would raise the rate of profit, or leave it unchanged – contrary to the expectations of generations of Marxist theorists. We can see these results even in our simple numerical example.

Let the economy be in the "equilibrium" described in question two, i.e. the rate of profit is 10%, and consequently the wage rate is 2.086, and $p(1)$ is 0.649 if $p(2) = 1$

---

9 For a proof that in a static Sraffa model *if and only* if the rate of profit is zero will there be a *one-to-one correspondence* between efficient, or socially productive, and cost reducing technological changes see theorem 4.9 in John Roemer, *Analytical Foundations of Marxian Economic Theory* (Cambridge University Press, 1981).

– as we calculated. Under these conditions the capital-using, labor-saving technical change in industry 1 we have been analyzing is cost-reducing, and will be adopted. Non-labor costs increase by: $(0.3-0.2)(1) = 0.1000$ as before, while labor costs decrease by $(0.1-0.05)(2.086) = 0.1043$, making the technology cost-reducing. The question is *not* if the capitalist in industry 1 who discovers the new technique will get a higher rate of profit than before right after she adopts it. Clearly she will since she was previously getting 10% and now will have lower costs than all her competitors, yet still receive the same price for her output as they and she did before, $p(1) = 0.649$. *Nor* is the question if all capitalists in industry 1 will receive a higher rate of profit if they copy the innovator as long as $p(1)$ holds steady at 0.649. Clearly, as long as prices and the wage rate stays the same, all those who implement the change will have lower costs per unit than before and therefore a higher rate of profit than before.

Instead, the question is what will happen to the rate of profit in the economy after capitalists from industry 2 move their investments to industry 1, because the profit rate is higher there, until the profit rates are once again the same in both industries? As long as $r(1) > r(2)$ capitalists will move from industry 2 to industry 1, thereby decreasing the supply of good 2 and driving $p(2)$ up, and increasing the supply of good 1 and driving $p(1)$ down until $r(1) = r(2) = r'$, the new, uniform rate of profit in the economy. We want to know if the *new uniform rate of profit* in the economy, r', under the *new equilibrium prices* will be higher or lower than the old rate of profit, r, assuming the real wage rate stays the same. To answer this question we simply substitute in the new technology for industry 1, set the wage rate equal to the old wage rate, $w = 2.086$, set $p(2) = 1$, as always, and solve for the new equilibrium price of good 1, $p'(1)$, and the new uniform rate of profit in the economy, r'.

$$(1+ r')[0.3p'(1) + 0.3(1)] + (0.05)(2.086) = p'(1)$$
$$(1 + r')[0.2p'(1) + 0.4(1)] + (0.2)(2.086) = 1$$

Solving these two equations in two unknowns yields $p'(1) = 0.644$ and $r' = 0.102$. So when the economy reaches its new equilibrium after the introduction of the cost-reducing new technology in industry 1, the price of good 1 relative to the price of good 2 is slightly *lower* ($0.644 < 0.649$) as we would expect since the cost-reducing change took place in industry 1, and the uniform rate of profit in the economy is slightly *higher* ($10.2\% > 10\%$). Since the change was capital-using and labor-saving this is contrary to Marx's prediction, but consistent with what Okishio proved would always be the case for any cost-reducing technical change as long as the real wage did not increase.

A Note of Caution

Microeconomic models are notorious for implicitly assuming all macroeconomic problems away. This means conclusions drawn from microeconomic models can be misleading when macroeconomic problems exist – which is the case with the Sraffa model of wage, price, and profit determination as well. Just because the rate of profit cannot go up unless the wage rate goes down in the Sraffa model as long as we hold technology constant does not mean this is always true in the real world. If an economy suffers from insufficient aggregate demand for goods and services leaving idle capacity, an increase in the wage rate which increases demand for goods and services and thereby increases capacity utilization can also revive profits, as both the short and long run macro models we study in Chapters 6 and 9 demonstrate. However, the simple Sraffa model does capture an important aspect of the relation between the wage rate and rate of profit: *If production and therefore income is held constant* (whether at full capacity levels, or below), the rate of profit and wage rate must be negatively related.

Producers and Parasites

The Sraffa model is a very useful framework for a number of "technical" reasons. It allows us to study a complex modern economy where we produce many different goods and services, and where many of the inputs we use in production processes are goods we must produce in other production processes. The simple "two good" model introduced here can easily be extended to as many goods as we want. It can also be generalized to include multiple *primary inputs*. The only input that is not produced in the simple model is labor. But in real economies there are other primary inputs beside labor which cannot be produced – raw materials we draw from the natural environment, such as fertile land and iron ore. Moreover, not all labor is equivalent. Sometimes we need a carpenter. But sometimes we need a welder, a computer programmer, a nurse, or a ditch digger. Unlike Marx's labor theory of value the Sraffa model can be easily generalized to include multiple primary inputs, including "heterogeneous" labor. In the general Sraffa model there will be wage rates for each category of labor as well as rental rates for every non-labor primary input. So no matter how many primary inputs, no matter how many different kinds of labor, and no matter how many goods and services, we can still use the Sraffa model to "explain" how wages, profits, rents, and prices are jointly determined and related to one another, and to analyze the effects of technical change.

But a more important advantage of the model is that it can teach us something very important about the essential nature of a modern economy – where the value of what we produce comes from, and therefore, who are producers and who are parasites. This is an issue economists have struggled to understand since Adam Smith first published *An Inquiry into the Nature and Causes of the Wealth of Nations* (underline added) – the actual title of his famous book. Following in the footsteps of Smith and other "classical" economists such as David Ricardo, Marx insisted that labor was the source of all "value" produced, and therefore all other classes must be parasites. Whereas neoclassical economists – following in the tradition of early "marginalists" such as Jevons, Walras, and Marshall – talk of the "marginal productivity" of different "factors of production," and conclude that when owners of a factor of production are paid its marginal product the payment is just and therefore "earned." No subject in economics has been more controversial, or more influenced by ideology and self-serving class interest.

What does the Sraffa model – or modern surplus approach – have to say on this subject? If a model could speak the Sraffa model would shout: "IT'S THE ECONOMY THAT'S PRODUCTIVE, STUPID!" In a modern economy multiple primary inputs are transformed by many different kinds of laboring activities into millions of different goods. If, after replacing all of the goods that were used up in this process, there is a physical surplus of various goods left over, then the economy was "productive."[10] What is it that makes the economy productive? It is the technologies that are symbolized in the Sraffa model by all of the a(ij)s and L(j)'s in all of the "recipes" for making all we make. And where did these recipes come from? They are what Joel Mokyr likened to "gifts of Athena"[11] from all generations who went before us, to all of us in the present generation. And whenever these a(ij)s and/

---

10 The issue of replacement of non-labor primary inputs used is admittedly thorny. By definition they cannot be produced, so how could they be replaced? And if they are not replaced, do we not deceive ourselves that our "surplus" is as large as it appears because we have not accounted for the fact that stocks of raw materials have been depleted? While we could not make this annoying problem go away when discussing sustainability and progress in Chapter 2, in the time honored tradition of economics when faced with a difficulty, we can make a convenient assumption here to allow us to move on: Let us assume for the moment that all the non-labor primary inputs are *renewable*, rather than non-renewable natural resources. For example, a forest grows every year, so that if we only harvest as many board-feet of timber from the forest as the forest grows every year, all we used has been effectively "replaced." So, for present purposes we will make the convenient assumptions that (1) all natural resources are renewable, and (2) we only use the amount of any non-labor primary input that "renews" each year.

11 Joel Mokyr, *The Gifts of Athena: Historical Origins of the Knowledge Economy* (Princeton University Press, 2003).

or L(j)s get smaller the economy becomes more productive, i.e. able to produce a larger surplus.[12]

But the economy is only *potentially* productive until we pick it up, so to speak, and work with it. Only when human beings put the productive potential of the economy to use by engaging in carpentry, welding, computer programming, nursing, and ditch digging labor do we actually produce a surplus of useful goods and services. So in this regard the modern surplus approach confirms the conclusion Marx came to a hundred and fifty years ago: The producers are the carpenters, welders, programmers, nurses, and ditch diggers; while those who don't work produce nothing, and therefore must be parasites if they receive any of the surplus produced by others.

What are we to make of a landowner who owns an acre of fertile land he rents out, or a capitalist who owns a shoe making machine he hires workers to work with? Neoclassical economists "predict" the landowner will receive rent equal to the size of the marginal product of his land and the capitalist will receive a quasi-rent equal to the marginal product of his machine, assuming land and machine markets are competitive. At this point most neoclassical economists do not hesitate to substitute the morally laden word "earn" for the neutral word "receive" with regard to rents and quasi-rents as long payments to their owners do not exceed the marginal product of the "factor of production" they own. But will the capitalist receive any profit in addition to her quasi-rent? According to neoclassical theory if all firms experience constant returns to scale, if all markets are competitive, and if there are no barriers to entry, in the long run profits should be reduced to zero on average, so any capitalist who receives a positive profit in the long run, above and beyond her quasi-rents, must be, like Yogi, smarter than the average bear and therefore deserve what they get.

Those of us who use the modern surplus approach see things quite differently. We do not dispute that the landowner and capitalist will receive payments. Nor do we dispute the fact that those who work would not be able to produce as much surplus without the land or machine. However:

12 In the general Sraffa system all of this information is contained in a matrix known as the "socio-technology matrix." It can be proved that if and only if the socio-technology matrix has a dominant eigenvalue less than one is the economy productive, i.e. capable of producing a physical surplus. It can also be proved that for a particular socio-technology matrix if and only if a technical change reduces the value of the dominant eigenvalue did the new technology make the economy more productive, i.e. capable of producing an even larger physical surplus of goods and services. The message, "It's the economy that's productive, stupid!" comes through loud and clear once we realize that a single number, the eigenvalue of the socio-technology matrix, summarizes how small the inputs have become, in general, to produce the outputs, and thereby tells us how productive the economy has become. See Robin Hahnel, *Income and Prices Distribution: Producers and Parasites*, forthcoming 2015.

(1) The Sraffa model makes clear that how much another acre of land or shoe making machine increases output depends not only on how fertile the acre or how well-designed the machine may be, but also on millions of other things – all of the a(ij)s and L(j)s that comprise the "gift of Athena" we all inherited – which *jointly* determine how productive the economy is.

(2) The Sraffa framework challenges neoclassical economists' prediction about how much landowners and capitalists will receive in the long run even if all firms experience constant returns to scale, all markets are competitive, and there are no barriers to entry. Whereas neoclassical theory predicts they will receive rents and quasi-rents equal to the marginal revenue product of fertile land and shoe making machines, provided land and machine markets are competitive, and zero profits on average in the long run, the Sraffa model predicts that depending on bargaining power there are many different possible combinations of rents, profit, and wages that are feasible in any given economy. According to the Sraffa model the productivity of the economy determines the size of the surplus available when labor is applied, and therefore what wages, rents, and profits can be in sum total; but how that surplus is divided is determined by the relative bargaining power of workers, landlords, and capitalists, which is in turn determined by a host of factors. So if the bargaining power of landowners, machine owners, and workers were high enough, capitalist profits might be zero, on average. But that would only happen if capitalists had no bargaining power whatsoever. Those of us who use the surplus approach believe that what is not only possible but far more likely is that profits will be positive, on average, in the long run even with constant returns to scale and under competitive conditions because capitalists are not powerless and therefore will appropriate part of the surplus produced, leaving rents and/or wages to be correspondingly less.

(3) Finally, political economists who use the Sraffa framework dispute the neoclassical interpretation that owners of natural resources "earn" their rents, and capitalists "earn" their quasi-rents and profits. In our view whenever profits are positive on average – which we insist they would be even in the long run with constant returns to scale under competitive conditions provided capitalists had not been rendered completely powerless *vis-à-vis* workers and resource owners – unless a capitalist joins in the human activity of working with the productive potential that is our common inheritance she has produced nothing. Which means her profit is *un*earned income, making her a parasite living off what those who do work produce. Similarly, even if rents and quasi-rents are not in excess of the marginal product of land and machines, unless

their owners work, *they* have produced nothing. So whatever they receive as rent or quasi-rent is also *un*earned income, making them parasites as well, living off the work of others.

But what do political economists say regarding the producers – the carpenters, welders, programmers, nurses, and ditch diggers? Unlike resource owners and capitalists they are clearly all producers, but are any of them also parasites, living off of others? This is where one must choose between maxim 2 and maxim 3 as discussed in Chapter 2. Are we going to try to measure whether some of the producers somehow produce more of the surplus than others, and judge whether wages are fair accordingly? Or are we instead going to try to measure differences in effort, or sacrifices among those engaged in a vast, cooperative division of labor and judge whether wages are fair on that basis? Readers already know why I believe the second approach makes more sense once we recognize that what is required is a *moral* argument for why some producers may deserve more than others.

6

Macroeconomics: Aggregate Demand as Leading Lady

Before the Great Depression of the 1930s there was only "economic theory." Thanks to the Great Depression and John Maynard Keynes we now have "microeconomics" *and* "macroeconomics." Economic theory bifurcated because some in the mainstream of the profession finally recognized that standard economic theory shed little light on either the cause or cure for the Great Depression. The old theory was relabeled "microeconomics" and preserved as the center piece of the traditional paradigm, and a new theory called macroeconomics was created to explain the causes and remedies for unemployment and inflation.

The leading lady in Keynes' new drama was *aggregate demand, the demand for all final goods and services in general.* By focusing on aggregate demand Keynes was able to explain why *the production of goods and services can fall,* why these economic "downturns," or *recessions,* can occur and become self-reinforcing, and what causes demand pull inflation as well. More importantly Keynes explained how government fiscal and monetary policies could be used to combat unemployment or inflation when these problems appear. Short-run macroeconomics can be understood using one new "law," one "truism," and simple theories of household consumption and business investment behavior.

The Macro "Law" of Supply and Demand

The new "law" is the macro law of supply and demand. It is the macro analogue of the micro law of supply and demand which is the key to understanding how markets for particular goods and services work. The macro law of supply and demand is the key to understanding how much goods and services in general the economy will produce, that is, whether we will employ our available resources fully and produce up to our potential, or we will have unemployed labor and factory capacity and consequently produce less than we are capable of. The macro law of supply and demand is also the key to understanding whether or not we will have inflation because the demand for goods and services in general exceeds the supply of goods and services the economy is capable of producing, resulting in excess demand which "pulls" up the prices of all goods and services.

The macro law of supply and demand says: *aggregate supply will follow aggregate demand if it can*. Aggregate supply is simply the supply of all final goods and services produced as a whole, or in the aggregate, which economists call gross domestic product, or GDP. It includes all the shirts and shoes produced, all the drill presses and conveyor belts produced, and all the MX missiles and swing sets for parks produced. Aggregate demand is the demand for all final goods and services as a whole. It includes the demand from all the **households** for shirts and shoes, the demand from all **businesses** for drill presses and conveyor belts, and the demand from every level of **government** for missiles and swings sets for parks. The rationale behind the macro law of supply and demand is as follows: The business sector is not clairvoyant and cannot know in advance what demand will be for their products. Of course individual businesses spend considerable time, energy, and money trying to estimate what the demand for their particular good or service will be, but in the end they produce what amounts to their best guess of what they will be able to sell. The business sector as a whole produces as much as they think they will be able to sell at prices they find acceptable. They don't produce more because they wouldn't want to produce goods and services they don't expect to be able to sell. And they don't produce less because this would mean foregoing profitable opportunities.

What if the business community is overly optimistic? That is, what will happen if the business sector produces more than it turns out they are able to sell? This does not mean that every business, or every industry is producing more than it can sell. No doubt some businesses, and maybe even entire industries, will have underestimated the demand for their product. But what if, on average, or as a whole, businesses overestimate what they will be able to sell? Most businesses will find they are selling less from the inventories in their warehouses than they are producing and therefore they are adding to inventories each month. While a business may decide this is a temporary aberration and continue at current levels of production for a time, if inventories continue to pile up in warehouses businesses will eventually cut back on production rates. When that occurs the supply of goods and services in the aggregate will fall to meet the lower level of aggregate demand – *aggregate supply will follow aggregate demand down.*

What if businesses are overly pessimistic? That is, what will happen if the business sector produces less than it turns out they are able to sell? They will discover their error soon enough because sales rates will be higher than production rates, and inventories in warehouses will be depleted. So even if they initially underestimate the demand for their products, businesses will increase production when they discover their error, and therefore production, or aggregate supply, will rise to meet aggregate demand – *aggregate supply will follow aggregate demand up.*

But there might be circumstances under which the business sector won't be able to increase production. What if all the productive resources in the economy are already fully and efficiently employed? In this case the increased labor and resources necessary for one business to increase its production would have to come from some other business where they were already employed, so the increased production of one business would be matched by a decrease in the production of some other business, and production as a whole, or aggregate supply could not increase. This is why the macro law of supply and demand says that aggregate supply will follow aggregate demand *if it can.* If the economy is producing the most it can, if it is already producing what we call potential, or full employment gross domestic product, aggregate supply will not be able to follow aggregate demand should the aggregate demand for goods and services exceed potential GDP.

Like the micro "law" of supply and demand, the macro "law" of supply and demand should be interpreted as the *usual* results of sensible choices people make in particular circumstances, rather than like the law of gravity that applies exactly to every mass in the presence of every gravitational force. The macro law of supply and demand derives from the common sense observation that, on average, when businesses find their inventories being depleted because sales are outstripping production they will increase production rates if they can; while if they find their inventories increasing because sales rates are less than production rates, they will decrease production.

Notice how this simple, common sense law provides powerful insights about what level of production an economy will settle on, and whether or not the labor, resources, and productive capacities of the economy will or will not be fully utilized. And notice how the answer to the question: "How much will we produce?" is not necessarily: "As much as we can." If the demand for goods and services in the aggregate is equal to potential GDP, then when aggregate supply follows aggregate demand we will indeed produce up to our capability. But if aggregate demand is less than potential GDP then, when aggregate supply follows aggregate demand, production will be less than the amount we are capable of producing, and consequently, there will be unemployed labor and resources, and idle productive capacity. This does not happen because the business community wants to produce less than it can. It is because it is not in their interests to produce more than they can sell. And while it is true that the owners of the businesses in a capitalist economy are the ones who decide how much we will produce, there is no point in blaming them for lack of economic patriotism when they decide to produce less than we are capable of, because any "patriotic" business that persisted in producing more than it could sell would be rewarded by being competed out of business by less "gung-ho" competitors.

The size and skill level of the labor force, the amount of resources and productive capacity we have, and the level of productive knowledge we have achieved, determine what we **can** *produce.* We call this level of output *potential,* or *full employment* **GDP.** But whether or not we *will* produce up to our capacities depends on whether there is sufficient aggregate demand for goods and services to induce businesses to employ all the productive resources available. If they have good reason to think they wouldn't be able to sell all they could produce, they won't produce it, and actual GDP will fall short of potential GDP. Any changes in the size or skill of the labor force, quantity or quality of productive resources, size or quality of the capital stock, or state of productive knowledge will change the amount of goods and services we *can* produce, i.e. the level of potential GDP. But what will determine the amount we *will* produce is the level of aggregate demand, and only changes in aggregate demand will lead to changes in what we *do* produce.

In sum: If aggregate demand is equal to potential GDP, actual GDP will become equal to potential GDP. But if aggregate demand is less than potential GDP, actual GDP will be equal to the level of aggregate demand and less than potential GDP. If aggregate demand is greater than potential GDP businesses will try to increase production levels to take advantage of favorable sales opportunities. But once the economy has reached potential GDP, as much as businesses might want to increase production further, as a whole they won't be able to. Instead, frustrated employers will try to outbid one another for fewer employees and resources than there is demand for – pulling up wages and resource prices. And frustrated consumers will try to outbid one another for fewer final goods and services than there is demand for, pulling up prices in what we call **demand pull inflation** – *a rise in the general level of prices caused by demand for goods and services in excess of the maximum level of production we are capable of.*

Aggregate Demand

Aggregate demand, AD, is composed of the consumption demand of all the households in the economy, or what we call aggregate, or *private consumption,* C, the demand for investment, or capital goods by all businesses in the economy, or what we call *investment demand*, I, and the demand for public goods and services by local, state, and federal governments, or what we loosely call *government spending*, G.

One of Keynes' greatest insights was that the forces determining the level of consumer, business, and government demand are substantially independent from the forces determining the level of production or output. He also pointed out that, even though businesses would try to adjust to discrepancies between aggregate demand and supply when they arose, in addition to the *equilibrating* forces described in the micro law of supply and demand, *disequilibrating* forces could operate in the economy as well. In particular, Keynes pointed out that weak demand for goods and services leading to downward pressure on wages and layoffs was likely to further weaken aggregate demand by reducing the buying power of the majority of consumers. He pointed out that this would in turn lead to more downward pressure on wages and more layoffs, which would reduce the demand for goods even further. The logical result was a downward spiral in which aggregate demand, and therefore production, moved farther and farther away from potential GDP. Keynes ridiculed his contemporaries' faith that excess supply of labor during the depression would prove self-eliminating as wages fell. He quipped that no matter how cheap employees became, employers were not likely to hire workers when they had no reason to believe they could sell the goods those workers would make. Keynes pointed out that the demand-reducing effect of falling wages on employment could outweigh the cost-reducing effect of lower labor costs on employment – particularly during a recession when finding buyers, not lowering production costs, is the chief concern of businesses. As a result Keynes rejected the complacency of his colleagues in face of high and rising levels of unemployment during the Great Depression based on what he considered to be their unwarranted faith that (1) demand *should* be sufficient to buy full employment levels of output, and (2) unemployment *should* be eliminated by falling wages.

If ever we needed an example of humans unlearning something we once labored hard to understand, we need look no farther than the sorry transformation of macroeconomic theory over the past thirty years. In the most famous economic book of the twentieth century, *The General Theory of Employment, Interest, and Money*, published at the height of the Great Depression in 1936, Keynes not only explained the causes of the Great Depression where his predecessors had failed to do so, he also explained what governments could do to reverse the downward spiral of too little demand for goods and services leading to layoffs, leading in turn to even less demand for goods and services, leading to more layoffs, etc. Challenging pre-1930 economic orthodoxy, Keynes preached that the government can increase aggregate demand directly by increasing its own demand for public goods and services, G, and/or induce an increase in consumer demand by reducing their taxes; and that monetary authorities can induce businesses to increase investment demand, I, by increasing the money supply to reduce interest rates, and thereby reduce the cost of financing investment projects. Focusing on the macro law of supply and demand and how to use fiscal and monetary policy to correct for undesirable levels of aggregate demand was the core of the Keynesian "revolution." However, all this wisdom, which was incorporated into mainstream macroeconomic theory and validated empirically as it was applied by governments throughout the world with great success for four decades, suddenly fell "out of favor" among mainstream macroeconomists beginning in the 1980s. Ever more complicated and mathematically sophisticated macroeconomic models whose intricacies PhD students were required to master in all the "top" economics departments became ever more divorced from reality. It is tempting to compare a macroeconomist trained in a mainstream program during the past few decades to an *idiot savant* whose impressive esoteric technical exploits are accompanied by a complete lack of basic understanding. The greatest economist of the twentieth century was literally purged from the macroeconomics curriculum before the century drew to a close. As we shall see, this has a great deal to do with why governments in Europe responded to the Great Recession with fiscal austerity rather than stimulus, and why fiscal stimulus fell victim to deficit reduction mania in the US, i.e. why governments have responded in the same counterproductive way to the Great Recession that Herbert Hoover did at the onset of the Great Depression eighty years earlier. A new generation of macroeconomists firmly in control of all the top departments were back to preaching the virtues of balancing budgets in any and all circumstances, just as Andrew Mellon as Treasury Secretary had preached to Herbert Hoover in 1930, leaving only a few grey beard "scolds" like Paul Krugman and Joseph Stiglitz, ostracized by the mainstream of the profession despite their Nobel prizes, to preach Keynes' wisdom when the crisis hit in 2008.

Consumption Demand

Keynes reasoned that the largest component of aggregate demand, household consumption, was determined for the most part by the size of the household sector's disposable, or after tax, income. He postulated that household consumption: (1) depended positively on disposable income, (2) that only part of any new or additional disposable income would be consumed because part of additional income would be saved, and (3) that even should disposable income sink to zero, consumption would be positive as people dipped into savings or borrowed against future income prospects to finance necessary consumption. No economic relationship has been more empirically tested and validated than the consumption income relationship. Countless "cross section studies" using data from samples of households with different levels of income and consumption in the same year, as well as "time series studies" using data for national income and aggregate consumption over a number of years in hundreds of different countries, all invariably confirm Keynes' bold hypothesis and intuition. The "consumption function" is far and away the most accurate indicator of economic behavior in the macroeconomist's arsenal. In its simplest, linear form: $C = a + MPC(Y - T)$ where C stands for aggregate consumption, Y stands for gross domestic income, GDI, T stands for taxes which are the part of income households can neither consume nor save since they are obligated to taxes, "a" is a positive number called "autonomous consumption" representing the amount the household sector would consume even if disposable income were zero, and MPC stands for the "marginal propensity to consume out of disposable income," that is, the fraction of each additional dollar in disposable income that will go into consumption rather than saving.

Investment Demand

The most volatile and difficult part of aggregate demand to predict is investment demand. First, note that in short-run macro models investment is treated as part of the aggregate demand for goods and services because what happens when businesses decide to undertake an investment project is they *first* must buy the machinery and equipment necessary to carry it out. That is, the first effect of investment is to increase the demand for what we call capital or investment goods. This is not to say that the *purpose* of investment is not to increase the ability of businesses to produce more goods and services. But while investment increases potential GDP, and may lead to an increase in the actual supply of goods and services in the future, its immediate effect is to increase the demand for investment goods. Second, Keynes himself had a very eclectic theory of investment behavior emphasizing the importance of psychological factors on business expectations and the rate of change of output as an indicator of future demand conditions. Moreover, political economists emphasize the importance of the rate of profit and capacity utilization in determining the level of investment as we will see in the long-run political economy macro model 9.5. But a simple relationship between investment demand and the rate of interest in the economy is sufficient to understand the logic of monetary policy, and all we need at present.

Businesses divide their after tax profits between **dividends**, *paid to stockholders*, and **retained earnings**, *income available for the corporation to use as it sees fit.* If a business wants to finance an investment project they generally use retained earnings first. But often retained earnings are not sufficient to finance a major investment project, and therefore a business must borrow money to add to its retained earnings to purchase all the investment goods a major project requires. A company can borrow from a bank or from the public by selling corporate bonds, but no matter how it decides to borrow it will have to pay interest. If interest rates in the economy are high, the cost of borrowing will be high. When the cost of borrowing is high the rate of return on an investment project will have to be high to warrant undertaking it given the high cost of borrowing required to finance the project. Presumably fewer investment projects will have this high rate of return, and therefore businesses will want to undertake fewer investment projects when interest rates in the economy are high.[1] We can express this negative relation between the rate of interest and investment demand most simply in a linear function such as: $I = b - 1000r$, where I is investment demand measured in billions of dollars, b is the amount of investment the business sector would undertake if the real rate of interest in the economy were zero, and r is the real rate of interest in the economy expressed as a decimal. While primitive, this investment function is sufficient to illustrate the logic of monetary policy we explore in Chapter 7. It says that whenever interest rates rise by 1% investment demand will fall by $10 billion, and whenever interest rates fall by 1% investment demand will increase by $10 billion.

Government Spending

If we ignore the foreign sector for the moment, the only other source of demand for final goods and services besides the household and business sectors is the government sector. We call the final goods and services demanded by national, state, and local governments G. While most state and local governments face restrictions on whether or not they can run a deficit, it is possible for the federal government to plan to spend either more or less than it collects in taxes.[2] *If the government spends less*

---

1 Even if a company can finance the entire investment project out of retained earnings, the opportunity cost of the project is high when interest rates are high because retained earnings could be deposited instead in a savings account paying a high rate of interest. So whether a company borrows or finances an investment project entirely out of retained earnings, it is less likely to undertake the project when interest rates are high, and more likely to invest when interest rates are low.

2 There are two easy ways to remind yourself that the Federal Government *can* spend more than it collects in taxes: First, it did so, in fact, every year from 1970 until 1998, and has resumed doing so again. Second, were it not possible for the government to spend more than it collects, politicians and economists would not bother debating the wisdom of passing a "balanced budget amendment" to the Constitution outlawing such behavior!

than it collects in taxes we say the government is running a **budget surplus**. If it *spends more* we say it is running a **budget deficit**. And *if it spends exactly as much as it collects in taxes* during a year we say the **budget is balanced**. Any individual or business can spend more than its income in a year if it can convince someone to lend it additional money, and the government can spend more than it collects in taxes by borrowing as well. The Federal Government usually borrows directly from the citizenry by selling treasury bonds to the general public.

So aggregate demand, AD, will be the sum of household consumption demand, C, business investment demand, I, and government spending, G – all measured in billions of dollars. Household consumption will be determined by household income and personal taxes. Business investment will be determined by interest rates in the economy, among other things we ignore for the time being. And the government can decide to spend whatever it wants independently of how much taxes it decides to collect, since the government can always run a surplus, and can finance deficits by selling treasury bonds. If AD ends up higher than current levels of production there will be excess demand for goods and services and businesses will try to increase production – successfully if current production is below potential GDP, but unsuccessfully if current production is already equal to potential GDP, in which case the excess demand will lead to demand pull inflation. If aggregate demand is below current levels of production there will be excess supply, businesses will reduce production to avoid accumulating unsellable inventories, and the economy will produce less than its potential and fail to employ all its productive resources.

The Pie Principle

One piece of the puzzle is still missing. How much income will there be in the economy? Just as we have to know the rate of interest before we can determine investment demand, we have to know the level of income before we can determine consumption demand. We can wait to see how interest rates are determined in Chapter 7 when we study money, banks, and monetary policy. But we cannot wait any longer to know what income will be if we want to know what GDP will become in the economy. The answer is given by a simple truism I call **the pie principle**: *The size of the pie we can eat is equal to the size of the pie we baked.* If we produced X billion dollars' worth of goods and services during the year, then we have X billion dollars' worth of goods and services available to use – not a dollar more nor a dollar less. Income is just a name for the right to use goods and services. So if we produced X billion dollars of goods and services, i.e. if gross domestic product or GDP is X billion dollars, then we also distributed X billion dollars of income to the actors in the economy, all told, i.e. gross domestic income or GDI is exactly X billion dollars as well.

This truism is easiest to see if we pretend for a moment the economy only produces one kind of good. Suppose we produce only shmoos – which we eat, wear, live in, and use (like machines) to produce more shmoos. If a shmoo factory produces 100 shmoos what can happen to them? Some will be used to pay the workers' wages. And those that are left over will belong to the factory owners as profits. How much did our shmoo factory contribute to gross domestic product? 100 shmoos. How much income was generated and distributed at the same time by our shmoo factory? 100 shmoos no matter how that income was divided between wages and profits. Suppose the workers were powerful and succeeded in getting paid 95 shmoos in wages. Then profits would be $100 - 95 = 5$ shmoos. Wages, 95 shmoos, plus profits, 5 shmoos, add up to $95 + 5 = 100$ shmoos of total income. On the other hand, suppose employers were powerful and only paid out 60 shmoos in wages. Then employers' profits would be $100 - 60 = 40$ shmoos. And wages, 60 shmoos, plus profits, 40 shmoos, add up to $60 + 40 = 100$ shmoos of total income again. The sum of the workers' wages and owners' profits cannot exceed 100 shmoos, nor can it be less than 100 shmoos. Since the same will hold for every shmoo factory, gross domestic product, measured in shmoos, and gross domestic income, measured in shmoos, have to be the same in an economy producing one good.

This conclusion extends to an economy that produces many different goods and services where we use some kind of money, like the dollar, to measure both the value of all the goods and services produced and the value of all the income generated and distributed in the process. The level of income in the economy will always be equal to the value of goods and services produced in the economy because the size of the pie we can eat is always equal to the size of the pie we baked. Which is why we don't need two different symbols for GDP and GDI in our model and equations. We can use the letter Y to stand for the value of all final goods and services produced, GDP, *and* for the value of all income paid out, GDI, since they always have the same value.

The Simple Keynesian Closed Economy Macro Model

We are ready to summarize our simple Keynesian macro model of an economy "closed off" from international trade and investment with the following equations:

(1) $Y = C + I + G$; (2) $C = a + MPC(Y - T)$; (3) $I = b - 1000r$; (4) $G = G^*$; (5) $T = T^*$

Equations 4 and 5 simply state what the chosen levels of government spending and tax collection are, allowing for the fact that they need not be equal to one another. Equation (3) tells us what investment demand will be depending on the interest rate in the economy. Equation (2) tells us what household consumption demand will be depending on income and taxes. And equation (1) is what we call the macroeconomic equilibrium condition. The Y on the left side of (1) is interpreted as GDP, or the aggregate supply of goods and services. The right side of equation (1) is the sum of private consumption demand, investment demand, and government demand, i.e. the total, or aggregate demand we will have in the economy. So equation (1) says that Aggregate Supply, AS, equals aggregate demand, AD.

The macro law of supply and demand says that the business sector will increase or decrease production (aggregate supply) until it is equal to the level of aggregate demand – if it can. We define *equilibrium GDP*, or **Y(e)**, to be *the level of production at which aggregate supply* **would** *be equal to aggregate demand.* Depending on how great aggregate demand is, it may be possible for the business sector to produce equilibrium GDP or it may not be. If AD is less than or equal to potential GDP, which we now call Y(f) for "full employment GDP," it is possible for the economy to produce Y(e), and the macro law predicts that actual GDP will eventually become equal to Y(e). But if AD is greater than potential GDP actual production cannot equal Y(e) but must stop short at Y(f). However, we can still ask: How high *would* GDP have to be in order for aggregate supply to equal aggregate demand? And the answer, Y(e), has great significance because when the business sector produces all it can, Y(f), Y(e) − Y(f) will be the amount of excess demand for final goods and services in the economy giving us a measure of how much "demand pull" inflation to expect.

For any given r*, G*, and T* we can use the equations in our simple model to find the equilibrium level of GDP. All we do is substitute equations (2), (3), and (4) into equation (1). If we use equation (1) we have stipulated that AS = AD. Therefore the Y we calculate when we use equation (1) is Y(e). Moreover, even though Y represents production, or aggregate supply on the left side of the equation, and Y represents income in the expression for disposable income in the consumption function on the right side of the equation, the pie principle assures us that Y as production and Y as income must have the same value on both sides of the equation. Substituting we get:

$$Y(e) = a + MPC(Y(e) - T^*) + b - 1000r^* + G^*$$

Which is a single equation in a single unknown, Y(e). Multiplying MPC through the parenthesis gives:

$$Y(e) = a + MPCY(e) - MPCT^* + b - 1000r^* + G^*$$

Subtracting MPCY(e) from both sides of the equation gives:

$$Y(e) - MPCY(e) = a - MPCT^* + b - 1000r^* + G^*$$

Factoring Y(e) out of each term on the left side of the equation gives:

$$Y(e)(1 - MPC) = a - MPCT^* + b - 1000r^* + G^*$$

Dividing both sides of this equation by $(1 - MPC)$ gives a "solution" for Y(e):

$$Y(e) = [a - MPCT^* + b - 1000r^* + G^*]/(1 - MPC)$$

If we know a, MPC, T^*, b, r^* and G^* we can calculate Y(e). If Y(e) is less than potential GDP, the macro law of supply and demand tells us the economy will settle at a level of production less than potential GDP equal to Y(e). If Y(e) is greater than potential GDP the macro law tells us that the economy will produce up to potential GDP, or Y(f), but the supply of goods and services will still fall short of the demand so we will have demand pull inflation. If Y(e) = Y(f) we will have neither unemployed labor and resources nor demand pull inflation, and we will produce all we are capable of given our present level of resources and productive know-how.

So after "solving" for Y(e) we can compare it with potential GDP, Y(f), to see if we will have an unemployment problem, an inflation problem, or neither. *If Y(f) – Y(e) is positive,* we say we have an **unemployment gap** in the economy of that many billions of dollars. The size of the unemployment gap represents the value of the goods and services that we could have made but did not make because there wasn't sufficient demand for goods and services to warrant hiring all of the labor force and using all the available resources and productive capacity. Another way of interpreting the size of an unemployment gap is as the value of the goods and services that those unemployed workers and resources could have produced but didn't because they were unemployed. *If Y(f) – Y(e) is negative,* we have an **inflation gap** in the economy because the level of aggregate demand which is equal to Y(e) is that many billions of dollars greater than the maximum value of goods and services the economy is presently capable of producing, Y(f).[3]

Fiscal Policy

We are now ready to understand the logic of *fiscal policy* defined as *any changes in government spending and/or taxes*. The microeconomic perspective on fiscal policy is that because of the free rider problem the government must step in and provide public goods since otherwise the economy will produce and consume too few public goods relative to private goods. In this view, according to the efficiency criterion the government should buy an amount of each public good up to the point where the marginal social benefit of another unit, MSB, is equal to the marginal social cost of producing another unit, MSC. Then the government simply collects enough taxes to pay for the public goods the government buys and makes available to the citizenry. But the macroeconomic perspective focuses on the fact that government spending and taxation affect aggregate demand, and therefore, by changing spending or taxes the government can change the level of aggregate demand in the economy.

If the economy is suffering from an unemployment gap – if there are people willing and able to work who can't find jobs and we are therefore producing (and consuming) less than we could – by increasing G* the government could increase aggregate demand and thereby reduce the unemployment gap. Or, by reducing spending the government could decrease aggregate demand and reduce the size of any inflation gap in the economy. Changing taxes will also have a predictable effect on aggregate demand. If the government increases taxes disposable income will fall and household consumption demand will fall. This would be helpful if the economy is suffering from demand pull inflation. If the economy has an unemployment gap, reducing taxes would be helpful because it would increase households' disposable income and induce them to consume more, raising aggregate demand and equilibrium GDP.

---

3 Suppose $a = 90$, MPC $= 3/4$, $b = 200$, $r^* = 0.10$ (or 10%), $T^* = 40$, $G^* = 40$, and $Y(f) = 900$: $Y(e) = 90 + 3/4(Y(e) - 40) + 100 + 40$; $Y(e) - 3/4Y(e) = 90 - 30 + 100 + 40$; $1/4Y(e) = 200$; $Y(e) = 800$. The business sector will eventually produce $800 billion worth of goods and services. Since the economy is capable of producing $900 billion worth of goods and services $(Y(f) = 900)$ we will fall short of "baking" as big a pie as we could have by $100 billion. We will have unemployed labor and resources that *would* have produced an additional $100 billion *had* they been employed – but they won't be because aggregate demand is only $800 billion so that's all the business sector can sell. For what it's worth the government budget is balanced $(T^* - G^* = 40 - 40 = 0)$, but the economy is in a recession, only producing 800/900 $= 0.89$, or 89% of all it is capable of.

However, before proceeding to analyze the macroeconomic effects of three different fiscal policies – changing only G, changing only T, and changing G and T by the same amount in the same direction – we stop to ask why most economists before Keynes were unable to see something that seems so straightforward and simple in retrospect. And we pause to unravel something surprising about the workings of the economy – the *multiplier effect*.

The Fallacy of Say's Law

Despite objections raised by the likes of Thomas Malthus and Karl Marx, most economists prior to the "Keynesian revolution" labored under an illusion regarding the relation between the level of production of goods and services in general and demand for goods and services in general. The misconception that undermined the ability of most economists before Keynes to understand the macro law of supply and demand, and therefore to understand depressions, recessions, and unemployment, went under the name of "Say's law," named after the nineteenth-century French economist Jean-Baptiste Say. According to *Say's law*, *in the aggregate, supply creates its own demand* – exactly the opposite of what Keynes' macro law of supply and demand says. Moreover, Say's law implies there can never be insufficient demand for goods in general, and governments therefore need not concern themselves with recessions which should cure themselves.[4]

The rationale for Say's law was best explained by the famous British economist and banker David Ricardo. In a series of famous letters to a concerned friend, Robert Malthus, Ricardo explained there was no cause for alarm nor need for the government to do anything about a serious recession in Great Britain at the time. Ricardo began by explaining the pie principle to Malthus, namely that every dollar of goods produced generated exactly a dollar of income, or purchasing power. When Malthus pointed out that people generally saved part of their income, and therefore consumption demand must inevitably fall short of the value of goods produced, leading inevitably to recession, Ricardo responded that savings earned interest only if deposited in a bank, such as his, and that he, like all bankers, was always at great

---

4 Amazing as it may seem, modern "rational expectation macroeconomics" once again falls under the spell of Say's law, as agents formulate "rational expectations" about the necessity of future tax increases to pay for any government deficits today, thereby neutering fiscal stimulus in theory. The fact that fiscal stimulus continues to work in reality becomes an anomaly to be ignored or explained away by today's mainstream macroeconomists.

pains to lend those deposits to business borrowers since otherwise his bank could make no profits. Ricardo explained that his business loan customers borrowed in order to invest, i.e. buy investment or capital goods, which meant that whatever consumption goods households failed to buy because they saved was made up for by business investment demand for capital goods. As long as the interest rate was left free to equilibrate the credit market, Ricardo concluded that any shortfall in aggregate demand due to household savings would be made up for by an exactly equal amount of business investment demand.

Ricardo's explanation of Say's law was appealing, so appealing in fact that it persuaded generations of economists who subscribed to it. But it contains a fallacy that fell to Keynes to point out. While it is true that every dollar of production generates exactly a dollar of income, or *potential* purchasing power (the pie principle), it is not necessarily true that a dollar of income always generates a dollar of demand for goods and services *this year*. This is one of those situations where timing is everything. Aggregate demand can be less than income this year if all actors in the economy as a whole spend less than current income, saving and adding part of current income to their stock of wealth. Or, aggregate demand can be greater than income this year if actors on the whole use previous savings, or wealth, to spend more than their current income, or borrow against future income.

What deceived Ricardo (and many others) was that just because the supply of loans is equal to the demand for loans at the equilibrium rate of interest, this does not mean that business demand for investment goods will necessarily be equal to household savings. The easiest way to see this is to recognize that not all loans to businesses are used to buy investment, or capital goods. Sometimes business borrowers use borrowed funds to buy government bonds, or shares of stocks in other businesses. When they do this they are borrowing someone else's savings only to "save" in a different form. For example, at the time it was made, a loan to USX Steel Company in the early 1980s was the largest loan in US history. But USX didn't use a penny of the loan to buy new steel-making equipment to replace obsolete equipment in its US plants because USX had decided that producing more steel in the US was no longer profitable. Instead USX used the "borrowed savings" to buy a controlling interest in Marathon Oil Company. This was a wise business decision, no doubt appreciated by USX stockholders. But buying all those shares of stock in Marathon Oil did not add a single dollar to the aggregate demand for investment goods, nor therefore for goods and services in general. So even though the interest rate may have equilibrated the market for lending and borrowing in this case, that did not mean the savings of households who did not buy consumer goods was translated into spending on investment goods by business.

Because it was so firmly entrenched among his fellow economists, Keynes went to great lengths to explain the fallacy of Say's law in *The General Theory*. He never tired of explaining that while the interest rate may equilibrate the market for borrowing and lending, this does *not* necessarily equilibrate savings and investment, and thereby guarantee that in the aggregate, supply will create its own demand. A given value of production *does* generate an equal value of income. But *when* that income gets used to demand goods and services can make a great deal of difference. If less income is used to demand goods and services in a year than were produced in that year, aggregate demand will fall short of aggregate supply, and production will fall as the macro law of supply and demand teaches. If the sum total of household, business, and government demand is greater than production during a year, production will rise (if it can), as Keynes' macro law teaches. It is simply not true that however much businesses decide to produce, exactly that much aggregate demand will necessarily appear to buy it. In any given year there may be either more or less demand since opportunities exist for whole economies to save and dis-save for months, or years.

Income Expenditure Multipliers

Since G is part of aggregate demand one would think that if the government increased G by, say $10 billion, aggregate demand would increase by $10 billion. Or if the government decreased G by $10 billion, aggregate demand would fall by $10 billion. But surprisingly, this is not the case. If G increases by $10 billion, aggregate demand can increase by a *multiple* of $10 billion.

Let's see how it would happen. Suppose the government increases spending by buying $10 billion more stealth bombers from Northrop Grumman. Assuming aggregate demand were equal to aggregate supply in the first place, as soon as the government buys $10 billion worth of invisible bombers aggregate demand will be $10 billion larger than aggregate supply. But the macro law of supply and demand tells us that production, or supply, will rise to meet the new demand, i.e. Northrop Grumman will produce $10 billion more bombers. But because the size of the pie we can eat is equal to the size of the pie we baked, income, or GDI, will now be $10 billion bigger than it was initially. Northrop Grumman will pay out more wages to its employees who made the new bombers, and more dividends to its stockholders. And since households consume more when their income is higher according to our theory of consumption, household consumption demand will rise once income has risen. This is a second increase in aggregate demand, above and beyond the original increase in government spending. This second increase in aggregate demand will take the form of an increased demand for shirts and beer by Northrop Grumman employees, and for sail boats and champagne by Northrop Grumman stockholders, whereas the first increase in aggregate demand was an increased demand for stealth bombers. It is an *additional* increase in aggregate demand, induced by, but clearly different from, the initial increase in government spending.

How much will consumer demand increase? Since production and income have risen by $10 billion, according to our consumption function households will consume MPC times $10 billion more than before. If the MPC were 3/4, then household consumption would rise by (3/4)($10) billion or $7.5 billion. But once again, the economy is now out of equilibrium. When production rose by $10 billion to meet the new government demand for $10 billion new stealth bombers, we were back to where aggregate supply equaled aggregate demand. But now that consumer demand has risen by an additional $7.5 billion, aggregate demand is, once again, higher than aggregate supply. The macro law of supply and demand tells us that production will again rise to meet this demand, if it can. But when production of shirts, beer, sail boats and champagne rises by $7.5 billion to meet this new demand, income will rise by $7.5 billion as well. And when income rises by $7.5 billion, household consumption will rise by MPC times $7.5 billion, and production will have to rise a third time for aggregate supply to again equal aggregate demand.

This **multiplier** chain of events goes on forever, but each additional increase in aggregate demand, and induced increase in aggregate supply, is smaller than the last.[5] The government spending multiplier just described is: $10B + MPC($10B) + MPC^2($10B) + . . . which can be rewritten: $10B[1 + MPC + MPC^2 . . .] The multiplier chain in brackets will sum to less than infinity as long as the MPC is a positive fraction – which it is as long as people save any of their new income. In high school algebra one proves that $[1 + d + d^2 + . . .]$ is simply equal to $[1/(1 - d)]$ provided $0 < d < 1$, which means our multiplier chain, neatly sums to $[1/(1 - MPC)]$, and the overall increase in aggregate demand that would result from an initial increase of $10 billion in government spending is $10B[1/(1 - MPC)]$. For MPC = 3/4, $10B[1/(1 - (3/4))]$ = $10B[4] = $40B. In other words, when the government raises spending by $10

---

5 These multipliers are called *income expenditure multipliers* – although "expenditure-income multiplier" would make more sense. They are also sometimes called Keynesian multipliers. Infinitely long series of positive terms can add up to infinity. After all, each term is positive and there is an infinite number of these positive terms. But if the terms diminish in size sufficiently, even though there is an infinite number of them, the sum total need not be infinite. It can, instead, be some finite number. Our government spending multiplier chain is of this second kind. As long as MPC < 1 successive terms will shrink fast enough so the overall increase in aggregate demand from an increase in government spending is finite.

billion, aggregate demand eventually rises by a multiple of $10 billion, a multiple of 4 if MPC = 3/4.[6] Hardly what one would have guessed at first glance!

The *government spending multiplier* is a logical necessity of: (1) the macro law of supply and demand which says if aggregate demand increases then production, or aggregate supply, will rise to meet it if it can; (2) the fact that the size of the pie we can eat is always equal to the size of the pie we baked, so when production increases income will increase by exactly the same amount; and (3) our theory of consumption behavior that says when income rises household consumption demand will rise by a fraction, MPC, of the increase in income. Which leaves us with our first policy multiplier formula. If we let ΔY represent the change in equilibrium GDP, or Y(e), and ΔG represent the change in government spending, then: $\Delta Y = [1/(1-MPC)]\Delta G$ and the expression in brackets, $[1/(1-MPC)]$, is called the government spending multiplier. It is what we have to multiply any change in government spending by to find out what the overall change in aggregate demand, and therefore equilibrium GDP, will be.

If, instead of changing G, the government chose to change T by ΔT, this would lead to an initial change in consumption demand of $-MPC\Delta T$. But this initial change in consumption demand would unleash the same multiplier process unleashed by the above change in government spending. The macroeconomy is an "equal opportunity respondent" – reacting to all initial changes in aggregate demand in the same way, irrespective of the source or nature of the initial change. So the overall change in aggregate demand from a change in taxes, ΔT, would eventually be $[1/(1-MPC)]$ times $- MPC\Delta T$, or $\Delta Y = [-MPC/(1-MPC)]\Delta T$.

Finally, if the government did change both spending and taxes at the same time, and if it changed them both by the same amount and in the same direction so that $\Delta G = \Delta T$, the government would be changing both sides of the budget by the same amount, $\Delta BB = \Delta G = \Delta T$. Under these conditions when we add the initial and induced effects of the two changes together we get:

$$\Delta Y = [1(1-MPC)]\Delta BB + [-MPC(1-MPC)]\Delta BB = (\Delta BB - MPC\Delta BB]/$$
$$(1-MPC) = \Delta BB(1-MPC)/(1-MPC) = [1]\Delta BB$$

Which gives us the third "fiscal policy" multiplier: if G and T are changed by the same amount in the same direction, aggregate demand and therefore equilibrium GDP will be changed by one times the change in both sides of the government budget.

---

6 We are implicitly assuming that production can keep rising in response to the sequence of increases in demand, i.e. that we were below potential GDP.

So we have three fiscal policy "tools": change government spending alone, change tax collections alone, and change both spending and taxes by the same amount in the same direction. Any of the three fiscal policies can be used to increase aggregate demand to combat an unemployment gap, or decrease aggregate demand to combat an inflation gap. *Deflationary policies reduce aggregate demand and inflationary pressures.* **Expansionary policies** *increase aggregate demand and raise production closer to potential GDP,* i.e. increase the size of the pie we bake. Economists define **equivalent macroeconomic policies** as *policies that change aggregate demand, and therefore equilibrium GDP, by the same amount.* So by definition equivalent fiscal policies have the same effect on the size of the pie we will bake or on inflationary pressures. But while different equivalent fiscal policies change the size of the pie we bake by the same amount, they have different effects on how the pie is sliced, that is, *the proportion of output that goes to private consumption, the proportion that goes to public goods, and the proportion that goes to investment goods,* or what economists call the **composition of output**. When we increase G the share going to public goods, G/Y, increases, while the shares going to private consumption, C/Y, and investment, I/Y, both decrease. When we reduce taxes the share going to private consumption, C/Y, increases, while the shares going to public and investment goods decreases. If we increase G and T by the same amount the composition of output shifts much more dramatically in favor of public versus private consumption.

Different equivalent fiscal policies also have different effects on government budget deficits or surpluses. Of course when both sides of the budget are changed by the same amount in the same direction there is no change in the government budget deficit or surplus. However, if G is increased a budget deficit will be increased, and if T is decreased a budget deficit will be increased as well. However, because the government spending multiplier is larger than the tax multiplier, a tax cut will have to be larger than a spending increase to achieve the same overall increase in aggregate demand. This means that reducing an unemployment gap by cutting taxes aggravates a budget deficit more than increasing spending does – a "truth" anti-tax conservatives seldom mention.

So besides looking at *who* gets a tax cut or pays for a tax increase, or whether it is human welfare or corporate welfare programs that are being increased or cut, it is important to consider the effects of different equivalent fiscal policies on the composition of output and the budget deficit when deciding which fiscal policy tool to use. Different classes and interest groups have different interests in these regards and therefore fiscal policy is always about more than simply the most effective way to combat unemployment or inflation. After adding monetary policy to our model in Chapter 7 we use our simple macro model 9.3 in Chapter 9 to explore the controversies surrounding US government macroeconomic policy in the aftermath of the Great Recession.

Other Causes of Unemployment and Inflation

While the simple Keynesian macro model is helpful for understanding *demand pull inflation* and unemployment caused by insufficient aggregate demand for goods and services, commonly called *cyclical unemployment*, there are other kinds of unemployment and inflation the simple Keynesian model does not explain. Beside cyclical unemployment there is *structural unemployment* and *frictional unemployment*. Cyclical unemployment is caused when low aggregate demand for goods leads employers to provide fewer jobs than the number of people willing and able to work. Structural unemployment results when the skills and training of people in the labor force do not match the requirements of the jobs available. In the case of structural unemployment the problem is not too few jobs, but people who are suited to jobs that no longer exist but not to the ones now available. Changes in the international division of labor, rapid technical changes in methods of production, and educational systems that are slow to adapt to new economic conditions are the most important causes of structural unemployment. But even if there were a suitable job for every worker there would be some unemployment. Frictional unemployment is the result of the fact that people do not stay in the same job all their lives, and changing jobs takes time, so when we "take a picture" of the economy the photo will show some people without jobs because we have caught them moving from one job to another even when there are enough jobs for everyone and people's skills match job requirements perfectly.

From a policy perspective it is important to realize that increasing aggregate demand for goods, and thereby labor, adds jobs, but mostly jobs like the ones that already exist. If the unemployment is largely structural, expansionary macroeconomic policy may not put much of a dent in it while increasing inflationary pressures. Instead, changes in the educational system and retraining and relocation programs are called for to combat structural unemployment. The true level of frictional unemployment, or what is sometimes called the "natural rate of unemployment," can have important implications for policy. If unemployment is only frictional, there is no need or purpose for government intervention. Adding more jobs or training people to better fit the jobs we have will not reduce frictional unemployment that results from the simple fact that people change jobs from time to time. Conservative economists have argued that the rate of frictional unemployment in the US rose from

3–4% in the middle of the last century to 5–6% by the beginning of this century. If this were true, it would imply that strong policy intervention is not warranted until unemployment reaches 7% in today's economy, even though all conceded that intervention was called for when the unemployment rate reached 5% in the past. But why should the rate of frictional unemployment have changed? Are job search methods *less* efficient than before? Are people *less* anxious to start their new jobs than before? Conservatives allude to changes in the composition and motivations of the US labor force insinuating that new entrants into the labor force – primarily women and minorities – have characteristics that lead them to have higher rates of frictional unemployment. But there is little scientific evidence to support the conservative claim which reduces to little more than prejudice and a strong wish to curb government initiatives aimed at reducing unemployment.

The important point is that employers benefit from unemployment. Employer bargaining power *vis-à-vis* their employees over wages, effort levels, and working conditions is enhanced when the unemployment rate is higher and there are more people willing and able to replace those working. Since capitalism relies on fear and greed as its primary means of motivation, a permanently low level of unemployment would reduce employees' fear and thereby pose serious motivational and distributional problems for employers. So it is hardly surprising that there is a "market" for economists who invent rationales to convince the government and the public to accept higher levels of unemployment as unavoidable. There is little more than this to the academic "debate" over changes in the "natural rate of unemployment."

There are also other causes of inflation beside excess demand for goods and services in general. Along with demand pull the most important kind of inflation is *cost push*. Imagine the following scenario. Employers and employees sit down to negotiate wage increases. At current price levels, employees need a 10% wage increase to get 80% of the value added in the production process – which let us assume is the least they think they deserve. Initially, employers resist these demands because they believe they deserve at least 30% of value added which cannot be achieved at current prices if wages rise at all. But faced with potential losses from a strike, employers finally agree to the 10% wage increase, only to turn around and "trump" the workers' play by raising prices 10%. Now that both wages and prices have risen by 10% the distribution of output is exactly what it was initially – 30% to the employers and 70% to the workers. Of course the workers cry "foul" and demand another 10% wage increase "to keep pace with the 10% inflation." If employers give in, only to increase prices again, we have a "wage-price spiral" and inflation as well. Notice that the cause of this inflation is not excess aggregate demand. The cause is an unresolved difference of opinion between employers and employees over who deserves what part of output that plays out in a way that causes wages and prices to spiral upward. Whether we call this "cost push inflation" – wages and profit "costs" are "pushing" prices up – "wage push" or we call it "profit push" depends on whose view we agree with regarding the distribution of output. If one agrees with labor that workers deserve 80% of output and employers only 20% the process would logically be called "profit push inflation" since the problem is obviously that employers keep trying to get more than they deserve by raising prices and voiding a non-inflationary and just settlement. If one agreed that owners deserved 30% and therefore workers only deserved 70% of output, the process would logically be called "wage push inflation" since the problem is that workers disrupt a non-inflationary, just settlement by insisting on a 10% raise.[7]

It is important to note that structural unemployment can exist in the presence of adequate aggregate demand for goods and services, and cost push inflation can exist even when aggregate demand does not exceed aggregate supply. There is no doubt that an increasing tendency toward **stagflation** – defined as *simultaneously increasing rates of unemployment and inflation* – plagued the US economy from the mid-1970s through the mid-1980s. Unlike today, when our simple Keynesian macro model very nicely explains both the cause of the Great Recession as well as why ill-conceived government policy has failed to overcome continued stagnation, our model does *not* help us understand how stagflation is possible. According to the simple Keynesian model the economy has *either* an unemployment gap, *or* an inflation gap, or neither. It cannot simultaneously have both too little aggregate demand – yielding cyclical unemployment – *and* too much aggregate demand – yielding demand pull inflation. Many anxious to dismiss Keynes and bury his wisdom six feet under seized on this failure to spread the unwarranted conclusion that "Keynes was wrong" – that a period of roughly ten years when the US economy suffered from stagflation had "proved Keynes wrong" – when it does nothing of the kind. Demand pull inflation can coexist with rising structural unemployment. And cyclical unemployment can coexist with increasing cost push inflation. An analysis that incorporates cost-push inflation and structural unemployment along with Keynes' insights about cyclical unemployment and demand pull inflation provides a perfectly sensible explanation for the stagflation that once plagued the US economy.

---

7 Mainstream economists try to label inflation "wage push" or "profit push" based on whether wages or prices rose first. But arguing over who hit who first is usually a pointless way to settle an ongoing conflict. More logically, it comes down to who one thinks has "right" on their side in the underlying disagreement.

The fact that the simplest Keynesian model fails to explain everything says nothing about whether it explains some important dynamics and issues brilliantly – which it does.

Myths about Inflation

Most Americans think inflation is bad for everyone while unemployment is bad only for the unemployed. In reality, the reverse is more the case – unemployment hurts us all and inflation hurts some but helps others. *Okun's law estimates that every 1% increase in the US unemployment rate reduces real output by 2%.* That is, the pie we all have to eat shrinks by 2% when 1% of the labor force loses their jobs. Moreover, a study prepared for the Joint Economic Committee of Congress in 1976 – back when someone still cared about such things – estimated that a 1% increase in the unemployment rate leads to, on average: 920 suicides, 648 homicides, 20,240 fatal heart attacks or strokes, 495 deaths from liver cirrhosis, 4227 admissions to mental hospitals and 3340 admissions to state prisons – each tragedy impacting a network of connected lives.

On the other hand, for every buyer "hurt" by paying a higher price due to inflation, there was necessarily a seller who must have been equally "helped" by receiving a higher price because of inflation. Moreover, we are all *both* sellers *and* buyers in market economies. How could you buy something unless you had already sold something else? But many people think of themselves only as buyers when they think about inflation, forgetting for example that they *sell* their labor, and therefore erroneously conclude that inflation necessarily hurts them – and everyone else whom they think of only as buyers.

This is how it really works: By definition *inflation means that prices are going up on average.* But in any inflation some prices will go up faster than others. If the prices of the things you buy are rising faster than the prices of the things you sell, you will be "hurt" by that kind of inflation. That is, your real buying power, or real income will fall. But if the prices of the things you sell are rising faster than the prices of the things you buy, your real income will increase. So for the most part, what inflation does is rob Peters to pay Pauls. That is, inflation redistributes real income.

I might object to inflation on grounds that it reduced *my* real income – that I happened to be one of the losers. More importantly, we might find inflation objectionable because those whose real income was reduced were groups we believe are deserving of having higher incomes, while those whose real incomes rose we consider less deserving. And this is often the case, because inflationary redistribution is essentially determined by changing relative bargaining power between actors in the economy. If corporations and the wealthy are becoming more powerful and employees and the poor are becoming less powerful, as has been the case for the most part over the past forty years, inflation will be one mechanism whereby the redistribution of real income becomes more inequitable. But this needn't be the case. Between 1971 and 1973 there was inflation in both the US and Chile. Yet wages rose faster than prices in Chile under the socialist government of Salvador Allende, while prices rose faster than wages in the US under Republican Richard Nixon. The redistributive effects of inflation *can* promote either greater equality or inequality.

Is the conclusion that inflation hurts us all then totally misguided? Not necessarily. We are all hurt whenever the production of real goods and services is less than it might otherwise have been. So if inflation makes the GDP pie we bake smaller than it would have been had there been less inflation, it would hurt us all – just like an increase in unemployment hurts us all. This can happen if inflation increases uncertainty about the terms of exchange to the point that businesses invest less and people work and produce less than they otherwise would have. When actors in the economy find inflation unpredictable and troubling this *can* happen. But to the extent that inflation is predictable and actors can therefore take it into account when they contract with one another there is little reason to believe it reduces real production and income.[8] On the other hand, if the government responds to fears of inflation with deflationary fiscal or monetary policy which does reduce production and output, the government reaction to inflation will "hurt us all." In sum, if the redistributive consequences of inflation aggravate inequities it is lamentable. Or, if inflation is so unpredictable and unsettling that real production falls it is a problem because it shrinks the pie we have to eat. Otherwise, most of us should think long and hard before joining corporations and the wealthy who put "the fight against inflation" at the top of their list of government priorities. The wealthy rationally fear that inflation can reduce the real value of their assets. And employers have an interest in prioritizing the fight against inflation over the fight against unemployment because periodic bouts of unemployment reduce labor's bargaining power regarding wages and working conditions. But when the rest of the American public enthusiastically joins the fight against inflation, it usually does so contrary to its own economic interests.

8 On the contrary, empirical studies overwhelmingly conclude that economic growth is positively correlated with mild inflation, which is understandable since mild inflation is indicative of robust aggregate demand keeping actual GDP close to potential GDP.

Myths about Deficits and the National Debt

Much popular thinking about federal government debt and deficits is based on the following analogy: "If I keep borrowing, going farther and farther into debt, I will eventually go bankrupt. Therefore, if the federal government keeps borrowing, i.e. running deficits, going farther and farther into debt, it will eventually go bankrupt too." But the analogy is false.

There is an important difference between the federal government and private citizens – or businesses and state and local governments for that matter. If anyone other than the federal government can't get someone to loan them more money, they cannot spend more than their income. But if the federal government's financial credibility bottoms out, and buyers in the market for new treasury bonds dry up, the federal government has one last resort. Unlike the rest of us who can be arrested and sent to jail for counterfeiting if we print up money to finance our deficits, the federal government could print up money in a pinch to pay for any spending in excess of tax revenues.

People in the know have long understood, even if the general public do not, that this is what a rational US government would do rather than fail to pay off treasury bonds when they came due, i.e. default on the national debt, since the disastrous consequences of a federal bankruptcy would be far worse than the inflationary effects of running the printing presses for a while. Which means that the "run the printing press option" never has to be exercised because there are always plenty of sophisticated big lenders willing to buy new bonds knowing that the US treasury would never default. But all this implicitly assumed that political sanity would prevail, i.e. that the US government would never choose to default even though it did not have to.

Debt ceilings, government shutdowns, furloughs, fiscal cliffs, and sequestration should all be understood for what they are – political insanity generated by partisan brinkmanship. The **debt ceiling** is a self-imposed limit on federal debt which began in 1917 as part of the Liberty Bond Act to finance World War I. The precise law governing the debt ceiling was modified in 1930, 1941, 1974, 1979, and 1995, but more importantly, whenever a self-imposed debt ceiling was reached Congress sensibly voted to raise the ceiling rather than leave the treasury unable to pay for spending authorized by a budget passed by Congress and signed by the President, or default on treasury bonds when they came due. However, in 1995, 2011, and 2013 a Republican-controlled House of Representatives turned the debt ceiling into a political football by refusing to raise it as the witching hour approached unless a Democratic President agreed to major political concessions. In 1995 federal employees were put on *unpaid furlough* and non-essential services were suspended for 27 days before the debt ceiling was raised. In 2011 the Government Accounting Office estimated that the delay in raising the debt ceiling had spooked investors enough to raise the government's borrowing costs by $1.3 billion in 2011 alone. Starting on December 31, 2012 the game of political chicken over debt and deficits forced the treasury to commence "extraordinary measures" to enable the continuing financing of the government. As part of the deal to end the previous debt ceiling crisis Democrats and Republicans passed the Budget Control Act of 2011 which stipulated that if the two sides could not agree on how to reduce the deficit by the end of 2012, commencing on January 1, 2013 there would be automatic, *across the board reductions in both defense and non-defense discretionary spending*, called **sequestration**, sufficient to prevent falling off the so-called fiscal cliff created by the Budget Control Act. In other words, *a self-imposed limit on the size of the budget deficit for fiscal year 2012–2013 – the fiscal cliff –* was added to the long-established self-imposed limit on the size of the national debt – the debt ceiling – thereby creating two witching hours and multiple opportunities to engage in political brinkmanship. Not surprisingly the game of chicken dragged on longer, with more twists and turns, more temporary postponements, leaving more self-inflicted damage in its wake. But however much all this has cost taxpayers in the form of higher interest payments on bonds because investors were spooked, and what amount to "late fees" for delayed payments of various sorts, so far the treasury has not failed to redeem any bonds when they came due, and *financial markets have continued to be willing to lend to the US government* so it can **rollover** the debt.

However, not all sovereign governments are as fortunate as the US government today which should always be able to find new buyers for its treasury bonds. Governments of small, less developed countries have long had to rely on foreigners to buy their bonds. These lenders are often not satisfied with domestic currency if it cannot be translated into foreign currencies, which means that holdings of gold or *foreign currency reserves* can become necessary for these governments to be able to roll over their debt. The US government was once such a government. In 1777 the Continental Congress had to secretly borrow $8 million from France and a quarter million from Spain to buy food, tents, guns, and ammunition for the Revolutionary Army since it could neither raise enough taxes nor convince US merchants to accept more Continental dollars. During the Civil War the Confederate Government was forced to resort to printing more and more confederate currency when they could no longer sell Confederate bonds – both of which became worthless when the South lost the war. But since the US has long been the world's largest economy foreigners are generally happy to hold dollars because there are plenty of US-made goods and assets one can use them to buy. Moreover, as the *international reserve currency*, US *dollars can also be used to buy goods or assets anywhere else.*

In any case, the national debt declined from a peak of almost 130% of GDP at the end of World War II to under 35% by 1980. But the Reagan era tax cuts and military spending increases raised the national debt from under 35% to over 75% of GDP between 1981 and 1991. This was totally unprecedented. Previously, the debt/GDP ratio had risen significantly only during major wars which caused government spending to increase dramatically, and during recessions or depressions when income and therefore tax revenues declined. The Reagan–Bush I era saw an unprecedented increase in the national debt during peace time and prosperity. It took nearly a century for the national debt to reach $1 trillion. Then the debt tripled in a mere decade in which there was neither war nor depression. The beneficiaries were the wealthy and corporations who saw their taxes cut dramatically, and the military industrial complex who fed at the Pentagon budget trough throughout the 1980s. Those who paid the consequences were the beneficiaries of social programs that were cut in the 1990s, and those whose taxes were increased to reduce the deficit from $290 billion in 1992 to $161 billion in 1995, to zero in 1998. The debt/GDP ratio declined throughout the two Clinton administrations, only to rise again for eight years during the two Bush II administrations despite economic prosperity. Obama has presided over the greatest recession since the Great Depression, during which the debt/GDP ratio climbed once again to over 100%.

However, it is important to remember who owns the debt. As of March 2013, 16% was owned by the two Social Security trust funds, 12% by the Federal Reserve Bank, 5% by the federal civil service retirement and disability fund, 3% by the military retirement fund, 1% by the Medicare hospital insurance fund, and another 4% by an assortment of federal government entities. In other words, the federal government owed 41% of the national debt . . . to itself! Another 3% was owned by state and local governments, meaning that governments in the US as a whole held 44% of the national debt. By 2013 the percentage owned by foreigners had risen from 22% in 1999 to 34% which means two-thirds of the national debt is still owed to ourselves. Moreover, the popular belief that "China now owns us" is highly exaggerated. As of 2013 China owned only 8% of outstanding US debt, which was only 1% more than Japan, and 4% less than was owned by the US Federal Reserve Bank.

The problem is *not* that the Federal government might go bankrupt, *nor* that we are hopelessly in hock to foreigners, or to China in particular. The problem is that interest payments on the debt can take up a lot of our tax dollars every year. In 1995 personal income taxes were $590 billion while net interest payments were $232 billion. In other words, before the government could buy *anything* with our tax dollars, it had to spend 40% of them simply to finance the debt. In 2000 interest payments on the national debt were 11% of all federal outlays while spending on *all* social programs was only 16%. With interest rates at historic lows over the past few years the debt service burden has eased somewhat, but the Great Recession has increased the debt substantially, so when interest rates rise again the debt burden "squeeze" on discretionary spending is likely to be worse than ever.

The problem is our ability to spend on social programs, and physical, human and community development is severely constrained not only by an absurdly unnecessary, obscene military budget,[9] but also by a debt service burden that is the legacy of the banquet Reagan, Bush I, and Bush II threw for their well-heeled supporters in the 1980s and 2000s but refused to pay for, and the Great Recession it led to. And the problem is that since the average bond holder is a lot wealthier than the average taxpayer, the escalating interest payments on the national debt are an increasingly regressive transfer of income from the have-less taxpayers to the have-more bond owners.

The Balanced Budget Ploy

In an op-ed piece published in the *Washington Post* on January 8, 1997 Robert Kuttner explained the "either/or budget fallacy" as follows:

How should the federal budget be balanced? By cutting aid to the poor? Or by reducing entitlements for the middle class? These, of course, are trick questions, since they leave out several options not on the menu: reducing defense spending; rejecting tax cuts which make budget-balance more difficult; cutting "corporate welfare," or not insisting on budget balance at all.

Ed Herman called it the balanced budget ploy: "The real aims of the push for a balanced budget are two-fold: to constrain macro-policy and prevent its use in ways that would increase pressures on the labor market . . . and to scale back the welfare state."

The Employment Act of 1946 and the Humphrey Hawkins Full Employment Act of 1978 nominally commit the federal government to whatever policies are necessary to provide jobs for all. And unlike the European Central Bank charter, the Federal Reserve Act directs US monetary authorities to conduct monetary policy

9 In 2012 US military spending was not only the highest of any government in the world, it was greater than the spending of the next ten governments combined!

so as to avoid *both* inflation *and* unemployment. Moreover, prior to the 1980s whenever unemployment rose above 5% public pressure mounted on the President, Congress, and the Federal Reserve Bank to fulfill these mandates by deploying fiscal and monetary policy tools to do something about it. However, efforts to make the President, Congress, and the Federal Reserve Bank responsible for guaranteeing Americans a right to a job were considerably watered down from the very beginning. Before they could be passed the guarantee of full employment had to be removed from the 1946 bill, and the goal of full employment in the 1978 bill was qualified as to be "consistent with price stability." So for many years Wall Street and the business community concentrated on fanning the public's irrational fear that the bonfires of inflation were about to consume the hard earned savings of us all as a means of rallying public pressure to oppose expansionary fiscal and monetary policy to reduce unemployment, and spending on social welfare programs in particular.

However, inflation has not actually been a serious problem in the US since the mid-1970s, as much as the usual suspects continue to insist that inflation is lurking around every corner. On the other hand, fiscally irresponsible tax cuts for the wealthy during the twenty years when Reagan, Bush I, and Bush II were in the White House, combined with excessive military spending by Republican and Democratic administrations alike from 1980 to the present, and most recently the Great Recession, have made it easier to stir up irrational fears about debt than inflation.[10] As a result the "balanced budget ploy" has become the favorite public relations tactic for those always in search of ways to convince the voting public to tolerate slashing programs like head start, food stamps, and social security even though polls consistently show voters overwhelmingly favor them. And if we judge by results "the budget must be balanced or we will go bankrupt" has been an even more effective rallying cry against expansionary fiscal policy than "inflation is going to eat your life savings." When politicians today wrap themselves in the patriotic banner of deficit reduction they are even less likely to be punished by discontented voters for presiding over a listless economy and draconian cuts to popular programs than when they used to march as crusaders against inflation.

The lines of interest are straightforward: Those who work for a living have greater bargaining power over wages and working conditions when the labor market is *tight*, because the more unemployed workers there are the more vulnerable are the employed. Employers, on the other hand, benefit from a *loose* labor market because they can find willing and capable workers more easily to use to threaten employees with replacement should they prove demanding. Similarly, the more humane and

---

10 For an amusing example of a typical deficit scare gimmick visit www.usdebtclock.org.

generous the welfare system, the more reasonable employers must be to induce people to work for them. When the "safety net" becomes less safe fear becomes a more powerful weapon in the hands of employers. This is not to say that employers do not suffer as well if a recession gets out of hand. Profits as well as wages took a hit when the Great Recession hit, although, as we saw in Chapter 2, profits rebounded quickly while wages have not. But in general employers have good reason to fear a successful application of Keynesian policies that stabilize the business cycle and keep labor markets permanently tight. Stabilization policies were particularly aggressive and successful in Sweden for thirty years after WWII, and labor's share of national income in Sweden rose steadily to a peak of 80% in 1976. In the US where opponents became more successful at obstructing active stabilization starting in the mid-1970s labor's share of national income has steadily declined.

For thirty years after WWII the ideological battle in the US was over prioritizing the fight against unemployment versus the fight against inflation, because, as we learned, demand management policies cannot battle one without aggravating the other. But now that inflation has not been a serious threat for more than a generation, the ideological battle has shifted to fighting joblessness versus balancing the budget. And those who fear tight labor markets have the ear of not only Republicans but "New Democrats" as well in the fight against budget deficits. While President Carter listened to the anti-inflation crusade out of one ear in the 1970s, President Clinton enlisted enthusiastically in the crusade to balance the budget in the 1990s, and with the economy still in the grip of the worst recession in over eighty years, President Obama made a crucial "pivot" from (too little) fiscal stimulus in 2009 to prioritizing deficit reduction in 2010. Obama collaborated with the usual suspects and used the Presidential bully pulpit to fan the flames of deficit mania when he should have been stumping tirelessly for a second stimulus which was clearly needed to speed recovery. He also appointed two austerity zealots, Erskine Bowles and Alan Simpson, as co-chairs of *his* National Commission on Fiscal Responsibility and Reform whose "findings" and recommendations have provided ammunition for Republican economic brinkmanship ever since. I suspect history will mark this ill-fated pivot as the defining moment of the Obama Presidency, since it guaranteed that a weak, sputtering, "jobless" recovery was the best that could be hoped for.

Wage-Led Growth

Mainstream macroeconomic theories invariably lead their users to expect a negative relationship between wage rates and the rate of economic growth in the long run. Even the few mainstream macroeconomists who still recommend aggressive expansionary fiscal and monetary policies to increase production in the short run see higher wage rates as an impediment to capital accumulation and therefore long-run economic growth. So how do political economists maintain that it is possible to choose a "high road" to higher rates of economic growth through higher wages, instead of the "low road" of increasing capital accumulation by suppressing wages?

Mainstream economists reason that wage increases in excess of labor productivity increases will squeeze profits and redistribute income from capital to labor. Since capitalists save more of their income than workers this will increase the proportion of output that goes to consumption, decrease the proportion available for accumulation, and thereby drive the growth rate down. Therefore, to increase growth mainstream economists argue we must increase capital accumulation by suppressing wages. Political economists like Michael Kalecki and Josef Steindl argued that even in the long run the relationship between wages and growth is complicated by demand considerations, and consequently that higher wages and higher growth rates are not necessarily at odds.

The rate of growth of actual GDP depends not only on the rate of growth of potential GDP but also on how close actual GDP is to potential GDP over the long run. If we hold technology constant, assume no increase in the size of the labor force, and assume no improvements in the *quality* of either capital or labor inputs, the rate of growth of potential GDP is determined entirely by the rate of capital accumulation. But for a given increase in the growth rate of *potential* GDP, the rate of growth of *actual* GDP will depend on the level of capacity utilization over the long run. For example, if potential GDP grows at 3%, but capacity utilization drops by 3%, actual GDP will not grow at all. Depressing wages, and thereby consumption, does leave more output available for capital accumulation, but by lowering the demand for goods and services it can also decrease capacity utilization. Kalecki pointed out that depressing wages may allow for greater capital accumulation, but it may also lead us to use less of the capital we have. He argued that if depressing wages lowered capacity utilization sufficiently it could lower the rate of growth of actual GDP even while increasing the rate of growth of potential GDP. Steindl pointed out that as corporations become larger and increase their monopoly power in the markets where they sell their goods to consumers, they can increase their "mark ups" over costs, raising prices and thereby diminishing the real wage. In other words, Steindl pointed out that real wages can be driven down when corporate power increases over consumers, not only when corporate power increases over workers.

In Chapter 9 we study a formal, political economy, long-run macro model 9.5 that captures the insights of Kalecki and Steindl, incorporates Keynes' insights about the effects of capacity utilization and the rate of profit on business investment demand, and allows class struggle as well as labor productivity to affect wage rates, as Marx insisted it would. Model 9.5 demonstrates how depressing wages can retard the rate of economic growth through its negative effect on long-run capacity utilization, and conversely why raising wages can increase the rate of economic growth through its positive effect on capacity utilization. In other words, the model demonstrates the logical possibility of "wage-led growth" even in the long run. In mainstream long-run models, where actual production is assumed always to be equal to potential output, there is a "zero sum game" between consumption and growth, and between the wage rate and profit rate. By allowing capacity utilization to vary the political economy model allows for "win-win" scenarios and "lose-lose" scenarios as well. Anything that increases capacity utilization over the long run will increase actual production and income over the long run as well. This makes it possible to have more consumption goods *and* more investment goods, and have a higher real wage rate *and* a higher rate of profit. Anything that decreases capacity utilization, output, and income means that *both* consumption and growth, and *both* the wage rate and profit rate may fall.

One of the distinguishing features of capitalism in the advanced economies over the last twenty years has been the dramatic increase in corporate power. At the same time, even before the recent disastrous crisis, we had witnessed lower rates of economic growth in the advanced economies than during the first thirty years after WWII. The work of political economists like Michael Kalecki and Josef Steindl exploring the effects of income distribution on aggregate demand, and incorporating Keynes' insights about the importance of aggregate demand into long-run models, provides a plausible explanation of declining growth rates in the advanced economies worthy of consideration: As corporations have increased their power *vis-à-vis* both their employees and their customers they have been able to keep real wages constant over the past thirty years even while productivity continued to grow. While this increased profits, making more potentially available for capital accumulation, it also prevented aggregate demand from increasing as fast as potential production and led to falling rates of capacity utilization and lower rates of economic growth. The work of Keynes, Kalecki, and Steindl and model 9.5 might also help explain how the Scandinavian economies could have had higher rates of economic growth than most other advanced economies during the middle third of the twentieth century *despite* higher tax rates and lower rates of technological innovation than many less successful advanced economies. Could it be that strong unions, high real wages, and high taxes to finance high levels of public spending, by keeping capacity utilization high, are not detrimental to long-run growth at all, but quite the opposite?

7

Money, Banks, and Finance

A bank is a place where they lend you an umbrella in fair weather and ask for it back when it begins to rain.

Robert Frost

It is ironic that money and banks top the list of economic subjects that most baffle students. Money is just a clever invention to save time, and bankers, contrary to their stodgy reputations, substitute bigamy for proper marriages between borrowers and lenders – with predictably disastrous consequences when both wives press their legal claims. Once the financial industry is understood for what it is, the Savings and Loan crisis of the 1980s, international financial crises of the 1990s, and the biggest global financial crisis since 1929, triggered when Lehman Brothers went bankrupt on September 15, 2008, are not difficult to understand. After which the logic of monetary policy and quantitative easing and tapering are easy to understand as well.

Money: A Problematic Convenience

It is possible to have exchange, or market economies, without money. A barter exchange economy is one in which people exchange one kind of good directly for another kind of good. For instance, I grow potatoes because my land is best suited to that crop. My neighbor grows carrots because her land is better for carrots. But if we both like our stew with potatoes *and* carrots, we can accomplish this through barter exchange. On Saturday I take some of my potatoes to town, she takes some of her carrots, and we exchange a certain number of pounds of potatoes for a certain number of pounds of carrots. No money is involved as goods are exchanged directly for other goods.

Notice that in barter exchange the act of supplying is inextricably linked to an equivalent act of demanding. I cannot supply potatoes in the farmers' market without simultaneously demanding carrots. And my neighbor cannot supply carrots without simultaneously demanding potatoes. Having learned how recessions and inflation can arise because aggregate demand is less or greater than aggregate supply, it is interesting to note that in a barter exchange economy these difficulties would not occur. If every act of supplying is simultaneously an act of demanding an equivalent value, then when we add up the value of all the goods and services supplied and demanded in a barter exchange economy they will always be exactly the same. No depressions or recessions. No demand pull inflation. It's enough to make one wonder who was the idiot who dreamed up the idea of money!

Sometimes ideas that seem good at the time turn out to cause more trouble than they're worth. Maybe finding some object that everyone agrees to accept in exchange for goods or services was just one of those lousy ideas that looked good until it was too late to do anything about it. But let's think more before jumping to conclusions. Barter exchange seemed to do the job well enough in the above example. But what if I want potatoes and carrots in my stew, as before, but my carrot growing neighbor wants carrots and onions in her stew, and my onion growing neighbor wants onions and potatoes in her stew? We would have to arrange some kind of three-cornered trade. I could not trade potatoes for carrots because my carrot-growing neighbor doesn't want potatoes. My carrot-growing neighbor could not trade carrots for onions because the onion grower doesn't want carrots. And the onion-growing neighbor could not trade her onions for my potatoes because I don't want onions. I could trade potatoes for onions which I don't really want – except to trade the onions for carrots. Or, my carrot-growing neighbor could trade carrots for potatoes she doesn't want – except to trade the potatoes for onions. Or, my onion-growing neighbor could trade onions for carrots she doesn't want – except to trade for potatoes. But arranging mutually beneficial deals obviously becomes more problematic when there are three goods, much less thousands.

There are two problems with barter exchange when there are more than two goods: (1) Not all the mutually beneficial, multiparty deals might be discovered – which would be a shame since it means people wouldn't always get to eat their stew the way they want it. And (2) even if a mutually beneficial multiparty deal is discovered and struck, the transaction costs in time, guarantees, and assurances might be considerable. Money eliminates both these problems. As long as all three of us agree to exchange vegetables for money there is no need to work out complicated three-cornered trades. Each of us simply sells our vegetable for money to whoever wants to buy it, and then uses the money we got to buy whatever we want.

Simple. No complicated contracts. No lawyers needed. But notice that now it *is* possible to supply without simultaneously demanding an equivalent value. When I sell my potatoes for money I have contributed to supply without contributing to demand. Of course, if I turn around and use all the money I got from selling my potatoes to buy carrots for my stew I will have contributed as much to demand as I did to supply when you consider the two transactions together. But money separates the acts of supplying and demanding making it *possible* to do one without doing the other. Suppose I come and sell my potatoes for money and then my six-year-old breaks his arm running around underneath the vegetable stands, I take him to the emergency room, and by the time we get back to the vegetable market it's closed. In this case I will have added to the supply in the Saturday vegetable market without adding to the demand. Nobody is seriously concerned about this problem in simple vegetable markets, but in large capitalist economies the fact that monetized exchange makes possible discrepancies between supply and demand in the aggregate can be problematic. Once a business has paid for inputs and hired labor they have every incentive to sell their product. But if the price they must settle for leaves a profit that is negative, unacceptable, or just disappointing, the business may well wait for better market conditions before purchasing more inputs and labor to produce again. The specter of workers anxious to work going without jobs because employers don't believe they will be able to sell what those workers would produce is a self-fulfilling prophesy that tens of millions of victims of the Great Depression, and now the Great Recession, can attest is no mere theoretical concern!

Banks: Bigamy Not a Proper Marriage

What if there were no banks? How would people who want to spend more than their income meet people who wish to spend less? How would businesses with profitable investment opportunities in excess of their retained earnings meet households willing to loan them their savings? If banks did not exist there would be sections in the classified advertisements in newspapers – or listings on ebay – titled "loan wanted" and "willing to loan." But matching would-be borrowers with would-be lenders is not a simple process. These ads might not be as titillating as personals, but they would have to go into details such as: "Want to lend $4,500 for three years with quarterly payments at 9.5% annual rate of interest to creditworthy customer – references required." And, "Want to borrow 2 million dollars to finance construction of eight, half million dollar homes on prime suburban land already purchased. Willing to pay 11% over thirty years. Well known developer with over fifty years of successful business activity in the area." But this entails two kinds of transaction costs. First, the creditworthiness of borrowers is not easy to determine. In particular, small lenders don't want to spend time checking on references of loan applicants. Second, not all mutually beneficial deals are between a single lender and borrower. Many mutually beneficial deals are multiparty swaps. Searching through ads to find all mutually beneficial, multiparty deals takes time – more than most people have – and guaranteeing the commitments and terms of multiparty deals takes time and legal expertise. One way to understand what banks do is to see them as "matchmakers" for borrowers and lenders. But it turns out they are more than efficient matchmakers who reduce transaction costs by informational economies of scale.

Perhaps banks could perform their service like the matchmaker in *Fiddler on the Roof* – collecting fees from the lender and borrower when they marry – but they don't. Banks don't introduce borrowers and lenders who then contract a "proper" marriage between themselves. Instead, banks engage in legalized bigamy. A bank "marries" its depositors – paying interest on deposits which depositors can redeem on demand. Then the bank "marries" its loan customers – who pay interest on loans which the bank can only redeem on specified future dates. But notice that if both the bank's "wives" insist on exercising their full legal rights, no bank would be able to fulfill its legal obligations! If depositors exercise their legal right to withdraw all their deposits, and if loan customers refuse to pay back their loans any faster than their loan contracts requires, every bank would be insolvent every day of the year. It is only because not all wives with whom banks engage in bigamy choose to simultaneously exercise their full legal rights that banks can get away with bigamy – and make a handsome profit for themselves in the process.

Many depositors assume when they deposit money in their checking account the bank simply puts their money into a safe, along with all the other deposits, where it sits until they choose to withdraw it. After all, unless it is all kept available there is no way the bank could give all depositors all their money back if they asked for it. But if that is what banks did they could never make any loans, and therefore they could never make any profits! To assume banks hold all the deposits they accept is to think banks offer a kind of collective safety deposit box service for cash. But that is not at all what banks offer when they accept deposits. Banks use those deposits to make loans to customers who pay the bank interest. As long as the bank collects interest on loans that is higher on average than the interest the bank pays depositors, banks can make a profit. But to realize the potential profit from the difference between the loan and deposit rates of interest, banks have to loan the deposits. And if they loan even a small part of the deposits obviously not all the deposits can be there in the eventuality that depositors asked to withdraw all their money.

Which leads to a frightening realization: Banks inherently entail the possibility of bankruptcy! There is no way to guarantee that banks will always be able to honor their legal commitments to depositors without making it impossible for banks to make profits. That is, no matter how safe and conservative bank management, no matter how faithfully borrowers repay bank loans, depositors are inherently at risk. But the logic of banking is even worse, which is why every government on the planet – no matter how *laissez faire* – regulates the banking industry in ways no other industry is subjected to.

How can a bank increase its profits? Profits will be higher if the differential between the rates of interest paid on loans and on deposits is larger. Every bank would like to expand this differential, but how can they? If a bank starts charging higher interest on loans it will risk losing its loan customers to other banks. If it offers to pay less on deposits it risks losing depositors to other banks. In other words, individual banks are limited by competition with other banks from expanding the differential beyond a certain point. Another way of saying the same thing is that the size of the differential is determined by the amount of competition in the banking industry. If there is lots of competition the differential will be small, if there is less competition the differential will be larger. But for a given level of competition, individual banks are restricted in their ability to increase profits by expanding their own differential. The other determinant of bank profits is how many loans they make taking advantage of the differential. If a bank loans out 40% of its deposits and earns $X in profits, it could earn $2X profits by lending out 80% of its deposits. Since there is little an individual bank can do to expand its interest differential, banks concentrate on loaning out as much of their deposits as possible.

Which leads to a second frightening realization: When stockholders press bank officers to increase profits, bank CEOs are driven to loan out more and more of bank deposits. Since insolvency results when depositors ask to withdraw more than the bank has kept as *reserves*, the drive for more profits necessarily increases the likelihood of bankruptcy by lowering bank reserves. It is true that stockholders should seek a trade-off between higher profits and insolvency since shareholders lose the value of their investment if the bank they own goes bankrupt. But stockholders are not the only ones who lose when a bank goes bankrupt. While stockholders lose the value of their investment, depositors lose their deposits. So when stockholders weigh the benefit of higher profits against the expected cost of bankruptcy they do not weigh the benefits against the entire cost, but only the fraction of the cost that falls on them. And even with regulations requiring minimum capitalization, it is always the case that the cost of bankruptcy to depositors is much greater than the cost to shareholders. This means that bank shareholders' interests do not coincide with the public interest in finding the efficient trade-off between higher profitability and lower likelihood of insolvency. Hence the need for government regulation.

This was a lesson that history taught over and over again during the eighteenth and nineteenth centuries as periodic waves of bankruptcy rocked the growing American Republic. Early in the twentieth century Congress charged the Federal Reserve Bank with the task of setting and enforcing a *minimum legal reserve requirement that prevents banks from lending out more than a certain fraction of their deposits.* In 1933 Congress also created a federal agency to insure depositors in the eventuality of bankruptcy in its efforts to reassure the public that it was safe to deposit their savings in banks during the Great Depression. Today the Federal Deposit Insurance Corporation (FDIC) will fully redeem deposits up to $200,000 in value if a bank goes bankrupt.

But federal insurance has created two new problems. First of all, as we discovered in the Savings and Loan Crisis of the 1980s, any substantial string of bankruptcies will also bankrupt the insuring agency! When the Savings and Loan Crisis was finally recognized there were roughly 500 insolvent thrift institutions with deposits of over $200 billion. The Federal Savings and Loan Insurance Corporation, FSLIC, had less than $2 billion in assets at the time. While the Federal Reserve Bank was anxious to shut the insolvent Savings and Loan Associations down to prevent them from accepting new deposits and creating additional FSLIC liabilities, neither Congress, led by Speaker Jim Wright from Texas, nor the Reagan White House wanted to declare the thrifts bankrupt because that would have required massive additional appropriations for FSLIC. Many of the insolvent thrifts were in Texas and they convinced Wright to lobby for delay of bankruptcy procedures. Owners of those insolvent thrifts had everything to lose from bankruptcy, whereas they could continue to collect dividends as long as they were permitted to accept new deposits and make new loans – regardless of whether or not there was any likelihood they would be able to overcome insolvency by doing so. The Reagan administration was not anxious to accept responsibility for the consequences of its financial deregulatory frenzy, and didn't want to have to raise taxes or cut defense spending to come up with the appropriations necessary to fund FSLIC sufficiently to pay off $200 billion to depositors – which the Gramm-Rudman Act limiting deficit spending would have required at the time. As a result the crisis was swept under the carpet for three more years, by which time the deposit liabilities of the insolvent thrifts had doubled. In other words, the politics of partially funded government insurance cost the American taxpayer additional hundreds of billions of dollars. Besides the $200 billion plus bailout itself, the Resolution Trust Corporation established by the Financial Institutions Reform, Recovery and Enforcement Act of 1989 to sell, merge, or liquidate insolvent thrifts, offered huge tax breaks as inducements to solvent financial institutions to take over failed institutions, thereby reducing tax revenues for many years and making it impossible to ever calculate what the total loss to taxpayers was from the S&L crisis of the 1980s.

Federal insurance also aggravates what economists call *moral hazard* in the banking sector. Bank owners and large depositors essentially collude in placing and accepting deposits in financial institutions that pay high interest on deposits which are used to make risky loans that pay high returns – as long as the borrowers don't default. But *when there are defaults on risky loans neither depositors nor shareholders are the major victims of insolvency and bankruptcy.* Lightly capitalized shareholders lose little in case of bankruptcy, while fully insured depositors lose nothing. Meanwhile both have been enjoying high returns while running little or no risk in the process. So government insurance compounds the problem that bank officers cannot be counted on to pursue the public interest in an efficient trade-off between profitability and risk by no longer making it necessary for depositors to monitor the lending activities of the financial institutions where they place their deposits. Apparently depositor fear of insolvency was an insufficient restraint on bank lending policy even before the advent of public deposit insurance since all governments had already found it necessary to charge their Central Bank with regulating minimum reserve requirements and monitoring the legitimacy of bank loans. Deposit insurance has the unfortunate effect of further weakening depositor incentives to monitor bank behavior.

Finally, notice that the existence of banks means the functioning money supply is considerably larger than the amount of currency circulating in the economy. If we ask how much someone could buy, immediately, in a world without banks the answer would be the amount of currency that person has. But in a world with banks where sellers not only accept currency in exchange for goods and services, but accept checks drawn on banks as well, someone can buy an amount equal to the currency they have *plus* the balance they have in their checking account(s). This means the "functioning" money supply is equal to the amount of currency circulating in the economy *plus* the sum total balances in household and business checking accounts at banks. For decades checking account balances in banks have been larger than the amount of currency in circulation, more than doubling the functioning money supply.[1]

1 More precisely, M1, referred to as the "basic" or "functioning" money supply, includes currency in circulation, "transactions account" balances, and travelers' checks. Beside checking accounts, transaction accounts include NOW accounts, ATS accounts, credit union share drafts, and demand deposits at mutual savings banks. The distinguishing feature of all transaction accounts is they permit direct payment to a third party by check or debit card. M2 and M3 are larger definitions of the money supply which include funds that are less accessible such as savings accounts and money market mutual funds (M2), and repurchase agreements and overnight Eurodollars (M3). By 2012 people held so much money in money market mutual funds and savings accounts that M2 had become more than four times larger than M1.

Which leads to our last frightening realization. Most of the functioning money supply is literally created by private commercial banks when they accept deposits and make loans. But as we have seen, when banks engage in these activities, and thereby "create" most of the functioning money supply, they think only of their own profits and give nary a thought to the sacred public trust of preserving the integrity of "money" in our economy.

Monetary Policy: Another Way to Skin the Cat

In Chapter 6 we studied three fiscal policies: changes in government spending, changes in taxes, and changing both spending and taxes by the same amount in the same direction. While they had different effects on the government budget deficit (or surplus) and on the composition of output, in theory, any one of them was sufficient to eliminate any unemployment or inflation gap. The alternative to fiscal policy is monetary policy which, in theory, can also be used to eliminate unemployment or inflation gaps. If the Federal Reserve Bank changes the money supply it can induce a rise or fall in market interest rates, which in turn can induce a fall or rise in private investment demand, which in turn will induce an even larger change in overall aggregate demand and equilibrium GDP through the "investment income expenditure multiplier." Just like fiscal policies, monetary policy can be either expansionary – raising equilibrium GDP to combat unemployment – or deflationary – lowering equilibrium GDP to combat demand pull inflation.

While fiscal policy attacks government spending directly, or household consumption demand indirectly by changing personal taxes, monetary policy aims indirectly at the third component of aggregate demand, private investment demand.[2] As explained in the previous chapter investment demand depends negatively on interest rates. The micro law of supply and demand tells us that changes in the money supply should affect interest rates, which are simply the "price" of money. Just as the price of apples

---

2 Our model and language oversimplify. While most federal taxes are personal taxes and therefore affect household disposable income, business taxes potentially affect investment decisions. Moreover, government transfer payments count just as much toward budget deficits as government purchases of military equipment, yet only the latter is part of the aggregate demand for final goods and services. And when the Fed cuts interest rates they make it cheaper for households as well as businesses to borrow. Beside business investment, monetary policy affects consumer demand for *big ticket items* like appliances, cars, and houses that people buy on credit. Nonetheless, a simple model, which we don't use to make actual predictions in any case, that assumes (1) all of G is demand for public goods, (2) taxes affect only household disposable income, and (3) monetary policy only affects business investment demand, is useful for "thinking" purposes and not terribly misleading.

drops when the supply of apples increases, interest rates drop when the supply of money increases. The Federal Reserve Bank – called the Central Bank in other countries – can change the money supply in any of three ways. It can change the legal minimum reserve requirement. It can conduct "open market operations" by buying or selling treasury bonds in the "open" bond market. Or it can change something called "the discount rate." By changing the money supply the Fed can induce a change in market interest rates to stimulate or retard business investment demand.

When the Fed lowers the legal minimum reserve requirement some of the required reserves held by each bank are no longer required and become excess reserves the banks are free to loan. As we saw, when banks make loans this has the effect of increasing the functioning money supply. By increasing the required reserve ratio the Fed can cause a decrease in the functioning money supply. Interestingly, changing the reserve requirement changes the money supply without changing the amount of currency.

The Fed has its own budget and its own assets, which in March 2013 included roughly 12% of all outstanding US treasury bonds in an assortment of sizes and maturity dates. So instead of changing the reserve requirement the Fed could take some of its treasury bonds to the "open" bond market in New York and sell them to the general public who, for simplicity, we assume pays for them with cash. The market for treasury bonds is "open" in the sense that anyone can buy them, and anyone who has some can sell them. While new treasury bonds are sold by the Treasury Department at what are called "Treasury auctions," previously issued treasury bonds are "resold" by their original purchasers who no longer wish to hold them until they mature, to purchasers on the "open bond market." When we talk about the Fed engaging in "open market operations" we are talking about the Fed buying or selling previously issued treasury bonds, that is, we're talking about the bond "resell" market rather than Treasury Department auctions of new bonds. When the Fed sells bonds this isn't a transfer of wealth from the Fed to the private sector or vice versa. It is merely a change in the form in which the Fed and private sector hold their wealth, or assets. Whereas the Fed used to hold part of its wealth in the form of the bonds it sells, now it holds that wealth in the form of currency it was paid for the bonds it sold. Whereas the private sector used to hold part of its wealth in currency, now it holds that wealth in the form of treasury bonds. When the Fed engages in open market operations it does change the amount of currency in the economy – increasing currency in the economy by buying bonds and decreasing currency in the economy by selling bonds.

So-called *quantitative easing* is a slight variation on this theme. As part of its attempts to rescue banks from insolvency in the aftermath of the financial crisis of

2008 the Fed under Chairman Ben Bernanke dramatically increased *Fed purchases of assets from banks*, thereby providing banks with more money and relieving them of troublesome assets. The policy was also intended as expansionary monetary policy, making it easier for banks to make loans to businesses and thereby stimulate the stagnant economy. *Tapering* refers to *a reduction in the amount of quantitative easing the Fed engages in each month*. Tapering, which was postponed several times when new data revealed that the economy was still sputtering, was the eventual response of the Fed to diminished fears of a recessionary relapse in 2013. Except for the fact that the Fed is purchasing assets from banks, rather than treasury bonds in the open market, quantitative easing and tapering are similar to traditional open market operations.

Finally, the Federal Reserve Bank loans money to private commercial banks that are members of the Federal Reserve Banking System.[3] If these commercial banks borrow more money from the Fed and then loan it out, the money supply will increase. If they borrow less from the Fed the money supply will decrease. Just like any other lender, the Fed charges interest on loans – in this case loans it makes to private banks that are members of the Federal Reserve System. And just like any other borrower, these banks will borrow more from the Fed if the interest rate they have to pay is lower, and less if the interest rate they pay is higher. *The name for the interest rate the Fed charges banks who borrow at its "discount window" is the* **discount rate**. So by lowering its discount rate the Fed can induce commercial banks to borrow more money, thereby increasing the currency circulating in the economy, and by raising the discount rate the Fed can discourage borrowing, thereby decreasing the amount of currency circulating in the economy.

In sum, the logic of monetary policy is as follows: The Fed can increase or decrease the functioning money supply, M1, by changing the minimum reserve requirement, through open market operations, including so-called quantitative easing, or by changing its discount rate. By changing the money supply the Fed can induce changes in market interest rates, leading to changes in investment demand, leading to even greater changes in aggregate demand and equilibrium GDP. When monetary authorities fear economic recession they increase the money supply, as then Chairman Alan Greenspan and the Fed did from mid-1999 through early 2002 when they regularly lowered the discount rate by a quarter and sometimes half percent

---

3 At the height of the financial crisis some of the largest financial institutions the Fed was most anxious to "bail out" were not commercial banks, but Wall Street investment banks which were not members of the Federal Reserve Banking System. Rules on who could borrow at the discount window were relaxed at that time to allow these banks to borrow from the Fed to avoid panic among their creditors.

every month or two, further aggravating a housing bubble Greenspan vehemently denied existed; and as Chairman Bernanke and the Fed did from 2008 through 2013. International Monetary Fund conditionality agreements, on the other hand, routinely insist that monetary authorities reduce their functioning money supply in exchange for emergency IMF bail out loans, for reasons we explore next chapter.

Since neither increasing nor decreasing the money supply affects government spending or taxes directly, monetary policy has no *direct* effect on the government budget. Of course if expansionary monetary policy lowers unemployment and thereby decreases government spending on unemployment compensation and welfare programs, it will indirectly lower G. And if expansionary monetary policy increases GDP and GDI, and thereby increases tax revenues collected as a percentage of income, it will indirectly raise T. So monetary policy does have an *indirect* effect on the government budget. But unlike fiscal policy, changing the money supply has no direct impact on the government budget. As far as the composition of output is concerned, expansionary monetary policy increases the share of GDP going to private investment, I/Y, and decreases the shares going to public goods, G/Y, and private consumption, C/Y. Deflationary monetary policy has the opposite effect – it chokes off private investment relative to public and private consumption. In Chapter 9 we explore the effects of *equivalent* monetary and fiscal policies in a simple, short-run, closed economy macro model 9.3.

The Relationship between the Financial and "Real" Economies

Increasingly the economic "news" reported in the mainstream media is news about stocks, bonds, and interest rates. During the stock market boom in the late 1990s the media acted like cheer leaders for the Dow Jones Average and NASDAQ index. It was not uncommon for the major US media to report with glee that stock prices rose dramatically after a Labor Department briefing announced an increase in the number of jobless. In the aftermath of the East Asian financial crisis the media reassured us that stock indices and currency values had largely recovered in Thailand, South Korea, and Indonesia – as if that were what mattered – neglecting to report that employment and production in those economies had *not* rebounded – as if that were unimportant. And ever since the financial crisis of 2008 and the Great Recession that followed in its wake the media is full of cheery news about the recovery in the stock market ignoring that jobs and wages in the real economy have failed to rebound. What should we care about, and what is the relationship between the financial sector and the "real" economy?

In Chapter 2 we asked, "What should we demand from our economy?" The answer was an equitable distribution of the burdens and benefits of economic activity, efficient use of our scarce productive resources, economic democracy, solidarity, variety, and environmental sustainability. Nowhere on that wish list did rising stock, bond, or currency prices appear. This does not mean the financial sector has nothing to do with the production and distribution of goods and services. But it does mean the only reason to care about the financial sector is because of its effects on the real economy. If the financial sector improves economic efficiency and thereby allows us to produce more goods and services, so much the better. But if dynamics in the financial sector cause unemployment and lost production, or increase economic inequality, or hasten environmental deterioration, that is what matters, not the fact that a stock index or currency rose or fell in value. In an era when the hegemony of global finance is unprecedented, it is important not to invert what matters and what is only of derivative interest.

How can money, lending, banks, hedge funds, options, buying on margin, derivatives, or credit default swaps increase economic efficiency? Simple: by providing funding for some productive activity in the real economy that otherwise would not have taken place. If monetized exchange allows people to discover a mutually beneficial deal they would have been unlikely to find through barter, money increases the efficiency of the real economy. If I can borrow from you to buy a tool that allows me to work more productively right away, whereas otherwise I would have had to save for a year to buy the tool, a credit market increases my efficiency this year – and the interest rate you and I agree on will distribute the increase in *my* productivity during the year between you, the lender, and me, the borrower. If banks permit more borrowers and lenders to find one another, thereby allowing more people to work more productively sooner than they otherwise would have, the banking system increases efficiency in the real economy. If options, buying on margin, credit default swaps, and derivatives mobilize savings that otherwise would have been idle, and extend credit to borrowers who become more productive sooner than had they been forced to wait longer for loans from more traditional sources in the credit system, these financial innovations increase efficiency in the real economy.

But while those who profit from the financial system are quick to point out these *positive* potentials, they are loath to point out ways the financial sector can *negatively* impact the real economy. Nor do they dwell on the fact that what the credit system allows them to do is profit from *other people's* increases in productivity. In 2002 when the first edition of the *ABCs of Political Economy* was published popular interest in learning about the downside potentials of financialization was limited. The mood was "let the good times roll," and those like me who insisted on weighing the dangers of financial liberalization were shunned as kill-joys and scolds. What a difference the greatest financial crisis in eighty years makes! What a difference it makes when the financial crisis strikes in New York City not Bangkok or Buenos Aires, and hits the US and Europe harder than the developing world. And what a difference it makes when people finally begin to notice and care about rising inequality, and ask if financialization may have something to do with it.

At its best what the credit systems does, in all its different guises, is allow lenders to appropriate increases in the productivity of others. Why do those whose productivity rises agree to pay creditors part of their productivity increase? Because the creditors have the wealth needed to purchase whatever is necessary to increase their productivity while they do not. Moreover, if they wait until they can save sufficient wealth to do without creditors, borrowers lose whatever efficiency gain they could have produced in the meantime. But even when the credit system works well, that is, even when it generates efficiency gains rather than losses in the real economy, absent strong intervention the credit system will increase the degree of inequality in the economy. As the simple corn model in Chapter 3 demonstrates, if the laws of supply and demand are allowed to determine interest rates there is every reason to expect more than half of the increase in the borrower's efficiency will go to the lender, thereby increasing inequality.

But besides increasing inequality the credit system can also generate efficiency losses instead of gains in the real economy. In Chapter 9 we look at a model 9.1 that makes clear how rational depositors can cause bank runs. We then look at a model 9.2 of a real corn economy with banks that shows how banks may generate efficiency gains when all goes well, but will make the real economy *less* efficient if there is a run on the bank. When depositors have reason to fear they will lose their deposits if they fail to withdraw before others do, the model demonstrates how banks will produce efficiency losses, not gains, in the real economy. In a second application of model 9.2 we show how international finance can generate efficiency *losses* as well as gains in a "real" global corn economy for similar reasons. The general lesson from models 9.1 and 9.2 is when borrowers and lenders become accustomed to finding each other through bank mediation and banks fail, it is possible for *fewer* borrowers to find lenders than otherwise would have, and therefore for the real economy to become less efficient than it would have been without banks. Similarly, when more highly leveraged international finance makes it more likely that international investors will panic, and capital liberalization makes it easier for them to withdraw tens of billions of dollars of investments from emerging market economies and sell off massive quantities of their currencies overnight, tens of millions can lose their jobs and decades of economic progress can go down the drain as banks and businesses in emerging market economies go bankrupt. This is how liberalizing the international credit system can make real less developed economies *less* efficient than they were when international finance was more restricted, as it was during the Bretton Woods era. And as citizens in advanced economies have recently discovered, these are among the potential *downsides* of lashing their real economies more tightly to the back of a credit system when the credit system proves unstable.

Banks, futures, options, margins, derivatives, credit default swaps, and other "financial innovations" all either expand the list of things speculators can buy and sell, or permit them to increase their **leverage** – *use less of their own wealth and more of someone else's when they invest.* In other words these, and whatever new financial instruments speculators dream up in the future, simply extend the credit system. If the extension provides funding for some productive activity that would otherwise not have been funded, it can be useful. But all extensions increase dangers in the credit system by (1) increasing the number of places something might go wrong, (2) increasing the probability that if something does go wrong investors will panic and the credit system will crash, or (3) compounding the damage if the credit system crashes. New financial products add new markets where bubbles can form and burst. Increased leverage makes financial structures more fragile and compounds the damage from any bubble that does burst.[4]

There are two rules of behavior in any credit system, and both rules become more critical to follow the more leveraged the system. Rule #1 is the rule all participants want all *other* participants to follow: DON'T PANIC! If everyone follows rule #1 the likelihood of the credit system crashing is lessened. Rule #2 is the rule each participant must be careful to follow herself: PANIC FIRST! If something goes wrong, the first to collect her loan from a debtor in trouble, the first to withdraw her deposits from a troubled bank, the first to sell her option or derivative in a market when a bubble bursts, the first to dump a currency when it is "under pressure," will lose the least. Those who are slow to panic, on the other hand, will take the biggest baths. Once stated, the contradictory nature of the two logical rules for behavior in credit systems makes clear the inherent danger in this powerful economic institution, and the risk we take when we tie the real economy ever more tightly to a credit system financial

---

4   For example, derivatives can disguise how many are speculating in a market. Frank Partnoy, a derivative trader turned professor of law and finance at the University of San Diego, described this problem as follows when explaining East Asian currency crises: "It's as if you're in a theater, and say there are 100 people and you have the rush-to-the-exit problem. With derivatives, it's as if without your knowing it, there are another 500 people in the theater, and you can't see them at first. But when the rush to the exit starts, suddenly they drop from the ceiling. This makes the panic all the greater." Quoted by Nicholas Kristof in his column in the *New York Times* on February 17, 1999.

businesses and politicians have conspired to make more unstable and fragile over the past three decades.

The Financial Crisis of 2008: A Perfect Storm

The financial crisis that struck Wall Street in the fall of 2008 was *not* simply the result of some mortgage loans that should never have been made because the borrowers were not sufficiently creditworthy. Less than 20% of mortgages were in arrears when the crisis hit, which means that 80% of mortgagees were current with their payments. Only because unsustainable macroeconomic imbalances were permitted to evolve, only because prudent regulation of the banking industry dating back to the Great Depression was systematically dismantled under pressure from the financial industry, only because people like Laurence Summers and Timothy Geithner actively intervened to prevent regulation of highly speculative Wall Street investment banks and hedge funds, was it possible for the worst financial crisis in eighty years to unravel when a housing bubble – which had to come to an end at some point – finally burst. There were seven steps that led to what I call the *perfect economic storm*, which also contained a surprise ending for banks and those who tried to rescue them.

Traditionally, people in the US applied to local banks for mortgage loans, and the bank approving the loan held the loan for 30 years. Under these conditions banks insisted on collateral – 20% down was the standard for decades – and banks checked carefully to be sure applicants had a secure job, income sufficient to make their mortgage payments, and a good credit rating – because if a mortgagee defaulted the bank who authorized the loan would suffer the adverse consequences. This worked well enough for all involved for over half a century, except the big Wall Street banks were not involved in a major way and therefore weren't making much money off the huge US housing market.

Step 1: The banks reviewing mortgage applications no longer kept the loans themselves. Instead, by the late 1990s most mortgages were sold within a few days of being approved to someone else, and often resold, and resold again many times within a few months, thereby creating a perverse incentive for the banks evaluating loan applications to no longer do their work carefully. Since local lenders were no longer holding the mortgages they no longer had an incentive to turn down applicants who were, in fact, poor credit risks. But why did large brokerage houses and investors buy these mortgages if many of them were now of dubious quality?

Step 2: Large Wall Street banks bought up huge numbers of mortgage loans from every region of the country and did something very creative with them. They chopped these loans up into tiny little pieces, and *packaged together thousands of pieces of different loans* into **securitized debt instruments** which they usually sold off to institutional investors, but sometimes kept as assets on their own books as well. But why did institutional investors buy these fancy mortgage-based securities if at least some of them contained poor quality loans?

Step 3: There are rating agencies who rate the riskiness of different securities. But the agencies do not provide this service for free, nor do the buyers of the securities pay for the evaluation. Instead, the agencies rating the securities are paid by the Wall Street banks who package the securities together for sale, which created a second perverse incentive. The Wall Street banks had little trouble getting almost all of their mortgage based securities rated Triple A – the highest rating, supposedly meaning the lowest risk for a buyer – by agencies that did not get hired and paid unless Wall Street banks were happy with their ratings.

At this point we had transformed a simple, straightforward and largely local home mortgage industry that worked well for half a century into an incredibly lucrative international business, because the Wall Street banks also sold their fancy Triple A rated mortgage-based securities to institutional investors and large banks in Europe and elsewhere. However, the whole business was now riddled with two, serious perverse incentives, with the Wall Street banks at the center raking in handsome fees for their securitization work which they proudly described to anyone who expressed concern as minimizing systemic risk by spreading risk more broadly.

Step 4: Fearful that the housing bubble in the US could not go on forever, in 2006 institutional investors, particularly in Europe, started to get cold feet and became more reluctant to buy the mortgage-based securities that had become the life blood of a global financial bubble. This is where what we might call "good old Yankee ingenuity" came to the rescue. A medium sized insurance company few had ever heard of named American International Group offered to sell insurance policies against the event that a securitized debt instrument proved to be of little value. Worried that the mortgage-backed securities you bought might be worthless due to defaults? No problem. All you have to do is buy an insurance policy from AIG.

Step 5: Almost overnight AIG became the largest insurance company in the world selling *insurance to buyers of mortgage-backed securities*, but what come to be known as **credit default swaps** were not classified as insurance, and thereby fell outside the purview of US government agencies regulating the insurance industry. As a result AIG was not required to set aside any significant amount of the handsome premiums they collected for the credit default swaps they sold. Instead they expanded their business and paid lavish dividends to their stockholders. Moreover, what quickly became a multi-trillion dollar market in credit default swaps not only fell outside all regulation, there was not even an information clearing house where one could determine the size of the market or who owned credit default swaps against what.

Of course as long as home prices kept rising this giant house of cards economists call a *Ponzi scheme* was not in jeopardy. But as soon as home prices peaked, and people whose financial plan relied on the price of their house continuing to rise because they could not afford their loan under other circumstances started to default, the whole house of cards began to unravel.

However, a 20% default rate on what came to be known as *sub-prime mortgages* would never have led to anything like the financial crisis that occurred had not the conditions for a perfect storm been permitted to evolve in the first place. The damage done by the inevitable burst of the housing bubble was magnified many fold because the financial sector was permitted to turn the reasonably profitable but reasonably safe home mortgage industry into a mammoth, global Ponzi scheme generating record profits for its players while it lasted. In other words, when the housing bubble burst what would have been a medium wave hitting only American coasts was turned into a tsunami that swept around the globe by the multiple perverse incentives described above. And what allowed these perverse incentives to evolve was a truly monumental failure to regulate key aspects of the mortgage, banking, financial, and insurance industries.

Step 6: But we were not done yet. A major surprise was still in store, first for the Wall Street banks, and then for the Bush and Obama administrations who both tried to clean up the mess by using taxpayer dollars to buy up the toxic assets on the books of the banks. The real economy you and I live in is completely reliant on the functioning of the credit system. Few of us can buy a house without getting a loan. Many of us pay for most of what we buy using a credit card – whose balance we either do, or more often do not pay off at the end of the month. Even more importantly, the businesses that employ us need loans to buy the intermediate inputs we need to work with, and finance shipping the goods we produce. As a result, when the credit system breaks down – as it did in the fall of 2008 – the real economy quickly begins to suffer as well.

Of course that is another way to understand the problem underlying this whole mess. Whereas the credit system should serve the real economy consisting of production and consumption, what is now referred to as financialization is the reversal of this relationship. Over the past forty years the financial sector has increasingly subjected production, consumption, and investment in new machines and equipment to its own purposes, and we have now discovered how badly that can work out for most of us. In effect the tail is now wagging the dog, and the dog is increasingly uncomfortable!

In any case, the point is our real economy will not function for us when the credit system seizes up – which is what happened in the fall of 2008. The credit system froze up because the big players at the top of the credit system, the Wall Street banks, were no longer willing to lend to one another because they knew that the fancy mortgaged backed securities many of them had kept on their own books were anything but triple A safe. In other words, the banks knew only too well that what came to be called their *toxic assets* were of questionable value. And when the Wall Street banks could no longer get credit from one another, credit froze up for the rest of us farther down the credit chain.

Understanding why the big banks suddenly would not lend to one another in the fall of 2008 and winter of 2009 is not only a fascinating story in and of itself, but also the key to understanding why the government had such a difficult time putting Humpty Dumpty back together again despite hundreds of billions of dollars of transfusions of taxpayer dollars via the Troubled Asset Relief Program, or TARP, launched by Treasury Secretary Paulson in October 2008, and trillions of dollars of commitments US taxpayers took on as the program was tweaked and ramped up by President Obama's new Treasury Secretary, Timothy Geithner in the years that followed.

Nobody wants to discover they were the last to lend to someone who goes bankrupt the next day. Ordinarily Wall Street banks are happy to lend to one another large amounts, generally for short periods of time. Suddenly after the Lehman Brothers bankruptcy they were not. The reason was simple. Wall Street banks feared that the bank they lent to might be on the front pages of the newspapers the next morning as the latest Wall Street Bank to go bankrupt. They had good reason to fear this because all of them had kept substantial amounts of mortgage backed securities on their books that were no longer really worth what they were supposed to be, and because it had become clear that any credit default swaps they had purchased from AIG were worthless because AIG was virtually bankrupt by September 2008, and the Fed was intervening to keep the crisis in the credit default market from bringing down major investment banks around the world.

In truth the CEOs of the Wall Street banks knew very little about the actual work done in their own securitization departments since it was a recent and technically complex financial innovation. So a CEO had to call in the much younger head of his own securitization department to ask him how he could know if another Wall Street bank asking for a loan was on shaky ground because their securities were toxic. And this was the shocking answer he got: "There is no way to know. Just like they have no way to tell what is really in the packages we have put together, and therefore whether our assets are toxic or not, we have no way to tell what is really in their packages, and therefore if their assets are toxic or not." How toxic were these mortgage backed security assets the big banks had on their books? On average they were worth 20% less than they once were because 20% of mortgage payments were now in arrears or default. So even a full write down meant that *on average* the assets *should* have been worth 80% of what they once were – which is bad news, but not a complete disaster. But to the banks surprise they discovered that the market price for the securities was practically nothing.

While the PR departments of the Wall Street banks were busy assuring the world that they were managing risk in a smarter way by spreading it out more, what the math whizzes the big banks hired to work in their securitization departments were actually doing was a brilliant job of hiding risk. In the process of chopping and packaging the different mortgages some of the securities they created contained 95% good loans and only 5% bad loans. But some of the securities contained only 5% good loans and the remaining 95% were bad. And only the people who created the packages had any way of knowing which were which. As long as defaults were few, as long as *all* of the securities had a Triple A rating, and as long as people assumed that credit default swaps really did provide insurance, hiding the risk was not a problem and worked for everyone. But as soon as the housing bubble burst and 20% of the underlying mortgages were in arrears things changed dramatically. The fact that the risk had been hidden so well, and nobody except the person who had done the chopping and packaging in the first place could tell where it was, turned a problem into a total disaster. The market price for the mortgage based securities did not fall by 20%, but instead fell by much more until nobody was willing to buy any of them except at fire sale prices, because no buyer, as an outsider, could distinguish the securities that were 95% good from the ones that were 95% bad.

Suddenly Wall Street banks were no longer willing to lend to one another, which froze the entire credit system. Moreover, if their securities were valued according to their going market prices all the Wall Street banks would be revealed as hopelessly insolvent – which is why the banks fought vehemently against proposals for *mark to market* accounting procedures for evaluating the assets on their books, and their protectors at the Fed testified against this proposal at hearings on Capitol Hill.

In sum, the Wall Street banks found to their shock that they had hoisted themselves on their own petard. Only the grave diggers knew where they had buried the risk, and clearly they could not be trusted to tell outsiders where it was. In effect the Wall Street banks had witlessly turned assets that should have been worth 80% of their former value on average into assets with very little, if any market value at all. The more clever a securitization department had been at playing this game of liar's poker, the more the bank found itself in checkmate with nobody willing to buy its assets or extend it any loans. So what did the government do to try to unlock and fix the credit system, and why did it prove so difficult?

Step 7: First the Bush administration – under the leadership of his Secretary of the Treasury, Henry "Hank" Paulson Jr., Chairman of the Federal Reserve Bank, Ben Bernanke, and Chair of the New York Branch of the Fed at that time, Timothy Geithner – and later the Obama administration, under the leadership of his Chief Economic Advisor, Laurence Summers, his Secretary of the Treasury, Timothy Geithner, and Ben Bernanke – tried to rescue the Wall Street banks from the mess they created for themselves by taking their toxic assets off their books. Since the market price for these assets was quite low the whole idea was to have a buyer pay the banks far more than their toxic assets were then worth. First the taxpayer bailout of the banks took the form of direct US Treasury purchases of toxic assets through a "reverse auction" that was so hampered by perverse information asymmetries and conflicts of interest that Secretary Paulson could not achieve lift-off for his plan before leaving office. The Obama administration tried to disguise the taxpayer subsidy in the form of what they called "private public partnerships" where the Treasury Department, FDIC and the Fed provided free insurance against downside risk to induce private party participation in purchases of assets from troubled banks.

In the end neither of these attempts to rid the banks of their toxic assets at public expense worked very well. What finally stabilized the situation was Bernanke simply flooded the big banks with cash to keep them afloat, first by reducing the discount rate and opening the discount window to large non-commercial banks for the first time, and later through quantitative easing. In these and other ways Bernanke made clear that the Fed would not permit any of the remaining Wall Street giants to fail, which made it safe for them to start lending to one another again, unlocking the credit system. Once the banks no longer had to sell assets buyers could not evaluate quickly to stay alive, the value of their assets had time to rise closer to the roughly 80% on average they were worth. More importantly, after a couple of years of borrowing massively from the Fed at zero interest to buy risk free treasury bonds paying over 3% and lend to emerging market economies for even more, bank profits were once again soaring. But while the crisis is now over for the banks, the financial system is just as prone to crisis as it was before 2008 because (1) the Dodd-Frank Wall Street Reform and Consumer Protection Act was more fig leaf than reform, and does very little to prevent behavior that is profitable for banks but dangerous for the rest of us, and (2) the financial system is now crowned by a smaller number of even larger big banks who can be even more bold and reckless because they can be more sure than ever that they will be regarded as "too big to be permitted to fail." Not to speak of the fact that all of the "real" North Atlantic economies remain stagnant, with high unemployment, and living standards for most Portuguese, Irish, Greeks, and Spaniards continue to spiral downward toward conditions we normally associate with the third world.

8

International Economics: Mutual Benefit or Imperialism?

Mainstream economics emphasizes the positive possibilities of international trade and investment to such an extent that most economists have difficulty imagining how more free trade, more international lending, or more direct foreign investment could possibly be disadvantageous. They understand why colonial relations might be detrimental to a colony. When Great Britain prevented its North American colonies from trading with Spain, and required them to buy only from England at prices set by England, mainstream economic theory recognizes that Great Britain was benefited, but her New World colonies may well have been made worse off. But mainstream economists point out that the era of colonialism is behind us. They point out that under free trade any country that is not benefited by trade with a particular trading partner can look for other trading partners, or not trade at all. They point out that when all are free to lend or borrow in international credit markets any country that is not benefited by the terms of a particular international loan is free to search for other lenders offering better terms, or not borrow at all. Mainstream theory teaches that as long as international trade and investment is consensual and countries do not mistake what the effects will be, no country can end up worse off, and all countries should end up better off. So now that colonialism is behind us the only reason mainstream economists can see why less developed countries would be damaged by international trade or investment is if *they* make a mistake. Only if *they* think a good or service they import will be more beneficial than it turns out to be, only if *they* think an international loan will improve their economic productivity more than it really can, can developing economies be disadvantaged in the eyes of most mainstream economists.

Political economists, on the other hand, argue that international trade and investment are often vehicles through which more developed countries (MDCs) at the "center" of the global economy exploit less developed countries (LDCs) in the "periphery" – long after the latter cease to be their colonies. Third world political economists in particular argue that "unequal trade" enriches more advanced economies at the expense of less advanced ones. Many political economists emphasize that direct foreign investment allows multinational companies from advanced economies to take advantage of plentiful raw materials and cheap labor in less developed economies, and to take over lucrative markets from domestic producers. And many political economists point out that international borrowing can ensnare poor countries in debt traps from which it is impossible for them to escape.

Mutual benefit or imperialism? Global village or global pillage? First we explore the logic behind each view – taking pains when reviewing mainstream theory to "render unto Caesar what is Caesar's." Then we see if mainstream and political economists are destined to talk about international economics in different languages with little hope of communication, or if we can sort out the sense of where things lie. We will discover that while international trade and investment *could, in theory,* improve global efficiency and reduce global inequality it would do so only in a very different global economic system than the one we have today, and that what is predictable is that more neoliberal, capitalist globalization *will* continue to do just the opposite if not stopped.

Why Trade Can Increase Global Efficiency

When we use scarce productive resources to make one good those resources are not available to make another good. That is the sense in which economists say there are **opportunity costs** of making goods. The *opportunity cost of making a unit of good A, for example, can be measured as the number of units of good B we must forego because we used the resources to make the unit of A instead of using them to make good B.* Opportunity costs are important for understanding the logic of international trade because whenever the opportunity cost of producing a good is different in two countries there *can* be positive benefits, or efficiency gains from specialization and trade. And as long as the terms of trade distribute part of the benefit of specialization to both countries, trade *can* be beneficial to both trading partners.

Suppose, for example, by moving productive resources from the shirt industry to the tool industry in the US shirt production falls by 4 shirts for every additional tool produced, while moving resources from the shirt industry to the tool industry in Mexico results in a drop of 8 shirts for every new tool produced. The opportunity cost of a tool in the US is 4 shirts while the opportunity cost of a tool in Mexico is 8 shirts. Conversely, since moving productive resources from the tool to the shirt industry in the US leads to a loss of 1/4 tool for every new shirt produced, while moving resources from the tool to the shirt industry in Mexico leads to a loss of 1/8 tool for every new shirt produced, the opportunity cost of a shirt in the US is 1/4 tool while the opportunity of a shirt in Mexico is 1/8 tool. Suppose the terms of trade were 6 shirts for one tool, or what is the same thing, 1/6 tool for one shirt. The US would be better off producing only tools – trading tools for any shirts it wanted to consume – because instead of using the resources necessary to produce 4 shirts, the US could instead produce 1 tool and then trade the tool for 6 shirts. So if the terms of trade are 1 tool for 6 shirts the US is always better off using its resources to produce tools and never shirts, even when it wants to consume shirts. Mexico, on the other hand, would be better off producing only shirts – trading shirts for any tools it wants – because instead of using the resources necessary to produce 1 tool, Mexico could instead produce 8 shirts and trade the 8 shirts for 1/6 tools per shirt, times 8 shirts, or 1 and 1/3 tools. So if the terms of trade are 1 tool for 6 shirts Mexico is always better off using its resources to produce shirts and never tools, even when it wants to consume tools. Generalizing we have the central theorem of mainstream trade theory: As long as opportunity costs are different in two countries, (1) specialization and trade *can* increase global efficiency, and (2) there are terms of trade that *can* distribute part of the efficiency gain to both trading partners, thereby making both countries better off.

Comparative, Not Absolute, Advantage Drives Trade

When David Ricardo first explained the logic of trade he was not concerned with why opportunity costs might be different in different countries. Instead he wanted to dispel the myth that mutually beneficial trade could only take place when one country was better at making one good while the other country was better at producing the other good. Ricardo showed that even if *one country was more productive in the production of both goods*, that is, even if one country had an **absolute advantage** in the production of both goods, the more productive country, not just the less productive country, could gain from specialization and trade. Ricardo demonstrated that the more productive country could benefit by importing the good in which it was relatively, or comparatively less productive, and exporting the good in which it was *relatively, or comparatively more productive*. In other words, Ricardo showed that **comparative advantage** – not absolute advantage – was the crucial factor driving trade.

Suppose in the above example it only takes 1 hour of labor to make either 1 tool or 4 shirts in the US, but it takes 10 hours of labor to make 1 tool or 8 shirts in Mexico. In this case the opportunity costs of tools and shirts in both countries is exactly the same as before, but the US is 10 times more productive than Mexico in tool production and 5 times more productive than Mexico in shirt production. In other words, the US is more productive than Mexico in producing *both* tools and shirts, and enjoys an *absolute advantage* in both industries. Before Ricardo, economists believed a country like the US would have no incentive to trade with a country like Mexico. Certainly the US would not import tools from Mexico because it is 10 times more productive than Mexico in tool production. But why would the US import shirts from Mexico when the US is 5 times more productive than Mexico in shirt production? Notice that the conclusion we derived above – both Mexico *and* the US are better off specializing in the good where they have the lower opportunity cost, or comparative advantage, and trading 6 shirts for 1 tool – still holds. We assumed nothing about how productive either country was when we derived this conclusion. Since the logic was airtight, the conclusion holds even if the US is more productive in the production of both tools and shirts, i.e. has an absolute advantage in both.

Where, you might ask, did the terms of trade, 1 tool for 6 shirts, come from? Mainstream theorists hasten to point out that in one sense it does not matter where it came from. If there is even one term of trade that distributes part of the efficiency gain from specialization and trade to each country, all the conclusions of mainstream trade theory we derived above follow. But there is more we can say about terms of trade that is very important to political economists concerned with the distributive effects of trade. In our example as long as 1 tool trades for more than 4 shirts but less than 8 shirts both countries will benefit from specialization and trade. If 1 tool traded for less than 4 shirts the US would have no incentive to trade because instead of producing 1 tool and importing less than 4 shirts from Mexico, the US could simply move resources from its own tool industry to its own shirt industry and get 4 shirts for each tool it loses. So the opportunity cost of a tool in the US, 4 shirts, forms a lower bound on the **feasible terms of trade**, i.e. *terms of trade that leave both countries better off*. On the other hand, if 1 tool traded for more than 8 shirts Mexico would have no incentive to trade. By moving resources from its own shirt industry to its own tool industry Mexico only has to give up 8 shirts to get a tool. So Mexico has no reason to trade more than 8 shirts to get a tool from the US, and the opportunity cost of a tool in Mexico, 8 shirts, forms an upper bound on the feasible terms of trade. Any terms of trade in the feasible range – 1 tool trades for more than 4 shirts but less than 8 shirts – leave both countries better off because it distributes part of the efficiency gain from international specialization to each country. Unless Mexico were a US colony and had no choice, it would presumably refuse to trade more than 8 shirts for 1 tool, and unless the US were a colony of Mexico it would presumably refuse to trade 1 tool for less than 4 shirts. We will return to the all important question of where within the feasible range the actual terms of trade will end up when we take up the distributive effects of trade later. But note for now that since Mexico is going to be exporting shirts it is better off the *fewer* shirts trade for a tool. That is, Mexico gets a greater share of the efficiency gain the closer the terms of trade are to the opportunity cost of tools *in the US* (4 shirts). Conversely, since the US will export tools, the US is better off the *more* shirts trade for a tool. That is the US gets a greater share of the efficiency gain the closer the terms of trade are to the opportunity cost of tools *in Mexico* (8 shirts).

To review: What Ricardo proved, to the surprise of his fellow nineteenth-century economists, was that differences in opportunity costs are both a necessary and sufficient condition for mutually beneficial trade, and comparative, rather than absolute advantage was the determining factor in what countries should and should not produce. In our example the opportunity cost of a tool is lower in the US (4 shirts) than it is in Mexico (8 shirts) – which gives the US a comparative advantage in tools. The opportunity cost of a shirt is lower in Mexico (1/8 tool) than it is in the US (1/4 tool) – which gives Mexico a comparative advantage in shirts. As we proved above, if the terms of trade are 1 tool for 6 shirts – or more generally 1 tool for more than 4 shirts but less than 8 shirts – each country is better off specializing in the production of the good in which it has a comparative advantage and importing the good in which it has a comparative disadvantage.

Ricardo also proved that absolute advantage plays no role in determining whether mutually beneficial specialization and trade is possible, nor in determining who should produce what. Instead, opportunity costs and comparative advantage are determinant. The intuition in our example is as follows: The US is more productive than Mexico producing tools and shirts, but is *relatively* more productive making tools: Whereas the US is only 5 times more productive than Mexico making shirts, it is 10 times more productive making tools. That is why the US should produce tools and let Mexico produce shirts. Mexico is less productive than the US producing tools and shirts, but is *relatively* less productive making shirts: Whereas Mexico is only 5 times less productive than the US making shirts, it is 10 times less productive making tools. That is why Mexico should produce shirts and let the US produce tools – provided terms of trade can be agreed on that distribute part of the efficiency gain to each country.[1]

---

1 We have implicitly assumed we cannot move Mexican workers to the US where they become as productive as US workers. If we could move all Mexican workers to the US and they instantly became as productive as US tool and shirt makers, it would be efficient to do so and make all shirts and tools in the US. But as long as some workers must remain in Mexico it is more efficient to have them produce something rather than nothing, and more efficient to have them produce shirts rather than tools.

Trade theory since Ricardo has focused on reasons opportunity costs differ between countries. Differences in climate or soil are obvious reasons countries might differ in their abilities to produce agricultural goods. Differences in the accessibility of deposits of natural resources are obvious reasons for differences in the opportunity costs of producing oil, coal, gas, and different minerals in different countries. And differences in technological know how – with significant effects of "learning from doing" – obviously give rise to differences in opportunity costs of producing different manufactured goods. A more subtle source of differences in opportunity costs is different factor endowments. Even if technologies are identical in two countries, and even if the quality of each productive resource is the same, if countries possess productive factors in different proportions the opportunity costs of producing final goods will differ – giving rise to potential benefits from trade.

Why Trade Can Decrease Global Efficiency

It is pointless to deny that if opportunity costs of producing goods are different in different countries there are potential efficiency gains from specialization and trade. The theory of comparative advantage (CA) is logically sound when it teaches that global efficiency is increased when countries specialize in making the goods they are relatively better at producing, and import the goods some other country is relatively better at producing. But this does not mean specialization and trade always improve global efficiency.

Inaccurate Prices Can Misidentify Comparative Advantage

If commercial prices inside countries do not accurately reflect the true social opportunity costs of traded goods, free trade can produce a counterproductive pattern of specialization, yielding global efficiency losses rather than gains. If commercial prices in a country fail to take account of significant external effects they may misidentify where the country's comparative advantage lies.[2] And if international specialization and trade are based on *false* comparative advantages

---

2 As discussed in Chapter 4, neoclassical economists do not like to focus attention on externalities because they imply markets do not allocate resources efficiently. So when mainstream economists discuss discrepancies between commercial costs and social costs which might give rise to counterproductive international divisions of labor they most often cite government subsidies as the cause of the discrepancy.

it can lead to international divisions of labor that are less productive than the less specialized patterns of global production they replace.

For example, we know the social costs of modern agricultural production in the US are greater than the private costs because environmentally destructive effects such as soil erosion, pesticide run-off, and depletion of ground water aquifers go uncounted or are undervalued. This translates into commercial prices for corn in the US that underestimate the true social cost of producing corn in the US. On the other hand, when corn is grown in Mexico farmers live in traditional Mexican villages that are relatively disease and crime free, and where centuries-old social safety nets exist when family members fall on hard times, whereas producing shoes in Mexico requires a Mexican to live in an urban slum or maquiladora zone where disease and crime are higher and safety nets absent. The positive external effects of rural village life when corn is produced in Mexico are undercounted in the commercial price of Mexican corn. So we know the commercial price of corn divided by the commercial price of shoes is lower than the social cost of corn divided by the social cost of shoes in the US, but higher than the social cost of corn divided by the social cost of shoes in Mexico.

If the external effects are large enough, relative commercial prices in the two countries can *misidentify* which country truly has a comparative advantage in corn and which country truly has a comparative advantage in shoes. While the ratio of the commercial price of corn to the commercial price of shoes make it appear that the US is relatively more productive in corn production and Mexico relatively more productive in shoe production, it may be that the comparative advantage of the US is really in shoe production and Mexico's comparative advantage is actually in corn production if all costs were taken into account. The problem is that even if external effects are significant enough so that taking them into account means it is more efficient to continue producing corn in Mexico and shoes in the US, free trade will lead to counterproductive specialization in which the US expands environmentally damaging corn production, importing more shoes from Mexico, while Mexico moves its population from traditional rural villages to urban slums and maquiladoras to increase shoe production, importing more corn from the US. Efficiency losses like this can happen when treaties like NAFTA increase trade because who *will* specialize in what is based on differences in relative *commercial prices* rather than on true, relative *social costs* – which can be substantially different.[3]

---

3 Environmentalists argue that international transportation is a service where commercial prices greatly underestimate true social costs. "Remember the Exxon Valdez!" is the environmentalist's equivalent of "Remember the Alamo!" The discrepancy between social and commercial costs of international transportation always makes it appear that specialization and trade is more efficient than it really is.

Unstable International Markets Can Cause Macro Inefficiencies

Even if international prices for traditional exports from less developed economies did not decline over the long run compared to prices they pay for imports, if prices for LDC exports are highly volatile this can damage their economies leading to global efficiency losses as well. During the first half of the twentieth century there were years when the international price of sugar was ten times higher than in other years. In years when Cuba exported sugar at 20 to 30 cents per pound the Cuban economy ran on all cylinders, but in years when sugar prices fell to 2 to 3 cents per pound the Cuban economy sputtered. The international price of tin experienced similar fluctuations during the same time period, periodically wreaking havoc with the Bolivian economy. One problem is that once the export sector reaches full capacity levels of output there is no way to take further advantage of price spikes. But unfortunately, when the bottom falls out of a traditional export market there is no lower limit on how many people can be thrown out of work and how many businesses can go bankrupt. So even if large drops in export prices in bad years were canceled entirely by equally large increases in good years, LDC economies cannot benefit from price spikes as much as they get hurt when prices crash in their traditional export markets. Another problem is that economic development requires a degree of stability. If once every decade a crash in the price of sugar or tin means local businesses selling to the growing domestic market go bankrupt as well, it is difficult to develop new sectors of the economy. In short, greater reliance on trade can lead to efficiency losses when international prices for your exports prove very unstable.

Adjustment Costs Are Not Always Insignificant

The adjustment costs of moving people and resources out of one industry and into another can be considerable. If adjustment costs are large they can cancel a significant portion of the efficiency gain from a new pattern of international specialization – irrespective of who pays for them. If people must be retrained, if equipment is scrapped before it wears out, if new industries are located in different regions from old ones so people must move to new locations requiring new schools, parks, libraries, water and sewage systems, etc., leaving perfectly useable social infrastructure idle in "rust belt" regions they vacate, all this duplication and waste should be subtracted from any efficiency gains from further specialization and trade. Since a great deal of the adjustment costs are not paid for by the businesses who make the decisions about whether to specialize and trade, the market fails to sufficiently account for adjustment costs. Consequently, when productivity gains from some new international division of labor are meager and adjustment costs large, we can easily get net efficiency losses from trade.

Dynamic Inefficiency

Finally, the theory of comparative advantage is usually interpreted to imply that a country should specialize even more in its traditional export products, since those would presumably be the industries in which the country enjoys a comparative advantage. But LDCs are less developed precisely because they have lower levels of productivity than other economies. If less developed economies further specialize in the sectors they have always specialized in, it may well be *less* likely they will find ways to increase their productivity. In other words, increasing *static* efficiency by specializing even more in today's comparative advantages may prevent changes that would increase productivity a great deal more, and therefore be at the expense of *dynamic* efficiency.

The hallmark of the **Asian development model,** pioneered by Japan and later imitated with great success by South Korea, Hong Kong, Taiwan, and Singapore, and most recently by capitalist China, was that they *did not accept their comparative advantages* at any point in time *as a fait accompli.* Instead *they aggressively pursued plans to create new comparative advantages in industries where it would be easier to achieve larger productivity increases.* Japan moved from exporting textiles, toys, and bicycles right after WWII, to exporting steel and automobiles in the 1960s and early 1970s, to exporting electronic equipment and computer products by the late 1970s and early 1980s. This transition was not the result of a *laissez faire* policy by the Japanese government. This successful transition to a different role in the international division of labor was accomplished through an elaborate system of differential tax rates and terms of credit for businesses in different industries at different times, planned by the Ministry of International Trade and Industry (MITI) and coordinated with the Bank of Japan and the taxing authorities. The whole point of the process was to create new comparative advantages in high productivity industries rather than continue to specialize in industries where productivity growth was slow. Neither Japan nor any of the other countries which followed the Asian development model allowed relative commercial prices in the free market to pick their comparative advantages and determine their pattern of industrialization and trade for them. Had they done so it is unlikely they would have enjoyed as much economic success as they have.[4]

---

4 In *Kicking Away the Ladder* (Anthem Press, 2002), Ha Joon Chang makes a compelling historical case that none of the advanced economies whose governments preach the benefits of free market principles to LDCs today followed free market principles themselves when they were first developing. In all cases protection and subsidies played key roles in historical development success stories.

Why Trade Usually Aggravates Global Inequality

While mainstream trade theorists are adamant in their insistence that freer trade always yields efficiency gains, and practically blind to reasons outlined above why this may not be the case, they are much quieter about the distributive effects of trade. When forced to address this unpleasant topic the academy admits to the following: (1) How any efficiency gains from trade will be distributed between trading partners depends, of course, on the terms of trade. (2) While any feasible terms of trade make both countries better off, this does not mean all groups within each country are benefited. There will usually be losers as well as winners from trade. (3) In the short run owners and workers in exporting industries benefit and owners and workers in importing industries are worse off. (4) In the long run, after resources have moved from industries where imports rise to industries where exports increase, the internal distributive effects of trade favor the owners of relatively abundant factors of production and disadvantage the owners of relatively scarce factors of production. Unfortunately, these dispassionate observations about the predictable distributive effects of trade scarcely do justice to unprecedented increases in global inequality over the past forty years.

Unfair Distribution of the Benefits of Trade between Countries

While it is true that trade *could* take place on terms anywhere in the feasible range – which means trade *could* reduce inequality between countries if the terms distributed more of the efficiency gains to poorer countries – unfortunately, the international terms of trade *usually* distribute the lion's share of any efficiency gains to countries that were better off in the first place, and thereby aggravate global inequality. The most important reason they do this is that as long as capital is scarce globally, that is, as long as having more machines and equipment would allow someone, someplace in the global economy to work more productively, there is good reason to believe the terms of trade will distribute more of the efficiency gains from trade to capital-rich countries. Interested readers should see Appendix B in my *Panic Rules! Everything You Need to Know About the Global Economy* (South End Press, 1999) for a simple model that demonstrates this point. There I adapt the simple corn model from Chapter 3 of this book to include a second good, machines, to provide a good for which corn can be traded, and to play the role of "capital." The only difference assumed between countries in the model is that "northern" countries begin with more machines than "southern" countries.

Consistent with CA theory, the model predicts a global efficiency gain when northern countries specialize in machine production which is relatively capital intensive, export machines, and import corn, while southern countries specialize in corn production which is relatively labor intensive, export corn, and import machines. But the model allows us to go beyond CA theory to determine where in the feasible range the terms of trade between corn and machines will fall if left to be settled by the laws of supply and demand. The central conclusion from the model is that as long as capital (machines, in the model) is scarce globally, *even when international markets for corn and machines are both competitive* free market terms of trade give more of the efficiency gain from trade to northern countries than to southern countries, aggravating global inequality.

The intuition is straightforward: When northern countries specialize in producing machines in which they have a comparative advantage, and southern economies specialize in corn which is their comparative advantage, there should be an efficiency gain. But as long as machines are scarce compared to labor globally, the southern economies compete among themselves for scarce machines, turning the terms of trade against themselves and in favor of the northern countries. The implications are profound: *Even if international markets are competitive, free market terms of trade will tend to aggravate global inequality in the normal course of events.*[5]

Political economists from the Global South have identified additional factors that adversely affect the terms of trade for southern exports compared to southern imports. (1) If capital intensive industries are characterized by a faster pace of innovation than labor intensive industries, the simple corn–machine model discussed above predicts the terms of trade will deteriorate for southern countries. (2) When income rises the fraction of income spent on different goods often changes. Unfortunately, many less developed countries export goods people buy less of when their income rises and import goods people buy more of when their income rises. This erodes the terms of

---

5 In our simple corn model in Chapter 3 the interest rate distributed the efficiency gain from the increased productivity of borrowers when their borrowed seed corn allowed them to use the more productive CIT instead of the less productive LIT. In that model as long as seed corn was scarce, borrowers competed among themselves and bid interest rates up to the point where the *entire* efficiency gain went to the lenders. In the simple corn–machine model of international trade the terms of trade distribute the efficiency gain when imported machines allow southern countries to produce corn using a more productive technology. In this model as long as machines are scarce, southern countries compete among themselves to import more machines by offering to pay more corn for a machine until the terms of trade become favorable to northern machine exporters, who thereby capture most of the increased efficiency in the southern economies. However, there is one interesting difference: If capital is scarce free market terms of trade will distribute more of the efficiency gain to better off northern countries aggravating global inequality, but they do not generally distribute the *entire* efficiency gain to the northern countries. One way to interpret this difference is to conclude that international trade is sometimes a less "efficient" means of international exploitation than international credit markets.

trade for LDCs as world income increases. (3) If trade unions are stronger in more developed than less developed economies, wage costs will hold steadier in MDCs than LDCs during global downturns, leading to deterioration in the terms of trade for LDCs. And finally, (4) if MDCs export products that are more differentiated, or MDC exporters have more market power than LDC exporters, the terms of trade will be even more disadvantageous to LDCs than would be the case if international markets were perfectly competitive.

All this leads to the conclusion that if left to market forces and power imbalances that generally favor richer countries the terms of international trade will continue to award more developed economies a greater share of any efficiency gains from increased international specialization and trade. But this does not mean that trade must aggravate inequality between countries. Ironically, the easiest way to reduce global inequality is simply by setting the terms of trade to distribute more of the efficiency gain to poorer countries than richer ones. *The existence and size of any efficiency gain from specialization and trade does **not** depend on the terms of trade.* The terms of trade merely distribute the efficiency gain between the trading partners. The efficiency gain they distribute is the same size no matter where in the feasible range the terms of trade fall. So there are just as many mutually advantageous terms of trade that reduce global inequality as terms that increase global inequality. Moreover, unlike foreign aid, where donors do not gain materially,[6] even terms of trade that give poor countries let us say two-thirds of the efficiency gain, and thereby reduce inequality between countries, would still give their more wealthy trading partners one-third of the efficiency gain, and therefore leave wealthier countries better off as well. But this will not happen if the terms of trade are left to market forces. This will not happen as long as non-competitive international markets favor richer countries. This can only happen if international terms of trade are determined through political negotiation where all parties share a commitment to reducing global inequality as well as benefiting themselves. In short, the only reason trade cannot be used to reduce global inequality is because the political will to do so is lacking among MDC governments.

Unfair Distribution of the Costs and Benefits of Trade within Countries

When the gap between rich and poor countries increases, global inequality rises. But when the gap between the rich and poor *within* countries increases, global inequality

---

6 I abstract here from the seamy side of foreign aid where strings are attached to extract material advantages such as reductions in tariffs and capital controls, relaxation in restrictions on foreign ownership, and purchase agreements that materially benefit businesses in the donor country.

rises as well. The recent rise of the BRICS – Brazil, Russia, India, China, and South Africa – relative to Europe and North America has reduced inequality somewhat between countries recently. Unfortunately inequality of wealth and income inside MDCs, LDCs, and BRICS has been rising steadily over the past twenty years, and there is good reason to believe the expansion of trade is partly to blame. To understand why trade has aggravated inequalities inside MDCs we need go no farther than mainstream trade theory itself. After David Ricardo's theory of comparative advantage, the most famous theory in international economics is due to two Scandinavian economists, Eli Heckscher and Bertil Ohlin. According to Heckscher-Ohlin theory, countries will tend to have a comparative advantage in goods that use inputs, or factors of production, in which the country is relatively abundant. But this means trade increases the demand for relatively abundant factors of production and decreases the demand for factors that are relatively scarce within countries. In advanced economies where the capital–labor ratio is higher than elsewhere, and therefore capital is "relatively abundant," Heckscher-Ohlin theory predicts that increased trade will increase the demand for capital, increasing its return, and decrease the demand for labor, depressing wages. Of course this is exactly what has occurred in the US, making the AFL-CIO a consistent critic of trade liberalization. In advanced economies where the ratio of skilled to unskilled labor is higher than elsewhere, Heckscher-Ohlin theory also predicts that increased trade will increase the demand for skilled labor and decrease the demand for unskilled labor and thereby increase wage differentials. In a study published by the Institute for International Economics in 1997, William Cline estimated that 39% of the increase in wage inequality in the US over the previous twenty years was due solely to increased trade.

However, Heckscher-Ohlin theory cannot explain rising inequality inside the lesser developed economies. As a matter of fact, Heckscher-Ohlin theory predicts just the reverse. Increased trade should increase returns to labor, and unskilled labor in particular, since those are relatively abundant factors in most LDCs, while reducing the returns to capital and skilled labor since those are relatively scarce factors in underdeveloped economies. In other words, Heckscher-Ohlin theory predicts that increased trade should aggravate inequalities within advanced economies, but should ameliorate inequalities within third world economies.

The problem is not with Heckscher and Ohlin's logic – which like the logic of comparative advantage theory is impeccable. The problem is that all theories implicitly assume no changes in other dynamics the theory does not address. Economic theories are famous for the qualifying phrase *ceteris paribus* – all other things remaining equal. When the real world does not cooperate with the theorist, and allows other dynamics to proceed, we often find the predictions of some particular theory are not borne out. That is not necessarily because the theory was flawed. It can simply be because the predicted effects of the theory are overwhelmed by the effects of some other dynamic the theory never pretended to take into account. In this case I believe the dynamics unaccounted for have to do with how globalization has affected third world agriculture.

First, the so-called "Green Revolution" in agricultural technology made much of the rural labor force redundant in the third world. Then neoliberal globalization accelerated the replacement of small scale, peasant farming for domestic production by large scale, export-oriented agriculture dominated by large landholders, and increasingly by multinational agribusiness. To be sure, third world peasants always made a miserable living on the land by first world standards. But they often make a better living than their cousins thrown off the land who crowd into every major city in the third world from Lima to Sao Paulo to Lagos to Cape Town to Bombay to Bangkok to Manila. While cash incomes are meager in third world agriculture, they are better than joblessness and beggary in third world cities.[7] Three decades ago large amounts of land in the third world had a sufficiently low value to permit billions of peasant households to live on it producing mostly for their own consumption, even though their productivity was quite low. The Green Revolution, globalization, and export-oriented agriculture have raised the value of that land. Peasant squatters are no longer tolerated. Peasant renters are thrown off by owners who want to use the land to produce more valuable export crops with capital intensive technologies. Even peasants who own their family plots fall easy prey to local economic and political elites who now see a far more valuable use for that land and have become more aggressive land-grabbers through a variety of legal and extralegal means. And finally, as third world governments succumb to pressure from the IMF, World Bank, and WTO to relax restrictions on foreign ownership of land, local land sharks are joined by multinational agribusiness, adding to the human exodus. The combined effect of these forces has driven billions of peasants out of rural areas into teeming, third world megacities in a very short period of time. This means there are many more ex-peasants applying for new labor intensive manufacturing jobs produced by trade liberalization in third world countries than there are new jobs. Even a casual glance at the scale of the human exodus from traditional agriculture explains why unemployment is increasing, not decreasing, and wage rates are falling, not rising, in less developed economies. So political economists need not deny that NAFTA

7 Interested readers should see the world acclaimed *Apu* film trilogy by Satyajit Ray, whose main character experiences this painful transformation in Indian village life.

has created new manufacturing jobs in Mexico – as Heckscher-Ohlin theory predicts. Instead we should point out that disastrous changes in Mexican agriculture accelerated by NAFTA have overwhelmed small beneficial Heckscher-Ohlin effects on employment and wages, which explains the large increase in overall *un*employment and the dramatic *fall* in real wages that have occurred since the Mexican government signed the NAFTA treaty twenty years ago.

Why International Investment Could Increase Global Efficiency

International investment can take the form of *multinational companies (MNCs) from MDCs building subsidiaries in LDCs.*[8] This is called **direct foreign investment**, or DFI. Alternatively, international investment can take the form of *multinational banks from MDCs lending to companies or governments in LDCs, or wealthy individuals or mutual funds from MDCs buying stocks of LDC companies, or bonds of LDC companies or governments.* This is called **international financial investment**, or IFI. As was the case with international trade, mainstream economic theory focuses on the potentially beneficial effects of both kinds of international investment and largely ignores the potentially damaging effects.

If machinery and know-how increase productivity more when located in a subsidiary in a southern economy than they do when located in a plant in the home country of the MNC, DFI increases global efficiency. If a loan to a foreign borrower increases productivity more abroad than it would have if lent in-country, IFI increases global efficiency. Mainstream theory assumes if profits are higher from DFI than domestic investment this is *because* the investment raises productivity more abroad than at home. So according to mainstream theory when MNCs invest wherever profits are highest they will serve the interest of global efficiency as well as their own interest. Similarly, mainstream theory assumes if foreign borrowers are willing to pay higher interest rates than domestic borrowers this is *because* the loan raises foreign productivity more than it would domestic productivity. So mainstream international finance teaches when multinational banks lend wherever they can get the highest rate of interest they serve the social interest as well as their own interest. Of course this is nothing more than Adam Smith's vision of a beneficent invisible hand at work in some new settings. It is the potential upside potential of IFI illustrated by

8 While most international investment still takes place between northern countries, I focus on north–south investment because that is of greater interest to political economists concerned with global inequality.

model 3.2 we studied in Chapter 3, where we implicitly assumed northern lenders all found southern borrowers whose productivity was actually enhanced by the loans they received.

Why International Investment Often Decreases Global Efficiency

Where mainstream economists see only beneficent invisible hands at work, political economists notice malevolent invisible feet lurking near by. Political economists focus on why the social interest may not coincide so nicely with the private interests of multinational companies and banks. Just because DFI is more profitable does not necessarily mean the plant and machinery are more productive than they would have been at home. DFI might be more profitable because the bargaining power of third world workers is even less than that of their first world counterparts. Or DFI might be more profitable because third world governments are more desperate to woo foreign investors and offer larger tax breaks and lower environmental standards to businesses locating there. Neither of these reasons why profits from DFI might be higher than profits from domestic operations imply that the plant, machinery or know-how raises productivity more abroad than it would have at home. In the opposite case more DFI will decrease global efficiency not increase it, even if profits from foreign operations are higher than from domestic operations.

It is also not necessarily the case that just because foreign borrowers are willing to pay higher rates of interest, loans are more useful or productive abroad than at home. When a dictator in Zaire borrowed billions in US credit markets over a thirty-year period, often at exorbitant interest rates, he used the loans mostly to line the pockets of his family and political allies and buy weapons to intimidate his subjects. There was no increase in economic productivity in Zaire, and consequently little with which to pay back international creditors after Mobutu Sese Seko departed in 1997. At the same time Mobutu was successfully borrowing billions in US credit markets without raising productivity in Zaire one iota, many technological innovators in the US trying to launch start-up companies to revolutionize communications systems worldwide were being turned down for loans in those same credit markets.

But a more serious problem with international lending turned out to be that when production in developing economies is tied more tightly to the international credit system and the credit system breaks down, real economies and their inhabitants suffer huge losses of production, employment, and accumulation of productive capital needed for economic development. Even before the latest and worst financial crisis in 2008, financial crises were inflicting serious damage on real economies over and over again. In Mexico in 1995, in Thailand, Malaysia, Indonesia, South Korea, and Singapore in 1997, in Russia in 1998, in Brazil and Ecuador in 1999, in Turkey in 2000, and in Argentina in 2001 when international investors panicked and sold off their currency holdings, stocks, and bonds in these "emerging market economies" there were huge efficiency losses in their "real" economies, and therefore the "real" global economy as well.

In a second international corn model in Chapter 9 we explore the downside potential of international finance by appending an international financial sector with downside as well as upside potentials to our simple international corn model. It is popular to dismiss market panics as aberrations, and the result of irrational, "herd-like" behavior. First we use model 9.1 to demonstrate that investors who "panic" are engaging in extremely rational behavior, and it is those who fail to panic who behave irrationally. Model 9.2 goes on to illustrate graphically how this perfectly rational behavior on the part of investors which can lead to a financial crisis makes the real global economy less efficient. The intuition is quite simple: When all goes well in the international financial system it *can* increase the number of loans, which *can* increase economic productivity, as mainstream theory and model 3.2 highlight. But there is a downside as well as an upside potential. What proponents of international financial liberalization don't like to admit is that increasingly footloose international lending has greatly exacerbated the likelihood and severity of asset bubbles in emerging market economies. And when we tie real emerging market economies ever more tightly to an international credit system which facilitates flight whenever a bubble bursts – as all bubbles eventually must – the crash is made worse and leads to even greater efficiency losses in real emerging market economies, as our second model 9.2 illustrates. What neoliberals in power at the IMF, World Bank, WTO, OECD, and US Treasury Department tout as "international financial reform" has not only lashed emerging market economies more tightly to the international credit system, it has made the international financial system a great deal more unstable and dangerous, literally *creating accidents waiting to happen.*

Why International Investment Usually Aggravates Global Inequality

Model 3.2 illustrates how international lending *can* increase global efficiency, but also why it *usually* increases global inequality as well even when it increases global efficiency. Global efficiency rises if international loans from northern economies raise productivity more in southern economies than they would have raised productivity domestically. But when capital is scarce globally, as it long has been, competition among southern borrowers drives interest rates on international loans up to the point where lenders capture the greater part of the efficiency gain. So even when international financial markets work smoothly and efficiently and do increase global efficiency, they *usually* increase income inequality between countries as well.

Model 9.2 where we append a more realistic version of international finance to a global corn economy demonstrates how international financial crises cause efficiency losses in "real" developing economies. But lost employment, production, and productive capital in Thailand, Malaysia, Indonesia, and South Korea were not the only casualties of the East Asian financial crisis of 1997–1998. That crisis, in particular, highlighted how liberalizing international finance can increase global wealth inequality as well as global income inequality. What I called the "Great Global Asset Swindle" when writing about it in *Z Magazine* in the aftermath of the Asian financial crisis works like this: International investors lose confidence in a third world economy, and dump its currency, bonds, and stocks. At the insistence of the IMF, the central bank in the third world country tightens the money supply to boost domestic interest rates to prevent further capital outflows in an unsuccessful attempt to protect the currency. Even healthy domestic companies can no longer obtain or afford loans so they join the ranks of bankrupted domestic businesses available for purchase. As a precondition for receiving the IMF bailout the government abolishes any remaining restrictions on foreign ownership of corporations, banks, and land. With a depreciated local currency, and a long list of bankrupt local businesses, the economy is ready for the acquisition experts from Western multinational corporations and banks who come to the fire sale with a thick wad of almighty dollars in their pockets.

In conclusion, international investment *can* increase global efficiency if it helps allocate productive know-how and resources to uses where they are more valuable. But it *can also* decrease global efficiency, particularly if it ties real economies ever more tightly to an unstable credit system that crashes with increasing frequency. International investment *could* reduce global inequality if interest rates on international loans were low enough to distribute more of the efficiency gain to borrowers than to lenders. After all, there is no economic "law" that says international borrowing *must* increase global inequality. Just as there are always fair terms of trade that diminish global inequality, there are obviously interest rates that would permit southern economies to enjoy more of the benefits of improved global efficiency. But those interest rates are not going to be generated by the laws of supply and demand in the international credit market.

Unfortunately, agencies like the Inter American Development Bank and World Bank have cut back on loan programs charging poor countries below market rates of interest. Worse still, so-called "subsidized" loans from international agencies are now mainly used as carrots to go along with the stick of international credit boycotts used to cajole and threaten debtor nations reluctant to subject their citizens to the deprivations of IMF austerity programs, and place their most attractive economic assets on the international auction block at bargain basement prices. So, unfortunately international investment *will* increase inequality when interest rates are determined by market forces in a world where capital is scarce, and where international financial crises create bargain basement sales for third world business assets no longer off limits to foreign bargain hunters. In the late 1990s and early 2000s the positive potential of liberalizing international investment was superseded by the negative potential in one LDC after another. In 2008, residents of the US and Europe whose governments were primarily responsible for international financial liberalization learned how the downside potential feels when chickens came home to roost.

Before the financial crisis of 2008 and the Great Recession that followed in its aftermath most mainstream economists believed neoliberal globalization had produced significant efficiency gains, while admittedly increasing global inequality. Evidence of escalating inequality was so overwhelming that nobody dared deny it, and for all who wished to see, it stood out as the most salient characteristic of the global economy from 1978 to 2008. After seven years of recession and stagnation those who continue to press for yet more of the same policies find it increasingly difficult to convince the public there are efficiency gains from neoliberal globalization. But even before the latest debacle, during the supposed "good times," there was no evidence whatsoever suggesting efficiency gains from neoliberalism. As a matter of fact, there was overwhelming evidence that neoliberal policies had slowed global growth rates significantly for anyone who cared to look.

A report prepared by Angus Maddison for the Organization for Economic Cooperation and Development (OECD) titled *Monitoring the World Economy 1820–1992* published in 1995 refuted the popular impression that neoliberal policies had increased world economic growth. Maddison documented that the average annual rate of growth of world GDP per capita during the neoliberal period from 1974 to 1992 was only *half* what it had been during the previous Bretton Woods era from 1950 to 1973. In *Scorecard on Globalization 1980–2000: Twenty Years of Diminished Progress* the Center for Economic Policy Research updated Maddison's work and reconfirmed his conclusion that neoliberal policies continued to be accompanied by a significant *decrease* in the rate of growth of world GDP per capita up through 2000. If dismantling the Bretton Woods system while promoting capital and trade liberalization had really produced more efficiency gains than losses, it is hard to imagine how world growth rates would have been cut in half! Ignoring overwhelming evidence of diminished performance, focusing only on the beneficial *potentials* of trade and capital liberalization, and downplaying catastrophic effects on global inequality were all part of the "free market jubilee" that began in the 1980s and continues to be celebrated by a majority of mainstream economists as well as the world's intellectual and governing elites despite its increasingly obvious disastrous consequences.

Open Economy Macroeconomics

In Chapters 6 and 7 we learned how aggregate demand explains the causes of some kinds of unemployment and inflation, and studied the logic of fiscal and monetary policies designed to alleviate these problems. But in those chapters we assumed the economy did not participate in, or was "closed" off from, international economic activities. Since fiscal and monetary policy affect a country's exports, imports, international investments, and the value of its currency, we need to extend our thinking when an economy is "open" to international trade and investment. Similarly, while the closed economy macro model 9.3 is sufficient for some purposes, we need the open economy macro model 9.4 to understand things like the logic and effects of IMF conditionality agreements, and austerity policies the European Commission imposes on the PIGS. But before we can build our simple open economy macro model we must first have a basic understanding of how international currency markets work.

International Currency Markets

Countries usually have their own currencies, with rare exceptions like monetary unions such as the *European Monetary Union* (EMU), or **Eurozone** discussed later. The US has dollars, the UK has pounds, Argentina has pesos, Japan has yen, etc. There are international currency markets where again, with rare exceptions, anyone who wants to buy or sell a particular currency can do so. But if I want to buy yen, for example, what do I use to pay for them? I use some other currency, such as the dollar or the pound. So the international currency market is not a market where a good or service is bought and sold, or where assets like stocks and bonds are bought and sold, but a market where people use one currency to buy a different currency. Which is why the "price" of a currency is quoted in terms of how many units of some other currency one must pay to buy it. For example, when I went on line to a currency calculator at 2:33 p.m. EST on February 11, 2014 I was told that if I wanted to buy one British pound I would have to pay 1.644926 US dollars. If an Englishman had checked at the same time on the same day he would have been told that if he wanted to buy one US dollar he would have to pay 0.607930 British pounds. When I visited the same currency calculator at 9:35 a.m. EST on February 12, 2014 I was told I must pay 1.65536 dollars to buy a pound, and an Englishman would have been told he could buy a dollar for 0.604099 pounds. So in less than 24 hours the dollar had declined, or *depreciated* in value relative to the pound, and the pound had increased, or *appreciated* in value relative to the dollar.[9] But what determines what the "value" of a currency will be?

For the most part the "laws" of supply and demand we studied in Chapter 4 determine what the values of currencies will be. Which means that when the demand for a currency increases, or when the supply of a currency decreases, its "price" will tend to rise, i.e. it will appreciate in value. While a decrease in demand for a currency or increase in its supply will cause the currency to depreciate in value.

But where do the supplies and demands for currencies come from? For example, where does the supply of British pounds and demand for British pounds in international currency markets come from? Any foreigner who wants to buy British exports must buy pounds in the international currency markets to do so, creating demand for British pounds. Any foreign MNC that wants to open a subsidiary in the UK, and any foreign mutual fund that wants to buy British Treasury bonds must buy pounds to do so, creating demand for British pounds. And any British MNC that wants to repatriate profits from its subsidiaries abroad must buy pounds to do so, creating demand for British pounds. Conversely, anyone in the UK who wants to purchase an import from abroad must use pounds to buy foreign currency to do so, adding to the supply of pounds in international currency markets. Any British MNC that wants to engage in direct foreign investment, and any British mutual fund that wants to engage in international financial investment must use pounds to buy foreign currency to do so, adding to the supply of pounds in international currency markets. And any foreign MNC that wants to repatriate profits from its subsidiary in the UK must use pounds to buy foreign currency to do so, adding to the supply of pounds in international currency markets.

9 It is common to speak of the dollar "losing value." But there are two different ways in which the dollar might "lose value" which are not the same at all. If my dollar buys me fewer beers in the US it is common to say it has "lost value." But economists already have a name for this – inflation. So when economists say the dollar has lost value we mean it has depreciated relative to other currencies, not that its domestic buying power has decreased. This distinction is important because it is quite possible, for example, for there to be inflation in the US – the dollar buys fewer beers – at the same time that the value of the dollar is rising in international currency markets – the dollar buys more British pounds.

Aggregate Supply and Demand in the Open Economy Model

In an open economy, besides domestic production, imports add to the supply of final goods and services available. And besides the demand that comes from the domestic household, business, and government sectors, foreign demand for exports adds to the demand for final goods and services. So when we write the equilibrium condition for an open economy we have:

$$Y + M = AS = AD = C + I + G + X;$$

which is traditionally written:

$$Y = C + I + G + X - M$$

Where M stands for imports and X stands for exports, and X – M is called net exports. Imports depend positively on the value of a country's currency, on its rate of inflation, and on the country's income. If the currency appreciates imports become cheaper compared to domestic goods. If the inflation rate is higher than it is in a country's trading partners, imports also become cheaper than domestic goods. Finally, just as consumers will buy more domestically produced goods when their income is higher, they will buy more imported goods as well. Exports depend negatively on the value of a country's currency and on its inflation rate compared to the inflation rates in its trading partners. If a country's currency appreciates its exports become more expensive to foreign buyers. If the inflation rate is higher than it is in a country's trading partners, it also becomes more expensive for foreigners to buy its exports. In the simple open economy macro model in Chapter 9 we express imports only as a positive, linear function of domestic income:

$$M = m + MPM(Y); m > 0; 0 < MPM < 1$$

Where MPM is the **marginal propensity to import** out of income, and m is the amount a country will import independent of fluctuations in its national income.

Income Expenditure Multipliers in the Open Economy Model

There is an important change in the size of the income expenditure multipliers when we change from a closed to an open economy model. In a closed economy when production rises to meet new demand and income rises as a result, the new income can go into new taxes, savings, or consumption. To the extent that new income goes into taxes or savings there is no further stimulus to aggregate demand, and no "multiplier effect." To the extent that new income goes into consumption spending it stimulates further production. But in an open economy not all consumption spending stimulates domestic production. If consumers buy domestically produced goods there is still a "multiplier effect" *vis-à-vis* the domestic economy. But to the extent that consumers buy imported goods, their new demand stimulates production abroad, not in their home economy. This implies that income expenditure multipliers in the open economy model must be smaller than in the closed economy model. The open economy income expenditure multiplier, $[1/(1 - MPC + MPM)]$, is smaller than its closed economy counterpart, $[1/(1 - MPC)]$. This also means that multipliers for "trading" economies like the UK will be smaller than multipliers for more self-sufficient economies like the US. The marginal propensity to import in the US is roughly 14% while the MPM in the UK is roughly 32%, more than twice as high, which means the multiplier effect of changes in aggregate demand are significantly greater in the US than in the UK. So in an open economy where part of any new income is spent on imports, the overall change in equilibrium GDP, ΔY, is equal to this new, somewhat smaller multiplier times whatever the initial change in aggregate demand may be. If the government changes its spending by ΔG, we multiply this times the new multiplier to find out how much equilibrium GDP will change, ΔY. If the government changes taxes by ΔT we multiply $-MPC\Delta T$ times the new multiplier. If business investment demand changes by ΔI we multiply this by the new multiplier. Finally, there is a new component of aggregate demand that might change initially: exports. If foreign demand for exports changes by ΔX we multiply this by the new multiplier $[1/(1 - MPC + MPM)]$ to find out how much equilibrium GDP will change as a result.

Capital Flows in the Open Economy Model

As explained, exports create demand for a nation's currency in international currency markets while imports add to the supply. If the value of exports exceeds the value of imports we say a country has a trade surplus, while if imports exceed exports we say the country has a trade deficit. Notice that a UK trade deficit of 10 billion pounds means that the supply of pounds in international currency markets has increased by 10 billion pounds more than the demand for pounds as a result of the UK's trading activity during a year, which tends to make the pound depreciate in value. While a trade surplus of 10 billion pounds means the demand for pounds has increased 10 billion more than the supply of pounds in international currency markets, which tends to make the pound appreciate. We can express the effect of a nation's trading activity on the net demand for its currency as: TNDC = X − M = X − [m + MPC(Y)].

We have also seen that international investment activity contributes to both the demand and supply of a nation's currency in international currency markets. A simple model cannot account for a variety of influences on decisions about DFI and repatriation of profits and earnings. But fortunately these aspects of international investment are far less volatile than international financial investment. And fortunately choices about whether to buy foreign or domestic bonds are particularly sensitive to one variable: differences in domestic and foreign interest rates. As regulations on international "capital flows" have largely been removed, as the pool of liquid global wealth has grown, and as communication technology facilitates 24-hour trading, tens of billions of dollars often move in a matter of hours in response to small changes in relative interest rates in different countries. When domestic interest rates fall relative to interest rates in the rest of the world fewer foreigners will invest their financial wealth in a country, and more domestic wealth holders will invest abroad where interest rates are higher. Conversely, a rise in domestic interest rates relative to the rest of the world induces an inflow of foreign financial investment in response to the higher interest payments, and reduces the outflow of domestic financial investment. So even in a simple open economy model we can account for how international investment activity affects the net demand for a nation's currency in international currency markets using a simple linear function: IINDC = 1000r − k where r is the domestic rate of interest expressed as a decimal. This simple relationship is sufficient to capture the major cause of changes in the most volatile part of net demand for a country's currency from international investment activity. Combining the trade effects with the investment effects, we have the overall net demand for a nation's currency in international currency markets:

$$ONDC = TNDC + IINDC = X − [m + MPC(Y)] + 1000r − k$$

With these additions, besides unemployment or inflation gaps, the composition of output, and government budget deficits or surpluses, we can calculate changes in the overall net demand for a nation's currency for any "state" of the economy. We can also calculate the effects of fiscal and monetary policy on trade, international financial investment, and the net demand for a nation's currency.

In the next chapter we use this simple open economy macro model 9.4 to illustrate the predictable effects of IMF conditionality agreements and understand why they give rise to such controversy. In exchange for a "bail out loan" that allows the country to pay off international loans coming due that it would otherwise have to default on, IMF "conditionality agreements" typically demand that the recipient government reduce spending and increase taxes, and that the central bank reduce the money supply – in addition to demanding removal of restrictions on international trade and investment and foreign ownership. Since the economy is invariably already in recession, fiscal and monetary "austerity" further aggravate the recession. Reducing government spending and increasing taxes both decrease aggregate demand and therefore decrease employment and production. Reducing the money supply raises interest rates, which reduces domestic investment demand and further decreases aggregate demand, employment, production, and additions to productive capital. This is why IMF programs commonly called "structural adjustment agreements" in the 1980s and "conditionality agreements" in the 1990s and early 2000s elicited strong opposition from citizens of less developed countries, often resulting in "anti-IMF riots."

But it would wrong to assume that IMF economists are ignorant of standard macroeconomic theory, or that the IMF is gratuitously sadistic. The IMF policies are designed to increase the probability that the country will be able to repay its international creditors, and makes perfect sense once one realizes this is their goal. If a government is in danger of defaulting on its "sovereign" international debt, forcing it to turn budget deficits into surpluses provides funds for repaying its international creditors. If the private sector is in danger of defaulting on international loans, anything that reduces imports and increases exports, or increases the inflow of new international investment will provide foreign exchange needed for debt repayment. Deflationary fiscal and monetary policy reduces aggregate demand and therefore inflation, which tends to increase exports and decrease imports. In reducing aggregate demand, deflationary fiscal and monetary policy also reduces output, and therefore income, which further reduces imports. Tight monetary policy raises domestic interest rates which reduces the outflow of domestic financial investment and increases the inflow of new foreign financial investment, providing more foreign exchange to pay off the international creditors whose loans are coming due. Finally, since all in the country who owe foreign creditors receive their income in local currency, anything that keeps the local currency from depreciating will allow debtors to buy more dollars with their local currency, which is what they need to pay their international creditors. In short, IMF austerity programs are well designed to turn stricken economies into more effective debt repayment machines as quickly as possible.

There is little doubt about what the short-run effects of fiscal and monetary austerity policies will be. Instead, we have a simple conflict of priorities: If the interests of international creditors are given priority, the IMF programs make perfectly good sense. They are only counterproductive if one cares about employment, output, productive investment, and prospects for economic development in economies where the poorest four billion people in the world live and suffer. This conflict of interest is demonstrated formally in model 9.4 where we apply our simple open economy macro model to a stylized IMF conditionality program for Brazil.

Monetary Unions and the Eurozone

Just as austerity was the response by the powers-that-be to financial crises in less developed countries for the past thirty years, austerity has been the response of the European Commission (EC) and European Central Bank (ECB) to the financial crisis that struck Europe in 2008 as well. As we will see in the next chapter when we use our open economy macro model 9.4 to analyze the case of Greece, the predictable effects, and whose interests have been served or sacrificed, are very much the same. However, there are important differences worthy of note:

- Prior to 2008 draconian austerity as the policy response to financial crisis had been almost exclusively reserved for third world countries. Blatantly prioritizing the interests of creditors over the wellbeing of a majority of *first world citizens* had not been done since conservative champions of austerity like Herbert Hoover in the US and Stanley Baldwin in the UK were sacked by voters early in the Great Depression. This has now changed: As explained in Chapters 6 and 7, ever since the onset of the financial crisis in 2008 governments in the advanced economies – whether center-right or center-left – have chosen to spare no expense to bail out banks and creditors while simultaneously insisting that everyone else must tighten their belt. It appears we have entered a new era where governments subservient to the interests of the financial sector and large corporations are now willing to administer the same nasty medicine to whites and middle class people in more advanced economies that they formerly doled out only to poor people of color in less developed economies.
- Of the 28 countries that are currently members of the European Union (EU) 18 of them are also members of the European Monetary Union (EMU), or Eurozone, and share a common currency, the euro. No country in the EMU any longer has its own currency, and the supply of currency for the entire EMU is controlled by the European Central Bank (ECB).
- There are important structural differences between more and less developed countries within the Eurozone. Productivity is lower in countries like Portugal,

Ireland, Greece, and Spain than in countries like Germany, Belgium, and the Netherlands. Labels like "northern" and "southern" generally serve, with obvious exceptions like Ireland in the north which is structurally more like its fellow PIGS in the south.

Even prior to 2008 there were significant trade imbalances between northern and southern countries within the Eurozone due to differences in productivity. For example, Greece already had a large trade deficit with Germany or, what is the same thing, Germany had a significant trade surplus with Greece. This trade imbalance generated more employment in Germany and more unemployment in Greece than there would have been otherwise. How are trade imbalances and the imbalances in unemployment that accompany them between countries reduced if they have separate currencies? As we have seen, back when Greece had the drachma and Germany had the deutschmark, the Greek trade deficit with Germany would have increased the supply of drachmas in international currency markets, which would have driven the value of the drachma down, which would have made imports from Germany more expensive for Greeks and Greek exports to Germany less expensive for Germans, which would have reduced the size of the Greek trade deficit with Germany and also reduced unemployment in Greece. The German trade surplus with Greece would have increased the demand for deutschmarks in international currency markets, which would have driven the value of the mark up, which would have made imports from Greece less expensive for Germans and German exports to Greece more expensive for Greeks, which would have reduced the size of the German trade surplus with Greece and also increased unemployment in Germany. But starting in 2001 Germany and Greece shared the same currency, the euro, so exchange rate adjustments could no longer eliminate trade imbalances between the two countries, nor the imbalances in unemployment that accompany them.

When the global financial crisis triggered the Great Recession it was inevitable that unemployment would rise significantly in the EMU as a whole. However, without exchange rate adjustments to distribute unemployment more equally, the rise in unemployment has been distributed very unequally among countries in the Eurozone. For example, in July 2012 the unemployment rate in Portugal was 16.0%, in Ireland was 14.8%, in Greece was 25.3%, and in Spain was 25.8%; while the unemployment rate in Germany was 5.5%, and in the Netherlands was only 5.3%. These dramatic differences in unemployment rates in the EMU in 2012 are the result of unabated trade imbalances within the Eurozone that can no longer be abated by exchange rate adjustments and four years of draconian fiscal austerity imposed on the PIGS by the European Commission (EC).

Especially for smaller and less developed European countries the advantages of joining the EMU were obvious at the turn of the century when it was being formed. In a global economy where the frequency and severity of runs on small and weak country currencies was growing, attaching your wagon to the mighty euro to avoid currency volatility made a great deal of sense. It also made it easier and cheaper for the PIGS to borrow from international credit markets. The disadvantages of membership in the EMU were less obvious in the early years but have become painfully apparent since the onset of the crisis. As explained above, when trade imbalances are reduced via exchange rate adjustments deficit countries enjoy increases in employment. However, there is another way to reduce a trade deficit. As our simple open economy macro model makes clear reducing national income and/or inflation will also reduce imports and increase exports. Unfortunately using fiscal austerity to reduce trade deficits with countries like Germany and the Netherlands aggravates unemployment problems considerably in the PIGS.[10] The other obvious disadvantage of joining a monetary union is that a country "gives up" the monetary policy tool. As we saw in Chapter 7, monetary policy can be used to combat unemployment and inflation. There are times when particularly strong stimulus is needed and it is advantageous to be able to engage in expansionary fiscal and monetary policy at the same time. This was certainly what needed to be done in both Europe and the US in 2009. There can also be practical considerations that make it difficult to deploy expansionary fiscal policy, in which case having the option of expansionary monetary policy is very helpful. Since 2010 a Republican-controlled House of Representatives has vetoed fiscal stimulus in the US, but fortunately the Fed has been able to engage in considerable monetary expansion. The European Central Bank has done far less to expand the money supply in the Eurozone, which may have suited countries like Germany and the Netherlands with low unemployment rates, but certainly has not helped the millions of unemployed workers in the PIGS.[11]

10 This is sometimes talked of as the difference between "external devaluation" and "internal devaluation." In the first case it is simply the value of a country's currency that falls. In the second case it is the level of production and income in a country that falls – which is far more painful.
11 Under the leadership of Chairman Bernanke the Fed was considerably more expansionary than the ECB from 2008 to 2013, which is one reason why recovery in the US was stronger than in the EU.

9

Macroeconomic Models

This is the last of three chapters with formal models. The five models in this chapter illustrate important themes in finance, macroeconomics, and international investment. As before, readers who want to be able to analyze economic problems for themselves are strongly encouraged to work through the models in this chapter.

Model 9.1: Finance

Model 9.1 illustrates the neglected downside potential of the financial sector as well as the upside potential highlighted by mainstream financial theory. We first use it to explain the logic of **bank runs** where *depositors rush to make withdrawals leading to insolvency and bankruptcy* to the detriment of all. We then apply it to international financial investment in emerging market economies. Most importantly model 9.1 demonstrates that financial crises in all contexts can result from behavior that is quintessentially rational.

Bank Runs[1]

"That is my money inside that bank, mine!" cried Ramona Ruiz, 67, a retired textile worker who was trying to withdraw funds from an ATM in the city center of Buenos Aires today only to find it empty. "I was being patriotic by not removing my savings earlier. And now I see what a fool I was."[2]

---

1 This model is adapted from an excellent book by Robert Gibbons, *Game Theory for Applied Economists* (Princeton University Press, 1992).

2 Quoted in "Argentina Restricts Bank Withdrawals," by Anthony Faiola, *Washington Post*, December 2, 2001: A30.

Two people deposit D in a bank. The bank lends these deposits, 2D, to a borrower who, if all goes well, will repay the bank 2R on a future date 2, where R > D. On the other hand, if the bank is forced to sell this loan "asset" to another bank on date 1 before date 2, it will only receive 2r from the sale of the loan where 2D > 2r > D. Depositors can withdraw their money on either date 1 or date 2. For simplicity we assume depositors have a zero rate of time discount, i.e. if the amount of money is the same the depositors don't care if they get it on date 1 or date 2.

If even one depositor withdraws on date 1 the bank has to liquidate its loan because it has nothing to repay depositors on date 1 without doing so, receiving 2r from the sale of the loan. If both depositors withdraw on date 1 each gets half of what the bank has, r, which is less than each deposited, D. If one withdraws on date 1 but the other does not, the one who withdraws gets D while the other depositor gets the remainder, 2r – D.

If neither depositor withdraws on date 1, the bank does not need to liquidate its loan asset before it reaches maturity and the bank is paid 2R > 2D on date 2 by its loan customer. If both depositors withdraw on date 2 each receives R. Or, if neither withdraws on date 2 the bank pays each depositor R. However, if one depositor withdraws on date 2 while the other does not, the one who does not withdraw is simply paid D and the one who does withdraw is paid the remainder, 2R – D.

The **payoff matrix** for the two depositors on date 1 is:

	Date 1	
	Withdraw	Don't Withdraw
Withdraw	(r, r)	(D, 2r – D)
Don't Withdraw	(2r – D, D)	(?, ?)

The payoff matrix for the two depositors on date 2 is:

	Date 2	
	Withdraw	Don't Withdraw
Withdraw	(R, R)	(2R – D, D)
Don't Withdraw	(D, 2R – D)	(R, R)

As in the Price of Power Game, model 5.2 in Chapter 5, we work backwards beginning with date 2. Both depositors will withdraw on date 2 if the game gets that far. If the other depositor withdraws I get R from withdrawing but only D if I do not. Since R > D I should withdraw if the other depositor withdraws. If the other depositor does not withdraw I get 2R – D by withdrawing but only R by not withdrawing. Since 2R – D > R I should withdraw if the other depositor does not withdraw. So *no matter what the other depositor does, I should withdraw* on date 2, and so should she. In other words, withdrawal is a **dominant strategy** for both players on date 2. Presumably *each player will play their dominant strategy* and we can expect the outcome to be what is called the **dominant strategy equilibrium**.[3]

This allows us to fill in the missing payoffs in the south-east cell of the payoff matrix for date 1. If neither depositor withdraws on date 1 then the game goes to date 2. But now we know that if the game does go to date 2 both depositors will withdraw and each will receive R. So we can fill in R as the payoff to each depositor if both don't withdraw on date 1, replacing (?, ?) with (R, R), and proceed to analyze the date 1 game.

On date 1 if the other depositor withdraws I get r from withdrawing and 2r – D if I do not. Since r > 2r – D I should withdraw if the other depositor withdraws. If the other depositor does not withdraw I get D by withdrawing but eventually R by not withdrawing. Since R > D, on date 1 I should not withdraw if the other depositor does not withdraw. There is no dominant strategy equilibrium on date 1. Each depositor's best move depends on what the other does. If I think the other depositor is going to withdraw, I should withdraw. Moreover, if that's what happens – we both withdraw – neither one of us would have any regrets over our own choice, and therefore if we had it to do again we would both presumably withdraw again. On the other hand, if I thought the other depositor was not going to withdraw on date 1, I should not withdraw either. Moreover, if we both don't withdraw, neither will have any regrets and wish to change our choice.[4] So *either* mutual withdrawal or mutual

---

3 It is easy to see why this outcome can be thought of as a kind of "equilibrium." If either player deviated from their dominant strategy they would regret having done so, and presumably correct their behavior. However, a dominant strategy equilibrium to a game should not be confused with the equilibrium outcome in a market. The two contexts are completely different, and the forces at play which presumably lead a market to its equilibrium are different from what generates a dominant strategy equilibrium outcome in a game. Besides the fact that analysts feel a certain degree of confidence in "predicting" the outcomes in both cases, the only other similarity is that analysts assume actors behave in their individual self-interest, i.e. "rationally."

4 What I have just explained means that both (withdraw, withdraw) and (don't withdraw, don't withdraw) are Nash equilibria (after the mathematician John Nash) to the date 1 game. They are both *outcomes where neither party would regret their choice after the fact*, so presumably if either outcome occurred, it would keep occurring – hence the word "equilibrium" again. Neither of the other two possible outcomes is a Nash equilibrium: If I withdrew on date 1 and you did not, you would regret your choice and withdraw next time if you assumed I was going to continue to withdraw on date 1. I might also regret my choice and not withdraw next time if I could be sure you weren't going to change to withdraw because I'd just burned you. Similarly, if I don't withdraw but you do we would each want to change our choice if we felt the other was not going to change their choice.

non-withdrawal are possible stable outcomes. But only one of these stable outcomes is efficient. Since (R, R) is better than (r, r) for both depositors (and the bank!), it is unambiguously more efficient. What we have discovered, unfortunately, is that this is only one of two equilibria. The other equilibrium outcome, mutual withdrawal on date 1, where each depositor withdraws for fear the other may withdraw, is inefficient and illustrates the logic of bank runs.

Notice that the model does not predict bank runs, any more than it predicts that depositors will always leave their deposits in banks until bank loans mature and all depositors get back more than they deposited in the first place. Instead, the model helps us see why *both* outcomes are possible – the outcome where the bank promotes economic efficiency by helping both depositors do better than had they hidden their D < R under their mattresses, and the socially counterproductive outcome where bank failure leaves both depositors worse off than had they hidden their D > r under their mattresses. The model also makes clear the importance of depositor expectations about the behavior of other depositors in a banking system. If depositors trust other depositors not to make early withdrawals all benefit (R > D, R > D), whereas if depositors are suspicious that others may make early withdrawals all lose (r < D, r < D).[5] One approach to thinking about deposit insurance and the minimum legal reserve requirement is to see them as ways to improve the likelihood that depositors will not panic and, therefore, that the banking system will generate efficiency gains rather than losses.

International Financial Crises

Model 9.1 can also be applied to international finance and help explain international financial crises and **contagion,** where *a financial crisis in one country triggers financial crises in other countries.* I chose the title *Panic Rules!* for a book about the global economy written right after the Asian Financial Crisis of 1997–1998 because the "panic rules" described in Chapter 7 were a useful way to begin to think about what had happened in those unfortunate Asian economies. Recall there are two rules of behavior in any credit system: Rule #1 is the rule every participant wants all *other* participants to follow: DON'T PANIC! However, Rule #2 is the rule each participant must be careful to follow herself: PANIC FIRST! These "panic rules"

---

5 Notice there is nothing more or less rational about either response. Don't withdraw is the rational response if you believe the other depositor is not going to withdraw. But withdraw – often called "panic" and portrayed as irrational behavior – is the rational response if you have reason to believe the other depositor is going to withdraw.

succinctly summarize both the promise and the dangers of any credit system. If you substitute "international investors" for the word "depositors," and "emerging market economy" for the word "bank" in the previous application of model 9.1 it nicely explains both the promise and danger inherent in today's liberalized international financial system. Or, if you substitute "currency speculator" for "depositor," and "emerging market currency" for "bank" you can learn much from the model about the potential benefits *and* dangers associated with making a currency *convertible*, i.e. *available for all to buy and sell*, and eliminating *capital controls*, which *restrict who can buy or sell how much of a currency, or when they can do so.*

Model 9.1 when applied to international finance illustrates why the international financial system has both "upside" *and* "downside" possibilities. The international financial system could increase global efficiency by expanding the number of mutually beneficial international deals that get struck when international investors obey Panic Rule #1 and (don't withdraw, don't withdraw) leads to the more efficient Nash equilibrium (R, R). But a fragile, highly leveraged, international financial system can also decrease global efficiency if international investors obey Panic Rule #2 and (withdraw, withdraw) leads to the less efficient Nash equilibrium (r, r).

Conclusion

Before asking if some financial institution or innovation distributes efficiency gains equitably between users, we need to ask if it is likely to yield efficiency gains rather than losses. As the above model makes clear, there is *always* a possibility in *any* financial arrangement that we could suffer efficiency losses (r < D, r < D), rather than enjoy efficiency gains (R > D, R > D), if participants obey Panic Rule #2 rather than Rule #1. Those who speak of the benefits of finance, financial deregulation, and new financial "instruments" invariably assume the positive alternative for their "product" and seldom warn of downside possibilities. It is true that *if* R is sufficiently greater than D, *if* r is not much less than D, and most importantly, *if* the probability of participants obeying Rule #1 and not Rule #2 is sufficiently high, the expected value of the effects of the credit system will be positive. However, the last "*if*" in particular cannot simply be *assumed*, but must be carefully weighed. Insurance programs, reserve requirements, a lender of last resort, rules of disclosure, capital controls, and a host of other factors all affect the probability that participants will obey one rule rather than the other – which model 9.1 makes clear is the all important issue. When these safeguards are absent or weak, as they are in today's international credit system, *rational* investors are more prone to obey Panic Rule #2 and the chances of efficiency losses are correspondingly greater. And *when investors use less of their own money and more of other people's money*, i.e. when smart investors **leverage** their investments to a greater extent to magnify their gains and shift more of the risk of losses onto others, this also makes smart investors more prone to panic because it means that r is smaller, making one's loss, 2r − D, even more frightening if other investors withdraw but you do not.

Model 9.2: Finance in Real Corn Economies

By combining the insights from model 9.1 about bank runs with the domestic corn model 3.1 from Chapter 3 we can illustrate how banks can increase economic efficiency in the real domestic economy, but also how they might lead to efficiency losses. By combining the insights from model 9.1 as applied to international financial crises with model 3.2 of a real global corn economy we can illustrate how international financial markets can increase economic efficiency in the real global economy, but also how they might lead to global efficiency losses.

Banks in a Domestic Corn Economy

As before the economy consists of 1000 members. There is one produced good, corn, which all must consume. Corn is produced from inputs of labor and seed corn. All are equally skilled and productive, and all know how to use the two technologies that exist for producing corn. We assume each person needs to consume exactly 1 unit of corn per week, after which they want to maximize their leisure. We assume people only accumulate corn if they can do so without loss of leisure. As before there are two ways to make corn: a labor intensive technique (LIT) and a capital intensive technique (CIT):

Labor Intensive Technique:
6 days of labor + 0 units of seed corn yields 1 unit of corn

Capital Intensive Technique:
1 day of labor + 1 unit of seed corn yields 2 units of corn

As always we measure the degree of inequality in the economy (imperfectly) as the difference between the maximum and minimum number of days anyone works, and efficiency as the number of days it takes on average to produce a unit of net corn.

We examine a situation where 100 of the 1000 people have 5 units of seed corn each, while the other 900 people have no seed corn at all.

Autarky

Under autarky each seedless person will work 6 days in the LIT and each seedy person will work 1 day in the CIT. The degree of inequality will be: $6 - 1 = 5$. The efficiency of the economy will be: $[900(6) + 100(1)]/1000 = 5.500$ days of work needed on average to produce a unit of net corn.

Imperfect Lending without Banks

Before we implicitly assumed that if borrowing and lending were made legal all mutually beneficial loans would be made. Financial economists explain this is a naïve and unwarranted assumption. It ignores the fact that there are considerable "transaction costs" associated with lenders and borrowers finding one another and successfully negotiating deals. Enthusiasts point out how banks reduce transaction costs for borrowers and lenders by allowing lenders to simply deposit funds at a single location where the rate of interest on bank deposits is taken as a given, and by allowing borrowers to apply at a single location where the rate of interest on bank loans is taken as a given. Want to borrow or lend? Easy to do, nothing to negotiate. So we overcome our naïvity and assume that without the assistance of banks only half of the mutually beneficial loans would be made. In other words, we assume only 50 of the 100 seedy would find borrowers, and the other 50 would fail to do so without the mediation of banks.

The rate of interest would still be 5/6 since any borrower would be willing to pay that much but no more. Consequently the seedless would work 6 days, as before, whether or not they borrowed and worked in the CIT, or did not borrow and worked in the LIT. The 50 seedy who lend out their corn would each collect $(5)(5/6) = 4.167C$ interest, consume 1C, accumulate 3.167C and not work at all. The seedy who did not find borrowers would work 1 day in the CIT, consume 1C, and accumulate no corn.

The efficiency of the economy would be $[900(6) + 50(1) + 50(0)]/[1000 + 50(3.167)]$ $= 4.705$ days on average to produce a unit of net corn. This is an improvement from autarky where the average number of days worked to produce a unit of net corn was 5.50. The degree of inequality would be 6 as compared to 5 under autarky – even without accounting for the 3.167C the 50 seedy who lend out their corn and do not work at all accumulate.

Lending with Banks When All Goes Well

We open a bank and assume this permits all 100 seedy people to find borrowers simply by depositing their seed corn in the bank. The bank will be able to charge an interest rate of 5/6 on loans of seed corn to the seedy, but to make a profit suppose the bank only pays 4/6 on deposits. If there is no legal reserve requirement, the bank could loan out all 500 units of seed corn deposited by the seedy, and the bank would get $(1/6)(500) = 83.33C$ in profits. Each of the 100 seedy depositors gets $(4/6)(5) = 3.33C$ interest, consumes 1C, and accumulates 2.33C without working at all. Each of the seedless works 6 days whether they borrow from the bank or do not, consume 1C, and accumulate none. The efficiency of the economy with a bank where all seedy deposit their corn, where none panic and make early withdrawals, where all corn deposits are loaned out to the seedless who use them productively to work in the CIT, and where all seedless repay their loans, plus interest, at the end of the week is: $[900(6) + 100(0)]/[1000 + 83.33 + 100(2.33)] = 4.101$ if we assume for convenience that there are no days worked at the bank. Of course this is the same degree of efficiency we calculated back in Chapter 3 when we assumed naïvely that all mutually beneficial deals between borrowers and lenders took place without a bank. The degree of inequality remains 6, although the seedy no longer accumulate 3.167C, instead they accumulate 2.33C and the bank has profits of 83.33 for zero work.

Lending with Banks When All Does Not Go Well

Suppose the seedy must deposit their seed corn in the bank before 12 p.m. on Saturday of the previous week in order to get their 4/6 weekly rate of interest, and suppose the bank lends seed corn to the seedless borrowers beginning Monday morning at 9 a.m. Over the weekend a rumor spreads among the seedy depositors that the weather bureau is predicting no rain for the week, in which case harvests from corn grown in the CIT will be depleted to the point where borrowers will not only be unable to pay interest owed the bank, they will not even be able to pay back all the principal they borrowed: ($r << D$). Our bank run model makes clear why rational depositors would switch from "don't withdraw" before the week begins but only at week's end, to "withdraw" immediately if they believe bad weather will prevent the seedless from being able to pay the bank back the principal, much less interest on their loans the following Sunday. So this Sunday all the seedy run (rationally) to find an ATM machine and withdraw their 5 units of corn from the bank. However, to everyone's surprise a soaking rain begins at 2 a.m. Monday morning, and by the time the work day begins Monday morning it is clear productivity in the CIT during the week will be as high as always.

In the extreme the bank would have no corn to lend on Monday morning, and if the seedy had lost the habit of searching for borrowers themselves so none of them found borrowers before the week's work began, the economy would sink back into autarky. But this means the economy would be even less efficient than before the bank was opened! In the extreme no seed corn would be lent in the aftermath of a bank panic – through either the bank or private arrangements – and the average days worked per unit of net corn produced would rise from 4.101 when the bank-credit system worked perfectly all the way back up to 5.500 under autarky. But 5.500 days on average to produce a unit of net corn is *worse* than 4.705 days on average to produce a unit of net corn which is what the imperfect credit market achieved before we opened a bank. This means the real economy is less efficient when the bank fails than when there was no bank at all and some, but not all lenders found borrowers on their own. In other words, it is possible that an imperfect, informal credit market where some lending takes place without bank mediation can be more efficient than a bank credit system when there is a bank crisis. To the extent that not all the seedy make withdrawals, and those who do find borrowers themselves, the efficiency loss would be less. But it is certainly possible that if bank panics are deep enough and occur often enough the economy could end up less efficient with a banking system than it would have been without one. What this simple model illustrates is how instability in the financial sector might obstruct more productivity enhancing loans than it facilitates, and thereby make the real economy less, rather than more efficient.

International Finance in a Global Corn Economy Revisited

Model 3.2 of a global corn economy predicted that opening an international credit market will increase global efficiency even as it increases global inequality. But in model 3.2 we naïvely assumed that all mutually beneficial loans between northern and southern countries would be contracted informally without the benefit of international financial markets. We can correct for this by adding insights from model 9.1 in its international interpretation to model 3.2 of a real global corn economy. As we just did for banks and a real corn domestic economy, we could compare four possible outcomes: (1) international autarky, (2) informal and imperfect international lending without the "benefit" international financial markets, (3) international financial markets where investors do not panic, and (4) international financial markets where investors do panic. There is no need to repeat the exercise because the results are obviously the same: If we assume some but not all mutually beneficial international loans get made without international financial mediation there is a partial but not complete efficiency gain from lending without finance compared to autarky. If we assume the remaining mutually beneficial international loans would get made through financial mediation *provided investors do not panic,* and therefore the financial system settles on its efficient Nash equilibrium (R, R), we get a further efficiency gain from international financial mediation. But *if, instead, investors do panic,* so the international financial system settles on the inefficient Nash equilibrium (r, r), and if the ensuing international financial crisis causes lending to drop by more than the amount that would have occurred without financial intermediation, the international financial system causes efficiency losses rather than gains. In 1997 a half dozen East Asian economies discovered this little advertised fact about capital liberalization the hard way. Argentina provided yet another painful reminder in 2001 for any who failed to learn this lesson from East Asia only a few years earlier.

Model 9.3: Macroeconomic Policy in a Closed Economy

Model 9.3 is the simple short-run macroeconomic model for a "closed" economy inspired by Keynes as developed in Chapter 6 and amended in Chapter 7 to include monetary policy. It highlights the importance of aggregate demand and demonstrates how fiscal and monetary policies can reduce cyclical unemployment and demand pull inflation. Below we use the model to follow the US economy when the Great Recession hit and we illustrate the predictable effects of different policy responses. In the process we can see how political considerations influence policy choices, and what has been the "good, the bad, and the ugly" in US macroeconomic policy since the onset of the Great Recession. All figures are fictitious and in billions of dollars. We start in 2007 before the US housing market bubble burst and Lehman Brothers Holding Inc. collapsed.

$C = 90 + 3/4(Y - T)$ is the consumption function, indicating that the US household sector will consume $90 billion independent of income, and three-quarters of every dollar of after tax, or disposable, income they have.

$I = 200 - 1000r$ is the investment function where r is the rate of interest expressed as a decimal. It says investment depends negatively on the rate of interest. Whenever interest rates change by 1% investment demand will change by 10 billion dollars.

$G^* = 65$ and $T^* = 40$ is what the government was spending and collecting in taxes. Potential GDP, or Y(f), was 900.

$Y = C + I + G$ is the equilibrium condition for the economy saying that aggregate supply, the Y on the left side of the equation, equals aggregate demand, the sum total of household consumption demand, C, business investment demand, I, and government spending, G.

(1) Calculate Y(e) in 2007 if r was equal to 10%, i.e. $r^* = 0.10$

$Y(0) = 90 + 3/4(Y(0) - 40) + 200 - 1000(0.10) + 65$
$Y(0) - 3/4Y(0) = 90 - 30 + 100 + 65$
$1/4Y(0) = 225$
$Y(0) = 900$

(2) What was the state of the economy in 2007?

$Y(f) - Y(0) = 900 - 900 = 0$

So there was neither an unemployment nor inflation gap, and the economy was producing up to its potential. Of course there could have been cost-push inflation or structural unemployment, but the simple Keynesian model would not allow us to see that.

(3) Was there a government budget deficit or surplus? How much?

$T(0) - G(0) = 65 - 40 = -25$

So there was initially a budget deficit.

(4) What was the composition of output in 2007?

$G(0)/Y(0) = 65/900 = 7.22\%$; $I(0)/Y(0) = 100/900 = 11.11\%$; $C(0)/Y(0) = 735/900 = 81.67\%$

When the housing bubble collapsed in 2007 greatly reducing homeowner wealth, US consumers reduced their consumption demand. The new consumption function was: $C = 75 + 3/4(Y - T)$. When the credit system froze after Lehman Brothers collapsed in 2008 businesses had difficulty getting loans and investment fell as well. The new investment equation was: $I = 190 - 1000r$.

(5) Calculate the new Y(e) assuming r remains 10%.

$Y(1) = 75 + 3/4(Y(1) - 40) + 190 - 1000(0.10) + 65$
$Y(1) - 3/4Y(1) = 75 - 30 + 90 + 65$
$1/4Y(1) = 200$
$Y(1) = 800$

(6) What was the nature and size of the gap in the economy?

$Y(f) - Y(1) = 900 - 800 = 100.$

So there was a substantial unemployment gap in the economy.

(7) What was the government budget deficit?

$T(1) - G(1) = 40 - 65 = -25$ still

(8) What was the composition of output?

$G(1)/Y(1) = 65/800 = 8.125\%$; $I(1)/Y(1) = 90/800 = 11.25\%$; $C(1)/Y(1) = 645/800 = 80.625\%$

At this point our macro model tells us stimulus was clearly needed in 2009. The Fed was busy rescuing the big banks, moving from TARP I under Bush/Paulson to TARP II under Obama/Geithner. However, the Democratic Party controlled both houses of Congress as well as the White House who are jointly responsible for fiscal policy. So the debate in early 2009 was over how much and what form of fiscal stimulus to engage in.

(9) Suppose liberal Democrats had gotten their way and the policy response had been to increase government spending by enough to eliminate the entire unemployment gap. How much would the government have had to increase spending in 2009 to raise equilibrium GDP back up to $900 billion?

Using the government spending multiplier formula for our model from Chapter 6:

$\Delta Y = [1/(1-3/4)] \Delta G$
$100 = [4] \Delta G$
$\Delta G = 25$

(10) What would have been the deficit in the government budget in this case?

$T(2) - G(2) = 40 - [65 + 25] = -50$ billion

(11) What would the composition of output have been in this case?

$G(2)/Y(2) = 90/900 = 10\%$; $I(2)/Y(2) = 90/900 = 10\%$; $C(2)/Y(2) = 720/900 = 80\%$

(12) Republicans in Congress did not favor strong stimulus in 2009. But if there was going to be any stimulus they wanted it to be through tax cuts not spending

increases. What if they had gotten their way regarding the kind of stimulus, but not its size? By how much would the government have had to reduce taxes to eliminate the entire unemployment gap and raise equilibrium GDP back up to 900 billion?

Using the tax multiplier formula for our model from Chapter 6:

$\Delta Y = [-3/4/(1 - 3/4)] \Delta T$
$100 = [-3] \Delta T$
$\Delta T = -33.33$

(13) What would have been the deficit in the government budget in this case?

$T(3) - G(3) = [40 - 33.33] - 65 = 6.66 - 65 = -58.33$ billion,

which is not only larger than the pre-policy deficit, but larger than the deficit the policy preferred by liberal Democrats would have created.

(14) What would the composition of output have been in this case?

$G(3)/Y(3) = 65/900 = 7.22\%$; $I(3)/Y(3) = 90/900 = 10\%$; $C(3)/Y(3) = 745/900 = 82.78\%$

(15) Suppose those Paul Krugman calls "deficit scolds" had convinced Congress and the White House in early 2009 that any increase in the budget deficit was intolerable.[6] What could the government still have done to eliminate the entire unemployment gap *without increasing the budget deficit?*

Using the Balanced Budget multiplier formula for our model from Chapter 6:

$\Delta Y = [1] \Delta BB$
$100 = \Delta BB = \Delta G = \Delta T$

So if the government had increased G *and* T by 100 billion in 2009, making $G(4) = 165$ and $T(4) = 140$, aggregate demand and equilibrium GDP would have risen by 100 billion eliminating the entire unemployment gap without increasing the budget deficit from its initial 25 billion level.

6 After the 2010 election this is exactly what the deficit scolds did succeed in doing. As explained in Chapter 6, Obama appointed a bi-partisan debt commission of deficit scolds who shifted the national conversation from stimulus to its opposite, deficit reduction. Since the Republican-controlled House refuses to raise taxes, making it impossible to increase spending without increasing deficits, fiscal policy debate since 2010 has been over how much to reduce spending, on which programs. Disastrous levels of long-term unemployment and youth unemployment without end have been the result.

(16) What would the composition of output have been in this case?

$G(4)/Y(4) = 165/900 = 18.33\%; I(4)/Y(4) = 90/900 = 10\%; C(4)/Y(4) = 645/900$
$= 71.67\%$

Obviously different fiscal policies that are *equivalent* in the sense of eliminating the same size unemployment gap have different effects on the government budget. You can see from the answers to questions 7, 10, 13, and 15 that while increasing spending and taxes by the same amount does not change the balance in the government budget, increasing G alone increases the deficit, while decreasing T alone increases the budget deficit even more.

You can observe the different effects different fiscal policies have on the composition of output by comparing the answers to questions 8, 11, 14, and 16. Increasing G to eliminate the unemployment gap raises the share of public goods slightly and reduces the shares of private investment and consumption slightly. Cutting taxes increases the share of private consumption slightly and decreases the share of public goods and private investment slightly. Raising both G and T increases the share of public goods dramatically, decreases the share of private consumption dramatically, and decreases the share of private investment slightly. In sum, while any of the three fiscal policies can be used to eliminate an unemployment gap, *equivalent fiscal policies* do *not* have the same effect on either government budget deficits or the composition of output.

We can also use model 9.3 to illustrate what actually did happen in 2009. First, Laurence Summers, Obama's chief economic advisor, underestimated the size of the fiscal stimulus needed by roughly half. Second, President Obama started negotiations asking only for the size stimulus he wanted. When those in Congress who wanted less stimulus were through whittling the President down to size, we were only talking about a 10 billion dollar stimulus instead of the 25 billion stimulus sorely needed. Next, the Republicans negotiated successfully for much of the stimulus to be in the form of tax cuts. This meant the stimulus would arrive later, the increase in the deficit would be larger, and there would be less bang for every dollar of deficit since many frightened consumers used their tax rebates to pay down debt instead of consuming more. Republicans also got federal grants to state governments eliminated from the 2009 stimulus thereby ensuring that state governments would suffer budget crises and have to cut spending when the recession dried up state tax revenues. In terms of our model here, what we got in the end was the equivalent of a $6 billion federal spending increase and a $4 billion tax cut. From our model we can easily estimate the combined total stimulus:

ΔY (total) $= [1/(1 - 3/4)]\Delta$ G $+ [-3/4/(1 - 3/4)]\Delta$ T $= [4][6] + [-3][-4]$
$= 24 + 12 = 36$

Did the "Obama" fiscal stimulus of 2009 help? Of course it did. Eliminating a little over a third of the unemployment gap is far better than doing nothing at all. But it was not nearly enough. And when all fifty state governments cut spending when their tax revenues dried up and there was no help from Washington, much of the woefully insufficient federal stimulus was neutralized, prolonging the recession and contributing to a jobless recovery.

Matters would have been far worse had the Fed not engaged in monetary stimulus. Under the leadership of Chairman Bernanke the Fed increased the money supply considerably between 2009 and 2013. The Fed did this only partly because it was soon apparent the fiscal stimulus had been insufficient, and mostly because it was a crucial part of their bank rescue plan. But suppose the Fed had estimated that the fiscal stimulus was only sufficient to increase aggregate demand by $36 billion, as we calculated above, realized political gridlock had set in so no more fiscal stimulus was on the horizon, and had wanted to engage in enough monetary stimulus to eliminate the remaining $64 billion unemployment gap? How would it have gone about doing that?

(17) The investment multiplier is the same as the government spending multiplier because in the short run the macroeconomy doesn't know or care whether the initial increase in spending comes from the federal government buying more aircraft or from private business buying more capital equipment. Therefore, using the investment expenditure multiplier for our model:

$\Delta Y = [1/(1 - 3/4)]\Delta I$
$64 = [4]\Delta I$
$\Delta I = 16$

(18) How much must interest rates fall to produce a $16 billion increase in private investment? We initially used the fact that I = 190 − 1000r to solve for I when we knew r. We now use the same equation to see what the new rate of interest, r(n), must be to give us the new I we need to finish closing the unemployment gap, i.e. the old I plus $\Delta I = 16$. The old I was 90, so the new I we need is 90 + 16 = 106. Substituting into I = 190 − 1000r to find the new r(n) needed:

$106 = 190 - 1000r(n); 106 - 190 = -84 = -1000r(n); (-84)/(-1000) = +0.084 = r(n)$
$(r(n) - 0.10) = (0.084 - 0.100) = -0.016 = \Delta r$

We need interest rates to drop by 1.6%.

(19) Suppose interest rates in the economy fall by 1% whenever the functioning money supply, M1, increases by 50 billion dollars. Since the Fed wants interest rates to fall by 1.6% they would have to get M1 to increase by (1.6)(50) = $80 billion. The Fed could do this by purchasing bonds in the open market, decreasing its discount rate, quantitative easing, or reducing the legal minimum reserve requirement.

(20) When the Fed does any of the above there is no direct effect on the government budget at all because none of the above actions by the Fed change either G or T.[7] Therefore the government budget would not be affected directly by increasing M1 by $80 billion, and the composition of output would be shifted slightly away from private and public consumption toward private investment.

Model 9.4: Macroeconomic Policy in an Open Economy

The open economy macroeconomic model developed in Chapter 8 can be applied to analyze the predictable effects of a typical International Monetary Fund conditionality agreement with less developed countries. It can also be used to analyze the effects of a typical austerity program the European Commission has imposed on each of the PIGS.

An IMF Conditionality Agreement with Brazil

IMF conditionality agreements typically require countries to implement deflationary fiscal and monetary policies as a "condition" for obtaining an IMF "bailout loan" to prevent default. Model 9.4 shows us how deflationary fiscal and monetary policy can increase the net demand for a country's currency increasing its exchange value, and thereby increase the ability of the country to repay its international creditors. But model 9.4 also shows us why these policies will reduce employment, production, income, and domestic investment, and thereby sheds light on why the IMF has become so unpopular with citizens of debtor countries. Assume the following information characterized the Brazilian economy in the fall of 1998: All figures are fictitious and in billions of reales, Brazil's currency.

---

7 If expansionary monetary policy works it will increase production and income. Since a rise in national income will increase federal tax collections this will reduce the government budget deficit. But this is an *indirect* effect on the budget. Monetary policy has no *direct* effect on the budget. Moreover, in our simple model taxes are not a function of income so there is no indirect effect in our model.

$C = 60 + (4/5)(Y - T)$ is the Brazilian consumption function.

$I = 150 - 1000r$ expresses domestic Brazilian investment as a linear negative function of the real rate of interest (expressed as a decimal) in Brazil.

$G = 120$ is what the government spends initially: $T = 100$ is initial tax collections.

$M = 50 + (1/10)Y$ is the import equation where Y stands for national income in this expression. Brazilian people and businesses import more when national income is higher. Their marginal propensity to import out of income, or MPM, is $1/10$.

$X = 120$ is foreign demand for Brazilian exports.

$Y(f) = 1000$ is Brazil's potential GDP.

$Y + M = C + I + G + X$ is the equilibrium condition for the economy. Y is domestic production, and therefore also national income, and M is imports. So $Y + M$ represents the aggregate supply of final goods and services. C is household consumption demand, I is domestic investment demand, G is government spending, and X is foreign demand for exports. So $C + I + G + X$ represents the aggregate demand for final goods and services. The equilibrium condition says the aggregate supply of final goods and services is equal to the aggregate demand for final goods and services when the goods market is in equilibrium. It is traditionally written: $Y = C + I + G + (X - M)$.

$TNDC = X - M = 120 - [50 + (/10)Y]$ expresses the net demand for reales in international currency markets due to Brazilian trade activity. If TNDC is positive we say Brazil has a trade surplus. If TNDC is negative we say Brazil has a trade deficit.

$IINDC = 1000r - 60$ expresses the net demand for reales in international currency markets due to international investment activity and is a positive function of domestic interest rates. When interest rates are higher in Brazil more foreign financial investment is likely to flow into Brazil, attracted by the high interest rate paid, and less Brazilian wealth is likely to flow out. When the interest rate in Brazil is 6%, or 0.06, the net demand for reales from all international investment activity is zero. For interest rates higher than 6% the net demand is positive, and we say Brazil has a surplus on its capital account, and for interest rates below 6% the net demand is negative and we say Brazil has a deficit on its capital account.

$ONDC = TNDC + IINDC = X - [m + MPC(Y)] + 1000r - k$ gives the overall net demand for reales in international currency markets as the sum of the net demand for reales from trade activity, TNDC, and the net demand for reales from international investment activity, IINDC. If ONDC is positive the net demand for reales in international currency markets has increased by ONDC, and the real will appreciate in value. If ONDC is negative the net demand for reales has decreased by ONDC, and the real will depreciate in value.

Assume the international value of the real increases (decreases) by 1% whenever the overall net demand for reales in international currency markets increases (decreases) by 10 billion reales. In other words, if ONDC = + 10 the real will appreciate 1%, and if ONDC = − 10 the real will depreciate 1%.

Assume interest rates inside Brazil increase (decrease) by 1% whenever the functioning money supply in Brazil, M1, decreases (increases) by 20 billion reales.

As explained in Chapter 8, the government spending and investment income expenditure multipliers are both equal to $[1(1 - MPC + MPM)]$ in this simple open economy macro model reflecting the extra "leakage" in the multiplier chain caused by spending on imports.

(1) Calculate the initial equilibrium GDP if the interest rate in Brazil is 5% ($r = 0.05$):

$Y(1) = 60 + (4/5)[Y(1) - 100] + 150 - 1000(0.05) + 120 + 120 - [50 + (1/10)Y(1)]$
$Y(1) - (4/5)Y(1) + (1/10)Y(1) = (3/10)Y(1) = 60 - 80 + 100 + 120 + 120 - 50 = 270$
$Y(1) = (10/3)(270) = 900$

(2) How big is the unemployment gap in the Brazilian economy initially?

$Y(f) - Y(1) = 1000 - 900 = 100$ unemployment gap

(3) How big is the Brazilian government budget deficit initially?

$T(1) - G(1) = 100 - 120 = -20$

(4) How big is Brazil's trade deficit initially?

$TNDC(1) = X(1) - M(1) = 120 - [50 + (1/10)Y(1] = 120 - 50 - (1/10)900 = -20$

(5) How big is the deficit on Brazil's capital account initially?

$IINDC(1) = 1000(0.05) - 60 = -10$

(6) What is the overall net demand for reales in international currency markets?

$ONDC(1) = TNDC(1) + IICNDC(1) = (-20) + (-10) = -30$

(7) By how much and in what direction will the value of the real change?

$ONDC(1)/10 = (-30)/(10) = -3\%$

The value of the real would drop by 3%.

(8) What percentage of GDP in Brazil is devoted to investment initially?

$I(1)/Y(1) = 100/900 = 0.111$ or 11.1%

When Brazilians look at their economy they see an economy with too much unemployment, producing below its capacity, and perhaps devoting too little of its output to increase its capital stock so as to increase potential GDP in the future. When the IMF looks at the same economy they see a government budget deficit and worry it might not be able to pay foreign creditors when loans payable in dollars come due. And they see trade and capital account deficits increasing the net supply of reales in international currency markets, depreciating the value of the real, making it harder for everyone in Brazil to buy the dollars they need with the reales they have to pay off international loans due in dollars.

Where Brazilians and the IMF see eye to eye is that Brazil is not going to be able to meet its outstanding international credit obligations without an emergency loan of dollars from the IMF, and that the consequences of default will be disastrous for both Brazil and international investors. So, in the fall of 1998 the IMF insists that in exchange for an IMF bailout loan the Brazilian government must *decrease* its spending by 30 billion reales.

(9) How large will the unemployment gap in Brazil become?

The government spending multiplier is $[1/(1 - 4/5 + 1/10)] = 10/3$. We multiply $\Delta G = -30$ by $(10/3)$ to get $\Delta Y = -100$, the drop in equilibrium GDP. So equilibrium GDP falls by 100 from 900 to 800 billion reales, and the unemployment gap increases from 100 to 200 billion reales.

(10) What will be the deficit or surplus in the Brazilian government budget?

$T(2) - G(2) = 100 - (120 - 30) = +10$ billion real surplus

This provides the Brazilian government with something to pay foreign bond holders when those bonds come due. Even if the bonds are denominated in dollars, the Brazilian government can sell its 10 billion real surplus for dollars to make payments in dollars.

(11) What will Brazil's trade deficit or surplus be?

$TNDC(2) = X(2) - M(2) = 120 - [50 + (1/10)800] = -10$

(12) What will the deficit or surplus on Brazil's capital account be?

Since $r(2) = r(1) = 0.05$ there is no change in IINDC, and $IINDC(2) = IINDC(1) = -10$

(13) What will be the overall net demand for reales in international currency markets?

ONDC(2) = TNDC(2) + IINDC(2) = (–10) + (–10) = –20

(14) How much and in what direction will the value of the real change?

ONDC(2)/10 = (–20)/10 = –2%, and the value of the real will fall by 2%.

While the Brazilian government is presumably no longer in danger of defaulting on international loans since it now enjoys a budget surplus, the trade and balance of payments deficits continue to threaten Braziilians' ability to repay foreign creditors. And while the downward pressure on the real has eased slightly, if the real continues to fall, Brazilian businesses are more likely to default on dollar denominated loans, and even the government surplus may be insufficient to pay off public debt payable in dollars. So, despite complaints in Brazil about rising unemployment and falling income, the IMF decides more austerity is needed. When Brazil needs a further loan in the spring of 1999 another opportunity for additional conditions arises. In exchange for an additional IMF bailout loan in March, 1999 the IMF requires the Central Bank of Brazil to tighten up on the money supply. Specifically the IMF insists that the Central Bank sell enough reales on the Brazilian bond market to reduce the Brazilian money supply, M1, by 60 billion reales as an additional conditionality.

(15) How much will the rate of interest in Brazil rise?
Since every time the functioning money supply decreases by 20 billion reales interest rates in Brazil rise by 1%, a 60 billion decrease in the money supply leads to a 60/20 = 3% rise in real interest rates in Brazil, so: r(3) = 5% + 3% = 8%.

(16) How much will business investment fall in Brazil?

I(3) = 150 – 1000r(3) = 150 – 1000(0.08) = 70

a drop of 30 billion reales from 100

(17) What will the unemployment gap in Brazil be now?
The investment expenditure multiplier is the same size as the government spending multiplier which we calculated was [10/3]. So we multiply $\Delta I = -30$ by (10/3) which gives $\Delta Y = -100$, a further drop in Y(e). Y(e) had already fallen to 800 billion reales, It now falls another 100 billion reales, and

the new equilibrium GDP, Y(3), is 800 − 100 = 700 billion reales. This increases the unemployment gap to (1000 − 700) = 300 billion reales.

(18) What will Brazil's government budget deficit be?

Monetary policy does not affect the government budget deficit directly, so it would remain the same as it was after the decrease in government spending, a 10 billion real surplus. (Since the drop in GDP will reduce tax revenues, indirectly the government budget surplus would actually be less than 10 billion, and might even turn negative once again.)

(19) What will happen to Brazil's trade deficit?

$$TNDC(3) = X(3) − M(3) = 120 − [50 + (1/10)700] = 120 − 50 − 70 = 0$$

Brazil's trade is finally "balanced."

(20) What will happen to the deficit on Brazil's capital account?

$$IINDC(3) = 1000r(3) − 60 = 1000(0.08) − 60 = + 20$$

So what was initially a 10 billion real deficit has been turned into a 20 billion real surplus on Brazil's capital account. Instead of increasing the supply of reales in international currency markets, international financial flows are now increasing international demand for reales.

(21) What is the overall net demand for reales in international currency markets?

$$ONDC(3) = TNDC(3) + IINDC(3) = 0 + 20 = +20$$

So finally there is a positive net demand for reales in international currency markets.

(22) How much and in what direction will the value of the real change?

$$ONDC/10 = +20/10 = +2\%$$

Finally the downward pressure on the value of the real has been reversed, and the real will appreciate in value by 2%, making it easier for all Brazilian creditors to pay off dollar denominated international loans.

(23) What percentage of Brazilian GDP will now be devoted to investment?

$$I(3)/Y(3) = [150 − 1000(0.08)]/700 = 70/700 = 10\% < 11.1\% = 100/900 = I(1)/Y(1)$$

This means that Brazil is not only investing $(100 - 70) = 30$ billion reales less than it was before, it is devoting an even lower *percentage* of its output to increasing its capital stock, and thereby its potential GDP than before.

Presto! By the end of 1999 Brazil has been successfully turned into an international "debt repayment machine" – while the Brazilian economy sinks further and further into recession, and long-run economic development becomes an even more distant dream.

EC Austerity Policy and Greece

The European Commission, European Central Bank, and the IMF, unpopularly known as "the Troika," imposed successive rounds of fiscal austerity on Greece from 2009 through 2014.[8] Ironically, after seeing the effects of the first program, it was the IMF who belatedly cautioned against "too much austerity" while the EC persisted as the hardest taskmaster. How does model 9.4 help us understand what happened?

Model 9.4 predicts fiscal austerity will increase unemployment, and decrease production and income even further – and they certainly have in Greece. However, instead of turning Greece into a "debt repayment machine" as the Troika expected and model 9.4 predicts is possible, fiscal austerity turned Greece into an even bigger debt time bomb. Before the economic crisis and austerity budgets began the ratio of Greek public debt to Greek GDP was 107%. As ever more draconian fiscal austerity was imposed year after year the debt to GDP ratio in Greece rose to 130% in 2009, 170% in 2011, and 176% in 2013.

There are two reasons austerity has not "worked" even on its own terms in Europe. The first is that austerity causes income to fall which causes tax revenues to fall as well. This effect was ignored by Herbert Hoover when he ordered cuts in government spending in 1930 in a counterproductive attempt to restore balance to the US budget, and it is also ignored in our simple model 9.4 where tax revenues are not modeled as a positive function of national income. We can easily correct this by making $T = tY$ where T is tax *revenues* and t is the tax *rate*. Observe what now what happens when the Greek government cuts spending: In model 9.4 the government spending multiplier is $(10/3)$, which means that if the Greek government cuts spending by €0

---

8 While of course there were differences, this story of painful austerity imposed by the Troika, combined with failure to rein in PIGS' borrowing costs sufficiently, leading to an increase, not decrease in indebtedness, was very much the same in Portugal, Spain, and Ireland as in Greece.

billion euros Greek national income will drop by $(30)(10/3) = €100$ billion. If the tax rate, t, is 30% this means tax revenues, T, will fall by $(0.30)(100) = €30$ billion, and the human suffering caused by the loss of €30 billion of public goods and services has not reduced the Greek government budget deficit by a single euro!

The second reason austerity has been counterproductive in Europe has to do with some characters Paul Krugman calls the "international bond vigilantes" and the failure of the European Central Bank to rein them in. While membership in the EMU protected Greece from investors in international currency markets responding to negative news about the Greek economy by "panicking" and selling off Greek drachmas – as they had when they triggered runs in East Asia on the Thai baht, the Malaysian ringgit, the Indonesian rupiah, and the South Korean won – it did not prevent them from responding to negative news about the Greek economy by selling off Greek government debt, and thereby driving borrowing costs for the Greek government through the roof.

While the interest rates on the bailout loans themselves could be kept below levels that were so high as to be unpayable, and therefore self-defeating, the EC and ECB allowed interest rates that "bond vigilantes" demanded to loan the Greek government money to be determined for far too long by the laws of supply and demand in the "free" capital market. While the risk of default on Greek government bonds was certainly higher than the risk of default on German government bonds, bond vigilantes profited from exaggerating the difference, forcing the Greek government to pay interest rates that guaranteed that its national debt would rise no matter how much it struggled to reduce spending or increase tax collection. As rating agencies like Standard & Poor's and Fitch and Moody downgraded the "quality" of Greek debt, the government's borrowing costs soared to over 15% while the yield on two-year Greek government bonds in the secondary market topped 170% in February 2012. A larger write-off of the unpayable debt should have been authorized much sooner, and the EU should have ended the destructive reign of the bond vigilantes sooner than it did.[9] Unfortunately a sophisticated version of vicious class war, disguised under the banner of "responsible austerity," trumped common sense in Greece and the other PIGS from 2008 through 2014, and threatens to continue to do so.

---

9 At any time the German government could have borrowed at 5% less than the Greek government was able to borrow in private capital markets and loaned the Greek government at 2% above German borrowing costs. This would have given the Greek government access to private capital markets on reasonable terms and netted the German government a profit. When the EC also proved incapable of providing this simple "protection" to Greece against the ravages of the bond vigilantes, the ECB belatedly intervened to allow Greece to borrow on reasonable terms.

Model 9.5: A Political Economy Growth Model

As explained in Chapter 6, mainstream macroeconomic theories invariably lead their users to expect a negative relationship between wage rates and the rate of growth of the capital stock, and therefore potential GDP in the long run. Since workers don't invest but only consume, while capitalists do invest and save more of their income than workers do, how could raising wage rates *not* reduce the growth of the capital stock in the long run, even if it does reduce inequality and poverty in the short run? The political economy growth model 9.5 demonstrates how and why what seems to be an obvious conclusion may be dead wrong, and in fact, higher wages may lead to higher, not lower rates of capital accumulation in the long run. Establishing a logical case for a wage-led, or a "high road" growth strategy in contrast to a profit-led, or a "low road" growth strategy is of great importance.[10]

The General Framework

There is only one good produced, which we call a shmoo. It is an all purpose good that both workers and capitalists eat, wear, and live in. Moreover, shmoos are also used to produce shmoos. In other words shmoos are a consumption good and also an investment good, and the capital stock, K, with which labor works to produce shmoos, consists of shmoos. Let X be the number of shmoos produced per year and C be the number of shmoos consumed per year. We assume any shmoos not consumed are added to the capital stock, i.e. invested, I, and for convenience we assume the rate of depreciation of the capital stock is zero. L is the number of person-years employed during the year, and c is the number of shmoos consumed per person-year of employment *by both workers and capitalists*.[11] This means that total annual consumption of shmoos, C, is equal to cL. If we let g be the rate of growth of the capital stock, then total annual investment of shmoos, I, is equal to gK since we have assumed no depreciation. Our first identity says that all shmoos produced are either consumed or added to the capital stock, i.e. invested:

---

10 I hasten to point out to all who are concerned that growth of through-put is not environmentally sustainable that we need not be talking about that kind of undesirable growth here. Growth is good if it is growth of economic wellbeing per capita and is not environmentally damaging. So please interpret the "shmoos" in model 9.5 as a "good" that truly increases human wellbeing without inflicting damage on the environment.

11 In other words, c is not the amount workers consume per year of employment, it is the amount workers and capitalists *together* consume per year of employment.

(1) $X = C + I = cL + gK$

Next we assume a very simple "fixed coefficient" production function. To make a shmoo it takes a certain number of person-years of labor, $a(0)$ – the labor input coefficient – and it takes a certain number of shmoos of capital stock, $a(1)$ – the capital input coefficient. With fixed coefficient production functions there is no way to substitute more labor to make shmoos with less capital, or more capital to make shmoos with less labor. To make X shmoos it takes $a(0)X$ person years of labor and $a(1)X$ shmoos of capital stock. If we only have $a(1)X$ shmoos in the capital stock it will do no good to hire more than $a(0)X$ person-years of labor because only X shmoos can be produced in any case, and if only $a(0)X$ person-years of labor are hired only $a(1)X$ shmoos from the capital stock will be used, the rest will be idle.

So L will always be equal to $a(0)X$ since employers do not have to hire more workers than they need. If output, X, is low and the labor force, N, is large this may mean that $a(0)X = L < N$ and we have unemployed labor. Similarly, if output X, is low and the capital stock, K, is large it may be the case that $a(1)X < K$ and we will have unutilized capital stock. The difference is that whereas employers do not have to hire N if they only want $L < N$, they are stuck with the capital stock they have, K. If this proves to be more than they need to utilize to produce the amount they want to produce, $a(1)X$, then some of their capital stock will be idle at their expense, so to speak. Therefore, L/X always equals $a(0)$, but K/X equals $a(1)$ only at full capacity levels of output. When not all the capital stock is being utilized $K/X > a(1)$. It is useful to define an index of capacity utilization, $u = X/K$, which ranges from a minimum value of 0 when output is zero to a maximum value of $1/a(1)$ when X is full capacity output and therefore $K/X = a(1)$ and $X/K = 1/a(1)$. How changes in exogenous variables affect our capacity utilization index, $0 \leq u \leq 1/a(1)$, will prove crucial to the performance of the economy in our model.

We now divide equation (1) by X and simplify: $X/X = c(L/X) + g(K/X)$ to get equation (2):

(2) $1 = ca(0) + g/u$

Just as shmoos produced go either to consumption or investment, income goes either to workers or capitalists. Our second identity says that total income is equal to the sum of the income of workers and capitalists.

(3) $PX = WL + rPK$

Where P is the dollar price of a shmoo, W is the dollar wage rate per person-year of employment, and r is the rate of profit capitalists receive. PX gives the dollar value of production, or GDP, which, according to the pie principle, must be equal to the dollar value of income, or GDI in the economy. WL gives the dollar value of all wages paid. And since PK is the dollar value of the capital stock, multiplying the dollar value of the capital stock by the rate of profit on invested capital gives us the dollar value of capitalists' profit income. Again we divide equation (3) first by X: PX/X = W(L/X) + rP(K/X), giving P = Wa(0) + rP/u. We now divide both sides by P which gives equation (4):

(4) $1 = wa(0) + r/u$, where $w = W/P$, the real wage.

Next we assume that while capitalists save part of their income workers consume all their income, and we let "s" represent the fraction of their income capitalists save.[12] And we write our third, and last, identity: The value of total consumption must equal the value of workers' consumption plus the value of capitalists' consumption. Total consumption is cL so the dollar value of total consumption is PcL. Total employment is L so the dollar value of total labor income is WL, which is also the dollar value of workers' consumption since they consume all their income. The dollar value of total capitalist income is rPK, but capitalists only consume part of that income, (1–s)rPK, which gives equation (5):

(5) $PcL = WL + (1–s)rPK$

Dividing equation (5) by PX gives:

$PcL/PX = WL/PX + (1–s)rPK/PX$; $c(L/X) = w(L/X) + (1–s)r(K/X)$; $ca(0) = [wa(0) + (1–s)r/u]$

Substituting this expression for ca(0) into equation (2) gives:

$1 = [wa(0) + (1–s)r/u] + g/u$; but from equation (4) $wa(0) = [1 – r/u]$

which gives:

---

12 Assuming a zero rate of saving for workers is convenient. None of our results would change if workers did save part of their income, as long as their saving rate is lower than the saving rate of capitalists.

$$1 = 1 - r/u + (1 - s)r/u + g/u; \text{ or } 0 = - r/u + r/u - sr/u + g/u; \text{ or } sr/u = g/u$$

which yields equation (6):

(6) $g = sr$

We call equations (2), (4), and (6) our *General Framework*. It contains the logical implications of the basic framework of our long-run macro model. In our framework we assume shmoos not consumed are invested. We assume a zero rate of depreciation on the capital stock. We assume there are two classes, workers whose income consists entirely of wages, and capitalists whose income consists entirely of profits. And we assume capitalists save out of their income but workers do not. In this framework of assumptions we can write three tautologies which reduce to equations (2), (4), and (6):

(2) $1 = ca(0) + g/u$
(4) $1 = wa(0) + r/u$
(6) $g = sr$

There are five "endogenous" variables we want to solve for: c, g, w, r, and u. So far there are three "exogenous" variables, or "parameters," a(0), a(1) and s, which we take as "givens" when solving for the endogenous variables. At this point we cannot solve for the values of five endogenous variables with only three equations. We need more equations. Fortunately we have yet to make any assumptions about what motivates capitalists to invest more or less, or how the goods and labor markets function. By adding a political economy theory of business investment, and a political economy theory about the struggle between employers and employees over real wages, we can "close" the basic model with two more equations that allow us to solve our long-run political economy macroeconomic model for the values of the five endogenous variables.

A Keynesian Theory of Investment

Keynes provided key insights into business investment behavior. First, he argued that investment would depend in part on what he called capitalists' "animal spirits," i.e. psychological and speculative factors that he argued were impossible to explain using formal models. In our model we represent what Keynes called capitalists' "animal spirits" by $\alpha > 0$. When capitalists become more optimistic α increases, and when capitalists get more pessimistic α decreases. Second, Keynes reasoned that capitalists would want to invest more if the rate of profit on invested capital was higher. In our model we represent this relationship by βr with $\beta > 0$. Finally, Keynes observed that since the purpose of investment is to increase the capital stock, capitalists would be *less* likely to invest when the utilization rate of the existing capital stock was lower. Why add more to the capital stock when you are not using what is already available? In our model we represent this relationship by τu with $\tau > 0$, signifying that capitalists' desire to increase their capital stock is positively related to the current level of capacity utilization. These behavioral assumptions about the rate at which capitalists would like to expand the capital stock, g, are incorporated into equation (7):

(7) $g = \alpha + \beta r + \tau u$ with α, β, τ all > 0

A Marxian Theory of Wage Determination

Marx provided key insights into how the real wage is determined. He argued that beside labor's productivity, the real wage in capitalist economies will depend on the bargaining strengths of labor and capital. If employees become more powerful the real wage will increase, whereas if employers become more powerful the real wage will decrease. We will model the effect of bargaining power on the real wage by multiplying labor's productivity by a parameter whose value increases when workers' bargaining power increases and decreases when capitalists' power increases. The real wage is W/P or w. Labor productivity is $[1/a(0)]$. Our bargaining power parameter is $[1/(1 + m)]$ where $m > -1$, giving us equation (8):

(8) $w = [1/a(0)][1/(1 + m)]$, with $m > -1$.

When $m = 0$, $[1/(1 + m)] = 1$ and the real wage is exactly equal to labor's productivity. For $m > 0$ $[1/(1 + m] < 1$, and therefore workers receive less than their productivity. For $-1 < m < 0$ $[1/(1 + m)] > 1$, and therefore workers receive more than their productivity. When m increases workers' real wage declines, and when m decreases their real wage rises. Combining equations (7) and (8) with the three equations from our general framework we have:

(2) $1 = ca(0) + g/u$; with $0 \leq u \leq [1/a(1)]$
(4) $1 = wa(0) + r/u$
(6) $g = sr$; with $0 < s < 1$
(7) $g = \alpha + \beta r + \tau u$; with α, β, τ all > 0
(8) $w = [1/a(0)][1/(1+m)]$; with $m > -1$

Solving the Model

This gives us five equations with five unknowns: c, g, w, r, and u. The first edition of the *ABCs* performed the tedious algebraic manipulations necessary to solve these five equations for the values of the five unknowns in terms of the model's parameters: a(0), a(1), s, m, α, β, and τ. Since most readers are not interested in complicated algebraic manipulations we simply report the results here and refer readers interested in their derivation to the first edition. The symbol * indicates the equilibrium value of an endogenous variable, expressed below in terms of the values of only parameters:

(a) $w^* = 1/a(0)(1 + m)$

(b) $r^* = \alpha/[s - \beta - \tau(1 + m)/m]$

(c) $g^* = s\alpha/[s - \beta - \tau(1 + m)/m]$

(d) $u^* = \alpha(1 + m) / [m(s - \beta - \tau) - \tau]$

(e) $c^* = [1 - sm/(1 + m)]/a(0)$

Equations (a), (b), (c), (d), and (e) are called the "reduced form" of the model and give the equilibrium value of each endogenous variable in terms of only the values of parameters. We can use these equations to see how changes in the value of any parameter affects the equilibrium values of the endogenous variables. Of particular interest is how changes in the savings behavior of capitalists as wealth holders, changes in the investment behavior of capitalists as entrepreneurs, and changes in the bargaining power of workers versus capitalists affect consumption and growth and the values of our two distributive variables, the rate of profit and the real wage.

The easiest way to discover how a change in the value of any parameter affects the value of any endogenous variable in our model requires knowledge of differential calculus. Anyone with this skill can deduce the effect on any endogenous variable of an increase in the value of any parameter by taking the partial derivative of the reduced form expression for the endogenous variable with respect to the parameter of interest. The sign of the result immediately reveals if the value of the endogenous variable increases, decreases, or remains unchanged when the value of the parameter increases. Since I did not want to require any mathematical skills beyond algebra, in the first edition I demonstrated how it is possible to deduce in what direction endogenous variables must move in response to an increase in the value of a parameter by careful inspection. But while this requires no calculus, unfortunately "careful inspection" can become quite involved and mentally taxing for some relationships in the model. Readers interested in the derivation of what is called the "comparative statics" of the model without using calculus can find it in the first edition. In this edition I simply present the results accompanied by a brief explanation.

To understand the intuition behind the results of our political economy growth model 9.5 it is important to focus on the role played by capacity utilization, u. If u does not change in response to a change in a parameter then output, and income as well, cannot change. With income constant if w rises r must fall, and vice versa. With output constant if c rises g must fall, and vice versa. So if when a parameter changes u does not change the economy is what we might call a "zero sum game" in the long-run. It is a zero sum game between capitalists and workers when they fight over income shares. (Hold u constant in equation 4 to see this.) And it is a zero sum game between the present and future generation when they fight over how much output will go to present consumption, c, vs. how much will be added to the capital stock, g. (Hold u constant in equation 2 to see this.) But unlike neoclassical and neo-Marxist growth models which always predict maximum capacity utilization in the long run, our political economy growth model 9.5 is subtle enough to see that even in the long run u might be lower or higher depending on circumstances. Any event that causes u* to increase can create a "win-win" or "win-no-lose" outcome for the present *and* future generations since production is higher so there are more shmoos to consume and/or add to the capital stock. Similarly, any event that increases u* can create a "win-win" or "win-no-lose" outcome for capitalists *and* workers as well, since an increase in u* means that income will be higher so there is more income to be distributed to capitalists and/or workers. On the other hand, any event, or change, that causes u* to fall creates "lose-lose" or "lose-no-win" outcomes since there will be less production to distribute between consumption and investment, and less income to distribute between workers and capitalists.

An Increase in Capitalists' Propensity to Save

When capitalists' propensity to save, s, increases this reduces demand for shmoos and thereby reduces capacity utilization, u*. With fewer shmoos produced both c* and g* fall. With lower income r* must fall because w* remains constant since w* in our model depends only on labor productivity, [1/a(0)], and labor bargaining power, m, neither of which has changed. In other words, an increase in capitalists' propensity to save creates a lose-lose outcome for the present and future generations, and a lose-no-win outcome for capitalists and workers.

An Increase in Capitalists' Propensity to Invest

If capitalists become more optimistic and decide they want to invest more, i.e. if α increases, this will increase the demand for shmoos to add to the capital stock, which will increase capacity utilization, u^*. Higher capacity utilization raises production and income. Again, with no change in labor productivity or worker bargaining power, w^* cannot change. Which means that r^* must rise. Not surprisingly since an increase in α raises the demand for shmoos to be added to the capital stock, g^* increases while c^* remains constant. In other words, an increase in α creates a win-no-lose outcome for capitalists and workers, and a win-no-lose outcome for future generations and the present generation.

An Increase in Workers' Bargaining Power

What if workers increase their bargaining power while labor productivity remains constant? In our model an increase in worker power is represented by a decrease in m, which increases w^* – see equation (a). The rise in w^* would require r^* to decrease unless u^* increases – see equation (4). However, an increase in the real wage increases demand for shmoos since it increases worker income and workers consume a higher percentage of their income than capitalists do. This increases capacity utilization, u^*, which increases production and income, generating a win-win outcome for workers and capitalists, as r^* increases along with the increase in w^*, as well as a win-win outcome for the present and future generations, as c^* and g^* both increase.

Wage-Led Growth

The logical possibility of wage-led growth is of great practical and political importance. It demonstrates that less developed countries do not need to repress wages to hasten the growth of their stock of productive capital and become more developed. In other words, the long-run version of "austerity is necessary if you want a better future" turns out to be no more true than the short-run version peddled by deficit scolds. However, our political economy growth model 9.5 not only explains why "wage-led growth" is possible if redistributing income from capital to labor helps keep capacity utilization higher over the long run, it also explains how capitalists can "foul their own nest," so to speak, when their bargaining power over workers increases. Over the past forty years the bargaining power of capitalists has increased steadily in the developed economies for a host of reasons. As a result we have witnessed a remarkable failure of real wages to keep pace with labor productivity for the first time in history. We have also seen significantly lower economic growth rates over the past forty years compared to the "golden era of capitalism" from 1950 through the mid-1970s. Obviously stagnant real wages are bad for workers, and low rates of growth of productive capital are bad for future generations. But our model points out that the low wage, "neoliberal economy" was not even necessarily best for capitalists. Low levels of capacity utilization, which have also been characteristic of the neoliberal period, can lower profit rates for capitalists. As capitalists became ever more powerful and pushed real wages farther and farther below labor productivity, stagnant demand and idle capacity may well have created a negative sum game in which profits were lower than they might otherwise have been.[13]

13 Political economists who were pioneers in the kind of "structuralist macroeconomics" represented by model 9.5 include Stephen Marglin, *Growth, Distribution and Prices* (Harvard UP, 1987), Amitava Dutt, *Growth, Distribution and Uneven Development* (Cambridge UP, 1990), Lance Taylor, *Income Distribution, Inflation and Growth: Lectures on Structuralist Macroeconomic Theory* (MIT Press, 1991), *Reconstructing Macroeconomics: Structuralist Proposals and Critiques of the Mainstream* (Harvard UP, 2004), and Thomas Palley, *Post-Keynesian Economics* (Palgrave Macmillan, 1996).

10

What Is to Be Undone?
The Economics of Competition
and Greed

When Milton Friedman published *Capitalism and Freedom* (University of Chicago Press) in 1964 free market capitalism[1] was not yet ascendant. In the post WWII era Keynesian, social democratic capitalism was more dominant, and government regulation and guidance of the economy was generally considered necessary, prudent, and desirable. So Friedman was writing as a dissident when he argued that only free market capitalism can provide economic freedom, promote political liberty, allocate resources efficiently, motivate people successfully, and reward people fairly, and government intervention was usually unnecessary and counterproductive.

By 2002 when the first edition of *The ABCs of Political Economy* was published neoliberal capitalism stood triumphant over the demise of not only centrally planned Communism, but social democratic, Keynesian capitalism as well. Friedman's disciples were more confident than ever that free market capitalism was the best economy possible. Deregulation, privatization, and dismantling the social safety net had become the order of the day. Keynesians had been successfully isolated and silenced, and only a scattered tribe of "heterodox economists" any longer challenged Milton Friedman's claims about the virtues of free market capitalism.

What a difference twelve years can make! While neoliberal capitalism still clings to power almost everywhere in 2014, and especially within the economics profession, there are now many who doubt that free market capitalism is truly the best economic system for the vast majority. Six years after the worst financial

---

1 *Laissez faire* capitalism, free market capitalism, and neoliberal capitalism are different terms that have been used in different eras and settings for the same kind of capitalism. I will use these labels interchangeably, while acknowledging that there are sometimes differences.

crash in four generations the global financial system remains without adequate regulation, and is just as dangerous as it was before the collapse of Lehman Bros. Five years after the largest drop in GDP since the Great Depression unemployment remains high in all the advanced economies with no end in sight. And despite overwhelming evidence that we are on course to unleash disastrous climate change, carbon emissions continue to rise everywhere. While the tongues of all but a few critics were tied in 2002, there are now many voices bemoaning the loss of hard won reforms neoliberals assured us were counterproductive, no longer necessary, or unaffordable. Every day more people are realizing that we are on course for an ecological disaster of Biblical proportions. As our "old economies" continue to fail us, there is rising interest in a potpourri of initiatives that are self-consciously *not* business-as-usual economics, called the "new" or "future" economy. And finally, there is a notable stirring of renewed interest in alternatives to capitalism altogether. However, it is still instructive to begin a careful evaluation of free market capitalism with a point-by-point response to Milton Friedman's claims about its purported virtues that have grown to become popular myths about capitalism. After which we can see where criticisms raised by protest movements in Europe and the US during the past five years fit into the long, historic debate over the pros and cons of *laissez faire* capitalism.

Myth 1: Free Enterprise Equals Economic Freedom

Friedman says the most important virtue of free enterprise is that it provides *economic freedom*, by which he means *the freedom to do whatever one wishes with one's person and property – including the right to contract with others over their use of your person or property.* He says economic freedom is important in and of itself, but also important because it unleashes people's economic creativity and promotes political freedom.

Political economists believe that people should control their economic lives, and only when they do so is it possible to tap their full economic potential. We also believe economic democracy promotes political democracy. But we find Friedman's concept of economic freedom inadequate, his argument that free enterprise allows people to control their economic lives highly misleading, his claim that free enterprise is efficient, rather than merely energetic, unpersuasive, and his conclusion that free enterprise promotes political democracy preposterous.

In Chapter 2 I argued it is important for people to control their economic lives irrespective of the quality of decisions they make. In other words, beside efficient and equitable outcomes we want workers and consumers to have input into economic decisions in proportion to the degree they are affected by those decisions – we want economic *self-management*. Friedman plays on the obvious truth that it is good when people are free to do what they want to substitute the concept "economic freedom" for a more meaningful definition of economic democracy. Since this distortion is at the core of capitalist mythology it is important to treat it seriously.

The first problem with Friedman's concept of economic freedom is that in capitalism there are important situations where the economic freedom of one person conflicts with the economic freedom of another person. If polluters are free to pollute, then victims of pollution are not free to live in pollution free environments. If employers are free to use their productive property as they see fit, then their employees are not free to use their laboring capacities as they see fit. If the wealthy are free to leave their children large bequests, then new generations will not be free to enjoy equal economic opportunities. If those who own banks are free from a government imposed minimum reserve requirement, ordinary depositors are not free to save safely. So it is not enough simply to shout "let economic freedom ring" – as appealing as that may sound.

In capitalism whose economic freedom takes priority over whose is settled by the property rights system. Once we realize economic freedom as defined by Friedman is meaningless without a specification of property rights – that it is the property rights system in capitalism which dictates who gets to decide what – the focus of attention shifts to where it should have been in the first place: How does the property rights system distribute decision-making authority? Does the property rights system distribute control over economic decisions equitably? Does it give people decision-making authority in proportion to how much they are affected by an economic decision? Or, by giving priority to property rights over human rights, and by distributing property ownership unequally, does a property rights system leave most people little control over their economic destinies and award a few control over the economic fates of the many?

So the first problem with Milton Friedman's way of conceptualizing the notion that people should control their own economic lives is that it merely begs the question and defers all problems to an unspecified property rights system. The second problem is that while Friedman and other champions of capitalism wax poetic on the subject of economic freedom, they have remarkably little to say about what is a better or worse property rights system. Most of what little they do say reduces to two observations: (1) Whatever the distribution of property rights, it is crucial that property rights be clear cut and complete, since otherwise there will be inefficiency due to "property right ambiguity." (2) Since, in their opinion, it is

THE ECONOMICS OF COMPETITION AND GREED

difficult to argue that any distribution of property rights is preferable to any other on moral or theoretical grounds, there is no reason in their opinion to change the distribution of property rights history bequeathed us, except perhaps, in cases of theft or outright fraud. In sum, Friedman defends the property rights status quo and considers only clarification of ambiguities a legitimate area for public policy. What is entirely lacking is any attempt to develop criteria for better and worse distributions of property rights, not to speak of discussion of how property rights might be distributed to best approximate economic self-management.

However, conservatives' silence on the issue of what, besides clarity and respecting the status quo, constitutes a desirable system of property rights does not extend to the issue of employer versus employee rights. According to Friedman there is no conflict between employees' and employers' economic freedoms as long as employment contracts are agreed to by both parties under competitive conditions. As long as the employment relation is voluntary, and as long as labor markets are competitive so nobody is compelled to work for a particular employer, or compelled to hire a particular employee, the economic freedoms of all are preserved according to Friedman and his conservative followers. In their eyes, when an employee agrees to work for an employer she is merely exercising her economic freedom to do with her laboring capacities as she sees fit. She could use her "human capital" herself if she wished. But if she is offered what she decides is a better deal – relinquishing her right to use her laboring capacities to another for an agreed wage payment – she should be free to do so. What's more, if she were prohibited from making this choice her economic freedom would be violated, just as the economic freedom of the employer to use his productive property as he sees fit would be violated if he were barred from hiring employees to work with it under his direction. Accordingly, Friedman concludes that *union shops*, where *a majority of employees have voted that all employees must become members of the union, which represents them collectively in bargaining with their employer*, are violations of employee as well as employer economic freedom under capitalism. And worse still is socialism's ban on private enterprise, which Friedman criticizes as the ultimate violation of people's economic freedom to hire and be hired by one another should they so choose.

The first problem with this defense of private enterprise as the cornerstone of economic freedom is that not all people have, or could ever have, an equal opportunity to become employers rather than employees. In real capitalist economies a few will become employers, the vast majority will work for someone else, and some will be self-employed. Moreover, *who* will be employers, employees, or self-employed is determined for the most part *neither* randomly *nor* by people's relative preferences for self-managed versus other-directed work. In the corn model in Chapter 3 we discovered that *only* under egalitarian distributions of seed corn would relative preferences for self-managed work determine who become employers and who become employees. Under inegalitarian distributions those with more seed corn become employers and those with less become employees *irrespective* of people's relative preferences for self-management or aversions to being bossed around. One of the most profound insights provided by the simple corn model is that while it is true, in a sense, that employees "choose" alienated labor, they do not necessarily do so because they have a weaker desire for self-management than those they go to work for. The distribution of wealth "tilts" the private enterprise playing field so that some will benefit more by becoming employers and others will benefit more by becoming employees *independent* of work preferences.

The answer to this criticism by the champions of private enterprise is that anyone who wants to work badly enough for herself can borrow in the credit market whatever is necessary to become self-employed or an employer. But this line of reasoning (1) assumes more than any real capitalism can offer – credit on equal terms for all – and (2) ignores that even competitive credit markets can impose a steep price on the poor for self-management that the wealthy are not required to pay. In a world with uncertainty and imperfect information – not to speak of patents and technological and financial economies of scale – those with more collateral and credentials will receive credit on preferential terms while the rest of us will be subject to credit rationing in one form or another. To expect any different is to expect lenders to be fools. So being referred to the credit market is not going to level the playing field for the poor. And even if all did receive credit on equal terms, our simple corn model in Chapter 3 demonstrates that the poor who avoid the status of employer by borrowing in credit markets – where we generously assumed anyone could borrow as much as she wanted at the market rate of interest and nobody has access to credit for less – effectively pay their wealthy creditors for the right to manage their own laboring capacities – a right that should be as "inalienable" as the right to vote on political issues. The buck must stop somewhere: Those without wealth to begin with have an uphill road to avoid employee status in capitalist economies, with or without credit markets, no matter how close to perfect those credit markets might be.

But even if the capitalist playing field were level, and even if the probability of becoming an employer rather than an employee was exactly the same for everyone, this would not mean the employer–employee relationship was a desirable one. Of course random assignment would be a far sight better than having relative wealth determine who will boss and who will be bossed. But is it better than having neither bosses nor bossed, and instead *all* enjoy self-management? Here is a useful analogy: A slave system where slaves apply to be slaves for slave masters of their choice is better than one where slave owners trade slaves among themselves. A slave system where people are assigned randomly to be slaves or slave masters is better than one where blacks are slaves and whites are slave owners. But abolition of slavery is better than even the least objectionable kind of slavery. The same holds for wage slavery: A labor market where employees are free to apply to work for employers of their choice is better than one where employers trade employees among themselves, as Curt Flood argued in his landmark suit against Major League Baseball in 1970. A system where who become employers and who become employees is truly a random walk is better than one where the wealthy predictably become the employers and the poor predictably become employees. But abolition of wage slavery – replacing the roles of employer and employee with self-management for all – is better than even the least objectionable system of private enterprise.

Myth 2: Free Enterprise Promotes Political Freedom

Friedman goes on to argue that besides being good in itself, economic freedom promotes political freedom. His first argument is that in a free enterprise economy people have a choice of non-government employers. This means people are not reliant on the government for their economic livelihood and therefore will be free to speak their minds, and in particular, free to oppose government policies. Friedman's second argument is that if wealth were distributed equally none would have sufficient discretionary wealth to fund political causes. Since wealth is distributed unequally in capitalist economies, Friedman concludes there are always multiple funding sources available for any and all political causes.

Economic democracy *is* political democracy's best friend, and authoritarian economies *are* political democracy's worst enemy. But that does not mean private enterprise promotes political freedom and democracy. One problem with Friedman's first argument is that private employers can intimidate employees who are afraid to lose their jobs if they support political causes their employers disagree with – just as a government employer can. In other words, Friedman is blind to the dictatorship of the propertied, and sees government as the only conceivable perpetrator of coercion. A second fallacy with his first argument is that a monolithic state employer is not the only alternative to a wealthy capitalist employer. State monopoly on employment opportunities in Soviet style economies *was* a serious obstacle to freedom of political expression in those societies. But in the next chapter we will see that nobody has reason to fear for her job because of her political views in a participatory economy, or in an employee managed, market socialist economy since the state exerts no influence over who gets hired or fired in either of these economies. Comparing capitalism only to Communism, and implicitly assuming there are no other alternatives is the oldest play in the capitalist team play book.

The obvious problem with Friedman's second argument – that unequal wealth provides alternative sources of funding for political causes – is that by his own admission, those with vastly greater wealth will control access to the means of political expression. This effectively disenfranchises the poor who have no recourse but to appeal to the wealthy to finance their political causes. Jerry Brown was right when he argued in the 1992 Democratic presidential primaries that politicians in both major parties in the US are essentially bought and paid for by wealthy financial interests who pre-select which candidates can mount viable primary campaigns. Ralph Nader was right when he argued during the 2000 general election that both the Republican *and* Democratic parties had been effectively bought by corporations, and should be seen for what they are, two wings of a single party of business, the Republicrats. And Occupy is right when it points out that the *Citizens United v. Federal Election Commission* Supreme Court decision in 2010 opened the floodgates to corporate money in elections, and made a mockery of political democracy in the United States.

Every politician has to ask how her stand on an issue will affect both her voter appeal *and* her funding appeal, mindful that donations from wealthy contributors are ever more important because televisions ads are increasingly important to "electability." While we needn't feel sorry for them, more and more US Senators are choosing retirement in face of the daunting task of raising literally tens of thousands of dollars per day starting the day after they're elected in order to be viable candidates for re-election six years later. The fact that Ross Perot and Steve Forbes Jr. could gain serious public consideration for their mostly harebrained political ideas by financing presidential bids out of their own deep pockets, whereas 99% of the population cannot pay for a single ad in the *New York Times*, much less finance a credible presidential campaign, is hardly evidence that capitalism makes it possible for all political opinions to get a hearing, much less evidence of equal political opportunities under capitalism. Moreover, why does Milton Friedman think the economically powerful and wealthy will finance political causes aimed at reducing their wealth and power? At best, Friedman's view of the wealthy as "patrons of the political arts" would predictably provide more adequate funding for some schools of "political art" than others. Simply put, Friedman's attempt to make a political virtue out of the large disparities of economic power capitalism creates is ludicrous. Unequal economic power breeds unequal political power – not political democracy – as any school child knows.

Myth 3: Free Enterprise Is Efficient

Friedman and mainstream economists argue that free enterprise promotes technological and motivational efficiency. They point out that any capitalist who discovers a way to reduce the amount of an input necessary to make an output will be able to lower her production costs below those of her competitors, and thereby earn higher than average profits. Moreover, other producers will be driven to adopt the new, more productive technique for fear of being driven out of business by more innovative competitors. In this way they argue competition for profit promotes the search for and adoption of more efficient technologies. While competition sometimes drives entrepreneurs to seek and implement technological improvements, Friedman fails to point out there are compelling reasons to believe competition for profits also drives firms to make technological choices contrary to the social interest.

Monopoly and oligopolistic markets not only yield static inefficiencies by restricting supply to drive up market price, they promote dynamic inefficiencies as well. Examples of large companies conspiring to suppress technological innovations because it would depreciate their fixed capital, or because it would reduce opportunities for repeated sales because a product lasted longer are legion. While this cause of technological inefficiency in real capitalist economies riddled with non-competitive market structures is important, I concentrate below on a more subtle problem, namely that even when markets are competitive, capitalists will often make socially counterproductive choices of technology.

Biased Price Signals

In Chapter 4 we discovered that externalities lead to market prices that do not accurately reflect true social costs and benefits. Since capitalists understandably use market prices, not true social costs, when deciding if a new technology is cost reducing, inaccuracies due to external effects can lead to socially counterproductive decisions regarding technologies. For example, our current price system puts a zero price on carbon emissions despite the fact that the EPA says the social cost of carbon is at least $12 per metric ton released and may be as high as $109. As a result we not only produce far too much of our energy from fossil fuels and far too little from renewable sources, but private funding for research to improve our ability to find and burn fossil fuels has been too plentiful, while private funding for research to improve solar panels and wind turbines has been too meager. The Sraffa model of price and income determination in Chapter 5 reveals a completely different reason prices in capitalism are biased in a way that leads profit-maximizing capitalists to make inefficient choices regarding technology. The higher the rate of profit in the economy, and the lower the wage rate, the more likely it is that capitalists will implement new capital-saving, labor-using technologies that are profitable but socially inefficient, and reject new capital-using, labor-saving technologies that are socially efficient but unprofitable. In sum, the greater the prevalence and magnitude of external effects, and the greater the bargaining power of capital over labor, the more likely the price system will provide false signals leading to socially counterproductive choices of technologies.

Conflict Theory of the Firm

The "conflict theory of the firm" explains why profit maximization requires capitalists to choose less efficient technologies if more efficient technologies lower their bargaining power over their employees sufficiently. The logic reviewed informally here is illustrated formally in the application of model 5.2, The Price of Power Game, to the conflict theory of the firm in Chapter 5. There is an inherent conflict of interest between employers and employees over how high or low the wage will be, and how much effort employees will have to exert for that wage. If we define the real wage in terms of dollars of compensation per unit of effort expended this reduces to a struggle over the real wage. For the most part employers are free to choose among alternative technologies available and free to establish whatever internal personnel policies they wish. Or at least, employers have considerable discretion in these areas. Political economists from the conflict school point out that it would be irrational for employers to consider the impact of technological choices and personnel policies on productivity *only* when these choices *also* affect employers' bargaining power *vis-à-vis* their employees. Since profits depend not only on the size of net output, but also on how net output is divided between wages and profits, rational employers will consider how their choices affect *both* the size *and* distribution of the firm's net output.

Suppose technology A is slightly less productive than technology B, but technology A substantially reduces employees' bargaining power while technology B increases the employer's bargaining power significantly. A profit-maximizing employer would have no choice but to opt for the less productive technology A. For example, consider automobile manufactures' choice between assembly line versus work team technologies. Suppose when quality and reliability are taken into account, making automobiles in work teams is slightly more productive than making cars on an assembly line. But suppose team production is more skill enhancing and builds employee solidarity, while assembly line production reduces the knowledge component of work for most employees and reduces employee solidarity by isolating employees from one another. If the "bargaining power effect" outweighs the "productivity effect," competition for profits will drive auto makers to opt for assembly line production even though it is less efficient.

The disagreement between political economists from the conflict school and our mainstream colleagues is *not* whether or not employers and employees *have* a conflict of interest over wages and effort levels – since everyone recognizes that they do – but whether or not this conflict leads to economic inefficiencies. Beside leading to inefficient technologies, this inherent conflict of interest between employers and employees over how to distribute the net product, or value added, also wastes valuable resources and personnel on supervisory efforts, creates incentives for employees to resist innovation and technical change, and most importantly wastes the creative economic potentials of the vast majority of the populace whose conceptual capabilities go under used and repressed by their employers who cannot trust them, because while employers and their employees share an interest in greater efficiency, they have conflicting interests over the effects of firm policies on bargaining power.

Myth 4: Free Enterprise Reduces Discrimination

Mainstream economists insist that competition for profits among employers will reduce discrimination. They point out that if an employer has "a taste" for discrimination and insists on paying white employees more than equivalent black employees, or male employees more than equivalent female employees, the discriminating employer will have a higher wage bill than an employer who does not discriminate and pays equivalent employees equally. Mainstream theorists conclude that eventually employers who do not discriminate should compete those who do out of business. Similarly, they point out that the business of any employer who fails to hire or promote the most qualified people due to overt or unconscious discrimination will be less productive than businesses who hire and promote purely on merit. So according to mainstream economists a firm that engages in discriminatory hiring or promotion practices should also be competed out of business by firms that do not. While mainstream theory is quick to see the profit-reducing aspects of economic discrimination on the part of employers, it is blind to the profit-increasing effects of discrimination. By recognizing the importance of bargaining power in the ongoing struggle between employers and their employees over the distribution of value added, the conflict theory of the firm helps us see why profit maximization does not preclude, but in fact *requires*, economic discrimination even when employers operate in competitive labor, goods, and capital markets.

Discrimination in hiring, assignment, promotion, and payment have all been used
to aggravate suspicions and antagonisms that already exist between people of different
races and ethnic backgrounds as well as between men and women, and people with
different sexual preferences. Historical settings where ample reasons for suspicion and
mistrust already exist provide ready-made pressure points employers can manipulate
to "divide and conquer" their employees. When employees are mutually suspicious
they can be more easily induced to inform on one another regarding lackadaisical
efforts – making it easier for the employer to extract more "labor done" from the
"labor hired." When employees are unsupportive of one another they will be easier
for their employer to bargain with over wages when their contract comes up. What
the conflict theory reveals is that since discriminatory practices by an individual
employer have these positive effects on profits, profit maximization requires engaging
in discriminatory practices up to the point where the negative effects of discrimination
on profits – which are the exclusive focus of mainstream theory – outweigh the
profit-enhancing effects – which only political economists identify. In other words,
competition for profits will drive employers to engage in discriminatory practices
up to the point where the redistributive effect of discrimination – increasing the
employer's share of value added by decreasing employees' bargaining power – equals
the negative impact of discrimination on productivity or the wage bill.

The implications of discovering that economic discrimination is part and parcel
of profit maximization are enormous. First, since mainstream theorists are correct
that discrimination often reduces economic efficiency, it provides yet another
reason to believe that capitalism will not be efficient. But more importantly this
means that it is not the employers who discriminate who will eventually be driven
out of business by those who do not, but just the reverse. Employers who steadfastly
refuse to discriminate will be driven out of business by those who pay attention
only to the bottom line – and therefore engage in profit-enhancing discriminatory
behavior. The implication for public policy is huge. If mainstream economists were
correct, competitive labor, goods, and capital markets would tend to eliminate
discriminatory employment practices, at least in the long run. In which case, if
minorities and women were willing to continue to pay the price for society's patience,
we could expect discrimination to diminish without government involvement. But
the conflict theory demonstrates that even assuming no collusion among employers,
it is profitable for individual employers to aggravate racial antagonisms among their
employees up to the point where the costs of doing so outweigh the additional profits
that come from negotiating with a less powerful group of employees. Therefore it is
foolish to wait for capitalism to eliminate discrimination if unaided. Instead, laws
outlawing discrimination and affirmative action programs are absolutely necessary

if discrimination is to be reduced in capitalist economies. Moreover, the struggle against discrimination through active intervention must constantly "swim upstream" in capitalism because employers who do discriminate are rewarded with higher profits, and employers who refuse to discriminate are punished by shareholders who care only about their bottom line.[2]

The increasingly popular view in the US that government protection and affirmative action have done their job and are no longer necessary could not be farther from the truth.[3] As the government's anti-discriminatory efforts weakened, the discrepancy between the wages of equivalent black and white workers increased by 50% from 10.9% in 1979 to 16.4% in 1989.[4] A study by the Government Accounting Office released in January 2002 revealed that the female wage gap was no longer shrinking, but had widened significantly between 1995 and 2000. Shannon Henry reported in an article titled "Male-Female Salary Gap Growing, Study Says" published in *The Washington Post* on January 24, 2002:

> Female managers are not only making less money than men in many industries, but the wage gap widened during the economic boom years of 1995 to 2000, according to a congressional study to be released today. The study found that a full-time female communications manager earned 86 cents for every dollar a male made in her industry in 1995. In 2000, she made only 73 cents of the man's dollar.

The conflict theory merely explains what is readily apparent to anyone who wishes to see.

Myth 5: Free Enterprise Is Fair

Imagine a capitalist economy where discrimination was successfully outlawed and labor markets were competitive. Even under these best of circumstances private

---

2 See Michael Reich, *Racial Inequality* (Princeton University Press, 1981): 204–215 for a simple, yet powerful model proving that wage discrimination is a necessary condition for profit maximization for individual capitalist employers operating in competitive markets.

3 See Barbara Bergman, *In Defense of Affirmative Action* (Basic Books, 1996) for persuasive evidence that affirmative action programs *do* help groups that are discriminated against, and that discrimination quickly reappears in their absence.

4 Lawrence Mishel and Jared Bernstein, *The State of Working America: 1994–95* (M.E. Sharpe, 1994): 187. "Equivalent" means comparing black and white workers with the same level of education, work experience, etc.

enterprise market economies would distribute the burdens and benefits of economic activity according to the conservative maxim 1: to each according to the market value of the contribution of his or her labor and productive property. But we have already seen why capitalist distribution is inequitable. Distribution, according to the conservative maxim, means that the grandson of a Rockefeller who never works a day in his life will consume a thousand times more than a hard working doctor, simply because the former inherited ownership of large amounts of productive property. In a world where the 85 richest people have more wealth than the poorest 3.5 billion,[5] capitalist inequities can hardly be dismissed as a minor liability, which is what Friedman does. As long as there are feasible economies that distribute the burdens and benefits of economic activity more equitably than capitalism – and in the next chapter we will see that there are – those who offer rationalizations for inequities in capitalism are nothing more than accomplices in the crime of economic injustice.

Myth 6: Markets Equal Economic Freedom

Milton Friedman argues that the principal virtue of markets is they promote economic freedom. This claim is such an important part of capitalist mythology that it is worth quoting Friedman's argument at some length:

> The basic problem of social organization is how to coordinate the economic activities of large numbers of people. . . . The challenge to the believer in liberty is to reconcile this widespread interdependence with individual freedom. Fundamentally there are only two ways of coordinating the economic activities of millions. One is central direction involving the use of coercion – the technique of the army and of the modern totalitarian state. The other is voluntary cooperation of individuals – the technique of the market place. The possibility of coordination through voluntary cooperation rests on the elementary, yet frequently denied, proposition that both parties to an economic transaction benefit from it, *provided the transaction is bilaterally voluntary and informed.* So long as effective freedom of exchange is maintained, the central feature of the market organization of economic activity is that it prevents one person from interfering with another in respect of most of his activities. The consumer is protected from coercion by the seller because of the presence of other sellers with whom he can deal. The seller is

---

5 From data in Credit Suisse's *2013 Global Wealth Report.*

protected from coercion by the consumer because of other consumers to whom he can sell. the employee is protected from coercion by the employer because of other employers for whom he can work, and so on. And the market does this impersonally and without centralized authority.

(*Capitalism and Freedom*: 12–13)

The first problem is that it is not one person one vote, but one dollar one vote in the market place. Some claim this as a virtue: If I have a particularly strong preference for a good I can cast more dollar ballots to reflect the intensity of my desire. But this is confusing two issues. There is nothing wrong with a system of social choice that permits people to express the intensity of their desires. In fact, this is necessary if we are to achieve self-managed decision making. But, *there is something wrong when people have vastly different numbers of dollar ballots to cast in market elections.* Few would hold up as a paragon of liberty a political election in which some were permitted to vote thousands of times and others were permitted to vote only once, or not at all. But this is exactly the kind of freedom the market provides. Those with more income have a greater impact on what suppliers in markets will be signaled to provide than those with less income, which explains why "market freedom" often leads to outcomes we know do not reflect what most people need or want. Why are there so many plastic surgeons when many communities suffer from lack of basic family practitioners? How can the demand for cosmetic plastic surgery be so high and the demand for basic family healthcare so low? There are many more who vote in the healthcare market for basic healthcare than for plastic surgery. And the intensity of people's desires for basic healthcare is higher than the intensity of desires for plastic surgery as well. But those voting for plastic surgery have many more votes to cast for even their less pressing desires than most voting for basic healthcare have even for life and death needs. Hence the provision of medical services of marginal benefit, like plastic surgery, and the failure to provide essential medical services for the poor, when healthcare decisions are left to the market place.

Second, in the simple corn model in Chapter 3 we saw how exchanges in labor and credit markets that are bilaterally voluntary and informed can still lead to growing inequalities – even when employees and borrowers are supposedly "protected from coercion" by a multiplicity of employers and lenders to choose from. The lie behind Friedman's portrayal of market exchanges as non-coercive is that he ignores the importance of what those who confront each other in the market place arrive with. As we saw in the corn model, when some arrive at the labor market with seed corn and others have none, it is entirely predictable the seedy will end up being the employers and the seedless their employees. Moreover, as long as seed corn is scarce it is predictable the seedy employers will capture the lion's share of the efficiency gain from the labor exchange as profits, even though the employers don't work at all. Similarly, those who arrive at the credit market with more seed corn will lend to those with less, and as long as seed corn is scarce the lenders will capture the lion's share of the resulting increase in the borrowers' productivity as interest, even though the lenders don't work at all. Friedman can call these outcomes non-coercive if he wants, on the grounds that the seedless volunteered to exchange their laboring capacities for a wage, and borrowers agreed to pay interest knowing full well what the consequences would be. But this merely displaces the source of coercion. It is their seedlessness that "coerces" employees and borrowers to "volunteer" to be fleeced. Are we to believe they would have "volunteered" to be the ones who showed up at the labor or credit market seedless in the first place?

Friedman opens the door when he acknowledges that exchange under non-competitive conditions is coercive. Yet exchanges under non-competitive conditions are bilaterally voluntary, informed and mutually beneficial. So one has to wonder why Friedman agrees that exchanges in non-competitive markets are coercive, and objectionable. In a one company town since I am free to remain unemployed, I am presumably better off working than not working if you find me employed. In a one bank town since I am free not to borrow at all, I am presumably better off if I borrow than I would have been had I not. But not even Milton Friedman has the *chutzpah* to call these non-competitive market outcomes non-coercive – even though the agreement is voluntary and may be mutually beneficial in both cases. Once we recognize that voluntary exchanges under non-competitive conditions are coercive since only one party to the exchange has the opportunity to choose among *different* partners, it is easy to see how exchanges under competitive conditions can be coercive as well. *When initial conditions are unequal, voluntary, informed, and mutually beneficial exchanges will be coercive and lead to inequitable outcomes even if exchanges take place under competitive conditions.*

The third problem with Friedman's assertion that market decisions are free from coercion is that buyers and sellers often come to agreements with adverse consequences for third parties who have no say in the matter whatsoever. Friedman acknowledges that victims of what he calls "neighborhood effects" are coerced, but presumes these are minor inconveniences that seldom occur. As we saw in Chapter 4, political economists believe external effects are the rule rather than the exception in market exchanges, thereby leaving many disenfranchised and "coerced" when buyers and sellers make decisions that affect them without giving a thought to consulting their interests.

The fourth problem is that Friedman assumes away the best solution for coordinating economic activities. He simply asserts "there are only two ways of coordinating the economic activities of millions – central direction involving the use of coercion – and voluntary cooperation – the technique of the market place." In the next chapter we will explore how participatory, democratic planning works, and see how it permits all to partake in economic decision making in proportion to the degree they are affected by outcomes. According to Friedman participatory planning must fall into the category of "central direction involving the use of coercion." But as readers will see, this is most certainly not the case, invalidating Friedman's assertion that there are only two ways of coordinating economic activities – a crucial assumption for which Friedman offers no argument whatsoever.

Myth 7: Markets Are Fair

Is capitalism unfair only because people get unjustifiable income from ownership of productive property? Or, are labor markets also unfair? Even if wages and salaries were determined in competitive labor markets free from discrimination, a surgeon who is on the golf course by 2 p.m. would consume ten times more than a garbage collector working fifty hours per week, because the surgeon was genetically gifted and benefited from vast quantities of socially costly education. Free labor and capital markets mean that most who are wealthy are so *not* because they worked harder or sacrificed more than others, but because they inherited wealth, talent, or simply got lucky. In Chapter 2 we concluded that distribution according to maxim 2 – to each according to the value of her labor's contribution – is inequitable because income from human capital is unfair for the same reasons income from physical capital is unfair: Differences in the values of people's contributions for reasons *other than* differences in effort or sacrifice are beyond people's abilities to control, and carry no moral weight in any case. But wages in real world capitalism are more inequitable than marginal revenue product wages would be. Minorities and women are not paid the market value of their labor's contribution. Because of economic discrimination in hiring, promotion, and pay, because of occupational ghettos, and because of unequal educational opportunities inequities in real world capitalism are far worse than they would be in ideal models.

Myth 8: Markets Are Efficient

In Chapter 4 we explored all the reasons to believe markets are guided by a malevolent invisible foot as often as by a beneficent invisible hand when they allocate our scarce productive resources. We discovered that Milton Friedman and received wisdom notwithstanding, there are good reasons to believe markets allocate resources very inefficiently and concluded:

> Convenient deals with mutual benefits for buyer and seller should not be confused with economic efficiency. When some kinds of preferences are consistently underrepresented because of transaction cost and free rider problems, when consumers adjust their preferences to biases in the market price system and thereby aggravate those biases, and when profits can be increased as often by externalizing costs onto parties external to market exchanges as from productive behavior, theory predicts free market exchange will often result in a *mis*allocation of scarce productive resources. . . . Moreover, when markets are less than perfectly competitive – which they almost always are – and fail to equilibrate instantaneously – which they always do – the results are that much worse.

When pressed, all economists concede that externalities, non-competitive market structures, and market disequilibria lead to allocative inefficiencies. Since mainstream economists take capitalism for granted, the debate among them is whether "market failure" or "government failure" is worse. That is, mainstream economists argue among themselves over whether government policies aimed at reducing inefficiencies due to externalities, non-competitive market structures, and disequilibria create even greater inefficiencies than those they eliminate. Conservative mainstream economists emphasize the dangers of ***government failure*** *when politicians and bureaucrats sacrifice efficiency to their personal agendas.* Liberal mainstream economists emphasize how much inefficiency due to market failures can be reduced by responsible government policies, if only opposition from business special interests can be overcome.

Not surprisingly, political economists usually side with liberals in the mainstream in our attempts to ameliorate the inefficiencies and inequities of capitalism. But political economists also emphasize that as much as we try to reduce the ill effects of market failures, even the best efforts are likely to fall short of what a truly desirable economy could yield for a host of theoretical and practical reasons. While anti-trust policy can be used to make industries more competitive, they frequently sacrifice economies of scale and dynamic efficiency in service of allocative efficiency when they break up large firms. Moreover, even when the public interest is obviously served, anti-trust cases are hard to win when opposed by corporate power as the recent Microsoft anti-trust case attests. Using fiscal and monetary policies to "fine tune" real economies honeycombed with uncertainties and speculative dynamics impossible to capture in even the most elaborate macroeconomic forecasting models is far more difficult than theoretical models would lead one to suspect. Political economists also emphasize that an increasingly integrated global economy and powerful domestic business interests often obstruct effective fiscal and monetary policy.

Sectoral imbalances pose a different kind of disequilibria and inefficiency. When an industry expands less rapidly than industries it buys from and sells to, it can become a "bottleneck" retarding overall growth and underutilizing productive capacities in related industries. *Indicative planning* or *industrial policy* attempts to *reduce the inefficiency that results from sectoral imbalances by anticipating them and reducing them through differential tax and credit policies.* Industries identified as bottlenecks are favored with lower business taxes and preferential credit to stimulate their growth, while "surplus industries" expanding more rapidly than related industries are discouraged by higher taxes and credit rationing in some form or another. Whether the government can guess better than the market, whether differential tax and credit policies are an invitation to corruption, and whether indicative planning reduces economic democracy as economic elites dominate the planning process are questions posed by mainstream and political economists alike.

In sum, quite the opposite from what Milton Friedman would have us believe: Private enterprise and markets *both* cause unacceptable inequities. Private enterprise and markets *both* cause significant inefficiencies. And private enterprise and markets *both* disenfranchise the vast majority from participating in economic decision making in proportion to the degree they are affected, and stand as a growing danger to, rather than a bulwark of, political liberty. As we explore in the next chapter, much can be done to ameliorate these deficiencies, and when well-conceived interventions are applied outcomes can be considerably improved. But mitigating damage is not the same as solving the root cause of problems, and mitigation won through herculean effort and sacrifice is always at risk of being undone when reform movements falter, weaken, or simply grow old.

What Went Wrong?[6]

When the nineteenth century was drawing to a close economic radicals expected the twentieth century would be capitalism's last. They expected democracy and economic justice to advance in tandem and replace a wasteful system based on competition and greed with a more efficient, equitable economy in which workers and consumers planned how to cooperate among themselves. But the heirs to nineteenth-century

---

6 Readers interested in a fuller evaluation of what twentieth-century critics of capitalism got wrong, and right, should see Part II of *Economic Justice and Democracy* (Routledge, 2005).

anti-capitalism – twentieth-century Communism and social democracy – each failed to advance these causes. So instead of hearing its last hurrah, capitalism beat back all its challengers, leaving us with a particularly virulent neoliberal version of capitalism firmly in the saddle as we began the twenty-first century. The difference between capitalism today and a hundred years ago is that "born again" capitalism is poised to do in mother earth in short order since its "initial conditions" include 7 billion people, modern industrial technology, and an already badly damaged ecosystem. God has given capitalism the rainbow sign. No more water, the fire next time. What remains to be seen is whether reformers and anti-capitalists have learned enough to change outcomes, and how much stimulus for change the latest economic crisis will provide.

The Communist economy was a system of public enterprises governed by a procedure known as central planning. After spreading its influence over large parts of the global economy from 1917 to 1989, these economies vanished in only a few years before the end of the century. The Communist economic system did not suffer from the same deficiencies as capitalism. Instead the centrally planned economies of the Soviet Bloc were terribly flawed in other ways. While the fatal flaw in capitalism is its anti-social bias, the fatal flaw in central planning was its anti-democratic bias. It is clear centrally planned economies run by totalitarian political parties, largely immune from popular pressure, and increasingly free to feather the nests of its leaders and members, were not likely to produce the best outcomes. The marriage of the single vanguard party state and central planning was truly a marriage made in hell of two totalitarian dynamics, where political and economic democracy were the first victims. Combined with a more democratic political system, and redone to closer approximate a best case version, centrally planned economies no doubt would have performed better. But they could never have delivered economic self-management, would have proved slow to innovate as apathy and frustration inevitably took its toll, and would have always been susceptible to growing inequities and inefficiencies as the inevitable effects of differential economic power grew. Moreover, central planners and plant managers both had perverse incentives leading them to behave contrary to the social interest. However, central planning would have been incompatible with economic democracy even if it had overcome its information and incentive liabilities. And the truth is it survived as long as it did only because it was propped up by unprecedented totalitarian political power. In the end Communist parties sacrificed economic democracy along with political democracy in the name of economic justice and efficiency they never delivered.[7]

---

7   For a thorough critique of centrally planned economies published almost a decade before the "fall of the wall" see Michael Albert and Robin Hahnel, *Socialism Today and Tomorrow* (South End Press, 1981).

Social democracy avoided the totalitarian errors of Communism only to abandon its commitment to pursuing the economics of equitable cooperation. While social democratic reforms within some national economies gained ground for thirty years after World War II, these reforms proved ever harder to defend as capital became more mobile internationally, and as ideological and political opposition to capitalism crumbled with the "fall of the wall." To rephrase an old adage: It proved harder and harder to build social democracy in one country. But social democracy also abandoned its base among the disadvantaged by accepting, rather than challenging the ideological underpinnings of labor and capital markets, and made peace with capitalism by accepting privately owned corporations and markets, i.e. an economic system based on competition and greed. After more than a half century of alternating in and out of power, European social democratic parties lost sight of the difference between playing the role of reformer and the role of apologist for capitalism. Worse still, in the latest economic crisis in one country after another European social democratic governments have imposed the same punitive and useless austerity policies on their historic voting bloc as have right wing governments. Social democratic parties have offered precious little difference in substance when in power over the past six years, and any remaining difference in rhetoric is falling increasingly on deaf ears.

Neoliberal Capitalism in Crisis

When the first edition of *The ABCs of Political Economy* was published neoliberal capitalism, like Shakespeare's Julius Caesar, truly did "bestride the narrow world like a colossus," leaving Communism and social democracy to "walk under its huge legs, and peep about to find dishonorable graves." In 2002 it was difficult to imagine how we could move from a world celebrating the economics of competition and greed as never before to a world practicing the economics of equitable cooperation.

But that was before the financial crisis of 2008. That was before the Great Recession engulfed the advanced economies in Europe and North America. That was before median family wealth in the US dropped back to its level in 1990, "erasing two decades of accumulated prosperity" in the words of the Federal Reserve Bank. That was before the unemployment rate in the Eurozone hit an all-time high. That was before the unemployment rates in Spain and Greece surged past 20%, and over 50% for Spanish and Greek youth. In other words, that was before capitalism reminded us once again just how inhumane, unfair, and wasteful of economic potentials it can be.

That was also before demonstrations shook Greece, and voters in Iceland refused to pay to bailout creditors of Icelandic banks in 2009. That was before demonstrators outside the international climate meetings in Copenhagen in December 2009 denounced their governments for abandoning efforts to do anything meaningful to prevent climate change. That was before student strikes led to the rise of the Uncut movement in the UK in the fall of 2010. That was before the rise of "Los Indignados" in Spain in the spring of 2011. That was before the electorate showed right center and left center governments administering inhumane and futile economic austerity policies the door in every country in the Eurozone. That was before the people of Wisconsin occupied their State house in the winter of 2011 in protest against austerity and union busting. That was before the incredible Occupy Wall Street movement spread to thousands of cities and towns across the United States in the fall of 2011. That was before students rebelled in Quebec and Chile in the spring of 2012. That was before the wheels nearly came off the neoliberal austerity wagon in Greece when a new coalition of radical left parties called Syriza – pledged to repudiate unpayable debt, nationalize the banks, end inhumane and futile austerity, and pursue an altogether different economic model – came within an eye-lash of winning an election and forming a government in June 2012. In other words, that was before hundreds of millions of people began to shout: "ENOUGH! We can, and will do better than ruling elites, whom we will no longer tolerate."

In their own voices, and in their own ways, these demonstrators are saying they no longer buy Milton Friedman's fairy tale about the wonders of free market capitalism. They are saying what Keynes said many years ago:

[Capitalism] is not a success. It is not intelligent, it is not beautiful, it is not just, it is not virtuous – and it doesn't deliver the goods. In short, we dislike it, and we are beginning to despise it.

However, Keynes also spoke for many protesters today when he added: "But when we wonder what to put in its place, we are extremely perplexed." In the next and last chapter we look to see what political economists have to offer today to alleviate confusion about what can be done in both the short and long run.

11

What Is to Be Done?
The Economics of Equitable
Cooperation

What should we do if we had the opportunity to start over again? We could hold a lottery – or perhaps have a brawl – to decide who owns what productive resources. The unfortunate losers would have to hire themselves out to work for the more fortunate winners, and the goods the losers produced could then be "freely" exchanged by their owners – the people who did *not* produce them. Of course this is the capitalist "solution" to the economic problem which has been spreading its sway for roughly three centuries. While less "triumphant" than a few years ago, neoliberal capitalism remains stubbornly entrenched despite its latest crisis and absence of meaningful reform.

Alternatively, we could make the best educated – or perhaps the most ruthless among us – responsible for planning how to use society's scarce productive resources and for telling the rest of us what to do. But that was tried with unsatisfactory results. After a troubled three-quarters of a century Communism and "command planning" have been consigned to the dust bins of history, may they rest in peace.

Whether centrally planned economies caused more or less alienation, apathy, inefficiency, inequity, and environmental destruction than their capitalist rivals is now a moot point. The important conclusion from humans' most recent experiments in mismanaging our economic affairs is that neither the economics of competition and greed, nor the economics of command, are the answers to our economic problems. In this last chapter we explore the ideas of those who believe the economics of equitable cooperation are not beyond humanity's grasp.

Not All Capitalisms Are Created Equal

Not all versions of capitalism are equally horrific, and better versions are well worth fighting for. Moreover, since the capitalist ruling class shows no signs of relinquishing power as quickly and easily as Communist rulers did, creating the economics of equitable cooperation will have to go on inside capitalist economies for the foreseeable future. So first we ask, how can capitalism be humanized? After which we discuss why we must go beyond capitalism in order to build the economics of equitable cooperation, and how to do it.

Keynesian Reforms

After the demise of Communism free market capitalists quickly targeted a new enemy – Keynesianism. No doubt Lord Keynes would have been just as surprised to find himself replacing Communism as Enemy #1 as his Nobel prize winning disciples, Joseph Stiglitz and Paul Krugman, were to find themselves ostracized by the mainstream of the profession in the 2000s when they refused to recant their Keynesian roots. It is important for not only progressives but radicals as well to understand where their allegiance lies in this new ideological war: *When it comes to Keynesianism versus neoliberalism progressives and radicals must be pro-Keynesian with no "ifs, ands, or buts."* This does not mean progressives and radicals do not go beyond Keynesian reforms in our efforts to replace the economics of competition and greed with the economics of equitable cooperation. But what makes progressives and radicals different from Keynesians is not that we do not always support reforms Keynesians are for, but that Keynesians do not always support more far reaching changes that some progressives and radicals are for.

Taming Finance

What's good for the wealthy and the financial companies who serve their interests is *not* necessarily good for the rest of us. If we listen to advice from the financial industry we will never restrict any of their activities – to our detriment.

Those were the first two sentences in the section on "taming finance" of the first edition published six years before the latest financial crisis. Paul Volker, who served as Chairman of the Board of Governors of the Federal Reserve System from 1979 through 1987, had this to say about financial regulation as far back as 1999 in a luncheon address to the Organization for Economic Co-operation and Development on March 18, 1999:

I've been involved in financial supervision and regulation for about 40 of my 70 years, mostly on the regulatory and supervisory side but also on the side of those being regulated. I have to tell you from long experience, bank regulators and supervisors are placed on a pedestal only in the *aftermath* of crises. In benign periods – in periods of boom and exuberance – banking supervision and banking regulations have very little political support and strong industry opposition.

Because of deregulation pushed by Wall Street and passed by politicians in the Democratic and Republican parties alike, by the early 2000s the domestic and global economies were more vulnerable to financial bubbles and crashes than at any time since the roaring 1920s. Anti-reforms like repeal of Glass-Steagall in 1999, and various measures that go under the label of international capital liberalization orchestrated by the US Department of the Treasury and the IMF, eliminated minimal protections and safeguards dating back to the New Deal and the Bretton Woods Conference. However, unlike the financial crisis of 1929 which did lead to serious financial reform and passage of the Glass-Steagall Banking Act in 1933, the political power of the US financial industry had grown so great by 2008 that it was able to prevent meaningful financial reform in the aftermath of the financial crisis of 2008. For any who suffer under the illusion that the Dodd-Frank Wall Street Reform and Consumer Protection Act signed into law by President Obama in July 2010 offers any real protection, suffice it to say that Paul Volker, who was a principal figure in the original committee drafting a bill, was pushed aside by Obama advisors Summers and Geithner and conspicuously out of the country when it was signed into law. Most importantly, the so-called "Volker-rule" banning commercial banks which benefit from federal insurance and protection from the Fed from engaging in speculative "proprietary trading," and without which the Act has no teeth, continues to be weakened as to its interpretation and application. In the end Dodd-Frank was little more than a fig leaf for the financial industry and its political protectors to hide behind from outraged voters. To rub salt in the wound, the US Treasury under Obama, and the Fed under Chairman Bernanke, have persisted in sparing no expense in bailing out Wall Street while Main Street is told it must tighten its belt.

Even when there are no crises, as our simple credit corn model reveals an unbridled financial sector will almost always distribute the lion's share of efficiency gains from extending the credit system to those who were better off in the first place, and thereby widen wealth and income inequalities. But as explained in Chapter 7 and illustrated by models 9.1 and 9.2, free market finance is particularly dangerous and prone to crisis, as people as different as Keynes and Volker have warned us. Simply put, an unregulated or badly regulated financial sector is an accident waiting to happen.

Therefore it must be regulated in the public interest to diminish the likelihood of financial crises, and to distribute the costs of financial crises more equitably when they do occur. Right now the government provides free underwriting for Wall Street, which is allowed to reap obscene profits from what are often risky investments with little social benefit, while the taxpayer is "on the hook" to pick up the tab whenever panic strikes, since we "the people" also suffer if panic goes unchecked.

Long before the recent crisis financial reformers had warned of dangers from deregulation and offered many useful suggestions. Jane D'Arista, Tom Schlesinger, William Black, Gerald Epstein, Robert Blecker, Tom Palley, Dean Baker, John Eatwell, Lance Taylor, Dorene Isenberg, and Gary Dimsky are among the many political economists who long before 2008 had developed a cornucopia of financial reform proposals ranging from modest reforms that diminish outright corruption and thievery, to substantial reforms to protect the real economy from "financial shocks," to ambitious reforms that would redistribute the benefits of financial activities from the wealthy to the poor and democratize monetary policy. Unfortunately, because the financial industry has controlled the political response, those who were ignored or ridiculed before the latest crisis, but who proved to be most prophetic, have been entirely excluded from crafting meaningful reforms in its aftermath.

Progressives who work on financial reform must judge how a reform will affect efficiency and stability in the real economy, how it will affect income and wealth inequality, and whether it will give ordinary people more or less control over their economic destinies. Of course they must also consider how likely it is that any particular financial reform is "winnable." But perhaps the time has come to ask whether or not a private financial sector has now become too big for the rest of us to allow to fail, ever again. After the crash in 1929 we got meaningful financial regulation. After that the financial sector lobbied for deregulation twenty-four seven for seventy-five years, until it had once again created another accident waiting to happen. The rational response in 2008 should have been to ask, "Why should we leave the financial sector in private hands?"

There are many reasons to nationalize the financial industry: (1) Failure to properly regulate the financial industry causes more harm than failure to regulate other industries. (2) The financial industry is more adept at outmaneuvering regulations than other industries, so the alternative to nationalization – regulation – is always likely to unravel. (3) Right now the financial industry is so flush with profits that it has literally bought the allegiance of most politicians, not only making it impossible to pass regulations but making a mockery of political democracy as well. And finally, (4) if one is relieved of the burden of figuring out how to turn the simple business of lending people's savings to creditworthy borrowers into a giant casino, where the house rips off huge profits while customers cover house losses, it is a fairly straightforward business to run. Even government bureaucrats can count deposits and process loan applications for creditworthiness! One must be careful, however, not to socialize losses and privatize wealth. To nationalize troubled banks and absorb losses on their toxic assets, and then turn them back over to stockholders when they are once again solvent, is worse than no nationalization. Public banks should also be run differently than private banks. The purpose of a public credit system is to lend according to social rates of return, which is not the same as commercial profitability.

Full Employment Macro Policies There is no reason aggregate demand cannot be managed through fiscal and monetary policies to keep actual production close to potential GDP, and cyclical unemployment to a minimum. That is, there is no technical or intellectual reason. Of course there are political reasons that prevent governments from minimizing macroeconomic inefficiency. Because the wealthy fear inflation more than unemployment, they exert political pressure on governments to prioritize the fight against inflation even when inflation is not a danger, to the detriment of combating unemployment. Because employee bargaining power increases when labor markets are tight over long time periods, employers pressure governments to permit periodic recessions in the name of fighting inflation. In an increasingly integrated global economy where demand for exports is an important component of aggregate demand in most countries, and where differential interest rates produce large movements of wealth holdings from one country to another, fiscal and monetary policies must be better coordinated internationally, which admittedly is trickier. But as in the case of domestic stabilization, the primary reason international macroeconomic policy coordination is not done well is political not technical.

Improved use of macroeconomic stabilization policies would not only make economies more efficient, it would strengthen movements fighting for equitable cooperation in other ways as well. Wage increases and improvements in working conditions are easier to win in a full employment economy. Affirmative action programs designed to rectify racial and gender discrimination are easier to win when the economic pie is growing rather than stagnant or shrinking. Union organizing drives are more likely to be successful when labor markets are tight than when unemployment rates are high. The reason privileged sectors in capitalism obstruct efforts to pursue full employment macro policies – it diminishes their bargaining power – is precisely the reason those fighting for equitable cooperation should pressure for it.

Every progressive organization should work to punish elected officials who fail to vote for fiscal stimulus when it is needed to prevent unemployment. But it is important not to overestimate what this would accomplish. Even if everyone had a job, they would not necessarily have a job they could support a family on, much less one that paid them fairly for their sacrifices. Even if everyone had a job that paid a living wage with benefits, they would not necessarily have personally rewarding, socially useful work since most jobs in capitalism are more personally distasteful than necessary, and much work in capitalism is socially useless or counterproductive. So when we fight for full employment stabilization policies we should never forget to point out that what every citizen deserves is a socially useful job with fair compensation. We should never tire of pointing out that while capitalism is incapable of delivering on this, it is just as possible as it is sensible.

Industrial Policy The French practiced what they called "indicative planning" with such success in the 1950s that the British government tried to copy the policy (unsuccessfully) in the early 1960s.[1] The German model of capitalism, then the Japanese model, and finally what became known as the Asian development model all used **industrial policy** to great advantage. In brief the policy consists of *identifying key sectors in the economy that are important to prioritize in order to increase overall economic growth rates.* In the 1950s the French Commissariat Général du Plan identified "bottleneck sectors" whose sluggish growth was holding back the rest of the economy, and arranged with the Finance Ministry and a state-owned development bank for lower business tax rates and interest rates for firms investing in those sectors. During the heyday of the post WWII Japanese economic miracle, the Ministry of International Trade and Industry, MITI, identified "industries of the future" expected to be crucial to Japanese international economic success, and arranged with the Finance Ministry and Bank of Japan for firms in those industries to be taxed and receive credit on preferential terms. In effect MITI treated comparative advantage as something to be created rather than meekly accepted as "national fate." As a result Japan became a world power house, first in low cost light manufactured goods, then in high quality steel and automobiles, and eventually in electronics and computers.[2] Among the "Asian Tigers" South Korea and Taiwan

---

1 Andrew Shonfield provides an excellent evaluation of both the French policy and the failed British attempt to copy it in *Modern Capitalism* (Oxford University Press, 1974).
2 President Nixon created a commission to study *The United States in the Global Economy* in the early 1970s. Peter Gary Peterson who headed the commission was so impressed with the advantages of Japanese industrial policy that he added a special appendix to the GAO report titled "The Japanese Economic Miracle," in which he urged the US government to imitate Japanese industrial policy.

copied Japan's successful industrial policies most closely, with great success.[3] Finally, it was the "Asian development model" rather than *laissez faire* capitalism which the Chinese Communist government embraced three decades ago to produce the latest "economic miracle."

There are three things progressive reformers should bear in mind about industrial policy: (1) Real capitalist economies are often plagued by temporary disequilibria among sectors that cause inefficiencies, and many capitalist economies are trapped playing a role in the international division of labor that dooms them to produce goods where opportunities to increase wages and profits are minimal. Industrial policies can be used to eliminate short-run imbalances between sectors, or to guide an economy out of a "vicious cycle" of specialization onto a more "virtuous" long run development strategy. Neoliberals who dominate policy in all the major international economic institutions are oblivious to the static and dynamic inefficiencies of markets, and therefore see no purpose to such policies, label them "crony capitalism," and pressure governments to abandon them no matter how successful they may have been. In many ways one can interpret rules countries are now required to follow as members of the World Trade Organization as little more than attempts to outlaw use of industrial policy.[4] (2) Industrial policies to help create new comparative advantages are crucial if less developed economies are ever to break out of their vicious cycle of poverty, and therefore are a particularly important part of forging a path toward more productive economies in the third world and a more egalitarian global economy. Industrial policy is also crucial to redirect investment in advanced economies away from priorities overvalued by the market like private luxuries for the affluent toward priorities the market neglects like housing for the poor, education, and environmental protection. (3) However, it is important to realize that industrial policy is highly susceptible to being hijacked by the largest corporations with the aid of high ranking government bureaucrats. If this occurs industrial policy can further reduce the power of workers, consumers, farmers, and small businesses if they are excluded from the industrial policy planning "power game." In fact, it can be argued that successful industrial policies in France, Japan,

3 See Alice Amsden, *Asia's Next Giant: South Korea and Late Industrialization* (Oxford University Press, 1989), and *The Rise of "the Rest:" Challenges to the West from Late-Industrialization Economies* (Oxford University Press, 2001).

4 Ha Joon Chang has become the most visible critic of wealthy countries who once used these policies themselves to develop, but are now rewriting the rules for the global economy to prevent their use by poor countries today. See *Kicking Away the Ladder* (Anthem Press, 2002), *Reclaiming Development* (Zed Books, 2004), *The East Asian Development Experience* (Zed Books, 2006), *The Bad Samaritans* (Bloomsbury Press, 2007), and *23 Things They Don't Tell You About Capitalism* (Bloomsbury Press, 2010).

South Korea, and Taiwan made their economies *less* democratic, and the absence of democracy has facilitated its use in China. Industrial policy is a kind of capitalist planning, not to be confused with the kind of democratic, participatory planning discussed below. On the other hand, it was used effectively without reducing economic democracy in Norway, and if progressive reformers win disadvantaged sectors seats at the planning table it can improve investment priorities and increase rather than diminish economic democracy in capitalist economies.

Wage-Led Growth In capitalism the low-road growth strategy is to suppress wages to increase profits and hope the wealthy will plow those profits back into productive investments that expand the capital stock and increase potential GDP. As demonstrated by model 9.5, besides being inequitable, this strategy runs the risk that the wealthy will not invest their profits to expand the domestic capital stock but use them to (1) buy luxury goods, or (2) save them by buying assets either at home or abroad. In the former case socially useful investments lack for funds as resources are used to produce yet more consumer goods for the wealthy. In the latter case not only will profits not be used to add machines to the capital stock, aggregate demand may falter and reduce actual production farther below a stagnant potential GDP, or, as we have just seen, create conditions that increase the risk that when an asset bubble bursts the ensuing financial crisis will turn into a full blown crisis in the real economy as well.

The high road to growth in capitalism is to raise wages to keep aggregate demand high, trusting that if there are profitable sales opportunities capitalists will find ways to expand capacity to take advantage of them. Besides being more equitable, this strategy minimizes lost output due to lack of aggregate demand and reduces unemployment in economies where chronic underemployment is a major social problem. The only risk in this strategy is there will be too little savings to lend to businesses trying to expand their productive capacity, in which case a bold progressive government could always increase taxes on the wealthy to finance socially useful public investment.[5]

Progressives in developing economies and their allies in the advanced economies need to reject neoliberal, low-road growth programs peddled by the US Treasury, IMF, World Bank, and WTO and point out there *is* an alternative – wage-led growth and production oriented toward domestic basic needs. Every developing economy

---

5 The danger of insufficient savings to finance productive investment in a wage-led growth strategy appears more dangerous in our political economy growth model 9.5 than it need be in the real world. Readers should note that there is no government in model 9.5. If we add a government willing to tax capitalist savings which are not being used to finance productive investment and use the revenues to pay for public investment the principal danger in the "high road" to growth disappears.

needs some dynamic export industries if for no other reason than to import cutting edge technologies. But subordinating the entire economy to export and profit-led growth is a recipe for disaster. It was a disaster for LDCs when the IMF forced it on them in the 1980s, 1990s, and 2000s, and is still a disaster when the EC forces it on the weaker economies inside the EMU.[6]

A Mixed Economy The truth is that sectors like education, healthcare, and housing for the poor, sectors like telecommunications and energy where technology makes monopoly difficult to avoid, and sectors like the financial industry where perverse incentives generate systemic risk in excess of individual risk and social rates of return often deviate from commercial rates of return, often do *not* perform well in private hands. In Europe and many developing economies during the golden era of capitalism governments established public enterprises in these sectors producing a *mixed economy*, i.e. *an economy with a mixture of private and publicly owned firms*. Privatization of these public enterprises has been a major part of the neoliberal program everywhere.

Privatization was a major thrust of Thatcher governments in Great Britain during the 1980s, and has been a constant theme of neoliberals and the IMF over the past thirty years in developing economies. Battles to protect public enterprises from being privatized are often necessary simply to fight against corruption, especially when such privatizations function merely as fire sales to benefit political rulers' wealthy backers and/or foreign multinationals. But sometimes it is also necessary to preserve public services at equitable prices. The sale of the Bolivian water utility to Bechtel Corporation in 1998 led to such dramatic price hikes that it spurred a popular movement that forced the Bolivian government to rescind the deal, and contributed to the election of a populist government under Evo Morales. In Washington DC a coalition of progressive forces battled the Financial Control Board imposed by the US Congress to oversee city finances to prevent privatization of DC General Hospital, the city's last public hospital required by law to accept any patient in need. Unfortunately that battle was lost when DC General was shut down in 2001 after almost two hundred years of public service. Sometimes opposing privatization is necessary to keep public enterprises which are key allies for governments in their industrial or economic development strategies. Publicly owned banks have played important roles in guiding economies in settings as varied as France in the 1950s and

---

6 See Arthur MacEwan, *Neo-Liberalism or Economic Democracy* (Zed Books, 2000) for a comprehensive, wage-led growth program for developing economies emphasizing domestic production for basic needs. MacEwan goes a long way toward rebutting the taunt neoliberals hurl at their critics: TINA – There Is No Alternative.

a number of Latin American and African countries in the 1960s and 1970s. While technically private, many banks in Japan and South Korea were so reliant on support from those countries' central banks that they could be counted on to cooperate with government industrial policies that brought about the Japanese and Korean economic miracles. Over the past ten years the US government, with a large assist from the IMF in the case of South Korea, has seized on every opportunity to force Korea and Japan to rescind laws barring foreign ownership of their banking sector. Not only does this allow foreign banks to gobble up lucrative assets when crises hit, it eliminates government influence over banking policies that was once an important part of successful industrial policy.

In conclusion, subordinating finance to the service of the real economy rather than the reverse, pursuing full employment fiscal and monetary policies and intelligent industrial policies, embracing a wage-led rather than profit-led growth strategy, and accepting public ownership where practical is nothing more than a "full Keynesian program." It may seem radical in an environment of free market triumphalism, but it once fell well within the political mainstream. However, as important as it is for progressives and radicals to give the Keynesian program our full support whenever the alternative is neoliberal deregulation and austerity, it is important to understand what a full Keynesian program is not. Even a full Keynesian program falls far short of redressing the fundamental inequities and power imbalances in capitalism. Additional reforms are necessary to make capitalism more fair and humane.

Reducing Economic Injustice

Tax Reform Unless taxes are strictly **proportional**, that is, unless *everyone pays the same percentage of their income or wealth on the tax,* taxes will redistribute pre-tax income and wealth. *If those with higher income pay a higher percentage of their income on a tax than those with lower income pay,* we call the tax **progressive** because it redistributes income from those with higher incomes to those with lower incomes. While *if those with higher income pay a lower percentage of their income on a tax than those with lower income pay,* we call the tax **regressive** because it redistributes income from those with lower incomes to those with higher incomes. Similarly, a tax on wealth can be proportional, progressive, or regressive depending on whether it did not redistribute wealth (a proportional wealth tax), redistributed wealth from rich to poor (a progressive wealth tax), or redistributed income from poor to rich (a regressive wealth tax). It is important to note that if those with more income or wealth can shield a greater part of their income or wealth from a tax by claiming more deductions than those with less income or wealth, even if the rate on taxable income or wealth rises with income, the tax will be less progressive than it appears, and may actually be regressive. Studies show that the federal individual income tax is much less progressive than it appears to be from its rate schedule once exclusions of income, deductions, and credits are taken into account. These exceptions to the complete taxation of income, also known as loopholes or preferences, tend to be distributed disproportionately to higher income persons. The reason is that the greatest loopholes pertain to savings and capital income of various types, and higher income persons have greater capacity to save and larger shares of capital income.

Moreover, many federal taxes such as Social Security and Medicare, or FICA taxes, are highly regressive, and state sales taxes and local property taxes are regressive as well. It is generally believed that despite progressive income tax rates, federal taxes as a whole are barely progressive, and the overall tax system, including state and local taxes, is regressive. In other words, at present in the US taxes are used to redistribute income from the poor to the rich. Obviously equitable cooperation requires exactly the reverse. There are a number of organizations with tax reform proposals that would replace regressive taxes with more progressive ones and make progressive taxes even more progressive – Citizens for Tax Justice (www.ctj.org), United for a Fair Economy (www.ufenet.org), and the Center on Budget Policies and Priorities (www.cbpp.org) to name a few. Unfortunately we have been "progressing" rapidly in reverse in the United States over the past forty years, as the wealthy have used their growing political influence to shift the tax burden off of themselves, where it belongs, onto the less fortunate, where it does not.

Tax Bads Not Goods What makes more sense than taxing socially destructive behavior rather than behavior that is socially desirable? Economists have known ever since A.C. Pigou proved back in the 1920s that efficiency requires taxing polluters an amount equal to the damage their pollutants cause. Moreover, if governments did this they would raise a great deal of revenue. But even if the tax is collected from the firms who pollute, the cost of the tax will be distributed between the firms who pollute and the consumers of the products they produce. To the extent that firms pass the pollution tax on in the form of higher prices, consumers pay part of pollution taxes along with producers. There is nothing wrong with this from the perspective of efficient incentives. The reason pollution taxes improve efficiency in a market economy is precisely because they discourage consumption of goods whose production requires pollution by making those products more expensive for consumers.

But studies of **tax incidence** – relating to *who ultimately bears what part of a tax* – have concluded that lower income people bear a disproportionate share of the burden of many pollution taxes, including a carbon tax. In other words, many so-called "green" taxes are regressive, and therefore aggravate economic injustice absent countermeasures. Fortunately, countermeasures are readily available. As just explained federal, state, and local governments in the US already collect taxes that are highly regressive, and in many cases even more regressive than pollution taxes. In 2013 FICA taxes for Social Security and Medicare were the second-largest source of federal tax revenues. Thirty-five percent of all federal revenues came from FICA taxes, where employees contributed 7.65% of their wages up to $113,700, and employers contributed an equal amount. If every dollar collected in pollution taxes were paired with a dollar reduction in Social Security taxes paid by employees we would substitute taxes on "bads" – pollution – for taxes on "goods" – productive work – and make the federal tax system more progressive as well. Or, if part of the revenue from a carbon tax is rebated to lower income households, a carbon tax can be made progressive. A recent study by the Northwest Economic Research Center at Portland State University concluded: (1) An Oregon state tax of only $10 per ton of carbon dioxide equivalents would raise over $1 billion of additional revenue a year. (2) If 50% of the revenue was rebated to Oregonians in inverse proportion to their income, the state could (a) still raise revenues by more than $500 million a year, (b) protect all but the wealthy from being adversely affected financially, (c) substantially reduce Oregon's carbon emissions, and (d) make renewable energy and energy conservation projects in the state much more cost competitive. Of course if the revenue from a carbon tax is used to reduce Oregon corporate income taxes, as Oregon's four major business associations are pressing for, Oregon taxes as a whole will become much more regressive.

Living Wages Establishing a minimum wage, and raising it faster than the inflation rate, is both equitable *and* good economics. Had the federal minimum wage been raised sufficiently during the decades prior to 2008 the financial crisis might have triggered only an "ordinary" recession, instead of the "Great Recession." Failure to raise the minimum wage from 1997 to 2007 at the national level led to living wage campaigns in many American cities during the 2000s. After Occupy broke the taboo on discussing inequality, raising the federal minimum wage was at long last under discussion again inside the Washington Beltway in 2014.

Opponents invariably argue that minimum wage laws and increases in the minimum wage hurt the people they are supposed to help by increasing unemployment. Unless the demand for labor is infinitely inelastic, raising wages does decrease employment to some extent as simple supply and demand analysis reveals. However, as explained in Chapter 4, what opponents of minimum wages do not want to admit is that the demand for labor is, in fact, often inelastic in the short run, and even more importantly, raising the wage, unlike raising other prices, can be expected to shift the demand curve for labor to the right as well as move us up the demand curve for labor. Because workers spend a higher percentage of their income than employers, wage increases increase the aggregate demand for goods and services which will make employers *more* likely to hire workers because they will have less trouble selling the goods those workers make. While moving up a given labor demand curve reduces employment, shifting the labor demand curve out – as wage increases do – increases employment. That is also simple supply and demand analysis, but not the kind opponents of minimum wages want to engage in. Opponents of a minimum wage also neglect to mention that the wage rate, like the rate of profit, is a distributive variable, and as the Sraffa model 5.4 of wage, profit, and price determination demonstrates, there are an infinite number of combinations of long-run equilibrium wage rates and profit rates, with associated relative prices for goods and services, that are possible in any capitalist economy. The only difference between combinations where the wage rate is high and profit rate is low, and combinations where the profit rate is high and the wage rate is low, is that the former are more equitable and the latter less so! So in the long run increasing the minimum wage simply moves us to a more equitable distribution of benefits in capitalist economies. As long as appropriate macroeconomic policies are used to preserve full employment there need be no loss of employment from increasing the minimum wage in the long run.[7]

Opponents' criticism that living wage campaigns in a single city will cost jobs in that city as employers move to other locations is more compelling on theoretical grounds than arguments against raising the federal minimum wage. It is nothing more than an example of the "race to the bottom effect" critics of corporate sponsored globalization are right to warn against. For that matter, it is no different from making local environmental regulations stronger, or local business taxes higher. Anything that raises costs to businesses in one locale makes it more likely they will move their business and jobs to another locale. But the lesson those working on living wage campaigns need to draw from this is not to give up, but to expand the living wage into adjoining jurisdictions, and to press for restrictions on the right of businesses to pick up and move. Just as a national minimum wage is better than minimum wages

---

7 Thomas Palley provides an excellent defense of "the new economics of the minimum wage" in "Building Prosperity from the Bottom Up," in the September/October 1998 issue of *Challenge*.

in some states but not others, the more jurisdictions covered by a living wage, the less likely there will be job losses because businesses would have to move farther. And while it is common today to think "freedom of enterprise" means businesses are free to do whatever they want – including murderous releases of toxic pollutants and life-threatening working conditions – the fact is that corporations are licensed by governments and can be held accountable to community needs. In the 1980s the Ohio Public Interest Campaign collected enough signatures to get an initiative on the ballot to place serious restrictions on how quickly, and for what reasons, corporations in Ohio could shut down and move out of state. Unfortunately the initiative was defeated when businesses outspent supporters by more than ten to one.

Theory aside, there is strong empirical evidence that local living wages have *not* led to significant job losses where they have been enacted. Partly this is because living wage ordinances often only cover city employees and employees of private employers who do business with the city. Robert Pollin and Stephanie Luce present evidence regarding job loss along with an excellent analysis of a number of living wage campaigns in *The Living Wage: Building a Fair Economy* (The New Press, 1998). As of February 2002 seventy cities and counties in the US had adopted some form of living wage. Successful living wage campaigns also provide opportunities to press private employers not covered by a city ordinance to pay their employees a living wage. The living wage ordinance in the city of Cambridge helped workers, students, and progressive faculty at Harvard University win substantial wage concessions from a recalcitrant institution and its neoliberal president, Laurence Summers, in the winter of 2001 – after a long campaign including student occupations of university offices. A much less publicized campaign at American University in Washington DC issued a report in February 2002 titled "A Living Wage for Workers at American University: A Question of Fairness and Social Responsibility" recommending an hourly wage of $14.95 in 2001 dollars for a 35-hour work week based on standards for the DC metropolitan region developed by the Economic Policy Institute and Wider Opportunities for Women. Oakland passed one of the nation's first living wage ordinances in 1998, but due to the city charter this law did not apply to the Port of Oakland. In 2002 a ballot initiative known as "Measure I" was passed which broadened coverage to include 1,500 low wage workers at the Oakland airport and seaport.

Single-Payer Healthcare Because single-payer healthcare reform was defeated in 1948 when most advanced economies were adopting it after WWII, and because the US healthcare system ever since has been left in the hands of private providers and the private insurance industry, the US healthcare system was in shambles by 2008.[8] Passage of the Patient Protection and Affordable Care Act in 2010 was arguably the largest legislative "accomplishment" of Obama's presidency. But typical of all of Obama's legislative efforts, in failing to take on powerful interests, while "Obamacare" ameliorated some problems it perpetuated and even aggravated others.

In all reform campaigns there is always tension between those who want to hold out for more far reaching, significant changes and those who preach the practical necessity of a more incremental approach. Usually the debate reduces to how much better a far reaching solution is compared to how much more likely incremental changes are to be won. The jury is still out on whether well-known deficiencies in Obamacare will lead to further reform, or only further delay moving to a single-payer system in the US. However, one could argue that the struggle for healthcare reform in the United States is a rare case where the incremental approach is actually *less practical* than fighting for significant reform because there is simply no way to extend adequate coverage to all and control escalating costs through the private insurance industry.

Only a single-payer, government insurance program can provide universal coverage while containing costs by eliminating the considerable administrative expenses of private insurance "cherry picking" healthier people for coverage. Only a single-payer program can eliminate the paper work and confusion associated with administering multiple insurance plans – all of which are worse deals than provided through single-payer systems in every other industrialized country in the world. A single-payer system is best suited to use monopsony power to control drug prices and hospital fees. And only a system separated from the workplace and employers' choices about providing insurance can end the strife caused when some companies in an industry which do provide healthcare benefits to their employees must compete against other companies which do not. The fact is that providing healthcare through private insurance and managed-care organizations for profit is so inefficient that incremental reforms that leave those institutions in control of the health care system simply cannot succeed. Instead, there is a much better deal for healthcare recipients, healthcare professionals, taxpayers, and the business community as a whole – single-payer, government insurance. It's been there for the taking since 1948. The only losers would be private insurance companies, drug companies, and for-profit managed care organizations – in other words, those who continue to be responsible for the crisis in American healthcare.

8 For a brief introduction to healthcare reform see *Seeking Justice in Health Care: A Guide for Advocates*, available from the Universal Health Care Action Network, UHCAN, www.uhcan.org.

Save Public Education Like healthcare, public education in the United States is also in shambles. Progressives must fight for adequate and fair funding, and for parents, teachers, and students to take control of their schools from corrupt and bloated administrative bureaucracies. Mandatory standard testing and linking school funding and teacher salaries to test results move beyond blaming the victims to punishing the victims. Nor are charter schools and vouchers a program to rebuild the public education system. Instead they are strategies to further destroy it. Proponents of charter schools and vouchers cynically manipulate images of disadvantaged children trapped in overcrowded, ghetto schools with incompetent, tenured teachers to argue for "choice" and "competition." The problem is not that the images fail to accurately represent the educational abuse disadvantaged children do, in fact, suffer. The problem is that competition and choice are not remedies for these problems.

A sufficient reason to oppose these initiatives is that instead of being policies to make sure there will be "no child left behind," vouchers and charter schools are policies designed precisely to "leave the most disadvantaged children behind" so that educational resources can be concentrated on children from advantaged homes who will experience diversity only in the personage of a relatively few poor and minority children from upwardly mobile homes. *What happens to ghetto schools where some students use their vouchers to leave?* When ghetto schools are the predictable losers in school "competition," will they be shut down? Will there be no schools in poor neighborhoods? Will all children from poor neighborhoods be bussed out to wealthy areas of cities and the suburbs? Obviously this "solution" is unacceptable because it robs poor children of any chance to enjoy adequate schooling in their own communities and because it places the burden of transportation entirely on their shoulders. Severely disadvantaged families can barely function even when all the children in the family attend local schools. Severely disadvantaged families cannot adequately support children traveling into strange and distant neighborhoods.

But this solution is also unlikely to ever be permitted. Instead, what will happen is ghetto schools will be consolidated, become even more overcrowded, will be stripped of their better students and more active parents, and become even less able to mount the necessary political pressure to secure their fair share of educational resources. What will happen is the most dysfunctional ghetto schools will be auctioned off to private corporations to run, like jails, for profit, to be abandoned when opportunities for short-run profit taking have been exhausted, or when outraged parents revolt over the miserable education their children receive in charter schools. Proponents of competition and choice don't talk about the schools and children who will inevitably be left behind. All one has to do is imagine what conditions will be like in *those* schools for *those* children to understand why competition and choice is not an acceptable strategy for public education.[9]

Instead we must fight for good schools in *all* neighborhoods – and particularly in poor neighborhoods since that is where the least advantaged students live. Public schools in *all* neighborhoods must be adequately funded and staffed. Scandalous differences in per pupil expenditures must be eliminated.[10] Appropriate programs and curricula must be available for *all* children in *all* schools. Parents, teachers, and students of schools in *all* neighborhoods must be empowered to participate in the educational process. And as long as housing segregation by race and income is rampant, children and families of all races and incomes must share the burden of integrating schools by participating in a fair lottery whose losers must temporarily forego the advantages of attending a local school and be bussed to a more distant one. So-called "educational reforms" that distract us from accomplishing these formidable tasks should be soundly criticized and rejected.

A Safe Safety Net The Scandinavian economies in the 1960s and early 1970s were the only capitalist economies to ever provide a safety net worthy of the name. Lyndon Johnson's so-called "War on Poverty" in the 1960s established a welfare system that was most noteworthy for how bureaucratic, inefficient, and demeaning it was, and how pitiful it was compared to Scandinavian, German, and British, welfare programs. But even that was more than those who were fortunate enough not to need a safety net in the US could stand. The centerpiece of the Republican Party "Contract for America" in 1994 was to abolish welfare. Newt Gingrich found in New Democrat Bill Clinton a President willing to collaborate with the same House Republicans who voted to impeach him four years later to "end welfare as we know it" in the President's

9 In 1993 Edith Rasell and Richard Rothstein edited a large collection of essays in *School Choice: Examining the Evidence* (Economic Policy Institute) which argued that evidence suggested that choice of schools had neither raised student achievement nor enhanced equal opportunity. Martin Carnoy rebutted reports purporting to demonstrate that students using vouchers improve their academic performance, and that the threat of vouchers improves performance in public schools in *School Vouchers: Examining the Evidence* (Economic Policy Institute, 2001). And Fred Hiatt reported that a study by Emily Van Dunk and Anneliese Dickman, "School Choice and the Question of Accountability," released in February 2004, "found little evidence that the Milwaukee program, with 10,000 vouchers (about 10 percent of public school enrollment), had spurred improvement in the public schools" ("Limits and Lessons of Vouchers," *Washington Post* 2/23/04).

10 Differences in per pupil expenditures are due to the fact that unlike other countries where public education is financed out of national tax revenues, K-12 public education in the United States is provided by 14,000 local school districts and funded largely by local property taxes despite the fact that property values differ widely between districts. Often spurred by legal suits, some states now pool property taxes at the state level, to be redistributed to school districts on an equal per pupil basis.

infamous words. Max Sawicky and his co-authors provide an excellent analysis of the devastating human effects of slashing welfare in *The End of Welfare? Consequences of the Federal Devolution for the Nation* (EPI Books, 2000). Building a safety net for the victims of capitalism that is worthy of the name remains the most pressing domestic task facing those of us who would make US capitalism more equitable and humane.

However, not even a full Keynesian program complemented by progressive taxes, adequate minimum wages, single-payer healthcare, decent public schools, and a safety net that is truly safe is sufficient to establish an institutional framework conducive to equitable cooperation. Only "future economy" initiatives combined with more radical "imperfect experiments in equitable cooperation" which ultimately lead to an altogether different economic system that distributes decision-making power in proportion to how much people are affected, rewards people according to their sacrifices and needs, and adequately protects the natural environment can accomplish that.

Beyond Capitalism

Even the most efficient and equitable capitalist economies cannot restore the environment, provide people with economic self-management, distribute the burdens and benefits of economic activity equitably, and promote solidarity and variety while avoiding wastefulness. That is one reason we must go beyond capitalism to build the economics of equitable cooperation. Another reason that has become painfully apparent over the past forty years is that reforms to humanize capitalism are always at risk of being reversed. If we leave private enterprise and markets in place the economics of competition and greed will always threaten reforms and lead to renewed attempts to weaken restraints they place on capitalists.

In the United States, the Humphrey Hawkins Full Employment and Balanced Growth Act was signed in 1978 after decades of lobbying by organized labor and civil rights groups, only to become a dead letter under a Democratic President, Jimmy Carter, and a Democratic Congress as soon as the ink was dry. Financial regulatory reforms prompted by the Crash of 1929 and the Great Depression were scuttled first by the Reagan administration in the early 1980s, leading to the Savings and Loan crisis of the 1980s, and later by the Clinton administration, who invited the financial industry to rewrite rules that had long irked them but protected the rest of us leading to the repeal of Glass-Steagall in 1999 and laying the ground work for the financial crisis of 2008. Welfare reforms dating from the "War on Poverty" in the 1960s were rolled back when a Democratic President, Bill Clinton, collaborated with a Republican Congress in the mid-1990s. Privatization of Social Security was first raised by the Clinton White House, and Obama's attempt in early 2014 to reduce benefits through the ploy of a chain-weighted consumer price index was only nixed by an all-court press from an outraged liberal coalition.

In Great Britain in the 1980s Margaret Thatcher's Tory governments reversed reforms that had made British capitalism more stable and equitable. Tony Blair's "New Labor" governments continued the process of dismantling reforms "Old Labor" and its progressive allies once worked decades to win. And most recently the Cameron Tory/Liberal government has used the crisis neoliberal policies created as an excuse to dismantle the British welfare state even further.

But the most successful attempts to humanize capitalism were in the Scandinavian economies during the 1960s and early 1970s. Norway and Sweden had a full Keynesian program, the most generous welfare system to date, and the Meidner Commission in Sweden had even begun to press for significant worker participation in firm governance. However, starting in the mid-1970s all these reforms came under attack. First international competition, and now the economic crisis are the excuses given for why Scandinavians can "no longer afford" their welfare safety net, despite the objective fact that their economies are more than twice as productive as they were forty years ago. Like the triumph of free market over Keynesian capitalism in the United States and Great Britain, the backward trajectory of social democracy in Scandinavia also stands as a reminder why we must replace the rule of corporations and market forces and go beyond capitalism if we expect to sustain progress toward the economics of equitable cooperation.

Worker and Consumer Empowerment

The essence of capitalism is, of course, that those who own the means of production decide what their employees will produce and how they will do it. Capitalism denies workers and consumers *direct* decision-making power over how they work and what they consume, and gives them in exchange something mainstream economists call "producer and consumer sovereignty." Producer sovereignty supposedly operates through labor markets where the ability of employees to vote with their feet provides incentives for their employers to take their wishes into account when deciding what they order them to do. Consumer sovereignty supposedly operates through goods markets where the ability of consumers to vote with their pocket books provides incentives for capitalists to take their wishes into account when deciding what they order their employees to produce. If labor and goods markets are competitive, the story goes, workers and consumers will exert *indirect* influence over issues that concern them. However, as we have seen, this indirect influence operates far from perfectly even when markets are competitive, and much less effectively when they are not. The "point" of capitalism is that economic power is concentrated in the hands of employers who own the means of production, or in modern capitalism, in the hands of corporations. Modern capitalism means corporate power.

But since humans want control over their lives, and work better when they have more control over the economic decisions that affect them, the essence of capitalism is problematic and gives rise to the following dynamic: Employees sometimes try to win some of the direct power capitalism denies them. Employers sometimes pretend to give their employees some direct power because their employees work better if they think they have power. *Employee stock options, total quality programs, joint worker-management committees*, and a host of programs that go under the all-embracing title **co-determination** in Europe, are the outgrowth of this dynamic. The secret to evaluating different forms of worker and consumer empowerment in capitalism is to try to distinguish between appearance and reality. Anything that *really* enhances employee or consumer power moves us toward the economics of equitable cooperation. But programs that increase employers' ability to get more of what they want out of their employees by deceiving them into thinking they have some power when, in fact, they do not, promote the economics of competition and greed, not the economics of equitable cooperation. Unfortunately it is not always easy to know which is which, or when a concession has been won by employees rather than bestowed by employers like the Trojan horse.

Worker-Owned Cooperatives

Cooptation of employees by their employers is impossible when there are neither employers nor employees, which is the case in **worker-owned**, or **producer cooperatives** *where employees are the sole owners of their enterprises*. But the argument for worker ownership is much stronger than as a means to avoid cooptation. As we have seen in capitalism people are rewarded according to the value of the contribution of the productive capital they own as well as the value of the contribution of their labor, so a Rockefeller heir who never works a day in his life can enjoy an income hundreds of times greater than that of a skilled brain surgeon. For this reason many political economists believe private ownership is incompatible with economic justice and must be abolished. Similarly, political economists who believe people have a right to manage their own labor call for the abolition of private enterprise because giving absentee owners the legal right to decide what their employees will produce and how they will produce it violates a more fundamental human right of their employees.

Market Socialism

Some support a mixture of public and private enterprise for the pragmatic reason that private enterprise has proven ill-suited to provide even minimally acceptable results in certain industries and situations. However, others support mixed economies as an incremental strategy for replacing private enterprise altogether, leading eventually to a public enterprise economy where property income no longer exists and workers, rather than absentee owners, choose their managers or manage themselves. All political economists who espouse public enterprise market models, or what is frequently called "market socialism," do so because they believe private enterprise is inherently incompatible with economic justice and democracy, and therefore must eventually be replaced by worker ownership. Yugoslavia was a living example of a workers' self-managed, market economy from 1952 until the collapse of Yugoslavia in the late 1980s. Few today are aware that the Yugoslav economy had the highest rate of economic growth in the world over much of that time period – even higher than Japan during the heyday of the "Japanese economic miracle."[11]

Democratic Planning

Others of us believe that not only must private enterprise eventually be replaced by worker ownership, but the market system must be replaced as well by participatory, democratic planning by worker and consumer councils and federations if we are to provide an institutional environment conducive to the economics of equitable cooperation. While differences obviously remain between those who advocate replacing capitalism with market socialism and those who favor participatory planning, recently some long associated with opposing sides in this historic "debate" have discovered a great deal of common ground.[12] There are also differences of opinions within each "camp." Whether publicly owned enterprises should be entirely under the management of those who work there, whether to introduce and how to go about investment planning, and whether to provide a guaranteed basic income even for those who do not work are among the subjects debated among

---

11 Benjamin Ward, Branko Horvat, and Jaroslav Vanek provided excellent theoretical analyses of Yugoslav-type, market socialist economies in the 1960s and 1970s. David Schweickart (*After Capitalism*, Rowman & Littlefield, 2002) and Michael Howard (*Self-Management and the Crisis of Socialism*, Rowman & Littlefield, 2000) are two recent proponents of employee managed, public enterprise, market economies.

12 For example, see Robin Hahnel with Erik Olin Wright, *Alternatives to Capitalism: Proposals for a Democratic Economy* (New Left Project, 2014).

market socialists. The spring issues of *Science & Society* in 2002 and ten years later in 2012 were both devoted to models of democratic planning. In his introduction to the 2002 issue Pat Devine[13] explained:

> [The authors] and I all share a commitment to democratic, participatory planning as the eventual replacement for market forces. But while there are many other points of agreement among all or some of us, there are also disagreements over fundamental principles and values as well as details.

Spurred first by the demise of Communism, and more recently by the ecological and economic crises in the advanced economies, there is also growing interest in **community based economy** alternatives to capitalism. Left Greens such as Howard Hawkins and social ecologists like Murray Bookchin propose replacing environmentally destructive market relations with *planning by semi-autonomous municipal assemblies* who they argue would have reason to preserve the ecological systems necessary to their own survival and wellbeing.[14] There has also been renewed interest in classic writings from the anarchist and utopian socialist traditions[15] among young people dissatisfied with capitalism and Communism. All these economic visionaries believe equitable cooperation and environmental preservation require replacing markets with some kind of democratic planning.

To provide a concrete idea of what the economics of equitable cooperation might look like, I briefly describe how one of the most fully developed and best-known alternatives to capitalism, a *participatory economy*, could work.[16] Not to be confused with a transition program, or a strategy for replacing the economics of competition

---

13 Devine's own model of democratic planning as "negotiated coordination" was spelled out in his path breaking book *Democracy and Economic Planning* (Westview Press, 1988).

14 See Howard Hawkins, "Community Control, Workers' Controls, and the Cooperative Commonwealth" in *Society and Nature* 1, 3, 1993, and Murray Bookchin with Janet Biehl, *The Politics of Social Ecology* (Black Rose Books, 1998). For a sympathetic evaluation see Robin Hahnel, "Eco-localism: A Constructive Critique," *Capitalism, Nature, Socialism* 18, 2, June 2007: 62–78.

15 Some anarchists whose writings have been rediscovered are Michael Bakunin, Peter Kropotkin, Emma Goldman, Alexander Berkman, Errico Malatesta, Anton Pannekoek, Isaac Puente, Diego Abad de Santillan, and Rudolf Rocker. Utopian socialists whose writings seem more compelling in the aftermath of the death of Communism include William Morris, G.D.H. Cole, and Sidney and Beatrice Webb.

16 This model was first presented in *The Political Economy of Participatory Economics* (Princeton University Press, 1991) and *Looking Forward: Participatory Economics for the Twenty First Century* (South End Press, 1991), both by Michael Albert and Robin Hahnel. The model has been featured in every journal and symposium devoted to alternatives to capitalism over the past quarter century. It is most recently explained and defended in *Pareon: Life After Capitalism* (Verso, 2003) by Michael Albert, and in *Of the People, By the People: The Case for Participatory Economics* (Soapbox Press, 2013) by Robin Hahnel.

and greed, the "model" of a participatory economy should be thought of as a proposal for how we might eventually provide robust institutional support for the economics of equitable cooperation.

Participatory Economics

The major institutions in a participatory economy are: (1) *democratic councils* of workers and consumers, (2) *jobs balanced* for empowerment and desirability, (3) *compensation according to effort* as judged by work mates, and (4) a *participatory planning* procedure in which councils and federations of workers and consumers propose and revise their own activities under rules designed to yield outcomes that are efficient and equitable.

Production would be carried out in *workers' councils* where each member has one vote, individual work assignments are balanced for desirability and empowerment within reason, and workers' efforts are rated by a committee of their peers to serve as the basis for consumption rights. Every economy organizes work tasks into jobs. In hierarchical economies most jobs contain a number of similar, relatively undesirable and unempowering tasks, while a few jobs consist of relatively desirable and empowering tasks. But why should some people's work lives be less desirable than other's? Does not taking equity seriously require trying to balance jobs for desirability? And if we want everyone to have equal opportunity to participate in economic decision making, if we want to ensure that the formal right to participate translates into an effective right to participate, does this not require trying to balance jobs more for empowerment? If some people sweep floors year in and year out, while others review new technological options and attend meetings year in and year out, is it realistic to believe they have equal opportunity to participate in firm decisions simply because they each have one vote in the workers' council? Trying to balance jobs for desirability and empowerment does not mean everyone must do everything, nor an end to specialization. Each person would still do only a few tasks – but some of them will be more enjoyable and/or empowering and some less.

In economies where compensation is determined by competitive forces in labor markets, people are rewarded according to the market value of the contribution of their labor. But the market value of the services of a skilled brain surgeon will be many times greater than the market value of the services of a garbage collector no matter how hard and well the garbage collector works. Since people will always have different abilities to benefit others, those with lesser abilities will always be disadvantaged in economies where compensation is determined in the market place. Therefore, a participatory economy rewards people according to the effort, or sacrifice they make in work, rather than the value of their contribution. If someone works longer, harder, or at more dangerous, stressful, or boring tasks than others, then, and only then, would she be rewarded with greater consumption rights in compensation for her greater sacrifice.

In a participatory economy every family would belong to a *neighborhood consumers' council*, which, in turn, belongs to a *federation* of neighborhood consumer councils the size of a city ward or rural county, which belongs to a city or regional federation of consumer councils, which belongs to a state federation of consumer councils, which belongs to the national federation of consumer councils. The major purpose of "nesting" consumer councils into a system of federations is to allow different sized groups to make consumption decisions that affect different numbers of people. As we have seen, in market systems failure to arrange for all those affected by consumption activities to participate in choosing them not only entails a loss of selfmanagement, but a loss of efficiency as well. Having consumer federations participate on an equal footing with workers' and neighborhood consumers' councils in the planning procedure avoids this bias in a participatory economy.

Members present consumption requests along with the effort rating their workmates awarded them to their neighborhood consumption council. Using estimates of the social costs of producing different goods and services generated by the participatory planning procedure described below, the burden a consumption proposal imposes on others can be easily calculated. No consumption request justified by a person's effort rating can be denied. Neighborhood councils can also approve requests on the basis of need in addition to merit.

The participants in *participatory planning* are worker councils and federations, consumer councils and federations, and the Iteration Facilitation Board. Conceptually participatory planning is quite simple: The Facilitation Board announces current estimates of the opportunity costs for all goods, services, resources, categories of labor, and capital stocks. Consumer councils and federations respond with their consumption requests accompanied by average effort ratings for their members, while worker councils and federations respond with production proposals, listing the outputs they would provide and the inputs they would need to make them. The Facilitation Board calculates the excess demand or supply for each good and adjusts the estimate of the opportunity cost of the good up, or down, in light of the excess demand or supply. Using these more accurate estimates of social opportunity costs, consumer and worker councils and federations revise and resubmit their proposals until the proposal from each council and federation has been approved by all the other councils and federations.

Essentially this procedure whittles overly optimistic proposals that are not mutually compatible down to what economists call a feasible plan in two ways: (1) Consumer councils requesting more than their effort ratings warrant are forced to reduce their requests, or shift their requests to less socially costly items, to win approval from other consumer councils who reasonably regard their requests as too greedy. Just as the social burden implied by a consumption proposal can be calculated by multiplying items requested by their opportunity costs to be compared with members' average effort rating, the benefits of the outputs a worker council proposes can be compared to the social costs of the inputs the workers requests using the same estimates of opportunity costs from the planning procedure. (2) Worker councils whose proposals have lower than average *social benefit to social cost ratios* are forced to increase either their efforts or efficiency to win the approval of other workers. Moreover, because "communities of affected parties" are empowered to decide how much of any pollutant they are willing to tolerate, and worker councils who want to emit a pollutant must ask their permission to do so and pay for damages caused, the planning procedure only permits emissions whose social benefits outweigh their damages.

Of course much more needs to be explained, and many questions need to be answered. There is now a considerable literature discussing all this into which interested readers can dig.[17] But it is important for those who want "system change" to understand why many people are skeptical of proposals to replace capitalism. At the beginning of the twentieth century most socialists assured people that central planning would make rational use of productive resources and put workers in charge of their destinies. But revolutionary dreams turned into Stalinist nightmares, and promises of equitable cooperation among "associated producers" turned out to be just that – promises – that real world socialism came to resemble less and less as years went by. In light of twentieth-century history, people today have every right to demand that advocates of an alternative to capitalism provide concrete answers as to how they propose to make all the different kinds of decisions that must be made in any economy, and address doubts critics raise.

From Here to There

Before we will be able to replace competition and greed with equitable cooperation, before we can replace private enterprise and markets with worker and consumer councils and participatory planning, we will have to convince a majority of the

---

17 I would suggest interested readers look first at *Of the People, By the People: The Case for a Participatory Economy* (Soapbox Press, 2013), and then *Alternatives to Capitalism: Proposals for a Democratic Economy* (New Left Project, 2014).

population that they need and want a different kind of economy. The only way to do this is to combine reform work with work to establish and expand elements of the future economy, an economy that is environmentally sustainable, democratic, and just. Work to reform capitalism *and* work to create imperfect experiments in equitable cooperation are both necessary. Neither strategy is effective by itself.

Reforms alone cannot achieve equitable cooperation because as long as the institutions of private enterprise and markets are left in place to reinforce anti-social behavior based on greed and fear, progress toward equitable cooperation will be limited, and the danger of retrogression will be ever present. The culture of capitalism is firmly rooted in popular consciousness. Most employees – not just employers – believe that hierarchy and competition are necessary for the economy to run effectively, and that those who contribute more should receive more irrespective of sacrifice. And why should people not believe this? Even if you feel you haven't gotten a fair shake, or that people born with a silver spoon in their mouth don't deserve what they get, few are likely to reject a major linchpin of capitalist culture all on their own. We should not fool ourselves that capitalism teaches people about its failings or shows them how to live non-capitalistically – quite the opposite. The only sense in which capitalism serves as midwife for its heir is by forcing people to learn to think and live non-capitalistically in order to meet needs it leaves unfulfilled. It falls to us to learn and teach others how to do this – which is a monumental task. We can ill afford to repeat the error of our twentieth-century predecessors who failed to face up to the magnitude of this undertaking, looking instead for short cuts and excuses for why it would not be necessary.

On the other hand, concentrating exclusively on organizing alternative economic institutions within capitalist economies also cannot be successful. First and foremost, exclusive focus on building alternatives within capitalism is too isolating. Until a non-capitalist sector is large, the livelihoods of most people will depend on winning reforms in the capitalist sector, and therefore that is where most people will become engaged. But concentrating exclusively on experiments in equitable cooperation will also not work because the rules of capitalism put alternative institutions at a disadvantage compared to capitalist firms they must compete against, and because market forces drive non-capitalist institutions to abandon cooperative principles. Our experiments proving to ourselves and others that a "new world" is possible will always be fully exposed to competitive pressures and the culture of capitalism. Yet failure to find ways within advanced capitalist economies to build and sustain non-capitalist networks capable of accommodating the growing numbers who will be drawn to the economics of equitable cooperation will prove just as damaging to our cause as failure to wage successful economic reform campaigns and build mass economic reform movements. In short, concentrating exclusively on reforming capitalism, or focusing only on building the future economy within capitalism, are both roads that lead to dead ends. Only in combination will reform campaigns and movements, and a growing future economy of diverse experiments in sustainable and equitable cooperation, successfully challenge the economics of competition and greed in the decades ahead.

The Future Economy

Even before the latest economic crisis, the failures of neoliberal capitalism had spurred the growth of what came to be known as "the new economy." Deteriorating economic conditions in all the advanced economies ever since 2008 have greatly accelerated its growth. Since some elements, like worker and consumer cooperatives, are hardly new, it seems more accurate to call it the *future economy –a diverse array of economic institutions and innovations that reject business-as-usual to self-consciously address rising inequality, environmental degradation, and economic decline in one way or another.* The future economy includes triple bottom line corporations, certified B-corps, ESOPs, worker-owned cooperatives, agricultural co-ops, electrical co-ops, insurance co-ops, retail co-ops, healthcare co-ops, artist co-ops, collaborative consumption, recycled clothing exchanges, solidarity economic networks, local exchange and trading systems, regional food systems, community supported agriculture, greenbelts, organic farming, renewable energy and energy efficiency initiatives, socially responsible investment, crowd sourcing, credit unions, community development financial institutions, state-owned banks, community development corporations, eco-villages, egalitarian and sustainable intentional communities, affordable housing mandates, community land trusts, participatory leasing, municipal equity investments, transit linked development districts, walkable neighborhoods, new urbanism, anchor institution collaboration, urban growth boundaries, municipality-owned utilities, public internet networks, city-owned hotels and convention centers, social investments by state pension funds, participatory budgeting . . . and more.[18]

18 The "future economy" is only beginning to be seriously studied. Gar Alperovitz has done much to make people aware of the breadth and diversity of what is going on in several recent books: *America After Capitalism* (Democracy Collaborative, 2011), and *What Then Must We Do?* (Chelsea Green, 2013). The Community Wealth website of the Democracy Collaborative Project, http://community-wealth.org, provides information about resources available to future economy initiatives, as well as information about initiatives that come to their attention. And I evaluate the strengths and weaknesses of different "experiments in equitable cooperation" in Chapter 13 of *Economic Justice and Democracy*

Clearly some initiatives are larger and others smaller; some prioritize protecting the environment while others focus on economic justice, or participatory decision making; some deviate farther and some less from "business-as-usual"; and some are more "reproducible" and others less so. It is important not to put any particular experiment on a pedestal and blind oneself to its limitations. It is also important not to focus exclusively on the limitations of a particular experiment and fail to recognize ways in which it advances the cause of equitable cooperation. But it is most important not to underestimate the value of these living experiments in equitable cooperation in general. What is called for is to nurture and improve future economy experiments that exist, build new ones that can reach out to more people, and link experiments in equitable cooperation together to form a visible alternative to capitalism in its midst.

Conclusion

The question boils down to this: Do we want to try and measure the value of each person's contribution to social production and allow individuals to withdraw from social production accordingly? Or do we want to base differences in consumption rights on differences in personal sacrifices made in producing goods and services as judged by one's work mates? In other words, do we want an economy that obeys the maxim "to each according to the value of his or her personal contribution," or the maxim "to each according to his or her effort and sacrifice?"

Do we want a few to conceive and coordinate the work of the many? Or do we want everyone to have the opportunity to participate in economic decision making to the degree they are affected? In other words, do we want to continue to organize work hierarchically, or do we want jobs balanced for empowerment?

Do we want a structure for expressing preferences that is biased in favor of private consumption over social consumption? Or do we want it to be as easy to register preferences for collective as individual consumption? In other words, do we want markets or nested federations of consumer councils?

Do we want economic decisions to be determined by competition between groups pitted against one another for their wellbeing and survival? Or do we want to plan our joint endeavors democratically, equitably, and efficiently? In other words, do we

(Routledge, 2005). But as useful as all this information may be, it is no substitute for serious studies measuring how future economy initiatives are performing on a number of dimensions and their overall impact. Economics for Equity and the Environment only launched its "Future Economy Initiative" in early 2014, beginning by applying a preliminary analytical framework to study and evaluate a handful of future economy case studies.

want to abdicate economic decision making to the market or do we want to embrace the possibility of some kind of participatory planning?

Those willing to work for the economics of equitable cooperation need not agree now on how far we will have to go to secure it. At this point there is an overwhelming consensus among opponents of the economics of competition and greed on reforms needed to make capitalism more efficient and equitable. There is also a growing awareness of the importance of expanding and deepening the future economy. As we do both we will no doubt continue to discuss and reevaluate whether it is necessary to move beyond capitalism, how far beyond capitalism we must go, and what a sustainable economics of equitable cooperation will eventually look like.

A Green New Deal

Unfortunately all of the above will be for naught unless cataclysmic climate change is prevented. If the planet is rendered inhospitable whatever progress we may have made toward the economics of equitable cooperation will quickly unravel. Therefore, one of the great mass movements of the early twenty-first century must be a movement to secure an effective, fair, and efficient international climate treaty and launch a *Green New Deal* in all of the advanced economies before it is too late. Scientists warn us that unless global greenhouse gas emissions are reduced by at least 80% before midcentury we run an unacceptable risk of triggering irreversible, cataclysmic climate change. Yet emissions continue to rise while international negotiations and domestic climate policy go nowhere. The bad news is that the economic crisis has distracted attention from the looming crisis of climate change. The good news is there is a single solution to both the economic and ecological crises – a Green New Deal. Replacing fossil fuels with renewables, transforming not only transportation but industry and agriculture as well to be much more energy efficient, and rebuilding our built infrastructure to conserve energy will be an immense, historic undertaking. What is needed if we are to avoid unacceptable climate change is the greatest technological "reboot" in economic history.

Six years since the financial crisis catapulted us into the Great Recession unemployment remains unacceptably high in the US and is far worse in Europe. If we do not put hundreds of millions of people to work over the next few decades in Europe and North America making our economies much more energy efficient and replacing fossil fuels with renewable energy sources, we will literally broil ourselves to death at some point in the century ahead. But if we fail to create hundreds of millions of new jobs transforming our economies stagnation will drag on indefinitely and the young generation in Europe and North America will face a jobless future. Two problems. One solution. A massive Green New Deal.

As Van Jones, soon to be appointed special advisor to the President for green jobs, put it in 2008: "The generations living today get to retrofit, reboot, and reenergize a nation. We get to rescue and reinvent the US economy. The more aggressive we are, the better off we will be. There is a better future out there." Unfortunately Van Jones was dismissed by President Obama under pressure from conservatives after being on the job for less than six months. Much that progressive activists do over the next decade will revolve around building a domestic political coalition powerful enough to launch a massive Green New Deal.

Notice how the "growth versus. the environment" trade-off disappears in a Green New Deal. Whenever economic growth slows, the labor movement, quite understandably, clamors for more economic stimulus to put people back to work. But whenever the economy grows more rapidly, the environmental movement complains, also understandably, that more production puts more strain on the environment and is unsustainable. *But it depends on what we are producing!* If we are building more McMansions for the 1%, putting more cars in every garage, paving more roads and highways, and building new port terminals to ship more coal to Asia, then getting jobs by increasing production does put unsustainable pressure on the environment. But if we create more jobs for laid-off construction workers retrofitting office buildings and houses so they will be more energy efficient; if we rebuild and expand public transportation systems; if we create more teaching jobs to train the new generation to transform and operate a decentralized electric grid that welcomes electricity from hundreds of millions of rooftops and substitutes local sources for distant central generators wherever possible; if we put laid-off coal miners to work assembling wind turbines; if we put high school grads to work installing solar panels on roof tops . . . then the new jobs are producing things we desperately need to save the environment, not throughput intensive consumption goods that destroy the environment. In sum, only a Green New Deal can provide people with what they cannot find now, and want more than anything else: socially useful work. And only a Green New Deal will prevent climate change that unleashes unthinkable destruction.

However, none of this will happen domestically unless there is an effective international climate treaty for two simple reasons. (1) Climate change is a global problem and cannot be solved without cooperation from all countries. Even China, the most populous country with roughly a fifth of the world's population, only enjoys roughly one-fifth of the benefit from its own emission reductions. Every other country enjoys an even lower percentage, and therefore has an even greater incentive not to reduce its own emissions but ride for free on the reductions of others. (2) An effective, equitable, and efficient climate treaty is needed to create incentives for national governments to implement domestic programs to reduce carbon emissions.

The international climate meetings scheduled for December 2015 in Paris may be our last chance before it is too late. Massive popular pressure must be put on country governments to finally commit to doing what is needed: (1) Sign a treaty that enforces mandatory reductions on national annual emissions in every country sufficient to reduce global emissions by at least 80% by 2050. (2) Distribute national reductions fairly. To be fair national reductions should be set according to a country's historic responsibility for causing the problem (its cumulative per capita emissions), and its capability to contribute to solving the problem (per capita GDP of those above a poverty threshold). In less than five minutes anyone can use the equity calculator, available on the EcoEquity website www.ecoequity.org, to calculate what they believe are fair reduction quotas for every country in the world. Finally (3) many economists, including this author, believe that once fair caps are set on national emissions for all countries, allowing governments to authorize sales of emission reduction credits by sources within their territories to sources elsewhere can do a great deal to reduce the global costs of preventing climate change and thereby lower resistance to deep emission reductions, while simultaneously reducing global inequality.[19]

If we do not create a mass movement sufficiently powerful to prevent climate change the world may soon not be worth saving. There is a serious likelihood that global emissions reductions will not be sufficient. There is an even greater likelihood that even if humanity comes to its senses at the last minute and reduces global emissions enough to prevent cataclysmic climate change, the costs of doing so will not be distributed fairly. It is the job of the climate justice movement to see that the climate problem is not only solved, but is solved fairly. There is no reason it cannot be.

19 Model 5.3 demonstrates why international carbon trading can be helpful once national emission reductions are set fairly. Also see Robin Hahnel "Left Clouds Over Climate Change Policy," *Review of Radical Political Economics* 44, 2, June 2012: 141–159, "Desperately Seeking Left Unity on Climate Change Policy," *Capitalism, Nature, Socialism* 23, 4, December 2012: 83–99, and "An Open Letter to the Climate Justice Movement." *New Politics*, Winter 2014: 76–83.

Index

policy 290; spending 151, 154–5, 162–3; underwriting of Wall Street 284
government spending multiplier 164, 242
government transfer payments 186n.2
Grameen Bank, Bangladesh 119
Gramm-Rudman Act 184
Great Britain 200, 299
Great Depression 147, 151, 152, 181, 184, 225
Great Global Asset Swindle 217
Great Recession: counterproductive response to 152; and debt 174, 175; fiscal stimulus 239–40, 241–2; and neoliberal capitalism 279; and profits 176; and unemployment 181, 189, 226; US economy during 237–43; and wages 189, 292
Greece: budget deficit 250; debt 249, 250; demonstrations 280; EU austerity policy 249–50; living standards 199; unemployment 199, 279
green consumerism 101–2
Green Economics: Confronting the Ecological Crisis 44, 46
greenhouse gases 50, 121–30, 309
green new deal 309–11
Green Revolution, in agricultural technology 213
Greenspan, Alan 188–9
green taxes, regressive 292
Greenwood, Daphne & Wolff, Edward 29
gross domestic income (GDI) 153, 156
gross domestic product (GDP) *see also* aggregate supply: actual 150, 177; equilibrium GDP 157, 186, 188, 240; full employment GDP 150; global/decrease in 218; and growth 49, 51; potential GDP 149, 150, 151, 153, 165, 177
growth: in advanced economies 178; and corporate profit rates 23; and environmental problems 49–52; export led 288; global rates 218; and inflation 170n.8; less developed countries (LDCs) 289; and macroeconomic theory 176–7; neoclassical growth

theories 257; neo-Marxist growth models 257; profit-led 251, 288, 290; rate of/and actual GDP 177; Scandinavia 178; strategies 251; uneconomic 52; wage-led 176–8, 251, 258–9, 288–9, 290; and wages 177; in wealth 22

Hawkins, Howard 302
healthcare 273, 294–5
Heckscher, Eli 212
Heckscher-Ohlin theory 212, 214
hedge funds 193
Heilbroner, Robert 92, 101
Henry, Shannon 271
Herman, Ed 174
high road growth strategy 251, 288
historical materialism 1, 11, 16
homosexuality 18
Hong Kong 208
Hoover, Herbert 152, 225, 249
household consumption, and aggregate demand 152, 155, 162, 163
household demand 148
household savings, and business demand for investment goods 161
households, wealth of 22
housing bubbles 189, 193, 194, 195, 197, 238
housing market, US 108
human activity, and social institutions 8
human center 2–8; defined 7–8; and institutional boundary 10, 13, 14
human characteristics 5–6, 7
human consciousness 3–4, 9–10
human development effects, economic choices 40
human development, theory of 6
Human Harvest, The 4
humans: individualistic interpretation of 5; needs of 2; as self-conscious/self-creative/social species 2; as self-creative 2, 3, 7
human sociability 4–5
human society, as part of a natural ecosystem 45
human traits, and markets 110

Medicare hospital insurance fund, owning debt 173
Mellon, Andrew 152
Mexico 213–14
microeconomic models: Climate Control Treaties 121–30; and macroeconomic problems 142; old theory as 147; Price Of Power Game 114–21; Public Good Game 112–14; Sraffa Model of Income Distribution and Prices 132–46
microeconomic perspective, fiscal policy 159
micro law of supply and demand 87–90, 93, 94, 96, 98, 106–7, 137
military budget 174
military retirement fund, owning debt 173
military spending 174n.9, 175
Mill, John Stuart 44
minimum legal reserve requirement 184, 231
minimum wage laws 79, 292–3
Ministry of International Trade and Industry (MITI), Japan 208, 286
minority groups 167, 281
Mishel, Lawrence & Bernstein, Jared 22
mixed economy 289–90, 301
Mobutu Sese Seko 215
mode of production 12
modern surplus approach 143, 144
Mokyr, Joel 143
monetary authorities, increasing investment demand 152
monetary policy(ies) 186–9; and aggregate demand 152, 186; avoiding inflation 174–5; expansionary 188; and inflation 174–5, 186, 227; and unemployment 174–5, 186, 227
monetary stimulus, Federal Reserve Bank 242
monetary unions 225–7
money 179–81; and efficiency of real economy 190
money supply: and aggregate demand 188; changing of 186; and equilibrium GDP 188; and Federal

Reserve Bank 186, 187, 188, 242; and government budget 189; and investment demand 188; and recessions 188
Monitoring the World Economy 1820–1992 218
monopoly capital theory 135
Morales, Evo 289
moral hazard, and federal insurance 185
more developed countries (MDCs): and climate control treaties 121; exploiting less developed countries (LDCs) 200–1; inequalities within/and trade 212; and terms of trade 211
mortgage-backed securities: insurance to buyers of 194–5; market prices for 197
mortgage industry 195
mortgage loans: and financial crisis 193; poor credit risks 193; reselling of 193
mortgages, sub-prime 195
multinational companies (MNCs) *see also* corporations: and buying up of third world business assets 217, 218; and direct foreign investment 214; and exploitation of LDCs 201; and foreign currencies 220
multiparty deals, mutually beneficial 180, 182
multiplier chain of events 163–5, 245
multiplier effect 160, 222
mutually beneficial multiparty deals 180, 182

Nader, Ralph 266
NAFTA treaty 206, 213–14
Nash equilibrium 230, 232, 237
National Commission on Fiscal Responsibility and Reform 176
national debt: myths about 171–4; Reagan era 173
national federation of consumer councils 304
nationalization, of financial industry 284
natural capital, precautionary principle 47
natural environment 45–6
natural needs/potentials 2
natural rate of unemployment 166, 167

natural resources, owners of earning
    rents 169
need(s): for freedom 3–4; of humans 2;
    natural/species/derived 2–3; payment
    according to 33
neighborhood consumers' council 304
neighborhood effects 274
neoclassical economists 143, 144
neoclassical growth theories 257
neoclassical theory 145
neoliberal capitalism 260, 278, 279–80,
    281
neoliberal economy, low wage 259
neoliberal globalization 213, 218
neoliberalism 17, 79
neoliberals, and privatization 289
neo-Marxist growth models 257
net domestic product (NDP) 49, 50, 51
New Deal 283
new deal, green 309–11
new economy 307
new technology: and capitalists 136–7;
    and competition for profits 267;
    cost reducing 267; and economic
    efficiency 136; and employee
    empowerment 121; failing to
    implement 120, 121; inefficient choices
    regarding 267–8; and labor costs 139;
    and rate of profit 136, 140–1; and
    social interest 267; socially productive/
    counterproductive 138–9, 267, 268;
    and wage rates 139, 140, 141; and
    wages/profits/prices 136
Nixon, Richard 170
non-Annex-1 countries 121
non-labor primary inputs, replacement
    of 143n.10
North Atlantic real economies, stagnation
    of 199
northern countries, gaining from trade 209
Northwest Economic Research Center 292
Norway 288, 299

Obama administration: bail out of of
    Wall Street 283; debt/GDP ratio 173;

and environment 18; and financial
    crisis 195; and fiscal stimulation/deficit
    reduction 176, 242; healthcare 295;
    reducing benefits 299; taxpayer bailout
    of banks 198; Troubled Asset Relief
    Program (TARP) 196, 239
Obamacare 295
Occupy Wall Street 17, 19, 21, 78–9, 266,
    280, 292
Ohio Public Interest Campaign 294
Ohlin, Bertil 212
Okishio, Nobuo 140, 141
Okun's law 169
Ollman, Bertell 5
On Liberty 44
"open" bond market, treasury bonds 187
open economy: macroeconomics 219–25,
    243–50; model 221–5
open market operations, Federal Reserve
    Bank 187
opportunity costs: differing between
    countries 205; and mutually beneficial
    trade 204; of production 201–2, 203
Organization for Economic Cooperation
    and Development (OECD) 218
outcomes: under autarky 80; and credit/
    labor markets 69; Pareto optimal 34;
    and social relationships 77; under three
    international economic regimes 80–2;
    unjust/exploitative 76, 77
output: and capacity utilization 257; and
    unemployment 169
owners of land/machines, as parasites 146
owners of natural resources, earning
    rents 145

pain/gain 55n.4
panic, and depositors 231
Panic Rules 233
Panic Rules! Everything You Need to Know
    About the Global Economy 209, 231
panics, bank 236
parasites, and producers 142–6
Pareto improvement 34
Pareto optimality, and efficiency 34–5

securitization departments, Wall Street
  banks 197, 198
securitized debt instruments 194
self-conscious agents, people as 2, 40
self-creative, humans as 2, 3, 7
self-management 41–2; economic 262,
  263; and the economy 52; falling levels
  of 110; and individual freedom 4,
  41; preferences for 264; and property
  rights system 263; shifting to alienated
  labor 67, 69, 77; of work 57, 63
self-serving class interest 143
sellers: and inflation 169; power of 106;
  rent seeking at expense of 105;
  satisfaction of 89
semi-autonomous municipal assemblies,
  planning by 302
sequestration 172
Sharpe, M.E. 44
short-run imbalances between sectors, and
  industrial policy 287
simple Keynesian macro model 168
Simpson, Alan 176
Singapore 208
single-payer healthcare 294–5
Smith, Adam 83, 92, 95, 137, 140, 143, 214
sociability, human 4–5
social activity, spheres of 13
social benefits 37, 95, 98, 100
social change 13–14, 15
social consumption 110
social costs: Adam Smith 95; of
  agricultural production in US 206;
  of gallon of gas 99; of international
  transportation 206n.3; of making
  cars 97; and participation in activities 41;
  of production 36–7, 95
social democracy 279, 299
social democratic capitalism 260
social effects, of
  production/consumption 103
social fabric, thinning of 110
social inefficiency, of new technology 268
social instability 13, 14
social institutions 2, 8, 9–10, 12

social interest: and capitalists 137; and new
  technology 267
socialism, market 301
social life, four spheres of 11–12, 16
socially efficient level of output, of
  goods 137
socially productive/counterproductive, new
  technology 138–9, 267
social relationships 2, 4, 77
social roles 7, 43
social safety net see safety net
Social Security, privatization of 298–9
Social Security trust funds, owning debt 173
social species, humans as 2
social stability, and social change 13–14
social welfare programs, opposition to 175
society(ies): and people 1–2; stabilizing/
  destabilizing forces 13, 14
socio-technology matrix 144n.12
solidarity 42–3, 52, 268
South Africa 15–16
southern exports/imports, and terms of
  trade 210
South Korea 208, 286, 288, 290
Soviet Union 19
Spain 108, 199, 279, 280
specialization 201, 208, 287
species nature, and denial of self-
  management opportunities 42
species needs/potentials 2, 3
species rights, self-management as 57
spending: government 151, 154–5, 162–3;
  military 174n.9, 175
Sraffa Model of Income Distribution and
  Prices 132–46, 267, 293
Sraffa, Piero 131
stabilization policies 176, 285
stagflation 168
state governments, and loss of federal
  grants 241
state of nature 5, 26
state taxation, sales/local property taxes 291
static efficiency 137, 208
status quo, elites preserving 15
steady state economy 50